The Violent Hero

Also available from Bloomsbury

Euripides: Children of Heracles, Florence Yoon
Euripides: Heracles, Emma Griffiths
Gods, Demigods and Demons, Bernard Evslin

The Violent Hero

Heracles in the Greek Imagination

Katherine Lu Hsu

BLOOMSBURY ACADEMIC
LONDON • NEW YORK • OXFORD • NEW DELHI • SYDNEY

BLOOMSBURY ACADEMIC
Bloomsbury Publishing Plc
50 Bedford Square, London, WC1B 3DP, UK
1385 Broadway, New York, NY 10018, USA
29 Earlsfort Terrace, Dublin 2, Ireland

BLOOMSBURY, BLOOMSBURY ACADEMIC and the Diana logo are trademarks of
Bloomsbury Publishing Plc

First published in Great Britain 2021
This paperback edition published in 2022

Copyright © Katherine Lu Hsu, 2021

Katherine Lu Hsu has asserted her right under the Copyright, Designs and
Patents Act, 1988, to be identified as Author of this work.

For legal purposes the Acknowledgments on p. x–xi constitute an extension of
this copyright page.

Cover design: Terry Woodley
Cover image: *Hercules and Nessus*, Florence, Italy. Photography by Jeremy Villasis/Getty

All rights reserved. No part of this publication may be reproduced or transmitted
in any form or by any means, electronic or mechanical, including photocopying,
recording, or any information storage or retrieval system, without prior
permission in writing from the publishers.

Bloomsbury Publishing Plc does not have any control over, or responsibility for, any third-party
websites referred to or in this book. All internet addresses given in this
book were correct at the time of going to press. The author and publisher regret
any inconvenience caused if addresses have changed or sites have ceased
to exist, but can accept no responsibility for any such changes.

A catalogue record for this book is available from the British Library.

Library of Congress Cataloging-in-Publication Data
Names: Hsu, Katherine Lu, author.
Title: The violent hero : Heracles in the Greek imagination / Katherine Lu Hsu.
Description: New York : Bloomsbury Academic, 2020. | Includes bibliographical references and
index. | Summary: "This book uses the mythological hero Heracles as a lens for investigating the
nature of heroic violence in archaic and classical Greek literature, from Homer through to
Aristophanes. Heracles was famous for his great victories as much as for his notorious failures.
Driving each of these acts is his heroic violence, an ambivalent force that can offer communal
protection as well as cause grievous harm. Drawing on evidence from epic, lyric poetry, tragedy,
and comedy, this work illuminates the strategies used to justify, constrain, and deflate the
threatening aspects of violence. The mixed results of these strategies also demonstrate how the
figure of Heracles inherently – and stubbornly – resists reform. The diverse character of Heracles'
violent acts reveals an enduring tension in understanding violence: is violence a negative
individual trait, that is to say, the manifestation of an internal state of hostility? Or is it one
specific means to a preconceived end, rather like an instrument whose employment may or may
not be justified? Katherine Lu Hsu explores these evolving attitudes towards individual violence in
the ancient Greek world while also shedding light on timeless debates about the nature of
violence itself"— Provided by publisher.
Identifiers: LCCN 2020024299 (print) | LCCN 2020024300 (ebook) | ISBN 9781350153714
(hardback) | ISBN 9781350153721 (ebook) | ISBN 9781350153738 (epub)
Subjects: LCSH: Heracles (Greek mythological character) | Violence in literature. |
Greek literature—History and criticism.
Classification: LCC PA3015.R5 H448 2020 (print) | LCC PA3015.R5 (ebook) |
DDC 398.20938/02—dc23
LC record available at https://lccn.loc.gov/2020024299
LC ebook record available at https://lccn.loc.gov/2020024300

ISBN: HB: 978-1-3501-5371-4
PB: 978-1-3501-9170-9
ePDF: 978-1-3501-5372-1
eBook: 978-1-3501-5373-8

Typeset by RefineCatch Limited, Bungay, Suffolk

To find out more about our authors and books visit www.bloomsbury.com
and sign up for our newsletters

For Dave,

coniugi caro

Contents

List of Figures ix
Acknowledgments x

Introduction 1
  On Violence 2
  On Myth 6
  On Heracles 10

1 Heraclean Force and the Representation of Violence 19
  Introduction 19
  Heracles as Monster-slayer in Hesiod's *Theogony* 20
  The *Iliad*'s Heracles 23
  Conclusion 46

2 Hero or Monster? Justifying Violence against Geryon 49
  Introduction 49
  Eliminating the Monstrous: Praising Heracles' Civilizing Efforts against Geryon 50
  Violence Questioned in Stesichorus' *Geryoneis* 56
  Pindar's Heracles: *Nomos*, Justice, and Violence 68
  Conclusion 75

3 Heroic Competition and the Home in Sophocles' *Trachiniae* 77
  Introduction 77
  Heracles and Achelous: A Paradigm of Competition 79
  Heracles and Nessus: A Distorted Suitor Competition 82
  Heracles at Oechalia: Another Distorted Suitor Competition 85
  Iole and Deianeira Vie for Heracles 88
  The Death of a Victor 93
  Conclusion 104

4 Coping with Violence: Victory and Friendship in Euripides' *Heracles* 107
  Introduction 107
  Violence against Enemies 109

	Violence against Friends	116
	Violence against the Self	123
	Conclusion	129
5	Heracles the Fool: Laughing at Violence	131
	Introduction	131
	Victory and the Flesh: Renewing Violence through Laughter	133
	The Comic Heracles in Euripides' *Alcestis*	146
	A Polyphony of Genres in Aristophanes' *Frogs*	156
	Conclusion	171

Conclusion: Which Path Did Heracles Choose?	173
Notes	183
References	215
Index	237

Figures

1.1	Heracles and Apollo vie for the Delphic tripod. East pediment of the Siphnian Treasury, *c.* 525 BCE.	31
1.2	Athena leads Heracles to Zeus. Attic black-figure lip-cup, Vulci, 555–550 BCE.	43
2.1	Winged Geryon duels Heracles. Chalcidian black-figure neck amphora, Vulci, 540–530 BCE.	57
2.2	Heracles aims an arrow at Geryon from behind a stone. Attic black-figure lekythos, *c.* 500–480 BCE.	65
2.3	Heracles crowned. Niobid Crater, Attic red-figure calyx crater, Orvieto, *c.* 460–450 BCE.	70
4.1	Heracles' Labor at the Stables of Augeas. Metope from the Temple of Zeus at Olympia, *c.* 475 BCE.	118
4.2	Heracles and the Stymphalian Birds. Attic black-figure lekythos, *c.* 500–480 BCE.	120
5.1	Heracles among satyr performers. Pronomos Vase, Attic red-figure volute crater, *c.* 400 BCE.	137

Acknowledgments

I owe a huge debt of gratitude to many people for their guidance and support in bringing this book to publication. I remain forever grateful to Ruth Scodel, who advised me at the University of Michigan and supervised the dissertation from which this book evolved. Richard Janko has challenged me since my first semester at Michigan and has continued to support me since. Special thanks are due to Johanna Hanink, whose questions and insights pushed me to improve the work at crucial moments.

At Brooklyn College, David Schur and Brian Sowers showed me the ropes of being an academic and taught me what it means to be a colleague. I have been supported in various ways by the members of the Classics Department at Brooklyn College, including Dee Clayman, Danielle Kellogg, JoAnn Luhrs, Gail Smith, Philip Thibodeau, John Van Sickle, and Liv Yarrow. I honor the memory of Jim Pletcher, a friend and kind colleague whose wit and brilliant teaching will be missed. The faculty and staff of the Latin/Greek Institute have inspired and encouraged me throughout the years: Collomia Charles, Caleb Dance, Carlo DaVia, Daniel Dooley, Rita Fleischer, Patrick Glauthier, Zachary Hayworth, Benjamin King, Katia Kosova, Aramis Lopez, Jeremy March, Geoffrey Moseley, Bill Pagonis, Suklima Roy, Akiva Saunders, Aaron Shapiro, Christopher Simon, Jeff Ulrich, and Alice Phillips Walden. I will always be indebted to the mentorship of Hardy Hansen, who taught me Greek, then taught me how to teach Greek, and then modeled for me how to lead the Institute.

I received helpful feedback and criticisms from audiences at College of the Holy Cross, Rutgers University, Smith College, Columbia University, Brown University, Wellesley College, the CUNY Graduate Center, Butler University, Brooklyn College, Baylor University, Trinity College, Reed College, and Tulane University. I have also benefited greatly from conversations about this work with a wide range of colleagues and friends, including Sarah Barbrow, Shuen Chai, Joy Connolly, Susan Deacy, Elda Granata and Alex Conison, Kathryn Hampton, Joseph Howley, Athena Kirk, Isabel Köster, Mary Jean McNamara, Amy Burghardt Muehlbauer, Julie Park, and Jessica Seidman.

I am thankful to Alice Wright, who steered my manuscript through the review process at Bloomsbury, as well as her colleagues Lily Mac Mahon and Georgina

Leighton. My many thanks go to the publisher's anonymous reviewers, whose comments, suggestions, and criticisms have greatly improved the manuscript.

I gratefully acknowledge the gift of dedicated time to complete the manuscript afforded by the Career Enhancement Fellowship for Junior Faculty from the Woodrow Wilson National Fellowship Foundation and the Andrew W. Mellon Foundation, as well as a Faculty Research Award from the Professional Staff Congress, the union that represents CUNY faculty members and staff.

It is a pleasure to acknowledge and thank my family, without whom I never would have gotten this far. First, my parents, Calvin and Florence Lu, have loved and encouraged me, always. Stephen and Grace, Apphia, Matthias, and Junia Lu have provided much cheer in trying times. Peter Lu has supported the development of this book at every stage. I owe so much to Joy Gavin for the loving care that she has given to my daughter Madeleine since her infancy, allowing me to devote time and attention to Heracles. I am grateful every day for Maddie and Aaron, and the joy they have brought into our lives. And finally, I thank my husband Dave, without whose dedicated support and steadfast love I would not have reached this finish line. It is to him that this book is dedicated.

Introduction

In the ancient Greek world, violence defined the actions of its heroes. This is demonstrated nowhere else as clearly as in the myths of Heracles. He was by far the most popular of all mythological heroes; his fame was widespread, encompassing the whole of the Greek world, preceding the origin of writing and lasting for centuries. Narratives about Heracles form a rich and varied mythological tradition. At its core are the Labors: he defeats threatening beasts and grotesque monsters, punishes law-breaking villains, and imposes order upon a chaotic world. Through his incredible skill, endurance, and courage, he accomplishes seemingly impossible acts that exceed mortal limitations. For these victories and for his strength, he was celebrated in literature, the arts, politics, philosophy, and cult. And as the only hero to obtain immortality and an afterlife on Mount Olympus with his father Zeus, Heracles occupies a uniquely lofty place in Greek mythology. He comes to take on a position as an aspirational figure in, for example, the genre of epinician poetry, his role as the patron of athletes and the gymnasium, and his status as *alexikakos*, or "averter of evils."

But the vast range of Heracles' myths also includes stories in which he wields his strength towards less celebrated ends: he murders his own family in a fit of madness, destroys an entire city on a dubious pretext, and dares to attack the gods themselves. He also frequently plays the buffoon, a stupid glutton enslaved to a voracious appetite for food, drink, and sex; this Heracles is ripe for mockery and subject to laughter that brings him low. In these myths, his violence can be presented as troubling and problematic, making Heracles an example to avoid. Heracles is thus a figure of great contrast, characterized by excessiveness in all directions.

His exploits share in common a reliance on heroic violence. Just as Heracles' myths illustrate the extremities of heroic behavior, they also reveal the unsettled nature of heroic violence. In the hands of extraordinary individuals like heroes, violence can bring about communal benefit, through the elimination of threats to safety and harmony. Yet it can also result in grievous harm, through anti-social behavior or uncontrollable impulses that injure the innocent, create disorder, and transgress social norms, leaving a legacy of destruction in its wake. The widespread recognition that Heracles earns for his deeds positions him as an ideal lens for exploring the ambivalence of heroic violence.

The changing depictions of Heracles and his use of violence are the subject of this study, which draws its evidence from the literature and art of Greece from the seventh to fifth centuries BCE. Through an investigation of a variety of roles Heracles serves across multiple genres, this study articulates the motifs that constitute an episode of violence, motifs that can be shaped and constructed to influence the evaluation of the use of violence. Furthermore, through the shifting evaluations of violence, different frameworks for understanding violence emerge: depending on the episode, Heracles' violence can appear as an appropriate means to a legitimate end, or as a manifestation of an internal, unstable character, or something on a spectrum between these two poles. In confronting the range of the hero's violent behavior, poets and artists also explore methods of constraining heroic force, whether through interpersonal relationships and social values, the conventions of competition, the authority of the gods, or even laughter. Yet the persistence of Heracles' problematic violence demonstrates how the figure of Heracles inherently, and stubbornly, resists reform. The project of taming Heracles, then, is a never-ending struggle, one that also reflects the unstable relationship of the extraordinary individual with both his enemies and his own community.

On Violence

The study of violence is central to several fields of inquiry and is marked by a diversity of scholarly approaches. For example, the last decade has seen a surge of public interest in the historical development of violence, as seen in the blockbuster success of (and debates generated by) Steven Pinker's *The Better Angels of Our Nature: Why Violence Has Declined Over Time* (2011).[1] The landmark sociological study traces the influences that have caused various measures of violence to decrease on a per capita basis to the present day. Pinker's thesis remains controversial, but the work, which begins with the ancient civilizations of Greece, Mesopotamia, and Asia, eloquently demonstrates the importance of understanding the place of violence in the ancient world: a rich knowledge of the role of violence in the past is essential to the assessment of our modern existence.

"Violence" is a term with as many meanings as contexts in which it is found; its definition is inevitably culturally contingent. I take my basic definition from Werner Riess's *Performing Interpersonal Violence: Court, Curse, and Comedy* (2012), which defines violence as "a physical act, a 'process in which a human being inflicts harm on another human being via physical strength' or plots to do so."[2] This definition suits the presentation of Heracles in Greek mythology, as the hero's violence is of the most fundamental kind: primarily physical, enacted by his own hands or weapons. It is no coincidence that his name is associated with the word *bia*—the Greek term for the physical use of force—in archaic epic poetry.[3]

The bibliography on violence in the ancient Greek world is extensive. A particularly rich vein of the research has focused on historical inquiries about, for example, violence in warfare, violence in Homeric society, the legal and political regulation of violence in democratic Athens, or the shifting ethical values of Athenian society.[4] Violence against women and violence against slaves each constitute an urgent and vital field of research.[5] These concerns are treated together in Foraboschi's *Violenze Antiche* (2018), which explores individual and mass violence to ask whether violence is rooted in human nature or in unjust social relations.[6] In recent years, several edited volumes have brought together a diverse range of scholars to address a central topic related to violence. For example, Riess and Fagan's *The Topography of Violence in the Greco-Roman World* (2016) brings the "spatial turn" to the historical analysis of ancient violence, while Xydopoulos, Vlassopoulos, and Tounta's *Violence and Community: Law, Space, and Identity in the Ancient Eastern Mediterranean World* (2017) joins the fields of study on legal practices, civic identity, and physical space into a unified study.[7]

Research on ancient violence remains relevant for addressing our contemporary social concerns as well. Since the publication of psychiatrist Jonathan Shay's *Achilles in Vietnam: Combat Trauma and the Undoing of Character* (1994) and *Odysseus in America: Combat Trauma and the Trials of Homecoming* (2002), violence in Greek mythology has been used to understand the psychological effects of the contemporary veteran experience.[8] Shay's work argues that the behavior of heroes in Homer's *Iliad* and *Odyssey* reflects the symptoms of complex post-traumatic stress disorder (PTSD) and uses their example to explore ways of preventing and recovering from trauma. Greek tragedy has also proven fertile ground in this area: for example, Peter Meineck's Aquila Theatre company and Bryan Doerries' Theater of War Productions have engaged with ancient depictions of violence in tragedies centered around trauma in war. Through productions put on for military audiences and involving veteran performers and audience talkbacks, these performances highlight the therapeutic power of drama, as well as the essential connections between ancient and modern concerns about homecoming after war.[9]

My inquiry focuses on violence committed by a single individual largely against other individuals (though Heracles also engages in martial campaigns). This kind of violence was subjected to shifting scrutiny, as the position of the individual changed alongside the titanic social and political changes that occurred throughout the archaic and classical periods, a period that saw the formation of the *polis*, the rise and fall of tyrants, and the blossoming and failures of democracy and empires. As the individual's relation to his neighbor and community was reshaped repeatedly, his employment of violence was likewise examined. The cultural products arising out of this era were no doubt influenced by this historical process, reflecting through their own media the anxieties surrounding the utility and threat of individual violence in society.

This study focuses primarily on literary representations of violence through mythological narratives in a range of literary genres.[10] In contrast with historical studies, which uncover incidents of, attitudes towards, and responses to actual violence, this attention to representation is a step removed from everyday life in ancient Greece. Rather, the representation of violence is ideological; that is, it not only depicts acts of violence, but also ascribes to it context, meaning, and value.[11] Myths about violence, therefore, provide a platform for exploring both the meaning of violence and potential methods of constraining that violence to legitimate ends.

Each representation of violence thus constructs a framework for understanding the phenomenon of violence. Today, by long-standing practice in both psychology and the American legal system, acts of violence or aggression are often divided into two basic types: instrumental aggression, defined as acts premeditated and motivated by some other goal, and impulsive aggression, which is characterized by an angry, emotional desire to hurt someone.[12] This division is not restricted to legal decision-making; it reveals an enduring tension found also in the analysis of critical theorists. In her reflections in *On Violence*, Hannah Arendt states that "violence is by nature instrumental; like all means, it always stands in need of guidance and justification through the end it pursues."[13] This presentation suggests that violence itself is a neutral force and can only be evaluated by its purpose. Its legitimacy demands to be evaluated through a means–ends calculus: does the end justify the means of violence? The instrumental approach thus assumes an underlying rationality for the occurrence and evaluation of violence.

In his *Critique of Violence*, Walter Benjamin, on the other hand, makes a distinction between mediate violence, violence that is means towards an end, and nonmediate violence, which is a manifestation. Benjamin openly doubts whether violence can ever "be a moral means even to just ends," thus resisting a means–ends logic for understanding violence.[14] Instead, he appeals to the "every day experience" of a man who is "impelled by anger, for example, to the most visible outbursts of a violence that is not related as a means to a preconceived end. It is not a means but a manifestation."[15] This violence is a manifestation, an eruption that both defies restraint and cannot be rationalized.

These approaches are not mutually exclusive, as both are used to frame episodes of Heraclean violence in Greek literature. In fact, as we shall see, in the hands of different poets, the same episode of violence can represent different frameworks of understanding violence. The evolving character of Heracles' violent acts raises further questions: is violence the result of a state of internal hostility that constantly threatens to manifest itself at will? Or is violence merely a method, a means applied toward and controlled by specific ends? In either case, additional questions remain: how can violence be constrained to legitimate ends, and what constitutes "legitimate"? This study attempts to answer these questions by identifying the motifs that constitute an episode of heroic violence and then analyzing how those motifs are amplified, suppressed, and shaped to allow for an ethical evaluation of the encounter. Through this kind of careful close reading, I hope to avoid a potential pitfall of studies like this one, the danger of conflating ancient and modern ideas of violence. While using a modern theoretical framework, I aim to avoid applying contemporary judgments by allowing the evaluation of the poet, the poem's narrative, the narrator, or the focalizer, to hold primacy.

In establishing and tracing these motifs, this study reveals patterns in how archaic and classical Greeks thought about acts of individual violence. It thus follows on the work of Werner Riess's study of fourth-century Attic forensic oratory, in which he illuminates a "semantic grammar of violence" underlying how Athenians talked about violence.[16] Heroic violence, I argue, also has a "semantic grammar of violence," as filtered through the mythological roles the hero plays. Some of these roles are specific to genre—the role of epinician victor is especially important—but they are not restricted by genre. Mythological roles can cross literary genres, even as genres interact with each other, such as lyric and choral poetry within drama. Through the examination of a single mythological figure, this study shows how individual violence, the work of an extraordinary individual within a community, has its own "semantic grammar" that allows its evaluation.

The representation of violence in art is of special interest for this study; the presentation of violence in Attic vase painting has been the subject of active scholarly debate in recent years.[17] As several studies have shown, in the late archaic period violence becomes less graphic, depicted more as a threat than in action; in concert with this shift, violence is legitimized by the lack of blood and delegitimized by its lack of restraint.[18] Susanne Muth takes a minority view, arguing in a lengthy study that these images cannot be interpreted as historical evidence of the Athenians' attitude towards violence. Rather, the shift from explicit to implicit violence reflects the agonal culture of Athens through a focus on the stronger party's superiority and power for admiring eyes.[19]

But Muth's approach is not the final word; and certainly in the literary evidence, the problematization of heroic violence and the question of its legitimacy are explicit. In my view, mythological narratives about Heracles inevitably reflect the culture that produces them. In exploring the depictions of Heraclean violence in images and poems, this study aims to illuminate how ancient Greeks dealt with the perennial questions about violence's role in their own society.

On Myth

The many manifestations of Heracles in material culture, a wide range of literary genres, and performance contexts across centuries constitute a rich mythological tradition. The variation in Heracles' depictions reflects the general dynamism of Greek myth; from the earliest representations of myth, variation was valued alongside the maintenance of tradition. Before the practice of writing came to Greece, oral poets composed unique versions of epic narratives, each performance an opportunity to recite a new variation of a familiar tale.[20] The flexibility of mythic material allowed for even more extreme changes.[21] Many myths about Heracles have prehistoric origins, especially those connected with his defeat of fearsome beasts, such as the Nemean Lion or Lernaean Hydra.[22] In these oldest tales, he is a figure of overwhelming power and physical strength, courageous and clever at exposing and exploiting his enemies' weaknesses. It is no surprise that in the sixth century BCE he becomes a symbol of victory for athletic champions and the poets who celebrate them. Yet at the same time he takes on the persona of a glutton and a buffoon, capering across the comic stage in Sicily, Magna Graecia, and Athens. Furthermore, in tragedy he can become the murderous madman of his family or a hero distinguished by his cruelty and selfishness.

In tracing the transformations of Heracles' form and function, this work engages with the methods of reception studies. Mythological innovation results in new "refigurations" of Heracles, the result of a process of "selecting and reworking material from a previous or contrasting position" or "the adaptation of a legend or myth by the addition of new features."[23] To adopt the language of Hans Robert Jauss, every audience for Greek poetry and drama came to a work equipped with a "horizon of expectations" about Heracles.[24] Each new work challenges, surpasses, disappoints, or even reaffirms the audience's expectations, creating a dialogue between the established and the new, out of which new interpretations of Heracles can emerge.[25] The varied manifestations of Heracles and his uses of violence can be viewed, then, as a dialogic process in which Heracles' changing cultural position necessitates reformulation within mythic narrative, and mythic narrative reflects his changing cultural position.

This approach shares much in common with narratological character analysis, which emphasizes that literary figures like Heracles are narrative constructs and not real people, and therefore are allowed their many contradictory, conflicting, and inconsistent presentations. Like nearly all mythological figures, Heracles is "transtextual," in that he "is a character that is inherited from earlier tradition and/or from preceding texts—a character which, simply put, travels through literary history."[26] By tracing his appearances across texts, media, and genre, this study reveals the interplay between Heracles' static characteristics (e.g., physical strength and skill) and dynamic characteristics (e.g., savior or buffoon), shedding light on the way different genres shape and adapt his presentation.

This study views the refigurations of Heracles through two different lenses: that of mythological roles (e.g., monster-slayer, *theomachos*, epinician victor, comic buffoon) and literary genre (e.g., epic, lyric, tragedy, comedy). As will be discussed further below in the "On Heracles" section, role and genre are distinct categories, but their treatment in this study demonstrates how they interact and inform one another. By way of brief example here, Heracles plays the role of culture hero in epic poetry, such as Hesiod's *Theogony*, in which Heracles imposes order on chaos in service of Zeus' agenda. The same role is also prominent in comic performances in which Heracles is also a buffoon. The two roles work in tandem to achieve a comic effect: after being debased by his own degrading appetites, Heracles' victories against villains restore him, leading to a conclusion that all can celebrate. The transformations of Heracles from role to role and genre to genre, and the tensions they produce, thus demonstrate the limits of genre, as well as the elasticity of mythological roles. Perhaps equally significant are the aspects of Heracles that remain stable and consistent throughout this study: his association with the use of force and his unruly resistance to taming prove to be defining characteristics.

But the broadest of mythological roles that Heracles plays is that of hero, a multivalent term that encompasses different meanings in different contexts. The meaning of the Greek term *hērōs* (ἥρως) overlaps with, but is not identical to, the English term "hero," which in contemporary usage usually denotes some figure worthy of admiration for accomplishing great deeds or demonstrating morally upright character. In this study, however, the term "hero" refers to the Greek *hērōs*, a figure who is identified by his *kleos* (eternal fame, κλέος), not by his moral exemplarity.[27] Usually the descendant of a god or goddess, he (as heroes are nearly always men) becomes famous for his deeds of endurance or strength, his military prowess, his accomplishment of public acts worthy of being retold.

These figures rarely model enviable lives, however. Ajax commits suicide after he is humiliated before his peers; Agamemnon, at the triumphant moment of his homecoming or *nostos*, falls at the hands of his unfaithful wife and her lover; Oedipus saves the city of Thebes from the Sphinx, but nevertheless murders his father and marries his mother. Often, the very traits that compel a hero to success also lead to his destruction. For example, Odysseus' proud spirit contributes to the sacking of Troy, but also impels him to taunt the Cyclops, drawing a curse that extends his wandering and ensures the death of his companions. The behavior, actions, and predicaments of heroes encompass—perhaps even strain—the limits of human experience.

In the study of Greek religion, the term *hērōs* denotes any figure who receives hero cult worship.[28] The rituals of hero-cult are distinct from the worship of divinities, and are emphatically local; worship of a hero focuses on the geographic area where his tomb resides.[29] Sometimes heroes known from literature remain in intimate contact with their cult identities, but though their traditions are often in parallel, they are not entirely overlapping.[30] There are many types of hero cults, but the cult of athletic heroes is particularly relevant for Heracles, founder of the Olympic Games and patron of the gymnasium. Fontenrose has identified a common narrative pattern to the establishment of these cults: an athlete wins remarkable victories, suffers injury or disappointment, brings destruction upon fellow citizens in revenge, and is in turn punished or rejected. This draws the anger of the athlete after death, causing calamity for the athlete's city; his violence is appeased only by the god's direction to establish a continuous cult.[31] The power of the cult figure is connected to anger and destruction and requires propitiation, directly associating the aetiology of these cults with heroic violence.

The role of the hero in ritual and cult is not a focus of this particular study, but the presentation of heroic violence in literature reflects some of its tensions. The cult hero is an exceptional power who holds the potential for both protection and destruction, and the relationship between the cult hero and his local community remains unstable, requiring continuous attention. So too does mythic narrative emphasize the vexed position of the violent hero, whose strength can be used to benefit friends and harm enemies but also constantly threatens to transgress limits and leave collateral damage in its wake. Most importantly for this study, Heracles' status as hero means that he represents an extraordinary individual who already stands outside of the bounds of regular human life. Yet he, a mortal son of Zeus poised to become a god, dwells and toils within a human community that is affected by his use of force. Like that mythological community, historical Greek societies had an interest in constraining individual violence to ends deemed legitimate, while discouraging excessive force. Through stories about Heracles, therefore, archaic and classical Greek cultures could explore the benefits and drawbacks of individual violence and test methods of constraint.

Myths about Heracles' exploits thus served not only to entertain, but also to shape the ethical evaluation of violence. Violent narratives and images have natural entertainment value.[32] Myth also serves as a conveyor of values: as Charles Martindale puts it, "stories encode values, and our account of stories are always value-laden."[33] Mythological stories serve as a conduit that allows for cultural change in both directions: that is, myth can reflect changes in the culture that produced it just as much as it can be a vehicle used by artists, writers, philosophers, or rulers to shape the values of their surrounding culture. These two functions of myth are not, of course, mutually exclusive, nor are they often easily distinguished, given our spotty knowledge of the contexts in which so many Greek myths were produced and received.

The gruesome myth of Tydeus and his death illustrate this ambiguity. In broad outlines: Tydeus, who lived and fought in the generation prior to the Trojan War, is one of the great warriors counted among the Seven who attack the city of Thebes. The struggle against his opponent Melanippus would claim both of their lives. Melanippus deals Tydeus a fatal blow before he is decapitated by Amphiaraus. Tydeus, in an unspeakable rage, begins to gnaw on Melanippus' brains; Athena, Tydeus' patron and protectress, had intended to reward her favorite with immortality, but when she sees Tydeus' actions, she changes her mind in disgust.[34] On the one hand, Tydeus' loss of immortality is the result of his violation of a taboo against cannibalism. The myth encodes fundamental divisions between god, man, and beast: in consuming the brain of Melanippus,

Tydeus confuses humanity and bestiality, and therefore he is prevented from attaining godhood.[35] On the other hand, the myth of Tydeus serves a social function. It delineates the conventions that govern individual victory on the battlefield: a champion cannot do just anything he likes, even to the mutilated body of his enemy. By depicting the punishment of a great warrior for his violation of convention, representations of the myth of Tydeus reinforce those conventions to their audiences.

As the myth of Tydeus demonstrates, Heracles is not the only hero in Greek mythology who wields violence in questionable ways. Figures such as Theseus, Perseus, Odysseus, and Achilles are also well known for their use of force. But Heracles is far and away the strong man par excellence in the Greek imagination, a status reflected in his temporal, generic, and geographic ubiquity. Because many kinds of stories about him survive (the Labors, martial exploits, family drama, comic failures) in multiple poetic or performance genres, he permits a broader range of exploration of the problems of heroic violence. In contrast, much of Theseus' mythology is built in imitation of Heracles', and Perseus' mythological cycle is quite limited in comparison. Achilles and Odysseus are both prominent, pan-Hellenic heroes well represented in surviving evidence, but in my view Achilles' violence is mostly limited to war and its surrounding context, while Odysseus seems to have been most prominently used to explore the ambivalence of cunning rather than force. Heracles also typifies broader cultural trends: this study demonstrates how Greeks used Heracles as a lens for exploring and experimenting with constraints on violence. We can see echoes of this in other hero figures, but by subjecting the single figure of Heracles to extensive scrutiny, these various strategies come to light even more clearly.

On Heracles

In this section, I will discuss some aspects of Heracles' mythological tradition that make him an outstanding figure through which to examine the intertwining of violence and heroism—the myth of apotheosis, the very broad range of his exploits, and the corresponding ability of the focalizer to shape the value of those exploits—and situate and describe this study within the context of previous scholarship on Heracles. Heracles is set apart by the myth that he, though born a mortal hero, becomes a god: at the end of his life, his body is burned on a pyre on Mount Oeta and he ascends to Olympus as a god; there he is married to Hera's daughter Hebe, the personification of youth, and he enjoys an afterlife of ease and feasting.³⁶ The tradition of his apotheosis sets him apart from nearly all the other heroes, who, as sons of gods and mortals, may accomplish remarkable deeds but nevertheless must die. The evidence for this myth can be found in literature, visual images, and archaeological finds. Along with many scholars, I argue that the *Iliad* and *Odyssey* preserve a tradition that does not yet know of Heracles' apotheosis; the references to Heracles' divinity in the *Odyssey*, *Theogony*, and the Hesiodic *Catalogue of Women* are interpolations inserted to bring these older texts into alignment with later views. Yet by the time of Pindar, Heracles can occupy an ambiguous position as *hērōs theos* ("hero-god," *Nem.* 3.22), a figure with affinities to both the mortal and divine world.

The theme of Heracles' introduction to Olympus and marriage to Hebe is better represented in the art of the archaic period. A large number of Attic black-figure vases (550–500 BCE) depict Heracles' being introduced to Olympus on foot or riding a chariot to Olympus (see Figure 1.2 for an example).³⁷ While these vases would have been held in private homes, a limestone sculpture group of Athena leading Heracles to the throne of her father Zeus would have been observed in a very public place, on the archaic acropolis at Athens. Boardman has argued that the popularity of Heracles and changes in his iconography are linked with the political activities of Peisistratus and his sons.³⁸ An unusual Corinthian aryballos, however, pre-dating the bloom of Athenian images on this theme, depicts Heracles and Hebe together in a chariot, in a wedding procession among the gods.³⁹ The unique iconography demonstrates that the deification of Heracles, regardless of Peisistratid influence, had an independent artistic tradition represented outside of Athenian tyranny.

How this heroic–divine duality was expressed in cult worship remains debated.⁴⁰ Herodotus uses the example of the dual cults of Heracles to explain the difference between worship of heroes (chthonic forces) and gods (who dwell above).⁴¹ Emma Stafford's overview of ritual worship in mainland Greece and the islands highlights the rich variety of rituals related to Heracles' cult.⁴² In sharp contrast with local hero worship, which was typically centered at the site of a tomb, his cult was truly pan-Hellenic. Both Thebes and the Argolid claimed his origin, and his resting place had no location (though Mt. Oeta remained associated with his death).⁴³ Furthermore, Heracles occupies a benign, overtly positive cultural role not usually attributed to local heroes, in that his cult was associated more with deification than revenge. The unprecedented nature of his heroic and divine cults makes him especially conspicuous.

Among the heroes of myth, Heracles is extraordinary for both his ability to accomplish glorious feats and his tendency to be caught up in calamity. No hero experiences the depths to which Heracles falls when he slaughters his own wife and children in a fit of madness; nevertheless, he goes on to ascend the heights of Olympus to recline with the gods alongside a divine wife, as a reward for the completion of his Labors. Both his disasters and his glorification depend upon violence, and often the way the violence is depicted determines whether the action is evaluated as good or bad.[44] As a brief example, Heracles' acquisition of the apples of the Hesperides and slaughter of their guardian snake are praised in Euripides' *Heracles* (394–9). The chorus there includes the exploit in a hymn of praise of Heracles' deeds, emphasizing the snake's frightening appearance (πυρσόντων, "red-backed," 398) and fierceness (ἄπλατον, "unapproachable," 399). Yet when the same incident is depicted in Book 4 of Apollonius' *Argonautica*, one of the Hesperides, Aegle, decries Heracles as "most shameless" (κύντατος, 4.1433) and "utterly destructive in arrogance and strength" (ὀλοώτατος ὕβριν / καὶ δέμας, 4.1436–7). For the nymphs, the serpent served a positive purpose as guardian of the apples, and Heracles is nothing but a homicidal thief.[45] As startling as this sort of contrast is, it is not rare in our sources. Indeed, the sheer ubiquity of Heracles' presence—from the stage to coinage to temple sculpture—allows for a close assessment of the spectrum of heroic action.

The example of Heracles' force against the Hesperides' snake highlights the influence of the one telling the story. The chorus in Euripides' play offers a completely different perspective from the Hesperides, who experience the direct and negative impacts of Heracles' violence. My reading of these episodes thus also owes a debt to the fundamental insights of narratology, which establish how the act of narration itself entails focalization.[46] The significance of the focalizer suggests that the representation of heroic violence resists a neutral evaluation. Perhaps because violence typically entails harm enacted by one party on another, or because mythic narratives function as conveyors of social values, literary treatments reveal how violence invites appraisal and judgment.

Heracles thus proves a natural choice for a study of the dynamics of heroic violence. Furthermore, for the purposes of this study, two separate but related elements shape the presentation of Heracles' violence on a broader level: the role Heracles inhabits in the myth, and the literary genre in which it appears. His exploits cluster loosely around roles or identities that are often associated with specific functions. For example, myths about his killing of fantastic animals point towards a role as a monster-slayer; the same myths, along with his punishments of human evildoers like Busiris, serve as a foundation for his role as a civilizer. Stories about his eating habits and love of drinking, on the other hand, frame him as a comic buffoon. The relationship between myths and roles is mutually influential: Heracles' successful completion of extraordinary feats can be attributed to his identity as a favorite son of Zeus, while his status as Zeus' son is used in various myths to justify his violent acts, question why he suffers, or promote his apotheosis. While certain roles are in place already in early archaic material, others develop over time, such as his role as a deified hero or epinician victor. Although this study concludes at the end of the fifth century BCE, Heracles acquires new roles in the centuries and millennia that follow: he becomes a pederastic lover in poetry at the same time as he is claimed as an ancestor by Hellenistic rulers, and the stupid strongman of comedy is reborn as an eloquent speaker among Renaissance humanists.

The literary genres and performance contexts that transmit Heracles' myths also bear responsibility for the contours of his presentation.[47] The conventions of epic poetry allow for the depiction of heroes mercilessly killing each other on the battlefield and feasting in great halls, but certainly not the defecation that results from consumption—a frequent theme in comedy. Heracles' range further enables him to be used to push the boundaries of generic conventions. The genre of Euripides' *Alcestis* is a famously controversial topic, for reasons unrelated to Heracles—the play was performed in the position of a satyr play, after a trilogy of tragedies, but without a satyr chorus—but Heracles' prominent role as a buffoon as in comedy certainly complicates it further.

One particularly significant genre for Heracles is epinician poetry, poems commissioned by wealthy patrons to celebrate their victories in major athletic contests. Heracles' physical superiority and association with activities such as wrestling make him a natural choice as patron for athletes. In Pindar's epinician odes, Heracles is further transformed into the ultimate mythological *exemplum* for his victors, the hero most worth of emulation. In the role of epinician victor, his violence is generally highly constrained and particularly communally oriented. One marker of the influence of epinician is its interaction with other genres: for example, Sophocles' *Trachiniae* and Euripides' *Alcestis* and *Heracles*, I argue, all draw on Heracles' epinician persona in their examination of heroic violence. And in Aristophanes' *Frogs*, the Heracles of epic, tragedy, and comedy are set in conversation with each other. This study thus demonstrates how Heracles' many roles and generic identities allow for a complex investigation of violence, even as his violence serves to delineate (and stretch) the boundaries of the genres themselves.

My focus on Heracles' use of violence and approach to his forms and functions distinguish this study from previous scholarship on Heracles. The earliest scholarship consisted of attempts to draw a coherent biographical narrative from the manifold ancient testimony. By collecting and surveying Heracles' appearances across literary texts and images, these wide-ranging studies document the breadth of Heracles' appearances in Greek and Roman culture.[48] While a major improvement over the "mythological handbook" approach, these studies nevertheless do not offer much in the way of synthetic analysis. Beginning in the 1970s, interest in the evolving character of the traditions of Heracles began to grow. The most important of these studies is Karl Galinsky's *The Herakles Theme*, which aims to produce for Heracles what Stanford's landmark *The Odysseus Theme* does for Odysseus: a scholarly exploration of nearly every aspect of the Heracles cycle, from the earliest evidence in the archaic period to modern times.[49] His sensitive treatment remains indispensable, alongside Kirk's detailed discussion of the contradictions that distinguish Heracles from other mythological heroes.[50] More recently, Emma Stafford's *Herakles* approaches Heracles' life with a similar chronological breadth, organizing each chapter by "theme," like the other volumes in Routledge's "Gods and Heroes of the Ancient World" series.[51] Her text, aimed primarily at students, presents a comprehensive and detailed overview of Heracles' ancient mythical tradition.[52] The book concludes with a substantial analysis of post-classical variations of Heracles, which both distinguishes her study from others' and is most welcome. These studies reveal the extraordinary multiplicity of Heracles and his traditions and trace Heracles' evolution from a figure of terrifying violence to a model of moral endurance.

The many scholarly avenues of approach to Heracles make him a popular subject for volumes and conference proceedings. The proceedings of four conferences specifically on Heracles in the past twenty-five years are eloquent testimony to European (particularly Francophone) interest in the subject.[53] All four volumes are wide ranging, addressing Heracles from the perspectives of archaeology, art history, gender studies, and cultural studies. The post-classical life of Hercules is the subject of several edited volumes developed through Emma Stafford's "Hercules Project" at the University of Leeds, on topics ranging from *Herakles Inside and Outside the Church* (2020) to *The Modern Hercules* (2021).[54] The forthcoming *Oxford Handbook to Heracles* provides a scholarly overview of his major exploits as well as prominent themes related to his myths.[55] A handful of longer essays seek to place Heraclean heroism within the context of one or more genres.[56] And substantial in-depth studies of a single text, such as Papadopoulou's monograph on Euripides' *Heracles*, provide an insightful "snapshot" of Heracles' appearance on the Attic stage.[57] Meanwhile, the number of articles related to Heracles' mythical tradition is simply vast.

Literary scholarship on Heracles tends to fall into two types of studies: a small-scale study of Heracles in an individual text or a broadly wide-ranging survey of Heracles across multiple genres and even centuries. The overwhelming variety of Heracles' traditions tends to enforce this dichotomy. My study straddles the divide between the long-range survey and narrowly focused study of Heracles.[58] The foundation of my research is the fine-grained philological analysis of Heracles' roles in specific texts, with contemporary images providing additional evidence. By addressing multiple texts and images produced over a span of four centuries, the study will be synthetic in nature, able to trace a specific phenomenon through time and across genres. But because the inquiry is focused on a defined set of questions about the representation of heroic violence, this study stands apart from the broad surveys discussed above.

The structure of this study is built around case studies of individual texts, allowing for both a close engagement with an individual narrative and a broader perspective on a range of texts from different genres. In combination, this approach allows the many generic and thematic connections to emerge and build upon one another over the course of the book. The case studies are united by their focus not only on the various facets of heroic violence, but also on the tensions between Arendt's instrumental violence and Benjamin's nonmediate violence. In investigating the taming of Heracles over time, this research offers a new understanding not only of the mythological figure, but also of the shifting ethical boundaries governing violence in the archaic and classical periods.

The first chapter of this book articulates the motifs that define episodes of violence in the poetry of Homer and Hesiod, alongside other archaic poetry. Through the myths of Heracles' Labors, sacking of cities, attacks on the gods, and birth and apotheosis, several of his early roles come into view. He functions as a monster-slayer; an object of divine favor and hostility; a *theomachos* who dares to fight the gods; a warrior who can tear down a city nearly single-handedly; a suffering mortal; and a divine figure. The ambivalence of his violence can be observed even in this early evidence, sometimes even within the same role. For example, in *Iliad* 5, Dione condemns Heracles' attacks on Hera and Hades as an example of an overreaching mortal, one whose nonmediate violence cannot be contained. But in the Hesiodic *Shield of Heracles*, the poet portrays Ares as the combatant possessed by rage and contemptuous of the gods' decrees, while Heracles wounds Hades yet still obeys Athena's injunctions; his violence remains confined to justifiable ends. This analysis reveals the components of each episode—akin to Riess' "semantic grammar of violence"— that, in the hands of a particular poet or painter, can be manipulated to produce wildly divergent portraits of heroic violence.

The second chapter takes a deep dive into a single myth, the Labor of the Cattle of Geryon, in order to investigate the instrumental nature of violence. By tracing the problematization of Geryon's death through the work of three poets, the chapter shows how Heracles' violence is used to interrogate the justification of violence by its ends. In Hesiod's *Theogony*, Heracles' violence against Geryon falls under his role as monster-slayer, and the more ordered universe that results from Geryon's elimination serves to justify his use of violence against him. But in Stesichorus' *Geryoneis*, Geryon is humanized as a noble warrior, despite his monstrous form; this recharacterization undermines Heracles' claim to be a civilizer and presents a Geryon who resists the label "monster." The challenge to the justification for Geryon's death is extended further in two fragments of Pindar, a poet whose epinician odes typically extol Heracles as an example worthy of emulation. In these fragments, Pindar calls both the ends and the means of violence into question by praising Geryon and suggesting peaceful means for acquiring the cattle. This particular myth thus provides fertile material for questioning the fundamental heroic role of monster-slayer; furthermore, it demonstrates how a labor that serves to justify the instrumental use of violence can develop into the depiction of violence as a manifestation.

The next two chapters explore the treatment of Heracles' violence in tragedy, a genre which frequently looks at the world of heroes from the perspective of the home. The third chapter examines heroic competition, a cultural practice that constrains violence through conventions which typically entail two male opponents competing for a prize. In Sophocles' *Trachiniae*, a series of distorted, improperly defined competitions—between Heracles and Nessus, between Heracles and Iole's family, and between Iole and Deianeira—lead to the collapse of the *oikos* and Heracles' death. Heracles experiences a painful death, and this despite the fact that he never loses his status as victor, revealing an estrangement between community and victor that epinician aims to heal. The corruption of heroic competition and the disaster that ensues display violence's resistance to governance by convention, suggesting that even in the person of a glorious victor, violence is continually threatening to manifest itself.

The fourth chapter investigates the daring experiment in Euripides' *Heracles*, to encompass Heracles' greatest triumph and most horrific act—the successful capture of Cerberus from Hades and the murder of his wife and children—within a single treatment of the figure. I argue that the play accomplishes this by relying on two of Heracles' roles, the *kallinikos* victor of epinician poetry and the *philos* (or friend). Initially the two roles of *kallinikos* and *philos* firmly confine Heracles' violence to glorious ends, as he successfully completes his Labors and rescues his family from an evil tyrant. But a fit of madness imposed by Hera causes him to wield his dominating violence against his loved ones, rather than his enemies; in the decoupling of these roles, heroic violence is framed as a manifestation rather than an instrument. Heracles' friend Theseus arrives and prevents Heracles from committing suicide, an act of self-directed violence, by offering a material return for Heracles' earlier favor, which allows Heracles *kallinikos* to emerge once more. In giving comparable weight to Heracles' victories and his social relationships, the play promotes the power of communal values to control violence.

Heracles' ubiquity as a comic buffoon allows for an assessment of laughter as a powerful technique for deflating violence's threat. The fifth chapter explores Heracles as a figure of Bakhtinian carnival in fragments of Sicilian drama, satyr play, and Old and Middle Comedy in Athens. The emphasis on the appetites of the lower body arouses laughter, degrading him; however, in the comic plots that inevitably lead to his victory over villains, Heracles is recrowned as victor. A study of Euripides' *Alcestis* illustrates how Heracles' physical excesses can be harnessed to save his *philoi*, reconciling his comic and epinician roles. Aristophanes' *Frogs* plays with the idea of Heracles and all that he represents by putting his distinctive manifestations across the genres of epic, tragedy, and comedy into conversation with each other. The collision of these roles in the Underworld cannot be resolved, leading to the collapse of the Heracles costume. The play thus demonstrates the manifold, dialogical nature of Heracles, while also revealing the intractability of violence itself.

By examining the interplay of mythological roles and a range of literary genres, this series of case studies yields a fuller picture of strategies for shaping and constraining heroic violence: instrumental justification, heroic competition, glorious victory, friendship, and laughter. Yet these strategies' limitations and vulnerabilities are also exposed. The means–ends logic of instrumental violence is undermined by Heracles' unjust actions; heroic competition can be corrupted such that violence becomes unbound; glorious victory when decoupled from friendship leads to kin-killing; and even laughter cannot resolve the ambivalence of violence. Heroic violence proves an unruly force, even as it remains necessary.

The findings from this study form a useful template for understanding Heracles' later treatments. In the conclusion, I foreshadow the application, adaptation, or even abandonment of these strategies in Heracles' manifestations in later periods, as demonstrated by Prodicus' philosophical tale of Heracles at the Crossroads, an episode with a long and influential afterlife. Xenophon's account of Prodicus' allegory ends before Heracles makes his fateful choice between Arete and Kakia, leaving the audience in suspense and implying (I argue) that Heracles' choice of Arete is not inevitable. The allegory relies on the tension between his roles as, for example, epinician victor and comic buffoon, illustrating how even the new philosophical Heracles engages with earlier generic manifestations of Heracles as defined throughout this book. After assessing the various roles, genres, and methods of controlling heroic violence explored in the book, the Conclusion brings together the major advances the book accomplishes in understanding heroic violence: establishing the different generic approaches to containing violence (epic, lyric, epinician, tragedy, comedy) and especially the influence of epinician; the pervasive anxiety surrounding victory itself; and the way in which the understanding of violence as a manifestation consistently overpowers the approach of violence as an instrument. Ultimately, the limited success of the project of taming Heracles proves that he is not a problem to be solved, but a problem to think with.

1

Heraclean Force and the Representation of Violence

Introduction

Already in our earliest literary and visual sources, Heracles is a well-known, pan-Hellenic figure. He is a popular subject of early Attic vase paintings, and the brief allusions to his actions in archaic poetry seem to indicate that broad knowledge of his exploits could be assumed. Even in this early evidence, Heracles' violence is treated in diverse ways; for example, in Hesiod's *Theogony*, Heracles' use of violence functions as a civilizing force, while in the *Iliad*, Heracles' attacks on the gods are condemned as reckless and disgraceful. This chapter's analysis is structured around several roles or functions that Heracles frequently plays in early archaic poetry and art: a monster-slayer, a victim of Hera's divine enmity, a champion and protégé of Zeus and Athena, a *theomachos* (a hero who physically attacks a god), and a sacker of cities. In exploring how the dynamics of these roles influence the evaluation of his use of violence, this chapter establishes the motifs that constitute an episode of heroic violence, a task akin to Riess's "semantic grammar of violence."[1]

The very language that names Heracles in epic poetry identifies him with violence. He is commonly referred to by the epic periphrasis *biē Hēraklēeiē* (βίη Ἡρακληείη), which literally translates into "Heraclean force," but is more conventionally translated as "mighty Heracles."[2] Of the seven references to Heracles in Hesiod's *Theogony*, for example, five of them incorporate this periphrasis.[3] The semantic range of *biē* encompasses both the more neutral "force, strength, might" and the more ambivalent "violence."[4] This periphrasis reverses the more typical epic epithet, in which the name is modified by an adjective, such as "swift-footed Achilles" (πόδας ὠκὺς Ἀχιλλεύς).[5] Metrical considerations may certainly play a role: related forms of *biē Hēraklēeiē* consistently occupy the second half of the dactylic hexameter line. But the shift of Heracles' name into adjectival form also emphasizes the significance of the noun *biē* and demonstrates how essential the notion of force is to the conception of Heracles for an archaic audience.

Heracles was the subject of several substantial archaic epics, all of which, unfortunately, are lost.[6] Creophylus of Samos, likely of the early seventh century BCE, composed a *Sack of Oechalia*, of which only one line remains.[7] Pisander of Rhodes wrote a *Heraclea* which apparently included an account of Heracles' Labors.[8] The *Suda* credits Panyassis of Halicarnassis with a *Heraclea* of 9000 lines over fourteen books; later citations of the text suggest a poem that explored Heracles' myths in great depth, including his penchant for drinking and feasts.[9] What has survived are the mostly incidental occurrences of Heracles in the works of Homer, Hesiod, and poems attributed to Hesiod.[10] In these works, Heracles' use of violence spans a wide range of actions, establishing him as an ambivalent hero, a figure of unstable meaning. In the *Theogony*, Heracles kills monstrous beasts, accruing glory for himself and protecting nearby communities. But in the *Iliad*, Heracles is a warrior willing to attack the gods; and in the *Odyssey*, Heracles kills a guest-friend, violating the conventions of *xenia*, one of the poem's fundamental principles. Thus, from the start, Heracles conveys the complexity of heroic violence, a complexity which only deepens when the myth of Heracles' apotheosis becomes more established in the sixth century BCE, and he takes on a larger role as an exemplary figure.

This chapter begins with an exploration of how Heracles' destruction of monsters is justified in Hesiod's *Theogony*, which also touches on the tensions between his roles as divine victim and divine champion. These tensions inform the presentation of his myths in the *Iliad*, where he also serves as a *theomachos* and sacker of cities. By comparing the Iliadic material to other archaic poetry and visual material, this chapter seeks to identify the elements that construct the underlying narrative framework for episodes of violence. The interaction between Heracles' various roles allows for the emergence of moral judgments of violence, represented by praise and/or blame of his actions by the poet or speaker. Already in this early stage, heroic violence can be modeled both as an instrument and as a manifestation. This material establishes a foundation from which new ideas will spring, idea that have the potential to alter the calculus of violence, as we shall see in the following chapters.

Heracles as Monster-slayer in Hesiod's *Theogony*

The *Theogony* is a poem about the birth of the gods and the emergence of the Olympian order; it describes how the world came to be the way it is, with Zeus, the father of gods and men, at its head. The poem is thus especially concerned with the triumph of order over chaos and conflicts between generations. Heracles appears prominently among the generation of heroes who eradicate malformed, menacing beasts from the earth: he kills three-headed Geryon, together with his dog Orthus and herdsman Eurytion (289–94), the Lernaean Hydra (313–18), and the Nemean Lion (328–32). As a preeminent monster-tamer, Heracles plays an important role in advancing the agenda of order. In this poem, the conquering of beasts—later codified into a series of Labors—is uncontroversial, and his use of violence unquestioned.[11] The poem offers three motivations that justify Heracles' use of violence:

First, the most obvious justification for Heracles' violence against monsters is the fact that some of them prove a direct threat to human society. Not every beast poses an explicit danger to nearby settlements, but the Nemean Lion clearly does:

τόν ῥ' Ἥρη θρέψασα Διὸς κυδρὴ παράκοιτις
γουνοῖσιν κατένασσε Νεμείης, πῆμ' ἀνθρώποις.
ἔνθ' ἄρ' ὅ γ' οἰκείων ἐλεφαίρετο φῦλ' ἀνθρώπων,
κοιρανέων Τρητοῖο Νεμείης ἠδ' Ἀπέσαντος·
ἀλλά ἑ ἲς ἐδάμασσε βίης Ἡρακληείης.

328–32

Hera, the famous wife of Zeus, raised and settled [the Lion] in the hills of Nemea, a calamity for humans. For there it was living and destroying the tribes of humankind, lording over Tretus of Nemea and Apesas. But the power of Heraclean force conquered it.[12]

Within the economical phrasing of these epic lines are intimations of significant human suffering. The Lion is called a bane or calamity (πῆμα) on humankind; instead of targeting the flocks of the villagers, it destroys the people themselves. The danger of the Lion is countered by an overdetermined epithet of Heracles. The epithet—literally, "the power of Heraclean force" (ἲς ... βίης Ἡρακληείης)— relies on two separate words for force, emphasizing that it is a bravado show of physical power that leads to the death of the Lion. Heracles' violence leads directly to improvements in the lives of the villagers of the Argolid.[13] But his work is not simply local. As Jenny Strauss Clay has shown, Heracles' monster-slaying serves the larger function of reaffirming the hierarchy of humans over beasts.[14]

Secondly, Heracles functions as an enforcer of order against destabilizing chaos, thereby promoting the rule of his father Zeus. Just as Zeus defeats a primeval generation of immortals in order to establish his reign, so Heracles clears the earth of anomalous creatures, with their proliferation of limbs and mixed breeding. Although Heracles is himself a sort of hybrid, called both the son of Zeus and the son of Amphitryon, his monster-slaying identifies him closely as an agent of Zeus, an affiliation that imparts a sense of divine approval.[15] Further bolstering Heracles' status as a divine champion is Athena's involvement in his battle against the Lernaean Hydra. The poet includes Iolaus as an ally, but the pair are only able to defeat the Hydra "by the plans of spoil-driving Athena" (βουλῇσιν Ἀθηναίης ἀγελείης, 318). Her consistent presence throughout his myths marks Heracles as particularly favored, even among the most famous of heroes.

But if Heracles functions as a representative of Zeus, then the slaying of his father's eagle poses a thorny problem. Heracles shoots the eagle that Zeus has appointed to visit Prometheus daily and feast on his immortal, regenerating liver (523–7). Yet the eagle is no hybrid monster, nor does it prey on innocent humans. Moreover, in killing the eagle, Heracles interferes with the punishment that Zeus has established for Prometheus, a rebel who challenged Zeus' authority; his attack aligns him with subversive forces that would overthrow the reign of Zeus. Such an outrage would seem to demand an explanation, which the poet helpfully supplies: Heracles kills the eagle "not against the will of Olympian Zeus, ruling on high, in order that the glory of Theban-born Heracles might be greater still than it was previously on the much-nourishing earth" (οὐκ ἀέκητι Ζηνὸς Ὀλυμπίου ὕψι μέδοντος / ὄφρ' Ἡρακλῆος Θηβαγενέος κλέος εἴη / πλεῖον ἔτ' ἢ τὸ πάροιθεν ἐπὶ χθόνα πουλυβότειραν, 529–31). This justification prevents Heracles from being perceived as an overweening, wayward son; instead, he becomes the object of such great affection that Zeus is willing to accept the diminishment of his own status in favor of his *kleos*.[16] The rationale thus smooths over any doubts about Zeus' authority while showing how Heracles' violent victories can be made worthy of celebration, perhaps even of deification.[17]

Thirdly, Heracles' monster-slaying can be presented as self-defense against the attacks of Hera. Hera's enmity, a force that consistently counterbalances Zeus' favor, is clearly framed as the root cause of Heracles' conflict with the Lernaean Hydra, which "Hera the white-armed goddess reared, terribly resentful of mighty Heracles" (ἣν θρέψε θεὰ λευκώλενος Ἥρη / ἄπλητον κοτέουσα βίῃ Ἡρακληείῃ, 314–15). Her anger is not some passing emotion, but a deep-rooted passion for destroying him. Hera's continuous plotting against him thus serves as another justification for his violence, since Hera occupies the position of overt aggressor, and Heracles the reactor who does not willingly choose violence. As we will see later in greater detail, Hera's persecution of Heracles can frame the challenges Heracles faces as a source of suffering; Heracles' deeds appear to be committed under duress rather than of his own free will, and he becomes the innocent victim of an insatiably vindictive goddess.

The *Theogony*'s brief references to Heracles' relationships with Zeus, Athena, and Hera anticipate their increased significance in later myths. Even within a single role as monster-slayer, the extreme disparity in his divine relations is evident and affects the evaluation of Heracles' violence: an emphasis on Zeus' fondness for his son or Athena's support elevates him, while a focus on Hera's antagonism positions him as a divine victim. Just as he moves within the space between humans and gods, the meaning of his violence is also subject to change and fluctuation. Nevertheless, Heracles' defeat of monsters leads to a more orderly and well-formed universe, earning him a position as an agent of Zeus. These rationales confine his heroic violence, presenting it as a means or an instrument that can be justified.

The *Iliad*'s Heracles

The rest of this chapter will focus on four roles prominent in the *Iliad* and how those roles reflect on the treatment of violence: Heracles functions as a victim of divine hostility, a divine protégé, a sacker of cities, and a *theomachos*. As he oscillates between serving as the victim of Hera's hatred, Zeus' beloved, and Athena's champion, Heracles reflects the gods' investment in the conflict at Troy; the approval of Zeus and Athena or the instigation of Hera thus become an important frame for understanding Heracles' actions. Next, I set Heracles' physical attacks on the gods in the *Iliad* in contrast with Heracles' struggle with Apollo over the Delphic tripod and his fight with Ares in the Hesiodic *Shield of Heracles*; the latter incident demonstrates that even an attack on a god can be cast as a divinely approved act. Finally, Heracles also plays the role of a sacker of cities: a comparison of his earlier destruction of Troy in the *Iliad* with his sack of Oechalia in the *Odyssey* illuminates the dynamics of how to justify overturning a city.

Heracles' presence in the *Iliad* is no surprise: violence is essential to its themes. In Simone Weil's influential summation, "The true hero, the true subject matter, the center of the *Iliad* is force. The force that men wield, the force that subdues men, in the face of which human flesh shrinks back."[18] Weil's reading illuminates the way heroic force turns living beings into objects, inanimate corpses, and touches conqueror and conquered alike. Although Heracles does not loom large in Weil's analysis, he is a representative of force itself, and thus lies close to the epic's concerns. In the *Iliad*, Heracles is portrayed as a towering but troubling hero of a previous generation, an exemplum from what Grethlein calls the "epic plupast" or, in Bär's term, "epic memory."[19] The full sweep of Heracles' life is represented, from his birth to his adult adventures to his death, and the poet's allusions to his exploits assume a close familiarity with Heracles' myths (e.g., 15.638–40). Of the eighteen times Heracles is mentioned by name, eight examples involve the epic periphrasis βίη Ἡρακληείη and related forms ("Heraclean force," seven examples), and βίη Ἡρακλῆος ("force of Heracles," one example).[20] Heracles and his use of force, especially in his sack of Troy and attacks on the gods, come to form a fundamental part of the backdrop to the epic's events.

Heracles' utility in the *Iliad* seems to lie largely in his use as a paradigm, a foil to reflect the current predicaments of the main players. He hardly appears as an independent actor or speaker in his own right; he is described by the narrator and in speeches, where he is focalized (mostly negatively) through internal narrators.[21] The material of his mythological cycle provides a rich fabula on which a variety of speakers can draw, each for his or her own purpose.[22] The range of the hero's roles allows others to boast about his prowess or to condemn his actions. This flexibility demonstrates his value within the mythical tradition: even from the earliest stages in Greek literature, Heracles was good to think with.

The *Iliad*'s Heracles: Heracles between the Gods

Although Heracles plays a limited role as a monster-tamer in the *Iliad*, many of the same unstable dynamics surrounding his relationships with the gods remain. In this section, I explore the epic's portrait of Heracles as a beloved son, divine champion and protégé, and divine victim. The conflict between the gods over his fate serves as a model for the gods' taking sides and playing favorites in the conflict between Trojans and Greeks. This aspect of Heracles' example in the *Iliad* highlights the larger precariousness of a hero's life. Both his renown and his struggles can be attributed to the larger machinations of the divine powers around him, providing a shifting view of Heracles' Labors.

In this text, Zeus is consistently presented as Heracles' father, and Amphitryon barely registers, playing no role in his exploits, even at birth.[23] Zeus' special fondness for Heracles elevates the hero to a status closer to his fellow Olympians', blurring the distinction between mortal and divine. Indeed, Zeus' pride in and affection for his son have become paradigmatic for the heroes of the Trojan War: when Agamemnon expresses regret over his quarrel with Achilles, he blames *Atē* and compares his own frustration to Zeus's anger when his plans for Heracles' birth are frustrated (19.91–136). For Zeus had boasted on the day of Heracles' birth that he would rule Argos; but clever Hera, aided by *Atē*, delays Heracles' birth, allowing Eurystheus to be born first and take priority in rule. Thus when Agamemnon wants to express grief upon watching Hector slaughter the Greeks, he draws on Zeus' helpless fury upon seeing his "own dear son" (ἐὸν φίλον υἱόν, 19.132) subjected to a lesser man.[24] Agamemnon's appeal to Heracles as an exemplum is designed to exonerate his own errors, attributing them to a force so powerful and blinding that she could interfere even with Zeus' will for his beloved son.

In light of Agamemnon's tale, Heracles' Labors are no longer tasks accomplished for the purpose of benefiting humankind or acquiring glory. Rather, Heracles must bear "shameful toil under the Labors of Eurystheus" (ἔργον ἀεικὲς ἔχοντα ὑπ' Εὐρυσθῆος ἀέθλων, 19.133). The Labors are now an imposition, and he therefore operates under compulsion, his use of violence no longer a considered or independent choice. An emphasis on Eurystheus' dominance implies that the Labors cannot be a means to an end; they are an end of themselves, existing as a venue for Eurystheus to increase Heracles' suffering and for Hera to vent her spleen.

Athena's comments to Hera about her relationship with Heracles likewise provide a new viewpoint on the Labors. Athena, usually Heracles' champion, expresses strong antipathy towards him to build an alliance with Hera against Zeus, whom she portrays as an overly indulgent father. By diminishing Heracles' power and insulting Zeus' support, she reaffirms her commitment to protect the Greeks against the onslaught of Hector, in defiance of Zeus' direct order not to interfere in the battle (8.1–27).

> οὐδέ τι τῶν μέμνηται, ὅ οἱ μάλα πολλάκις υἱὸν
> τειρόμενον σώεσκον ὑπ' Εὐρυσθῆος ἀέθλων.
> ἤτοι ὁ μὲν κλαίεσκε πρὸς οὐρανόν, αὐτὰρ ἐμὲ Ζεὺς
> τῷ ἐπαλεξήσουσαν ἀπ' οὐρανόθεν προΐαλλεν.
> εἰ γὰρ ἐγὼ τάδε ᾔδε' ἐνὶ φρεσὶ πευκαλίμῃσιν
> εὖτέ μιν εἰς Ἀΐδαο πυλάρταο προὔπεμψεν
> ἐξ Ἐρέβευς ἄξοντα κύνα στυγεροῦ Ἀΐδαο,
> οὐκ ἂν ὑπεξέφυγε Στυγὸς ὕδατος αἰπὰ ῥέεθρα.
>
> 8.362–70

[Zeus] does not remember how many times I saved his son, burdened by the Labors of Eurystheus. Truly Heracles would keep on crying to heaven, and Zeus would send me down from heaven to defend him. If I had known these things in my prudent heart, when Eurystheus sent him to the realm of Hades the gatekeeper in order to lead out of Erebus the hound of hated Hades, he would not have escaped the sheer waters of the Styx.

Athena claims that Zeus' lack of gratitude has colored her view of her help to Heracles; she has become Heracles' unwilling and resentful protector, not the divine helper of a mortal but worthy partner. In her telling, Heracles is hardly a glorious conqueror of outsized heroic prowess, but a needy complainer, dependent on others' aid for his successes. Heracles, and by extension Zeus, owes his most significant triumph—the return from Hades with Cerberus—to an underappreciated Athena. By disparaging Heracles, Athena accomplishes two rhetorical goals: first, to demonstrate her independence from the aims of a foolish Zeus, and second, to frame herself as a natural associate of Hera, Heracles' most determined enemy.[25] The heroic victories of Heracles are reduced to the means by which Athena and Hera establish common cause, illustrating his relevance to defining alliances across Olympus and Troy.

Zeus' divine favor towards Heracles inevitably arouses the divine antagonism of Hera, a continuous struggle that animates a series of conflicts following Heracles' sack of Troy. In a study of the repeated appearances of Heracles, Mabel Lang shows that "there was a detailed tradition of Heracles as the object of divine favor and hostility, and, more important, that Zeus' and Hera's conflict over Hector was most likely modeled on that tradition."[26] Indeed, when Hera begs Hypnos to lull Zeus to sleep so that she can aid the Greeks, Hypnos refuses because he recalls the painful consequences of the last time he overwhelmed Zeus at Hera's request. Hera drove Heracles to Kos, and when Zeus awoke he nearly destroyed Hypnos.[27] Hypnos recalls the memory:

ἤματι τῷ ὅτε κεῖνος ὑπέρθυμος Διὸς υἱὸς
ἔπλεεν Ἰλιόθεν Τρώων πόλιν ἐξαλαπάξας.
ἤτοι ἐγὼ μὲν ἔλεξα Διὸς νόον αἰγιόχοιο
νήδυμος ἀμφιχυθείς· σὺ δέ οἱ κακὰ μήσαο θυμῷ
ὄρσασ' ἀργαλέων ἀνέμων ἐπὶ πόντον ἀήτας,
καί μιν ἔπειτα Κόωνδ' εὖ ναιομένην ἀπένεικας
νόσφι φίλων πάντων. ὃ δ' ἐπεγρόμενος χαλέπαινε
ῥιπτάζων κατὰ δῶμα θεούς, ἐμὲ δ' ἔξοχα πάντων
ζήτει. καί κέ μ' ἄϊστον ἀπ' αἰθέρος ἔμβαλε πόντῳ,
εἰ μὴ Νὺξ δμήτειρα θεῶν ἐσάωσε καὶ ἀνδρῶν·

14.250–9

... on the day when that overweening son of Zeus was sailing from Ilium after sacking the Trojan city. Then I sweetly spread over the mind of aegis-bearing Zeus, lulling him to sleep. But you contrived evil for him in your heart, inciting the blasts of harsh winds upon the sea, and then you carried him off to well-settled Kos, far from his all his friends. But Zeus was enraged when he awoke, tossing gods around the house, and looking above all for *me*. And he would have cast me down from heaven to be covered by the sea, if Nyx, tamer of gods and men, had not saved me.

Hera requires the aid of Hypnos in order to accomplish her plots against Heracles. Only when Zeus' vigilance is suspended through sleep can Hera harass the hero, and Zeus' response upon waking is exaggerated and violent.[28] No doubt Zeus is angered in part because he was tricked by Hera and Hypnos. But his concern for his son, which exceeds his loyalty towards his fellow immortals, appears paramount: when Hypnos is reluctant to help Hera once more, she scoffs, "Do you really think that far-sounding Zeus will aid the Trojans just as he raged on behalf of his own son, Heracles?" (ἦ φὴς ὡς Τρώεσσιν ἀρηξέμεν εὐρύοπα Ζῆν / ὡς Ἡρακλῆος περιχώσατο παῖδος ἑοῖο; 14.265–6). For Hypnos, Zeus' allegiance to Heracles epitomizes the gods' favoritism for particular mortals.

This episode remains vivid in Zeus' mind as well. Hera is able to bribe Hypnos into luring Zeus to sleep once more, but as soon as Zeus awakens again, he remembers his anger at Hera's previous plot and his punishment: he strung her up before all the gods as a public demonstration of his superiority over her, and personally whisked Heracles back to Argos (15.18–30). For Zeus, Hera's insubordination and Heracles' suffering cause deeply personal heartache; he recalls, "But not even this [punishment of Hera] relieved my heart of constant anxiety about god-like Heracles" (ἐμὲ δ' οὐδ' ὣς θυμὸν ἀνίει / ἀζηχὴς ὀδύνη Ἡρακλῆος θείοιο, 15.24–5). In describing Heracles as "god-like," Zeus elevates his son for a moment, promoting his safety and honor over Hera's dignity. Nevertheless, Zeus' concern for his son is undermined by his inability to protect him from Hera, a volatility that defines the life of Heracles as it swings from legendary successes to terrible sorrows.

This presentation of Heracles frames him as a kind of pawn, passed off from one god to another, buffeted by shifting alliances and unreliable support. While these fluctuations reduce Heracles' agency, they also underline Zeus' unreliability and the general fallibility of the gods. Athena rhetorically abandons Heracles to advance her own aims; Hera oppresses him, imposing Labors to increase his suffering; Zeus literally falls asleep on the job. That so extraordinary a hero as Heracles can experience such vicissitudes reflects the deep-seated dysfunction of Olympus. This "god's-eye view" of Heracles' career minimizes the question of Heracles' violence. Heracles' responsibility for his actions is reduced, framing his use of force as a compulsory response to externally imposed circumstances, rather than a reflection of a particular individual.

The *Iliad*'s Heracles: Heracles the *Theomachos*

The view of Heracles as a pawn of the gods is counterbalanced by his own propensity to attack them, a transgressive act of *hybris*. His role as *theomachos*—that is, a human warrior who fights against the gods—focuses attention on his interstitial position between mortal and immortal, and the audacity of his choice of adversary brings into question his control over his use of violence. In Book 5, Heracles' violence against the gods is recalled as a foil for Diomedes' unrestrained *aristeia*.[29] After Diomedes wounds Aphrodite in battle, Dione comforts her daughter Aphrodite with the reminder that even more bellicose gods have suffered wounds from mortals. In the eyes of Dione, Heracles' assaults on Hera and Hades are characteristic of a dangerous, overreaching hero:

τλῆ δ' Ἥρη, ὅτε μιν κρατερὸς πάϊς Ἀμφιτρύωνος
δεξιτερὸν κατὰ μαζὸν ὀϊστῷ τριγλώχινι
βεβλήκει· τότε καί μιν ἀνήκεστον λάβεν ἄλγος.
τλῆ δ' Ἀΐδης ἐν τοῖσι πελώριος ὠκὺν ὀϊστόν, (395)
εὖτέ μιν ωὐτὸς ἀνὴρ υἱὸς Διὸς αἰγιόχοιο
ἐν Πύλῳ ἐν νεκύεσσι βαλὼν ὀδύνῃσιν ἔδωκεν·
αὐτὰρ ὃ βῆ πρὸς δῶμα Διὸς καὶ μακρὸν Ὄλυμπον
κῆρ ἀχέων ὀδύνῃσι πεπαρμένος· αὐτὰρ ὀϊστὸς
ὤμῳ ἔνι στιβαρῷ ἠλήλατο, κῆδε δὲ θυμόν. (400)
τῷ δ' ἐπὶ Παιήων ὀδυνήφατα φάρμακα πάσσων
ἠκέσατ'· οὐ μὲν γάρ τι καταθνητός γε τέτυκτο.
σχέτλιος ὀβριμοεργὸς ὃς οὐκ ὄθετ' αἴσυλα ῥέζων,
ὃς τόξοισιν ἔκηδε θεοὺς οἳ Ὄλυμπον ἔχουσι.

5.392–404

But Hera suffered, when the mighty son of Amphitryon struck her right breast with a triple-barbed arrow, and incurable pain seized her. Giant Hades also suffered his swift arrow like the rest, when the same man, the son of aegis-bearing Zeus, struck him—at Pylos, among the dead—and gave him over to severe pains. But he went to the home of Zeus on high Olympus, grieved at heart, wracked with pain. The arrow driven into his stout shoulder distressed his spirit.

But Paion, applying numbing drugs to it, healed him, for nothing about him was mortal. Reckless, wrong-doing man, who has no regard for his evil-doing, but distresses with his arrows the gods who rule Olympus!

In her intent to console her daughter, Dione's condemnation of Heracles is absolute.[30] Her disapproval has a moralizing tone: Heracles is reckless (σχέτλιος), and the attacks themselves are unlawful and wanton (ὀβριμοεργός, 5.403); his heedlessness of his own actions (οὐκ ὄθετο) indicates an undisciplined temperament prone to unchecked force. Moreover, she provides limited backstory to contextualize the attacks, and her emphasis falls on the fact that Heracles has aimed his arrows at an inappropriate set of opponents, the Olympian gods. Only Dione in the whole of the *Iliad* refers to Heracles as a son of Amphitryon (though she also calls him a son of Zeus a few lines later). By highlighting Heracles' mortal parentage, Dione amplifies the transgressive nature of Heracles' attack on gods. The ends of his attack do not justify the means of violence; his theomachy is a manifestation of nonmediate violence.

Dione goes on to associate Heracles with another set of *theomachoi*—the Giants, Otus and Ephialtes, who trap Ares in a jar for months (5.385–91). On the verge of perishing, Ares is rescued at last by his fellow Olympian Hermes. The Gigantomachy belongs to an early mythological era when the Olympian hierarchy was not yet firmly established; even the supposedly immortal Ares appears vulnerable to death. The grouping of Heracles with Otus and Ephialtes heaps up hostility on Heracles' actions, framing them not only as overweening, but as primitive and destabilizing of the order that governs the universe—this despite the fact that Heracles is celebrated for *helping* the gods fight off the Giants (an episode acknowledged in 14.250–61).[31] This suggests that Heracles could present a similar threat to his father Zeus and the Olympians as Zeus posed to his own father Cronus. Dione's speech implies that Heracles the ambitious son may be poised to overthrow the regime and usurp the rule of his own father. Although Heracles never dares to defy Zeus, his attacks on Hades and Hera relate his violence more to upheaval than to order.

The sheer audacity of Heracles' attack on the Olympian gods blurs the boundaries between god and mortal.[32] Heracles' overreaching presents a real threat, as Dione emphasizes the severe pain Hera and Hades were forced to endure (τλῆ, ἀνήκεστον . . . ἄλγος, ὀδύνῃσιν, ὀδυνήφατα). By causing the gods to suffer physical distress, Heracles brings them low, closer to the mortal level. At the same time, by proving himself as an adversary worthy of the gods, he elevates himself to more of a peer status with them. But Dione strives to reinforce the distinction by describing the healing of Hades' wound as the privilege of the immortals (οὐ μὲν γάρ τι καταθνητός γε τέτυκτο, 5.402).³³ The *Iliad* presents the tradition that Heracles dies like a mortal, with no apotheosis foreshadowed in the text. Ultimately, the Olympian order remains unmoved, despite Heracles' aggression: the gods are healed, and Heracles dies.³⁴

While Heracles' actions as a *theomachos*, as focalized by Dione, arise from an arrogant grasping for power, they also represent the moment in the poem when he rises closest to immortality. The manifestation of *hybris* in his violent assaults on the gods is thus connected with his exceptionality. Furthermore, a motif of theomachy seems to recur in Heracles' early myths, emphasizing his status as an extraordinary warrior whose capabilities permit him to reach beyond normal human bounds. Two other incidents—his fight with Apollo at Delphi and with Ares at Pagasae—demonstrate alternative (and contrasting) ways of framing a *theomachos*' violence. These episodes explore the range of meaning that Heracles' battles with the gods permit, and how violence constructs and constrains his liminality.

The *Iliad*'s *Heracles: Heracles the* Theomachos *at Delphi*

In his conflict with Hera and Ares in *Iliad* 5, Heracles asserts his physical and martial dominance. But when Heracles wrestles with Apollo over the tripod at Delphi, Heracles seeks a different prize: divine knowledge. His failure to acquire the prophecy he seeks through theomachy calls into question both the means and the ends of his pursuit. Heracles' attack on Apollo at Delphi continues a tradition of competition over the oracle, and a comparison with the foundation myths of Delphi reveals that just as theomachy elevates Heracles above other mortals, it also reinforces his inferiority to the gods.

In Pseudo-Apollodorus' retelling (2.6.2–3), Heracles seeks an oracle that would instruct how he could be cured of the disease incurred by the pollution from his impious murder of his guest-friend, Iphitus.³⁵ When the Pythian priestess does not give him an oracle, Heracles becomes enraged and decides "to plunder the temple and, after carrying off the tripod, to establish an oracle for himself" (τόν τε ναὸν συλᾶν ἤθελε, καὶ τὸν τρίποδα βαστάσας κατασκευάζειν μαντεῖον ἴδιον, 2.6.2). Apollo confronts him, and while the two sons of Zeus are tussling over the tripod, Zeus separates them with a bolt of lightning. After the fight, Heracles receives his oracle, and is purified by being sold into slavery to Omphale and paying blood-money to Iphitus' father, Eurytus.³⁶ Although it seems to end with a relatively tidy conclusion, this episode reveals the insufficiency of Heracles' reliance on violence. The end goal of establishing a personal oracle for his own use is itself suspect and, moreover, the means of violence is also questionable: Heracles' violence arises as a first angry impulse, rather than last recourse, and is wrapped up in a sacrilegious effort to despoil Apollo's sanctuary.

In the artistic tradition, Heracles' fight with Apollo enjoyed significant popularity, appearing widely on black-figure vase paintings and even on the east pediment of the Siphnian Treasury at Delphi (525 BCE) (Figure 1.1).[37] The images of this episode consistently focus on the moment of Heracles' greatest transgression: the physical struggle between Heracles and Apollo. Boardman classifies the images in two predominate types: the "stand-up fight," an earlier schema in which Apollo and Heracles engage in a tug-of-war with the sacred tripod in the middle, and the "running fight," in which Heracles is carrying the tripod off under his arm, and Apollo tries to grab it.[38] The image is dynamic, and even in the examples in which Heracles appears to have gained possession of the tripod, the outcome of the contest remains in doubt. This emphasis on the struggle has been interpreted by scholars as a symbol of the political conflict between two competing cults or the First Sacred War.[39] Boardman has developed over a series of important articles an argument that connects changes in the

Figure 1.1 Heracles and Apollo vie for the Delphic tripod. East pediment of the Siphnian Treasury, *c.* 525 BCE. Credit: Delphi Archaeological Museum, Delphi © Hellenic Ministry of Culture and Sports/Archaeological Receipts Fund/Fokida Ephorate of Antiquities.

iconography of various depictions of Heracles with political developments during the sixth century.⁴⁰ But even if a specific event stands behind Heracles' image, or a particular historical figure can be charged with revising its iconography, the sheer number of images of Heracles and their continued popularity would seem to indicate that people also enjoyed those images for their own sake, inviting further investigation.

Heracles' struggle for the tripod participates in a longer history of violent competition for control of the oracle at Delphi, one of the most important sites in mainland Greece for the transmission of divine answers to mortal questions.⁴¹ The violence of Heracles' attempted usurpation of Apollo's authority imitates Apollo's own establishment of his oracle. The *Homeric Hymn to Apollo* connects the establishment of the oracle with Apollo's killing of the noxious Python (300–4, 356–74). By slaying the Python, Apollo relieves the neighboring peoples and their flocks of its harassment, an act which suggests a larger shift of power from chthonic forces to Olympian gods. The Homeric Hymn celebrates this act of foundation, but Euripides' later *Iphigenia among the Taurians* presents a version in which Apollo's triumph was not without controversy.⁴² In Euripides' choral ode, the temple servants present what Lloyd-Jones calls "undoubtedly the oldest story, Apollo forcibly dispossessed [Gaia]":⁴³ they describe how Apollo, while still an infant, acquired his prophecies by slaying the Python.⁴⁴ This offends Gaia, who had intended to hand over the oracle to Themis; Gaia therefore allows mortals to gain prophetic knowledge through dreams. Apollo supplicates his father Zeus, and Zeus intervenes to put an end to Gaia's defiance and restore Phoebus' prophetic power (1234–82).⁴⁵ Zeus thus settles the dispute in favor of his young son and exerts his authority over the older goddess, Gaia.

The Pythia in Aeschylus' *Eumenides* offers a rather different account of Apollo's gaining the oracle, one that overtly suppresses the elements of violence. She begins the *Eumenides* by framing the transfer of authority over the oracle as a peaceful and deliberate process. The Pythia omits the brutal slaying of the Python entirely, suggesting perhaps an underlying discomfort with the oracle's foundation on an act of Apollonian violence. In her telling, the power of prophecy passes from Gaia to Themis, as the narrative in the *IT* presents as Gaia's original intent, then from Themis to Phoebe, and from Phoebe to Apollo:

πρῶτον μὲν εὐχῆι τῆιδε πρεσβεύω θεῶν
τὴν πρωτόμαντιν Γαῖαν· ἐκ δὲ τῆς Θέμιν,
ἣ δὴ τὸ μητρὸς δευτέρα τόδ' ἕζετο
μαντεῖον, ὡς λόγος τις· ἐν δὲ τῶι τρίτωι

λάχει, θελούσης, οὐδὲ πρὸς βίαν τινός,
Τιτανὶς ἄλλη παῖς Χθονὸς καθέζετο
Φοίβη, δίδωσιν δ' ἣ γενέθλιον δόσιν
Φοίβωι· τὸ Φοίβης δ' ὄνομ' ἔχει παρώνυμον.

1–8

First in this prayer I privilege the first prophet of the gods, Gaia, and after her, Themis, who was the second to assume this oracular seat of her mother, as the story goes. And in the third appointment, by Themis' wish and by no force, another Titan, daughter of Chthonos, Phoebe, took the seat. And she gives it as a birthday present to Phoebus, who derives his name from hers.

The Pythia's prologue emphasizes the smooth and stately succession from one prophet to the next, ensuring continuity of the oracle's function and reputation.[46] The gift of prophecy, it turns out, does not reside in a tripod or in a specific geographic location, nor can it be acquired through victory in physical combat. Zeus remains intimately involved: he inspires Apollo's heart with prophecy and establishes him on the throne at Delphi, making him a "prophet of Zeus" (Διὸς προφήτης, 19). Where Apollo earlier proved his precocious excellence by defeating a dangerous beast and wresting control over the prophetic function of the place away from Gaia, he now graciously receives the freely offered authority of the Delphic oracle as a present. For the Pythia, the conciliatory, nonviolent process by which Phoebus acquires his oracular power is a point of pride. This innovation suggests a shift in the evaluation of Apollo's seizure of sacred power: that is, rather than being viewed as a necessary act of violence in the process of ordering a primitive universe, his violence becomes an unnecessary, potentially destabilizing, aggression.

Heracles' attack at Delphi may well provoke a similar anxiety. Heracles' violent attempt to secure the power of the oracle for himself threatens to upend one of the structures by which mortals glimpse the immortal mind. The potential seizure of prophetic power at Delphi presents him as a new Apollo, a fellow upstart who evicts the previous authority in order to establish his own. And in daring to challenge Apollo directly over the tripod, Heracles establishes himself as extra-human, a hero reaching nearly to Olympus itself. On the other hand, the presentation in Ps.-Apollodorus (our only surviving textual source) also undermines the comparison with Apollo. Heracles does not succeed in overcoming him in their tug-of-war. Moreover, Heracles' wish to plunder the temple marks him as little better than any number of impious bandits, including Cycnus, who is discussed below. Furthermore, it is not clear whether Heracles would even be able to receive the oracle he desires by stealing the tripod and setting it up elsewhere.[47] Apollo must be willing to provide the knowledge, which may stem ultimately from Zeus; Delphi itself is a sacred place; and the Pythia is the conduit through which the god speaks. Without the cooperation of Zeus, who supported and enabled Apollo's rise to power, Heracles' attempt to found an oracle using the Delphic tripod seems likely to come to nothing.

Heracles' struggle with Apollo demonstrates the extent to which he relies on the impulsive use of force to achieve his goals. But the true prize at stake—prophetic knowledge—cannot be won by coercion alone. Zeus intervenes between his two sons, and his restoration of order maintains the status quo: Apollo keeps both his tripod and his authority at Delphi. Heraclean violence thus falls short of the mark. His failure to achieve his ends ensures that his force remains unjustified, and his application of violence in a context where violence is unlikely to prove effective reveals his limited problem-solving skills.

Nevertheless, despite the impiety of his attack on Apollo's temple, the arrogance of his belief that he can establish an oracle without his father's consent, and his violent assault on an Olympian god, Heracles' journey to Delphi does not end in complete defeat. He ultimately learns the information he desperately seeks and is cured of his disease after enduring humiliating slavery and paying recompense. When Zeus interrupts the fight between his sons, he chooses to separate them with the lightning bolt, rather than blasting the mortal hero alone. Heracles is revealed to be no Apollo, but in simply surviving the conflict with him, Heracles proves his special status.

The Iliad's Heracles: Heracles the Theomachos in the Hesiodic Shield of Heracles

In contrast, the Hesiodic *Shield of Heracles* manages to package an episode of theomachy in such a way that avoids presenting Heracles as hotheaded or audacious and instead explicitly justifies the attack.[48] This likely sixth-century BCE poem celebrates Heracles' defeat of Cycnus, a son of Ares and lawless brigand preying on visitors to Delphi.[49] Cycnus is clearly defined as a threat to social order and religious devotion: "he used to lie in wait and violently plunder whoever would lead famous hecatombs to Pytho" (κλειτὰς ἑκατόμβας / ὅστις ἄγοι Πυθοῖδε βίῃ σύλασκε δοκεύων, 479–80).[50] The actual combat between Heracles and Cycnus is relatively brief (413–23): Cycnus' spear fails to penetrate

Heracles' much lauded shield, and Heracles kills him with a spear through the neck.[51] In killing Cycnus, Heracles champions ordinary pilgrims to the oracle of Apollo and, perhaps ironically, establishes himself as a pious defender of Apollo's sanctuary.[52] This act of violence thus falls squarely within his oeuvre of punishing evildoers, protecting local communities, enforcing order, and serving the interests of the gods. Heracles thus fulfills the purpose for which Zeus conceived him, to be "a defender from ruin for gods and bread-eating men" (θεοῖσιν / ἀνδράσι τ' ἀλφηστῇσιν ἀρῆς ἀλκτῆρα, 28–9).

What is perhaps more unusual is the way that the *Shield* frames Heracles' assault on Ares, an Olympian god, as a permissible and restrained act. The *Shield* accomplishes this by giving Athena an active role in communicating divine edicts to both combatants; Heracles obeys orders, but Ares does not. Before the fight, Athena appears to Heracles and assures him that Zeus will give him the victory. She also warns him:

εὖτ' ἂν δὴ Κύκνον γλυκερῆς αἰῶνος ἀμέρσῃς,
τὸν μὲν ἔπειτ' αὐτοῦ λιπέειν καὶ τεύχεα τοῖο,
αὐτὸς δὲ βροτολοιγὸν Ἄρην ἐπιόντα δοκεύσας,
ἔνθα κε γυμνωθέντα σάκευς ὕπο δαιδαλέοιο
ὀφθαλμοῖσιν ἴδῃς, ἔνθ' οὐτάμεν ὀξέι χαλκῷ·
ἂψ δ' ἀναχάσσασθαι· ἐπεὶ οὔ νύ τοι αἴσιμόν ἐστιν
οὔθ' ἵππους ἑλέειν οὔτε κλυτὰ τεύχεα τοῖο.

331–7

When you have deprived Cycnus of sweet life, then leave him and his armor, but you yourself closely observe Ares, destroyer of men, as he attacks. Where you see with your eyes that he is exposed beneath his well-wrought shield, there wound him with sharp bronze. But fall back: since not now is it fated for you to seize his horses or his famous armor.

Athena increases Heracles' courage for battle by ordaining his victory over Cycnus, but her advice for the aftermath of the duel is equally important. Her instructions require Heracles to restrain the impulse in the flush of victory to vaunt over Cycnus' body and strip his corpse of spoils. Furthermore, after he has injured Ares, he must refrain from pressing his advantage, mounting a second attack, and seeking the prizes of victory.[53] That is, he must remain in control of his violence even in the heat of a life-threatening duel, and respect the injunctions of one deity while another tries to kill him. That Heracles will curb his bloodlust is not a foregone conclusion: the suspense is heightened when Heracles boasts of a previous bout with Ares at Pylos in which he severely wounded him in the thigh and threatened to seize his "gory spoils" (359–67).[54]

After Heracles kills Cycnus, he heeds Athena's advice and waits for Ares' attack. In the moment before they clash, Athena intervenes, coming face to face with Ares.[55] She orders him,

> Ἄρες, ἔπισχε μένος κρατερὸν καὶ χεῖρας ἀάπτους:
> οὐ γάρ τοι θέμις ἐστὶν ἀπὸ κλυτὰ τεύχεα δῦσαι
> Ἡρακλέα κτείναντα, Διὸς θρασυκάρδιον υἱόν:
> ἀλλ᾽ ἄγε παῦε μάχην, μηδ᾽ ἀντίος ἵστασ᾽ ἐμεῖο.
>
> 446–9

Ares, restrain your strong passion and untouchable hands: for it is not lawful for you to kill Heracles, the bold-hearted son of Zeus, and strip off his armor. But come on, cease from battle, and do not stand in opposition to me.

Just as Athena invokes the higher force of allotted fate (*aisimon*) to Heracles, she here exhorts Ares to respect *themis*; Ares nevertheless ignores her entirely (450). Enraged at the death of his son, he attacks Heracles with spear and sword; Heracles evades Ares' assault and, following Athena's prompting, wounds Ares again in the thigh with a spear thrust underneath his shield.[56] Phobos and Deimos sweep in to rescue Ares and carry him back to Olympus, still living and in possession of his spoils, but humiliated nonetheless.[57]

The *Shield* poem presents Ares as the combatant more driven by unrestrained rage and less willing to be constrained by divine fate, an authority even higher than the Olympian gods. Heracles succeeds because he willingly submits to Athena and curbs his bloodlust, while Ares opens himself up to injury and defeat by rejecting her counsel. The *Shield* thus manages to pull off a tricky feat: Heracles becomes a bold warrior who attacks and injures a god while, at the same time, respecting his proper place in the divine order.[58] The *Shield*'s Heracles somehow reinforces the authority and order of the Olympians in his fight against Ares. This is in direct opposition with his theomachy in the *Iliad*, which Dione uses to condemn the violence of mortal heroes who believe themselves worthy opponents of the gods. While Heracles succeeds in wounding his opponents in these two texts, he fails to demonstrate his superiority in his conflict with Apollo at Delphi; his inability to procure divine knowledge by force reveals the limits of his violence. Each of these incidents places Heracles in a liminal space: he mediates between the gods and humankind not by ascending to Olympus as a god himself, but by daring to meet the gods as an equal and forcing them to acknowledge a hero's power.

The *Iliad*'s Heracles: Heracles the Sacker of Cities

If Heracles' role as *theomachos* focuses on a duel between a warrior and a god, his role as sacker of cities interrogates violence committed against an entire population. As a Greek who has previously sacked the city of Troy, Heracles serves as an important touchstone for the Greeks and Trojans battling on the Trojan plain. In contrast, the famous Labors, preoccupied as they are with fantastic creatures or far-flung quests, receive relatively little attention.[59] An examination of his sack of Troy in comparison with the *Odyssey*'s presentation of his razing of Oechalia shows how the brutal violence required for these acts can be justified or condemned.

The origins of Heracles' assault on Troy lie in Laomedon's refusal to pay Apollo and Poseidon the promised wage after they build the walls of Troy; Poseidon then sends a sea monster against the city in retribution. Heracles defeats this monster, and according to other sources, also rescues Laomedon's daughter Hesione. He later returns to sack the city when Laomedon refuses to hand over his divine horses as promised. The plain of Troy still bears the physical evidence of his conflict with the *kētos*: when Poseidon and Hera seek a suitable place to observe the battle, they sit on the wall constructed by the Trojans and Athena to shelter Heracles in his flight from the sea monster (20.144–8), like spectators at the top of a stadium. The wall has become a landmark, a physical marker of Heracles' earlier presence.

Heracles' defeat of the *kētos* is followed by Laomedon's second act of treachery—denying Heracles the promised mares—and Heracles' return to punish the city as a whole. In sacking the city to avenge Trojan duplicity, Heracles precedes the generation of Iliadic heroes besieging Troy in response to the actions of Paris, Laomedon's grandson. Yet, oddly, he is not specifically invoked as a significant *paradeigma* of success by any of the main heroes. It falls to his son Tlepolemus, a minor figure, to call upon the comparison between Heracles' sack and the Greek expedition. Tlepolemus boasts of the deeds of his father Heracles while taunting Sarpedon, a son of Zeus and Trojan ally:

ψευδόμενοι δέ σέ φασι Διὸς γόνον αἰγιόχοιο
εἶναι, ἐπεὶ πολλὸν κείνων ἐπιδεύεαι ἀνδρῶν
οἳ Διὸς ἐξεγένοντο ἐπὶ προτέρων ἀνθρώπων·
ἀλλ' οἷόν τινά φασι βίην Ἡρακληείην
εἶναι, ἐμὸν πατέρα θρασυμέμνονα θυμολέοντα·
ὅς ποτε δεῦρ' ἐλθὼν ἕνεχ' ἵππων Λαομέδοντος
ἓξ οἴης σὺν νηυσὶ καὶ ἀνδράσι παυροτέροισιν

Ἰλίου ἐξαλάπαξε πόλιν, χήρωσε δ' ἀγυιάς·
σοὶ δὲ κακὸς μὲν θυμός, ἀποφθινύθουσι δὲ λαοί.

5.635–43

They lie when they say you are the son of aegis-bearing Zeus, since you fall far short of those men who were born of Zeus in previous generations. But they say of a different sort was mighty Heracles, my father—brave in spirit, lionhearted. He once came here for the horses of Laomedon, accompanied by only six ships and fewer men, but he sacked the city of Ilium and desolated its streets. But *your* heart is cowardly, and your people are perishing.

Tlepolemus' invocation of Heracles not only establishes his genealogical claim to greatness, but also positions the Greek force as avengers once more of Trojan betrayal. As Kelly argues, "The Greeks, their position, their intentions and coming success, are the true parallels for Heracles' paradigmatic exploits. The Trojan past is being repeated in the present, as another member of the ruling family refuses to restore what he promised."[60] Heracles not only participates in the *Iliad*'s rich use of past examples to illuminate its present, he embodies the epic's central aspiration.[61]

Tlepolemus appeals to Heracles as a way to denigrate his opponent, but Sarpedon does not seem to take offense. Rather, he readily admits the legitimacy of Heracles' grievance:[62]

Τληπόλεμ' ἤτοι κεῖνος ἀπώλεσεν Ἴλιον ἱρὴν
ἀνέρος ἀφραδίῃσιν ἀγαυοῦ Λαομέδοντος,
ὅς ῥά μιν εὖ ἔρξαντα κακῷ ἠνίπαπε μύθῳ,
οὐδ' ἀπέδωχ' ἵππους, ὧν εἵνεκα τηλόθεν ἦλθε.
σοὶ δ'...

5.648–52

Tlepolemus, truly that man destroyed sacred Ilium because of the folly of a man, illustrious Laomedon, who upbraided with harsh speech the man who benefited him, nor did he hand over the horses for which he came from afar. But as for you...

Sarpedon responds to the taunt by distinguishing between Heracles, who suffered personal injury, and Tlepolemus through the use of an adversative *de*. Although an ally of the Trojans, Sarpedon affirms multiple reasons justifying Heracles' sack of the city: Heracles accomplishes a good work for Laomedon in killing the sea monster (εὖ ἔρξαντα), but Laomedon, already proven an unreliable party in the incident with Apollo and Poseidon, repeats his foolishness in breaking their agreement.[63] In addition to depriving Heracles of the promised reward of immortal horses, he adds literal insult to injury, training verbal abuse on a man he should have treated as an honored guest. When Heracles destroys Troy and nearly all of Laomedon's family in response, he punishes outrageous behavior and defends fundamental social codes. Heracles' example also seems to justify the asymmetry inherent in city-sacking: as the result of conflict between two elite men, the entire city is destroyed.

But Tlepolemus' boasting about Heracles proves ironic: Tlepolemus intends the comparison to insult Sarpedon, but it turns out to reflect poorly on himself. Heracles effectively takes control of Troy with a small force; the young Greek, on the other hand, is a little-known member of the much larger fighting force assembled by Agamemnon, an army that unsuccessfully lays siege to Troy for ten years. And unlike Heracles, who openly assaults and sacks the city, the Greek forces manage to overcome its walls at last only by means of a guileful trick.[64] Moreover, though Tlepolemus manages to wound Sarpedon severely, Sarpedon kills him. In defeating Tlepolemus, Sarpedon invalidates Tlepolemus' mockery of his lineage and affirms that he truly is a son of Zeus. The contrast between Tlepolemus and Heracles is stark and unflattering. The gulf between Heracles and the current generation of Greek heroes may explain why Heracles' example operates in the background, rather than the foreground, of the epic narrative: he makes it look too easy.[65]

The motivations provoking Heracles' sack of Oechalia, an episode that will be treated in greater detail in Chapter 3 of this book, are far more mixed. The sack of Oechalia is intimately connected with Heracles' death and merited its own independent archaic epic, now lost, attributed to Creophylus of Samos. On one level, Heracles' destruction of Oechalia seems in broad strokes to be analogous to his sack of Troy. One version has Eurytus, the king of Oechalia, insulting Heracles and refusing to award the promised prize for a victory in an archery contest, and Heracles sacking the city in revenge.[66] In denying Heracles' claim to the prize he has earned, Eurytus mimics Laomedon, inviting Heracles' justified vengeance. But the prize that Eurytus revokes is his daughter, Iole, who is perhaps rightly denied to a hero with such a troubled relationship history. It is desire for Iole that drives his assault of the city, arousing Deianeira's jealousy and setting his own doom into motion. In the surviving sources, the sack of Oechalia is treated as lamentable violence that destroys not only the family and wealth of Eurytus, but the very life of Heracles himself. In this way, the sack of Oechalia is a forerunner of Agamemnon's sack of Troy: even if the attack on the city can be justified, its eventual extermination proves ruinous for conqueror and conquered alike.

Furthermore, the sack of Oechalia is wrapped up in a series of disastrous events including the murder of Iphitus, a son of Eurytus. The murder of Iphitus receives an oblique mention in the *Odyssey* in connection with the bow that Odysseus uses in his final revenge over the suitors.[67] Book 21 describes how Iphitus gives the bow as a present to Odysseus when the two meet as young men. They form a friendship in Messenia when on parallel missions: Odysseus was seeking the return of sheep and herdsmen stolen from Ithaca; Iphitus was searching for his lost mares and colts. The gift exchange of Iphitus' bow for Odysseus' spear and sword establishes a relationship that is cut unfortunately short, for Heracles murders Iphitus before Iphitus and Odysseus can entertain each other at their respective homes (21.11–41).

In this episode, Odysseus and Iphitus serve to reinforce the proper functioning of *xenia*, the guest–host friendship so grossly violated by Penelope's suitors. But Heracles' involvement here aligns him more with the suitors than Odysseus.[68] The poet harshly criticizes Heracles' killing of Iphitus:

αἳ δή οἱ καὶ ἔπειτα φόνος καὶ μοῖρα γένοντο
ἐπεὶ δὴ Διὸς υἱὸν ἀφίκετο καρτερόθυμον,
φῶθ' Ἡρακλῆα, μεγάλων ἐπιίστορα ἔργων,
ὅς μιν ξεῖνον ἐόντα κατέκτανεν ᾧ ἐνὶ οἴκῳ,
σχέτλιος, οὐδὲ θεῶν ὄπιν αἰδέσατ' οὐδὲ τράπεζαν,
τὴν ἥν οἱ παρέθηκεν· ἔπειτα δὲ πέφνε καὶ αὐτόν,
ἵππους δ' αὐτὸς ἔχε κρατερώνυχας ἐν μεγάροισι . . .

21.23–30

[The mares] then became [Iphitus'] murder and doom, when he arrived at the home of the strong-willed son of Zeus, the man Heracles, experienced in great deeds. He killed him in his house, even though he was a guest-friend. Reckless, he honored neither respect for the gods nor his own table, which he had set before him, and then afterwards slew him. But he kept the strong-hoofed horses in his halls . . .

The poet condemns Heracles' violence because Iphitus is a guest friend (ξεῖνον): his transgression against hospitality is a crime against the gods and his own reputation as a host (τράπεζαν). In the larger tradition, the pollution incurred from this heinous act drives him into servitude to Omphale in Lydia, a situation so humiliating that it provides another motivation for his sack of Oechalia. In keeping Iphitus' horses for himself, Heracles adds theft to his crime of murder. The poet labels him "reckless" (σχέτλιος), the same term that Dione applies to Heracles in criticizing his attacks on the gods in *Iliad* 5; his assault on his guest is as grave a violation as his violence towards the gods. Heracles' brutality is wanton; the text does not acknowledge any basis for Heracles' hostility against Iphitus or his family, but rather focuses on his contravention of crucial social conventions. By suppressing potential justifications for hostility, the narrative presents his aggression as nonmediate violence of the sort that threatens to destabilize social order.

The *Odyssey*'s focus on Heracles' violation of *xenia* reflects the importance of the theme for Odysseus' narrative. The manner in which each host or society receives stranger-guests becomes a marker for distinguishing civilized from barbarian. Thus, Heracles' murder of Iphitus is especially devastating. Moreover, the fact that Heracles sets a feast for Iphitus before murdering him recalls Aegisthus' reception of Agamemnon, the epic's chief paradigm of the threat of a failed *nostos*.⁶⁹ By presenting Heracles as a representative of the epic's worst inversions of standard values, the poem also establishes him as a hero unfit for emulation. Heracles' killing of his guest-friend further frames him as a hypocrite: for part of his motivation for sacking Troy (Laomedon's harsh speech) and Oechalia (Eurytus' insults) appears to stem from his own sense of anger at being mistreated by his hosts. Thus, Heracles the sacker of cities functions as a model for exploring the justification and abuses of violence, whether he is too powerful to be compared to the *Iliad*'s heroes or too uncivilized to be a model for Odysseus.

The *Iliad*'s Heracles: The Death of Heracles

The tensions among the various roles of Heracles in early myth come to a head in the treatment of his death and afterlife. Inevitably his final fate—dying as a mortal hero or joining the Olympians as a god—shapes the evaluation of his actions in life. Despite the unparalleled status accorded to Heracles in the *Iliad*, he nevertheless experiences the fate of every mortal: death. So striking is the contrast between Heracles' peculiar glory and his common end that Achilles chooses him as the model for his own demise:

οὐδὲ γὰρ οὐδὲ βίη Ἡρακλῆος φύγε κῆρα,
ὅς περ φίλτατος ἔσκε Διὶ Κρονίωνι ἄνακτι·
ἀλλά ἑ μοῖρα δάμασσε καὶ ἀργαλέος χόλος Ἥρης.
ὣς καὶ ἐγών, εἰ δή μοι ὁμοίη μοῖρα τέτυκται,
κείσομ' ἐπεί κε θάνω.

18.117–21

> For not even mighty Heracles escaped his doom, although he was most beloved to lord Zeus, son of Cronus. But Fate, and the harsh anger of Hera, conquered him. So, too, I—if in fact a similar fate has been prepared for me—will lie there, after I am dead.

Achilles pits two of Heracles' roles against one another, beloved of Zeus and Hera's victim, and the outcome is clear: Hera wins. Achilles, who is also championed by certain gods, sees all too clearly that divine patronage ultimately cannot protect him against divine antagonism.[70] But Hera and Zeus are not the only forces in play; Achilles also attributes Heracles' death to a power even stronger than the gods, fate (*kēr*, *moira*). Regardless of the dramatic swings between rival divine alliances, whatever *kleos* Achilles achieves for himself, *moira* cannot be evaded. In the aftermath of Patroclus' death, Heracles' demise almost becomes a consolation: the greatest of heroes died, so Achilles may as well take vengeance on his enemies in the meantime, as his death cannot be avoided in the end.

Achilles' use of the epic periphrasis *biē Hēraklēos* (βίη Ἡρακλῆος) highlights Heracles' vitality and physical strength, even as Achilles expresses no doubt about Heracles' mortality.[71] The association between Heracles and *biē* makes him an especially fitting exemplum for Achilles.[72] As Nagy has argued, *biē* is closely associated with both (positive) *kleos* and (negative) *hybris*, becoming an ambivalent term that finds its fullest manifestation in Achilles himself.[73] Just as Achilles chooses to die young in exchange for *kleos*, so too does Heracles earn eternal *kleos*—as demonstrated in the poem's remembrance of him—at the cost of a life of suffering and a painful death. The mortal end of Heracles is thus characterized by constraint. Although he occupies a liminal space between gods and humans, any breaches into divine space are merely temporary. The good deeds he accomplishes for humans serve more to sate Hera's anger than to justify his cosmic elevation. Above all, Zeus' failure to preserve his son Heracles—as also seen in the death of Sarpedon in book 16—illustrates the limits that restrict even the father of gods and men himself.

Achilles' statement clearly establishes Heracles' status in early myth as a mortal hero, not a god, as he comes to be regarded in later centuries. Through artistic evidence, we can trace the development of the apotheosis myth in the archaic period. The earliest visual references to the apotheosis can be found on a Samian crater of the seventh century BCE and a Corinthian aryballos of the early sixth century (*LIMC* Herakles 3330 and 3331); these vessels depict Heracles riding in a chariot together with Hebe, the goddess of youth, in a marriage motif that indicates his divine status.[74] In the second half of the sixth century at Athens, the apotheosis motif becomes a popular subject in vase painting.[75] Here the

Figure 1.2 Athena leads Heracles to Zeus. Attic black-figure lip-cup, Vulci, 555–550 BCE. London BM 1867,0508.962. © The Trustees of the British Museum.

iconography is centered around Heracles' introduction to Zeus on Olympus on foot, as in Figure 1.2—an episode also represented on a limestone pediment from the archaic acropolis—or by chariot.[76] Yet ambiguity about Heracles' status persists in the literary tradition, captured by Pindar in the seemingly oxymoronic epithet "hero-god" in *Nem.* 3.22 (*hērōs theos*). In later treatments, Heracles' apotheosis is treated as an extraordinary reward for extraordinary accomplishments, as well as a boon in compensation for his earthly sufferings at Hera's hands.[77]

The different worlds embodied in Achilles' view of heroic mortality and the possibilities inherent to apotheosis sit uncomfortably side by side in *Odyssey* 11, when Odysseus meets Heracles in his final encounter in the Underworld.[78] In the troubled text handed down to us, Odysseus recounts meeting Heracles' ghost while the genuine Heracles feasts among the gods with his wife Hebe:

τὸν δὲ μέτ' εἰσενόησα βίην Ἡρακληείην,
[εἴδωλον· αὐτὸς δὲ μετ' ἀθανάτοισι θεοῖσι
τέρπεται ἐν θαλίῃς καὶ ἔχει καλλίσφυρον Ἥβην,
παῖδα Διὸς μεγάλοιο καὶ Ἥρης χρυσοπεδίλου.]
ἀμφὶ δέ μιν κλαγγὴ νεκύων ἦν οἰωνῶν ὥς,
πάντοσ' ἀτυζομένων· ὁ δ' ἐρεμνῇ νυκτὶ ἐοικώς,
γυμνὸν τόξον ἔχων καὶ ἐπὶ νευρῆφιν ὀϊστόν,
δεινὸν παπταίνων, αἰεὶ βαλέοντι ἐοικώς.

11.601–8

Then I recognized the mighty Heracles [—his image, that is—for he himself enjoys the festivities among the deathless gods and holds lovely-ankled Hebe, daughter of great Zeus and golden-sandaled Hera]. But around him went up a cry of the dead, like birds, fleeing in every direction. But he, like dark night, carrying a naked bow and an arrow on its string, glared about him fiercely, as if always on the verge of shooting.

Odysseus' narrative struggles to cohere: he seems to catch himself, correct himself with the awkwardly enjambed *eidōlon*; the unique mechanics of an image occupying the Underworld while the "real" deity inhabits Olympus remain difficult to explain. Lines 602–4 were suspected even by ancient commentators, one of whom attributes the lines to Onomacritus in the sixth century BCE.[79] Many modern scholars continue to view them as an interpolation, arguing persuasively that they reflect the later development of the apotheosis myth.[80]

Although these lines are likely a later addition, the discomfort they provoke in the midst of this passage is nevertheless productive to explore. One point of tension is the diametrically opposed evaluation of Heracles' fate.[81] The vision of Heracles on Olympus and his marriage to Hebe, the daughter of Hera, presumes a radical reconciliation with his most hated enemy, which is not suggested anywhere in the text. He is not presented as the beast-slayer who protects human communities or an ally of the gods against the Giants. Most of all, his genteel enjoyment of the civilized pleasures of a communal feast, bears no resemblance to the behavior of Heracles in the Underworld. He is a menacing, intimidating figure who constantly threatens those around him; even in the afterlife, he gives baleful glances at everyone who crosses his path, prepared to engage in a fight at any moment. This is not a hero at peace, confident that his final battles lie in the past. And the shades around him—even though they are *already dead*—are terrified by his potential violence against them. If the shades in the afterlife retain their most salient characteristics from life, Heracles' life would seem to have been defined by armed aggression.

Heracles' reflection on his life helps to explain his stance. This speech to Odysseus provides a rare example in early literary sources of Heracles' speaking for himself. Here his tone is characterized more by lament and grief, rather than triumph over adversity:

Ζηνὸς μὲν πάϊς ἦα Κρονίονος, αὐτὰρ ὀϊζὺν
εἶχον ἀπειρεσίην· μάλα γὰρ πολὺ χείρονι φωτὶ
δεδμήμην, ὁ δέ μοι χαλεποὺς ἐπετέλλετ' ἀέθλους.
καί ποτέ μ' ἐνθάδ' ἔπεμψε κύν' ἄξοντ'· οὐ γὰρ ἔτ' ἄλλον
φράζετο τοῦδέ γέ μοι κρατερώτερον εἶναι ἄεθλον.
τὸν μὲν ἐγὼν ἀνένεικα καὶ ἤγαγον ἐξ Ἀίδαο·
Ἑρμείας δέ μ' ἔπεμψεν ἰδὲ γλαυκῶπις Ἀθήνη.

11.620–6

> Even though I was the son of Cronus' son, Zeus, I experienced untold misery. For I served a man far inferior, who imposed harsh Labors on me. Once he even sent me to retrieve the Hound, for he did not think any other task could be more difficult for me than this. I dragged him and led him up from Hades. Hermes and owl-eyed Athena conducted me.

Heracles remains stung by his subjection to the inferior Eurystheus, and in his view his Labors do not offer an opportunity to acquire *kleos* for himself and safety for others; they are instead painful burdens to be endured. He mentions Zeus, Athena, and Hermes, his divine patrons, but even their allegiance does not alleviate his suffering in life or unhappiness in death. Heracles' view of his former accomplishments thus seems roughly analogous to that of Achilles, who famously maintains that he takes no pleasure in his former glory now among the dead (11.489–91).

Heracles illustrates his lament with the most daunting of his Labors: entering the Underworld, capturing Cerberus, and bringing him back to the upper world. Heracles refrains from linking his return from Hades to a figurative conquest of death.[82] The capture of Cerberus, impressive as it is, accomplishes no lasting results; even though Hermes and Athena escort him on the way, he does not boast of his success. Heracles finds himself an occupant of the same Hades from which he stole its three-headed guardian. Heracles concludes his speech by dashing off into the distance: the same hero who never earns a respite from the evil commands of cowardly Eurystheus continues to live by violence after his death.

This passage supplies the earliest example of a negative evaluation of Heracles' Labors, negative in that they are treated as an externally imposed punishment, associated only with pain and suffering, and do not benefit anyone. The Labors can be acclaimed as glorious victories, but, as is seen in this passage, they are also a source of shame and distress to Heracles. The framing of the Labors as terrors needlessly suffered seems here to obscure the possibility of apotheosis as a reward. For the Heracles of the *Odyssey*, even his greatest achievements represent nothing but a *kakos moros* (11.618). If in fact the disputed lines about Heracles' apotheosis are genuine, then the poet makes no attempt to force his violent hero to conform to the status of a hero who has earned deification through his benefactions to humankind.

This tension in the text between Heracles' dim view of the value of his own Labors and the ultimate reward of apotheosis illuminates the way in which the myth of apotheosis can exert pressure on the rest of the Heracles cycle. The

Iliadic Heracles—a great but mortal hero—can serve as a foil for the heroes of the Trojan War. He becomes a paradigm from the past for warriors who assault the gods, sack a city, and experience changing fortunes based on the whims of the gods. But when the deification of Heracles is introduced, his significance as an aspirational figure is amplified, and the demand for his Labors to have beneficial import becomes more pressing. Thus, when the *Odyssey* presents Heracles as a grim resident of the Underworld and the brutal slayer of Iphitus, the less savory aspects of Heracles' violence are emphasized, potentially stirring conflict with the claims of apotheosis in Olympus.

As the myth of apotheosis becomes more widespread in the sixth century BCE, Heracles' use of force draws increasing scrutiny. Fontenrose argues that the historical establishment of hero cult for victorious athletes is associated with a need to ward off anger and *tisis*; but the divine worship that is attributed to Heracles in literary sources is so unusual that it is nearly always associated with reward.[83] Heracles' almost unique status as a deified hero requires more overt justification and thus sits uneasily with the problematic aspects of his heroic violence. The development of Heracles as an exemplary figure for epinician praise in Pindar's poetry—and the difficulty Heracles' unnecessary uses of violence can pose to the project of praise—will be examined in the next chapter.

Conclusion

This chapter has moved to isolate and identify the elements that make up an episode of violence by examining several significant roles that Heracles plays in early Greek myth: monster-slayer, champion of Zeus, victim of Hera, protégé of Athena, *theomachos*, sacker of cities, even deified immortal. These roles are represented in the myths of other heroes as well, but here they point towards Heracles' extraordinary range. He is somehow both the most favored hero (as seen by his apotheosis) and the most persecuted hero (evidenced by the burden of the Labors); his tremendous capacity for violence is justified by its civilizing function, or terrifying because of his propensity for outbursts against inappropriate opponents (the gods or Iphitus). His violence may enforce or transgress fundamental social customs, while his battles may protect local communities or reflect only his own uncontrollable rage. Furthermore, the analysis of Heracles' roles brings to light the various components that influence the presentation of his violence. Violence's ends, its means, its motivation, the narrative framing, and even the emotional state of Heracles can be manipulated to produce a different

Heracles, from wanton aggressor to celebrated defender of the helpless.[84] Heracles' inherent ambiguity makes him an ideal figure for exploring violence's malleability, which renders it subject to interpretation and external evaluation.

My investigation of archaic poetry suggests that all of these aspects of violence—the roles, their components, the interaction of the roles with each other, and the external evaluation of the action by the poet or speaker—can come together to articulate a kind of "system" of violence. These aspects can serve as "variables" that can be adjusted to produce different "results," as it were, aligning each episode of violence within Arendt's framework for instrumental violence or Benjamin's nonmediate violence or manifestation. For example, Heracles' slaying of beasts is justified when the villagers who are saved are brought into the picture, but the treachery of Iphitus' murder is a useful element for highlighting the danger of heroic rage. The chapters that follow will introduce other roles that become more prominent for Heracles over time—for example, his role as epinician victor, friend, or buffoon—and will examine how they add new "variables" that influence and constrain (or fail to constrain) heroic violence. But already in our early sources, we can observe how the richness of Heracles' mythical material can be used to interrogate the ends, means, and manifestations of violence.

2

Hero or Monster?

Justifying Violence against Geryon

Introduction

This chapter executes a deep dive into a single myth, the seizure of the Cattle of Geryon, one of Heracles' Labors, in order to investigate the instrumental nature of violence. Between Hesiod's *Theogony* (287–94, 979–83) and Pseudo-Apollodorus (2.5.10), the basic narrative outline can be pieced together: at Eurystheus' command, Heracles travels to Erytheia in the far west, Geryon's home. After slaying Geryon's herdsman Eurytion and his dog Orthus (also spelled Orthrus), Heracles captures his quarry, Geryon's Cattle. Menoetes, herding nearby the cattle of Hades, reports these events to Geryon, who is slain in a duel with Heracles. Heracles drives the Cattle back to Tiryns, a journey that offers many opportunities for adventure.[1] The myth places Heracles in various roles: he is a monster-slayer, a traveler and colonizer, a victor returning wealthy with prizes, and a hero surpassing the geographic bounds of the known mortal world. In our exploration of instrumental violence, we will focus on the role of monster-slayer, one of the most fundamental roles of the Greek hero.

In its outlines, the myth depends upon Heracles' heroic violence for its success. The monster and his associates must be subdued, and the captured quarry serves as physical proof of Heracles' triumph. But Heracles' violence against Geryon can also be criticized. In the *Theogony*, Hesiod treats Heracles' killing of Geryon and acquisition of his Cattle as a fairly straightforward heroic accomplishment, one which results in the elimination of a monstrous hybrid, the acquisition of wealth and booty, and a more ordered universe under Zeus' rule. But Stesichorus' lyric poem *Geryoneis* problematizes Heracles' actions by humanizing the monster Geryon. While Heracles appears to have the gods and fate on his side, the poem's deeply sympathetic portrait of Geryon questions whether Heracles' violence is indeed civilizing, ordering, and just. It also places Heracles' victory in the wider context of Geryon's community, expanding the evaluation of heroic violence to include its collateral damage. In two fragments that address the myth of Geryon, Pindar hesitates to praise the violence of Heracles: in one fragment, Pindar lapses into silence out of respect for Zeus; in another, the famous fr. 169a, Pindar appeals to *nomos* as the principle that justifies the greatest violence.

As this chapter traces the problematization of the Labor, it also explores a conception of violence that is well summarized by Hannah Arendt. In *On Violence*, she writes, "Violence is by nature instrumental; like all means, it always stands in need of guidance and justification through the end it pursues."[2] The poems described above hold these aspects of violence up to the light for examination, interrogating the ends and means of Heracles' actions and evaluating the validity of their guidance and justification. By the time of Pindar, both the ends and the means of Geryon's death can be called into question, illuminating the ambivalence of one of Heracles' most fundamental roles, that of monster-slayer.

Eliminating the Monstrous: Praising Heracles' Civilizing Efforts against Geryon

In the *Theogony*, the Labor of the Cattle of Geryon provides the opportunity to exalt Heracles and his extraordinary accomplishments. As discussed in Chapter 1, Heracles is one of several heroes who play the role of monster-slayer, in which he functions to extend Zeus' ordering of the larger cosmos to the world of humans and beasts, a kind of succession myth itself. Violence is part and parcel of this mission: "Heracles 'civilizes' the earth by destruction."[3] In the first, more detailed of two accounts, the poet situates Geryon in a genealogical list of monsters descended from Phorcys and Ceto (270–336), emphasizing his monstrosity. Through his family tree, Geryon is associated with bizarre creatures like the fifty-headed Cerberus and snaky Echidna, each a strange "monster" or "prodigy" (πέλωρον, 296). Triple-headed Geryon too belongs to this category, since as Jenny Strauss Clay defines them, "monsters are hybrid creatures that unite normally disparate elements, for example, the human and the bestial, or combine distinct species. Frequently, too, they involve a multiplication of human or animal features, or, conversely, a subtraction and isolation of features that usually occur in pairs."[4]

The first of the two passages about him gives the fuller account of the myth:

Χρυσάωρ δ' ἔτεκεν τρικέφαλον Γηρυονῆα
μιχθεὶς Καλλιρόῃ κούρῃ κλυτοῦ Ὠκεανοῖο.

τὸν μὲν ἄρ' ἐξενάριξε βίη Ἡρακληείη
βουσὶ παρ' εἰλιπόδεσσι περιρρύτῳ εἰν Ἐρυθείῃ
ἤματι τῷ ὅτε περ βοῦς ἤλασεν εὐρυμετώπους
Τίρυνθ' εἰς ἱερὴν διαβὰς πόρον Ὠκεανοῖο
Ὄρθον τε κτείνας καὶ βουκόλον Εὐρυτίωνα
σταθμῷ ἐν ἠερόεντι πέρην κλυτοῦ Ὠκεανοῖο.

287–94

Chrysaor bore three-headed Geryon after he mixed with Callirhoe, the daughter of famous Oceanus. Mighty Heracles slew him for his rolling-gaited cattle in sea-girt Erytheia on the day when he drove the wide-browed cattle to sacred Tiryns, after he crossed the ford of Ocean, and killed Orthus and the cowherd Eurytion in the misty steading beyond famous Ocean.

The passage lays out a number of salient features of the myth: Geryon's name is preceded by the epithet "three-headed" (τρικέφαλον, 287), emphasizing his physically monstrous qualities; already he stands outside the realm of normal humans and Olympian gods. The description names not only his parents Chrysaor and Callirhoe, but also Orthus and Eurytion, members of his wider household. Heracles, meanwhile, appears as a monster-slayer, as well as a traveler who returns home laden with the spoils of victory.

In comparison, the second and briefer passage, which appears as part of the Catalogue of Women, appears relatively generic:

Καλλιρόη τέκε παῖδα βροτῶν κάρτιστον ἁπάντων,
Γηρυονέα, τὸν κτεῖνε βίη Ἡρακληείη
βοῶν ἕνεκ' εἰλιπόδων ἀμφιρρύτῳ εἰν Ἐρυθείῃ.

981–3

Callirhoe bore a child, the strongest of all mortals, Geryon, whom mighty Heracles killed for the sake of his rolling-gaited cattle in sea-girt Erytheia.

In this passage, Geryon's unusual anatomy goes entirely unmentioned. Instead, the passage underscores his enormous strength, which increases Heracles' glory in defeating him, and the Cattle that serve as the prize of victory. The reference to Erytheia, with its far-flung locale, enhances Heracles' courage. The elision of Geryon's characteristic features here elevates the significance of the Cattle to the Labor; the most important thing is that Heracles acquires such valuable booty through a difficult struggle.

A return to the first Geryon passage highlights the specificity of Geryon's monstrous genealogy. The prominence of Chrysaor is significant because he, not

Callirhoe, links Geryon to a complex family of primordial, untameable creatures who need to be eliminated in the process of the ordering of the universe.[5] While heroes like Perseus and Bellerophon kill Medusa and the Chimaera, Heracles is the most prominent in the account of this family. As Clay observes, "each sequence of monstrous births culminates in an exploit of Heracles: *Theogony* 270–94 (Geryon and Orthus), 295–318 (the Hydra), and 319–32 (the Nemean Lion)."[6]

This structural repetition invites a comparison between Geryon, the Lernaean Hydra, and the Nemean Lion, and how their deaths are justified. The Lernaean Hydra, for example, seems to exist primarily for the purpose of realizing Hera's hostility against Heracles:

> τὸ τρίτον Ὕδρην αὖτις ἐγείνατο λύγρ᾽ εἰδυῖαν
> Λερναίην, ἣν θρέψε θεὰ λευκώλενος Ἥρη
> ἄπλητον κοτέουσα βίῃ Ἡρακληείῃ.
> καὶ τὴν μὲν Διὸς υἱὸς ἐνήρατο νηλέι χαλκῷ
> Ἀμφιτρυωνιάδης σὺν ἀρηιφίλῳ Ἰολάῳ
> Ἡρακλέης βουλῇσιν Ἀθηναίης ἀγελείης.
>
> 313–18

Third, [Echidna] bore the hostile-minded Lernaean Hydra, a monster which the goddess white-armed Hera raised, angry at Heracles' strength. And the son of Zeus slew her with ruthless bronze, the son of Amphitryon—Heracles—along with Iolaus, dear to Ares, by the will of Athena, driver of spoils.

Hera's direct involvement establishes the Hydra as an existential threat to Heracles. Just as she sends the twin snakes against him as an infant, she nurtures a multiplicative, snake-like creature to kill him as an adult. Heracles' fight with the Hydra is thus not an independent choice, but a heroic necessity in defense of his own life. But Heracles is not cast as a helpless victim of divine hatred here; with the aid of Iolaus and Athena, Heracles triumphs. Furthermore, the Hydra is not a distant menace: it lives in the Argolid, posing a threat to a settled area. Heracles' violence thus also marks him as a defender of humans against powerful and hostile evils.

Even as this passage sets up the antipathy between Heracles and the Hydra, it also draws connections between the hero and Geryon. Heracles is called the son of Zeus and then the son of Amphitryon in the following line. In a genealogical poem, Heracles' double paternity indicates his own unsettledness: does he belong among the sons of immortal Zeus or the family lineage of the mortal Amphitryon? His true descent from Zeus is signaled by his participation in Zeus' ordering agenda and the personal enmity of Hera. If he were only the biological son of Amphitryon, she would have no reason to be so jealous. Heracles' mixed parentage is reflected in Geryon, the offspring of an immortal mother and mortal father.[7] And just as Geryon protects his Cattle with a posse of relatives, so Heracles fights with the help of his nephew Iolaus.

The poem presents the Nemean Lion more explicitly as a danger to human civilization:

> Ὄρθῳ ὑποδμηθεῖσα, Νεμειαῖόν τε λέοντα,
> τόν ῥ' Ἥρη θρέψασα Διὸς κυδρὴ παράκοιτις
> γουνοῖσιν κατένασσε Νεμείης, πῆμ' ἀνθρώποις.
> ἔνθ' ἄρ' ὅ γ' οἰκείων ἐλεφαίρετο φῦλ' ἀνθρώπων,
> κοιρανέων Τρητοῖο Νεμείης ἠδ' Ἀπέσαντος·
> ἀλλά ἑ ἲς ἐδάμασσε βίης Ἡρακληείης.
>
> 327–32

Overpowered by Orthus, [Chimaera gave birth to] the Nemean Lion, which Hera, the famous wife of Zeus, raised and settled in the hills of Nemea, a calamity for humans. For there it was living and destroying the tribes of humankind, lording over Tretus of Nemea and Apesas. But the power of Heraclean force subdued it.

This beast also harasses a local populace; a "calamity for humans," the Lion dominates the inhabitants of Nemea, a reversal of the human imperative to control nature. In killing the Lion and appropriating its skin as his own symbol, "Heracles restores the appropriate hierarchical order whereby men rule over beasts."[8] Hera is involved again in the Nemean Lion's rearing, thereby forcing its confrontation with Heracles, and her description as the "wife of Zeus" recalls her resentment against her husband's promiscuity, a constant thread throughout this genealogical poem. In his exploits against the Hydra and the Lion, Heracles acts as an agent of his father's agenda, the victim of Hera's hostility, and the protector of humans.

In contrast, while the Lion and Hydra pose a danger to people through their proximity to human habitation, one of Geryon's distinguishing features is the great distance that separates him from the known world. Erytheia's location across Oceanus is neither the Underworld nor the world of humans, a liminal space where "anomalous creatures, such as monsters, which defy categories applying to the normal flow of social time, find themselves *in perfect harmony* with the rules of the marginal landscape to which they belong."[9] Geryon seems content to inhabit this marginal space, making no effort to cross Oceanus himself. Geryon's threat to humans is downplayed and his physical abnormality is emphasized, while social concerns help to justify the deaths of the Hydra and Lion, and their unusual physical traits go unmentioned.

In place of a civilizing motive is the incentive of valuable spoils, Geryon's Cattle, which appear in both passages. The acquisition of the Cattle is presented as the prime motivation for Heracles' travel to Erytheia and killing of Geryon, while the spoils from the Lion and the Hydra are elided. The Labor participates in a long tradition of heroic cattle-raiding to prove one's worth.[10] The function of a successful cattle raid is illustrated by Nestor's long-winded tale in *Iliad* 11.670–760. By killing his enemies Itymoneus, Mulius, and many unnamed Elians, youthful Nestor proves his manhood. Moreover, the herds he captures and brings home serve as an external symbol of his victory and add to his wealth, as he offers them to the gods and to his community for food. Heracles too displays his excellence by returning to Tiryns with proof of his victory over Geryon.[11]

But this is no ordinary cattle raid: Heracles' return from Erytheia can also be figured as a successful return from the world of the dead, a signal of a victory over death itself.[12] The journey across Oceanus itself is specially marked as a transgression of the boundary between mortals and the dwelling of the dead or the gods: Beaulieu writes, "Heracles sails to a dimly lit location beyond the boundary of the mortal world in order to gain a token of immortality. The monsters that Heracles defeats there, the three-bodied Geryon and his triple-bodied dog Orthus, the brother of Cerberus, also suggest a quest in an infernal location, beyond the boundaries of death."[13] The association with immortality can also be found in the Labors of the Apples of the Hesperides and Cerberus, Labors which require Heracles to travel to unknown places, display incredible persistence, courage and strength, and return with proof of accomplishment.[14] Although Heracles' apotheosis is not explicitly foreshadowed in Hesiod's presentation of this Labor, its accomplishment allows Heracles to demonstrate how far he surpasses other heroes. The victory itself then almost serves as a justification for the Labor.

A choral ode in Aeschylus' *Heraclidae* demonstrates another way to make the Labor of Geryon praiseworthy: by pronouncing a moral judgment against Heracles' victims. The ode, which probably reviews Heracles' contributions to Greece, amplifies Geryon's fearsome physiology and thereby elevates Heracles' defeat of him, while also vilifying members of Geryon's household:[15]

ἐκεῖθεν ὄρμενος
ὀρθόκερως βοῦς ἤλασεν

ἀπ' ἐσχάτων γαίας Ὠκεανὸν περάσας
ἐν δέπαϊ χρυσηλάτῳ
βοτῆράς τ' ἀδίκους κτείνας
δεσπόταν τε †τριύτατον†
τρία δόρη πάλλοντα χεροῖν,
τρία δ' ἴτης σάκη προτείνων,
τρεῖς δ' ἐπισσείων λόφους
ἔστειχ' ἶσος Ἄρει βίαν.

fr. 74.1–10

Setting off from there, he drove the straight-horned cattle from the furthest reaches of the earth, having crossed Oceanus in a golden cup and after killing the wicked herdsmen and their triple-bodied master, who brandished three spears in his hands and boldly held three shields before him and shaking three crests, he approached, equal to Ares in force.

As in Hesiod, the Cattle take pride of place in the description of the Labor; but the bulk of the stanza is devoted to the conflict required to seize them. The exploit is made grand and worthy of retelling by the repetition of Geryon's tripled form, with three spears, three shields, and three crested helmets. His status as a warrior is increased by the comparison with Ares; *bian* is a word usually collocated with Heracles, but here it is transferred to his opponent. Geryon becomes a worthy if freakish adversary, requiring three times the skill and endurance to defeat as others. Furthermore, Geryon's herdsmen are called "unjust" or "wicked" (ἄδικοι), justifying Heracles' killing of them in pursuit of the Cattle. But what makes them wicked remains unclear. After all, they live on the other side of Oceanus, and no evidence that these herdsmen are a problem for other inhabitants of Erytheia is provided. The seemingly arbitrary attribution of a negative moral quality to the herdsman reveals its gratuitousness; the adjective is applied not to tell us more about the herdsmen, but rather to justify Heracles' violence against them.

These passages from Hesiod and Aeschylus thus exhibit aspects of the Geryon myth that make it worthy of celebration. These versions underscore the value of Geryon's Cattle, the great distance Heracles must travel to meet his enemy, and the monstrosity of Geryon's form. Hesiod's account links Geryon and his household closely to other anomalous, multiplied creatures whom Heracles, in his role as monster-slayer, kills in the process of civilizing the earth under Zeus' reign. Aeschylus's chorus emphasizes Geryon's fierceness and his tripled body, weapons, and armor, likewise increasing Heracles' courage and skill in overcoming him; furthermore, by calling the herdsmen whom Heracles kills "unjust," the chorus challenges any perception of injustice in Heraclean violence.

Violence Questioned in Stesichorus' *Geryoneis*

Stesichorus' *Geryoneis* alters the nature of the conflict between monster and hero, potentially bringing Heracles' violence and its glorification into question. Unfortunately, although the poem numbered at least 1300 lines, only fragments of it survive, making many aspects of the poem difficult to interpret.[16] But it is clear that this Geryon, though still physiologically a monster, is decidedly less monstrous. Stesichorus draws on Iliadic themes to create a sympathetic Geryon; as Davies and Finglass describe it, "Scenes and motifs which in Homer celebrate the greatness and pathos of human heroism are applied by Stesichorus to the terrifying Geryon, humanising the beast and encouraging the audience to admire his valour and to feel the tragedy of his predicament."[17] Stesichorus perhaps even goes so far as to use Geryon to represent the ideals of the Homeric *agathos*.[18] The humanization of Geryon illuminates the intrinsic difficulty of defining a "monster" over and against a "hero."

Based on an anthropological and ritual approach, Lada-Richards defines monsters as "creatures which do not fit neatly within their own culture's taxonomic system, creatures, that is, which in some way or other escape through the meshes of their own society's structural organization."[19] The concept itself is unstable; as a culture's taxonomic system shifts, the definition of monster is also subject to redefinition. If, as Clay argues for the Hesiodic universe, heroes and monsters are mirror-images of one another, one wonders then whether the definition of "hero" is equally fluid, and perhaps equally interrogated in this poem.[20] In recalibrating the opposition between "monster" and "hero," Stesichorus' presentation also calls into question the justification for Heracles' role as monster-slayer.

This kind of reframing of traditional myth is something that Stesichorus appears to do in other texts. In the *Palinode*, Stesichorus presents an innocent and virtuous Helen who never betrays her husband and arrives at Troy with Paris, a theme elaborated by Euripides in the *Helen*.[21] Closer to home, Stesichorus' *Cycnus* modifies the character of the conflict between Heracles and Cycnus in comparison with the pseudo-Hesiodic *Shield of Heracles*, as Richard Janko has shown.[22] Stesichorus' Cycnus not only preys on pilgrims to Delphi; he builds a temple with their skulls, a grisly detail not present in the *Shield*. Stesichorus contrives to make his Cycnus even more evil, and his Heracles, by contrast, even more pious, establishing his victory as more morally sound.

But before Stesichorus humanizes Geryon, he first amplifies his physical difference. In Hesiod, he is described as having three heads; the scholiast at that line (287) informs us that "Stesichorus says that he even had six arms and six legs and was winged" (Στησίχορος δὲ καὶ ἓξ χεῖρας ἔχειν φησὶ καὶ ἓξ πόδας καὶ ὑπόπτερον εἶναι).[23] The comment suggests that Stesichorus is responsible for the tripling of Geryon's limbs and the addition of his wings, a heightening of his physical monstrosity. While not necessarily related to our poem, a sixth-century Chalcidian amphora depicts a Geryon with a pair of large wings emerging from his outermost shoulders; because of the wings he occupies even more space on the vase than Heracles, magnifying his fearsomeness as an opponent (Figure 2.1).[24]

Yet he does not seem to be the kind of criminal who must be stopped and punished. His very remoteness and inaccessibility render him unthreatening to

Figure 2.1 Winged Geryon duels Heracles. Chalcidian black-figure neck amphora, Vulci, 540–530 BCE. Paris, Cabinet Médailles 202. Credit: Bibliothèque nationale de France.

others. Heracles requires a fantastic mode of transportation to cross Oceanus and reach Erytheia: the golden cup of the Sun (fr. 8a Finglass = S17).[25] How Heracles comes to possess the cup in Stesichorus' version remains unknown, but Geryon certainly has no such cup, and no evidence survives that indicates that Geryon showed any interest in leaving his home.

On the one hand, Heracles' journey frames him as an antecedent of Greek colonists or settlers: the poem is written by an inhabitant of a Greek colony in Sicily, confronting the larger, unknown western Mediterranean. Franzen argues that the poem was written from the perspective of the Other, Geryon, in order to create a collective mythology for Himerans, a hybrid community of Greeks and native Sicilians.[26] Even if we do not accept all of Franzen's conclusions, it's easy to see how this story, of Heracles' triumph in unfamiliar territory, may have been a comfort to colonists: "When the hero travels to Erytheia to steal the cattle he glorifies the Greek enterprise abroad and so paves the way for the pioneers of Greek civilization."[27] On the other hand, Geryon's isolation from Greek civilization underscores the distinction between himself and other monsters, like the Hydra and the Lion, which actively threaten local communities.

Though Geryon lives in an isolated location, he is far from an isolated creature. Surrounded by a network of family, members of the larger household, and neighbors, Geryon appears to live in a familiar social environment. In addition to his herdsman Eurytion and dog Orthus, Callirhoe, Geryon's mother, is nearby. She delivers a tearful and loving speech to her son in an effort to persuade him not to attack Heracles, who seems to have already slain Eurytion and Orthus and stolen the Cattle (fr. 17 Finglass = SLG S 13 = P.Oxy. 2617, fr. 11). Her appeal, as reconstructed by Barrett, Page, and others, unmistakably recalls Hecuba's plea to Hector in *Iliad* 22.[28] As Hector prepares to face Achilles, Hecuba loosens her robe, and cries, "Hector, my child, respect these (words) and pity me as well, if ever I offered you my soothing breast" ("Ἕκτορ τέκνον ἐμὸν τάδε τ' αἴδεο καί μ' ἐλέησον / αὐτήν, εἴ ποτέ τοι λαθικηδέα μαζὸν ἐπέσχον, 82–3). Callirhoe, too, expresses her grief at the possibility of watching her son die, describing herself as "miserable, wretched in childbearing, and suffering unforgettable things" (ἐγὼν [μελέ]α καὶ ἀλασ[τοτόκος κ]αὶ ἄλ[ασ]τα παθοῖσα, 2–3).[29] She also exposes her breast to Geryon, a gesture that asserts her intimate connection with her child and demands pity for the grief she will endure should she lose her son (μαζ[ὸν] ἐ[πέσχ~, 5).[30]

This interaction between Geryon and his affectionate, sympathetic mother is both broadly universalizing—all mothers and sons share a recognizable bond— and quite specific in its allusion to Hector. The reference to Hecuba's grief for her beloved son embeds Geryon within a loving nuclear family.[31] He is not loathed, feared, or rejected; on the contrary, he is the object of love and regard. And as Geryon chooses to fight with Heracles anyway, he departs with an aura of Hector's doomed nobility about him.

Callirhoe is not the only character who cautions Geryon about fighting Heracles. In the longest surviving fragment of the poem (fr. 15 Finglass = SLG S11 = *P.Oxy.* 2617 frr. 13a + 14 + 15), Geryon responds to someone, presumably Menoetes, who has just informed him that Heracles has killed Eurytion and Orthus and has stolen his Cattle.[32] This fragment presents the so-called "Dilemma of Geryon," who must choose either to confront the cattle thief and risk death or to allow him to abscond unchallenged. He poses an alternative question, something along the lines of "if, on the one hand, I am immortal and ageless ... if, on the other hand, I must die ..." The son of an immortal Oceanid nymph and the mortal (at least in Hesiod) Chrysaor, Geryon remains in doubt about his own status.[33]

The second alternative Geryon ponders—regarding being mortal—can be pieced together from fragmentary lines, something along the lines of, "if I am not immortal and must die, better to accept my fate and die fighting Heracles than to cast shame upon my family's honor."

αἰ δ' ὦ φι[λε —‿—‿ γῆ-
ρας [ἱκ]έσθαι,
ζώ[ει]ν τ' ἐν ἐ[παμερίοις ‿—
θε θ[ε]ῶν μακάρω[ν,
νῦν μοι πολὺ κά[λλιόν —‿—
ὅ τι μόρσιμ[ον —‿—‿‿—
καὶ ὀνείδε[—‿‿—
καὶ παντὶ γέ[νει ‿—‿—
ὀπίσω Χρυσ[άο]ρο[ς υ]ἱόν.

ll. 16–24

If, dear one, [it is necessary for me] to arrive at old age and to live among mortals, [apart from] the blessed gods, it is far more noble for me now [to endure] what is fated ... and insults ... and for my whole tribe ... hereafter the son of Chrysaor.

Geryon's commitment to his honor and the good fame of his family and father positions him again as a Hector who would prefer death over a reputation for cowardice.[34] He does not try to avoid his fate or defy his allotment, but prizes his own dignity above all.[35] So formulaic is this hero-talk that it almost becomes possible to forget that the speaker has three heads, six arms, six legs, and a pair of wings. One of Stesichorus' achievements, then, is to develop Hesiod's disorderly monstrosity into an admirable, aristocratic warrior.

But the first alternative dealing with immortality remains subject to vigorous scholarly debate.[36] Denys Page was first to connect Geryon's deliberation with Sarpedon's speech to Glaucon in *Iliad* 12:[37]

ὦ πέπον εἰ μὲν γὰρ πόλεμον περὶ τόνδε φυγόντε
αἰεὶ δὴ μέλλοιμεν ἀγήρω τ' ἀθανάτω τε
ἔσσεσθ', οὔτε κεν αὐτὸς ἐνὶ πρώτοισι μαχοίμην
οὔτε κε σὲ στέλλοιμι μάχην ἐς κυδιάνειραν·
νῦν δ' ἔμπης γὰρ κῆρες ἐφεστᾶσιν θανάτοιο
μυρίαι, ἃς οὐκ ἔστι φυγεῖν βροτὸν οὐδ' ὑπαλύξαι,
ἴομεν ἠέ τῳ εὖχος ὀρέξομεν ἠέ τις ἡμῖν.

332–8

Old friend, if, by escaping this war, we should become ageless and immortal, neither would I myself fight in the front lines, nor would I ever send you into glory-bringing battle. But now, since uncountable Spirits of Death stand about, whom it is impossible for a mortal to flee or escape, let us go forth, whether we offer glory to another, or he to us.

But Sarpedon's speech opens with an unattainable wish; immortality is not a possibility for Sarpedon or Glaucon. The invocation of immortality functions as a device that enables the interlocutors to reconcile themselves to the inevitability of death.

Geryon's consideration of immortality, though, seems less abstract. The verb of the protasis in his conditional is in the indicative mood, as the personal verb ending *-mai* shows.

αἰ μὲν γὰ[ρ ⏑ ἀθάνατος ⏓
μαι καὶ ἀγή[ραος – ⏑ – ⏑ –
ἐν Ὀλύμπ[ωι
κρέσσον[(⏑) – ⏓ – ⏓ – ⏑ ἐ
λέγχεα δ[– ⏓ –

ll. 8–12

For if I [am] immortal and ageless ... on Olympus, better ... disgrace[38] ...

The rest of the passage is woefully fragmentary and requires supplementation. Like Davies and Finglass, I follow W. S. Barrett, who builds on Page's work to suggest that Geryon muses, "if I am destined to be immortal *if not killed by Herakles*, then better not to fight."[39] Whether Geryon is aware of his mortal status or not, he clearly arrives at the conclusion that he must duel Heracles, against the advice of his interlocutor. Geryon, though surely not *kalos*, is nevertheless *agathos*.

Geryon's concern for his immortality serves as a point of comparison with his opponent Heracles.[40] In raising and then dismissing the possibility of life "on Olympus" (ἐν Ὀλύμπ[ωι], l. 10), Geryon also reminds the audience that such a future remains a possibility for Heracles as a consequence of the successful completion of his Labors. Or as Hanne Eisenfeld puts it, Geryon's musing "activates the audience's awareness of Herakles' destiny which, in turn, alters the implications of Geryon's ethical model. Even though Herakles is not yet immortal and may be justifiably fearful as he comes face to face (to face) with a three-headed opponent, Geryon's rhetoric begins to maneuver him into his future identity as a god."[41] If the "super-salience" of a divine Heracles occupies the immortal end of Geryon's dilemma, then it also leaves "Geryon alone to make the quintessentially mortal choice between glory and survival," making him a proxy for the audience's "empathy and self-recognition."[42]

While Geryon's dilemma may evoke Heracles' apotheosis, it also directly implicates Heracles in an unjust crime. One of Geryon's motivations for confronting Heracles is the insult of looking upon his own Cattle being "plundered" (κεραϊ[ζομεν – ⏑ – ⏑ ἁ]μετέρων, ll. 14–15). In highlighting the rightful ownership of the Cattle, the speech strongly focalizes the theft from Geryon's perspective, giving a clear assignment both of victim to Geryon and of aggressor to Heracles.[43] The juxtaposition of Heracles as a bandit with his future apotheosis is provocative.[44] In giving voice to Geryon's perspective and making it sympathetic, this passage also undermines the whole justification of Heracles' role as monster-slayer and raises the question, is it based on *this* sort of triumph that Heracles' admittance to Olympus is justified? Such a question comes perilously close to undermining the whole heroic endeavor.

Furthermore, Geryon's courage and blamelessness do not ensure a victory against Heracles, perhaps due in part to the influence of the Olympian gods. In another fragment (fr. 18 Finglass = *SLG* S14 = *P.Oxy.* 2617 fr. 3), Athena appears to engage with Zeus and then Poseidon about the outcome of the conflict. The context remains unknown: perhaps a council of the gods has just disbanded, or the Olympians are collectively observing the fight in progress. Athena, Heracles' champion and helper, no doubt advances his cause against Geryon, Poseidon's grandson. Athena speaks first to Zeus, who, as "king over all" (παμ[βασιλῆα, l. 2), holds final authority; perhaps she urges him to favor Heracles or approves of a pronouncement of his impending victory. Her conversation with Poseidon remains more obscure, though.⁴⁵ Whether Athena challenges Poseidon to help Geryon or reminds him to refrain from involving himself, the fragment emphasizes Athena's eagerness for the battle, reiterated in her presence at the conflict on several vases.⁴⁶ Moreover, the appearance of Iris alongside Athena on an Attic red-figure vase perhaps signals that Athena dispatched her to carry advice or an encouraging message to Heracles, an incident which may be related to this fragment.⁴⁷

The involvement of the Olympians in this conflict, which recalls the council of the gods in *Odyssey* 1 or the discussion preceding the killing of Hector in *Iliad* 22, implies that the ultimate outcome of the fight between Heracles and Geryon is predetermined.⁴⁸ Heracles' emergence as divine champion perhaps counterbalances his presentation as a marauder and pillager. Clearly, mythic tradition has already dictated the outcome—Heracles must defeat Geryon—but, by making the intervention of the gods explicit within the poem's narrative, Stesichorus instills even greater *pathos* in Geryon's deliberations about fighting and survival. Geryon nobly reconciles himself to death at Heracles' hands, if attempting to defend his Cattle from the latter will prevent dishonor from staining his family's name. His assessment draws the pity of the poem's audience, however, because the audience is aware that Geryon goes forth inevitably to his own death.⁴⁹

The fragments culminate in a description of the final battle between Heracles and Geryon (fr. 19 Finglass = *SLG* S15 + S21 = *P.Oxy.* 2617 frr. 1 + 4 + 5). The surviving text provides a smattering of details: Heracles deliberates before the duel begins, deciding in his mind (νόωι διελε[, l. 5) that the best approach is to fight by means of stealth (πολὺ κέρδιον εἶν . . . λάθραι πολεμε[ῖν, ll. 7–8). Geryon engages Heracles while equipped with a shield (ἀσπίδα, l. 12) and a helmet (ἱπ]πόκομος τρυφάλει', l. 16); Heracles, on the other hand, fights with the club (ῥόπαλον, fr. 20.3 Finglass = *SLG* S16 = *P.Oxy.* 2617 fr. 31) and bow and arrow (οἰ[σ]τός, fr. 19.40 Finglass = *SLG* S15 = *P.Oxy.* 2617 fr. 5). I have argued thus far that Stesichorus portrays a surprisingly sympathetic Geryon, and one question that these details raise is whether Heracles is presented somehow as "unheroic." The Homeric poems and vase paintings can provide material for comparison, but for reasons I explain further below, we should approach with caution.

The arming of each of the combatants presents a sharp contrast: Geryon does not attack with tooth or claw like the opponents in other Labors, but instead is "well-armed like a hoplite," the familiar Greek farmer-soldier prepared for war; Heracles' weapons are decidedly more rustic.⁵⁰ Geryon's armor is a symbol of more organized society, especially when associated with the communal efforts of hoplite formation. Even though Geryon fights one-on-one with his opponent, his armor may nevertheless make the monster more recognizable. It is Heracles' equipment of lion skin, bow, and club that is unusual. Although later it becomes iconic of the hero, it befits a primitive loner. He is able to travel lightly, attacking from a distance with arrows or up close with his club. Athenaeus quotes the Peripatetic scholar Megaclides, who asserts that this depiction of Heracles in fact originated with Stesichorus' poem:[51]

> τοῦτον οὖν, φησίν, οἱ νέοι ποιηταὶ κατασκευάζουσιν ἐν λῃστοῦ σχήματι μόνον περιπορευόμενον, ξύλον ἔχοντα καὶ λεοντῆν καὶ τόξα· καὶ ταῦτα πλάσαι πρῶτον Στησίχορον τὸν Ἱμεραῖον.
>
> 12.512f = Stes. fr. 281 Finglass
>
> [Megaclides] says that the recent poets dress up this man [Heracles], then, in the form of a robber, wandering about alone, carrying a club and lion skin and bow. And the first to shape him thus was Stesichorus of Himera.

Finglass provides evidence for being skeptical of Megaclides' claim.[52] Nevertheless, the general contrast between hero and monster is quite striking. Geryon is embedded in a network of relationships, while Heracles is solitary; Geryon rises in legitimate defense of own property, while Heracles is a bandit; and where Geryon wears conventional armor, Heracles fights in garb and with weapons that mark him as alien to Greek warfare.

The attack by bow and arrow is particularly problematic because archery is denigrated as less glorious in the *Iliad*.[53] This lies at the center of Diomedes' insults to Paris, when Diomedes disparages Paris' archery in comparison with his own implements of battle:

> τοξότα λωβητὴρ κέρᾳ ἀγλαὲ παρθενοπῖπα
> εἰ μὲν δὴ ἀντίβιον σὺν τεύχεσι πειρηθείης,
> οὐκ ἄν τοι χραίσμῃσι βιὸς καὶ ταρφέες ἰοί·
> νῦν δέ μ' ἐπιγράψας ταρσὸν ποδὸς εὔχεαι αὔτως.
> οὐκ ἀλέγω, ὡς εἴ με γυνὴ βάλοι ἢ πάϊς ἄφρων·
> κωφὸν γὰρ βέλος ἀνδρὸς ἀνάλκιδος οὐτιδανοῖο.
> ἦ τ' ἄλλως ὑπ' ἐμεῖο, καὶ εἴ κ' ὀλίγον περ ἐπαύρῃ,
> ὀξὺ βέλος πέλεται, καὶ ἀκήριον αἶψα τίθησι.
>
> 11.385–92
>
> You archer, worthless wretch, delighter in hair, girl-ogler! If, in fact, you should make trial of me, face to face, in armor, not, you know, would your bow and swift arrow help you: and now that you have scratched the bottom of my foot, you vaunt so. I do not care, as if a woman or thoughtless child struck me. For the

blunt arrow of a weakling is worthless. But in contrast, when I throw the spear, even if it grazes ever so little, it proves sharp, and quickly makes him lifeless.

The *Iliad*'s general characterization of Diomedes as a dependable killing-machine, and of Paris as useless and cowardly, serves to justify Diomedes' taunt. Heracles' arrows can hardly be called "blunt" (κωφόν) like Paris', especially given that Heracles dips them in the venom of the Hydra (fr. 19.31–6 Finglass). Nevertheless, this exchange reveals that, in the environment of an epic duel on the battlefield, the man dressed in armor and using weapons like the spear and sword better suits the Homeric model of an effective warrior.[54]

Heracles' club is also an unusual weapon. Heracles does not carry the club in Homer's poems, where the weapon seems a bit old-fashioned or archaic. In the *Iliad*, it appears prominently in a reminiscence by old Nestor, when he recalls a fight in the generation before his own. A warrior named Areithous earns the nickname "Maceman" for his iron club (τὸν ἐπίκλησιν Κορυντήτην, 7.138). But Lycurgus defeats him "by guile, not by strength" (δόλῳ, οὔ τι κράτεΐ γε, 7.142) by trapping him in a narrow pass, where Areithous is unable to swing the club. Areithous' death illustrates the limits of this particular weapon; as Kirk observes, his iron club "would be relatively useless in organized battle . . . since anyone with a thrusting spear, let alone a throwing-spear, lay out of range."[55] Oddly, when Lycurgus strips Areithous' armor and bequeaths it to his squire Ereuthalion, the famous club goes unmentioned, suggesting that Ereuthalion does not use it in his fight against Nestor.

A large number of vase images depicting the combat also provide comparanda. Heracles and Geryon were a popular subject in the sixth and early fifth centuries BCE, with about 130 images surviving and over 70 on Attic black-figure vases alone.[56] A survey of the paintings reveals a theme of Heracles and Geryon depicted in mid-fight, with a wide variation of iconography: vases from the mid-sixth century show Heracles drawing his bow at Geryon from a distance; later, a close fight with Heracles attacking Geryon with a sword or club predominates. Accompanying figures include the body of Eurytion or Orthus, Athena or other deities, a mourning woman, and the Cattle. Martin Robertson detects the direct influence of Stesichorus' poem on specific illustrations, especially a Chalcidian vase on which Geryon is depicted with wings, a rare variation (Figure 2.1).[57] We even have some images of Heracles aiming his arrow at Geryon from behind a rock, perhaps in response to Stesichorus' version of the myth (Figure 2.2).

But Philip Brize is more skeptical, arguing that these paintings should not be approached as "illustrations" of a text, but be taken on their own terms: "The artists

Figure 2.2 Heracles aims an arrow at Geryon from behind a stone. Attic black-figure lekythos, c. 500–480 BCE, London BM 1895.10-29.1 © The Trustees of the British Museum.

were bound, above all, by the traditions specific to each genre."[58] Susanne Muth builds on this conclusion in a thorough survey of the iconographic development of the fight, underlining how the depiction of Geryon emphasizes different aspects of Heracles' strength: when Geryon threatens to attack Heracles at close quarters, Heracles' courage is emphasized, and when Geryon's drooping, dying head marks him as a victim, Heracles' victorious dominance is apparent.[59] If these images developed mostly independently of the poetic tradition, then using them to inform our reading of Stesichorus' poem seems even more unreliable. Nevertheless, the range and variation of these images do demonstrate the tremendous interest and excitement the narrative of the fight might have generated.

Indeed the poem highlights graphic details about Heracles' attack on Geryon. Heracles dispatches one of Geryon's heads with an arrow smeared with venom, or as it is poetically described, "the agonies of the man-destroying, speckle-necked Hydra" (χολᾶι | ὀλεσάνορος αἰολοδε[ίρ]ου | ὀδύναισιν Ὕδρας, fr. 19.34–6 Finglass).[60] The addition of the Hydra's poison is a bit of (literal) overkill here, given that the arrow goes straight through one of Geryon's brains.[61] The innovative weapon and the vivid description of the arrow's silent path sets high expectations for the rest of the fight to follow. Perhaps Heracles runs into close range and fights hand-to-hand with a club or sword to defeat the other two bodies, as depicted in the vase paintings. Even if Heracles' stealthy approach and use of archery are uncharacteristic of the best of Homer's heroes, they are unlikely to be the only actions Heracles undertakes in the fight; the three stages of the fight allow the possibility for a variety of attacks, opportunity for demonstrating wit, courage, and skill.

But even as Heracles mounts a successful attack, the poem's concern for humanizing Geryon remains. After Heracles' arrow finds its mark, the narrative shifts in tone with a comparison of Geryon's slumping head to a dying poppy.

> ἀπέκλινε δ' ἄρ' αὐχένα Γαρ[υόνας
> ἐπικάρσιον, ὡς ὅκα μ[ά]κω[ν
> ἅτε καταισχύμοισ' ἁπαλὸν [δέμας
> αἶψ' ἀπὸ φύλλα βαλοῖσα. [
>
> fr. 19.44–7 Finglass

> And Geryon tilted his neck at an angle, just as a poppy, when it spoils its delicate body, suddenly dropping its petals ...

The contrast between the gory destruction of Geryon's head and the small flower draws attention to its own incongruity.[62] In an account that emphasizes weapons, blood, strategy, and death, the abrupt turn to a fragile blossom may be jarring. Page notes that Stesichorus' simile is based on the account of the death of Gorgythion by Teucer's arrow in the *Iliad*:[63]

> μήκων δ' ὡς ἑτέρωσε κάρη βάλεν, ἥ τ' ἐνὶ κήπῳ
> καρπῷ βριθομένη νοτίῃσί τε εἰαρινῇσιν,
> ὣς ἑτέρωσ' ἤμυσε κάρη πήληκι βαρυνθέν.
>
> 8.306–8

> But just as a poppy droops its head, which is weighed down by fruit and spring rains in the garden, so he bowed his head, weighed down by his helmet.

In her explication of the two similes, Maingon suggests that "the sudden transition to a peaceful image tends to intensify the horrors of war" in the Iliadic context, and perhaps a similar effect is intended in Stesichorus' version.[64]

Stesichorus' version alters an important detail, however: the Homeric poppy droops its head because it is in its prime; it is laden with fruit, which gathers more water in the rain. The Stesichorean poppy, on the other hand, drops its own petals, leaving its stem bare. According to Fowler, Stesichorus replaces the Homeric contrast between the simile and its context with coincidence, as "the poppy is dying."[65] To pursue this idea further: Stesichorus' poppy dies at the end of its season, naturally wilting, losing its petals because it has already finished its period in bloom. In a similar way, Geryon's time has come, as evidenced earlier by the Olympian interference in the duel's outcome. Yet the predetermined lifecycle of the poppy is balanced against the simile's use of the adverb "suddenly" (αἶψα). The mature poppy does not gradually wither, but is denuded all at once. Even for a bloom that was destined to fade, its end comes abruptly. Geryon, who had girded himself to face Heracles with a willingness to accept death, is likewise killed in a swift and final duel.

These few fragments of Stesichorus' lengthy poem provide only a tantalizing glimpse of his treatment of the myth of the Cattle of Geryon. Yet they are sufficient to outline at least some of the surprising ways in which the poem destabilizes the traditional dynamics between Heracles the hero and Geryon the monster. The poem makes Geryon more human, more Greek, and more heroic. While Hesiod's Geryon is grouped together with other malformed monsters who must be snuffed out by Heracles as an act of imposing order, Stesichorus presents a Geryon modeled on a Homeric *agathos*. Geryon lives in isolation, posing no direct threat to Greek settlements; he is the beloved son of a doting mother; and he is a brave warrior who deliberately chooses to risk death in defense of his honor, a decision that appears even more noble in the context of the gods' predetermining his death at Heracles' hands. Moreover, in his duel with Heracles, it is Geryon who wears the familiar armor of the Homeric warrior, and Heracles who attacks with unusual weapons and in a stealthy manner.

The socialization of Geryon in particular adds a further dimension by exposing the larger costs of Heracles' inevitable triumph. Not only is the sympathetic Geryon dead, but his mother is plunged into grief. Members of Geryon's household are struck down as impediments to Heracles' acquisition of the Cattle. By providing the perspective of Heracles' victims, the poem expands its view of heroic violence to include its broader consequences and the collateral damage it leaves in its wake.

By locating the most civilized ideals within the triplicated, aberrant body of Geryon, Stesichorus undermines Heracles' claim to a civilizing mission. The recalibration of the contrast between hero and monster thus challenges Heracles' role as a monster-slayer and culture hero whose violence is worthy of admiration. Yet even as Heracles is positioned as an aggressor and unlawful brigand, he is portrayed as the divine champion of Athena and the fated victor; perhaps even his apotheosis is foreshadowed. The ends of Heracles' Labor are inevitably accomplished: he kills Geryon and returns with the stolen Cattle to Greece. But the uncomfortable juxtaposition of marauder and future god casts doubt on the justification of the means.

Pindar's Heracles: *Nomos*, Justice, and Violence

In two fragmentary poems, Pindar uses Heracles' Labor of the Cattle of Geryon to acknowledge the difficulties of praising heroic violence. This might be a bit surprising because Pindar's work frequently extols Heracles to his patrons as the victor par excellence and an exemplum worthy of imitation.[66] A brief examination of Pindar's praise for the hero will help contextualize his criticism in the two fragments. Pindar famously calls him a "hero god" (ἥρως θεός, *Nem.* 3.22), a kind of oxymoron that encapsulates one of the many contradictions of Heracles.[67] On the one hand, Heracles is a hero closely connected with the foundation of the Olympic Games in honor of his father Zeus and victory in athletic competition. On the other, unlike other mortal heroes, he becomes a god upon his death. In *Nemean* 1, Pindar connects Heracles' exceptional excellence (*aretē*) with his future divinity. In preface to describing the infant Heracles' defeat of snakes sent by Hera, the poet declares, "I willingly hold on to Heracles among the mighty summits of glorious excellence" (ἐγὼ δ' Ἡρ- / ακλέος ἀντέχομαι προφρόνως / ἐν κορυφαῖς ἀρετᾶν μεγάλαις, 31–3). In response to this marvelous sign, Teiresias prophesies Heracles' apotheosis, presenting it as a reward he will earn for his "great toils":

> . . . αὐτὸν μὰν ἐν εἰρή-
> να τὸν ἅπαντα χρόνον ⟨ἐν⟩ σχερῷ
> ἀσυχίαν καμάτων μεγάλων
> ποινὰν λαχόντ' ἐξαίρετον
> ὀλβίοις ἐν δώμασι . . .
>
> 69–71

> . . . he himself in uninterrupted peace for all time would obtain quiet, a chosen recompense for his great toils, in the blessed halls . . .

Included among these toils are his slaughter of beasts on land and sea, killing of evildoers, and defense of the gods against the Giants. Unsurprisingly, each of these instances of violence is justified by its aim to protect mortals, benefit the gods, and maintain order in the universe.

Pindar also elevates Heracles by joining his Labors to socially beneficial work that requires no violence at all. In his third Olympian ode, Pindar describes the strange fact that Heracles makes *two* trips to the distant Hyperboreans.[68] The first, at the behest of Eurystheus (with Zeus' permission), finds Heracles chasing the Hind of Artemis from Arcadia to the far north:

τὰν μεθέπων ἴδε καὶ κείναν χθόνα πνοιᾶς ὄπιθεν Βορέα
ψυχροῦ. τόθι δένδρεα θάμβαινε σταθείς.
τῶν νιν γλυκὺς ἵμερος ἔσχεν δωδεκάγναμπτον περὶ τέρμα δρόμου
ἵππων φυτεῦσαι.

31–4

While pursuing her, he saw also that land beyond the gusts of freezing Boreas. Arrested, he marveled at the trees there. And sweet desire for them possessed him, to plant them around the boundaries of the twelve-coursed horse track.

Yet Heracles turns aside from this thought and applies his energy to capturing the Hind. It is only later, after the establishment of the Olympic Games in a harshly lit plain, that Heracles remembers the olive tree. His second trip serves as the occasion for him to address the Hyperboreans with persuasive words (πείσαις ... λόγῳ, 16):

πιστὰ φρονέων Διὸς αἴτει πανδόκῳ
ἄλσει σκιαρόν τε φύτευμα ξυνὸν ἀνθρώποις στέφανόν τ' ἀρετᾶν.

17–18

Trustworthy in intention, he was seeking, for the grove of Zeus open to all, a shady plant as a boon shared among men, and a crown of excellence.

There is a clear emphasis on the olive tree as a favor shared equally among all people (πανδόκῳ, ξυνόν). Equally important is the pacific nature of this acquisition: Heracles obtains the olive trees not by violent uprooting and assault, but through verbal persuasion.[69] By linking Heracles' voluntary kindness to the attendees at Olympia with his pursuit of the Hind, Pindar gives the Hind's capture a socially positive function within the larger narrative.[70] Moreover, the olive crown becomes the prize for the victor at Olympia, a constant reminder of Heracles' thoughtful largess and respect for his father. An example of a vase image of Heracles crowned as an athletic victor can be observed in Figure 2.3.

The poem further promotes the Labor of the Hind by giving it the express approval of two Olympian gods. Artemis herself receives Heracles at Ister (26–28); her welcoming presence ensures that the Hind does not appear to be kidnapped or stolen. Moreover, Eurystheus' order ultimately comes from Zeus (28), a detail that removes the stigma of enslavement from Heracles and instead frames him as an agent of Zeus. Even the Hind herself is not killed or sacrificed, but merely led (ἄξονθ', 29) to Eurystheus. Each of these details shows how divine imprimatur can constrain Heracles' violence to positive ends.

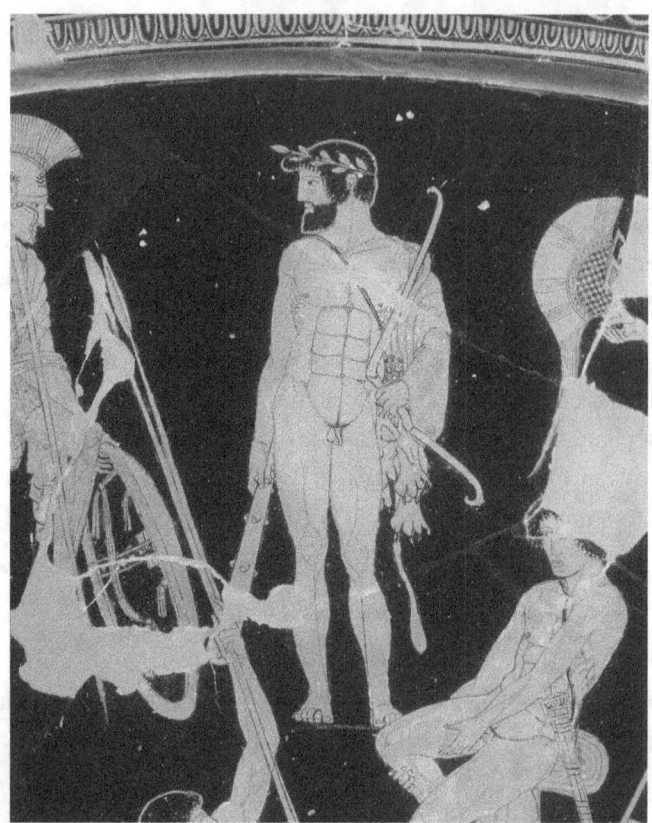

Figure 2.3 Heracles crowned. Niobid Crater, Attic red-figure calyx crater, Orvieto, c. 460–450 BCE. Musée du Louvre G341, Paris, France. Photo: Hervé Lewandowski. © RMN-Grand Palais/Art Resource, NY.

Yet when it comes to the Labor of the Cattle of Geryon, Pindar struggles to praise Heracles. Like Stesichorus' poem, Pindar's fragments bring out the problematic aspects of Heracles' violence against Geryon, emphasizing the ambivalence underlying Heracles' successful theft of the Cattle. In a fragment of a dithyramb, fr. 81, Pindar starts to show a preference for Geryon over Heracles, but then quickly silences himself.

> – ᵕ – – – σὲ δ' ἐγὼ παρά μιν
> αἰνέω μέν, Γηρυόνα, τὸ δὲ μὴ Δί
> φίλτερον σιγῷμι πάμπαν· – ᵕ – –

I, on the one hand, praise you, Geryon, in comparison to him [Heracles], but I should keep silence entirely about what is not dear to Zeus.

By elevating Geryon over Heracles, the poem begins to question the ends of Heracles' violence. If Geryon is more praiseworthy, more worthy of celebration, or superior to Heracles, then perhaps he does not deserve death at Heracles' hands, and Heracles has no right to take his Cattle. And if the ends of the Labor are no longer viewed as a great display of excellence, then the violence that enables their enactment can no longer be justified. But before this line of thought can be pursued, the poet lapses into silence.

Silence is a frequent phenomenon in Pindar's work. On the one hand, silence can simply be the absence of praise poetry, whose purpose is to commemorate wonderful deeds for posterity. For example, in fr. 121, Pindar says, "a noble deed, kept in silence, dies" (θνᾴσκει δὲ σιγαθὲν καλὸν ἔργον, 4); that is, hymns and songs function to keep alive the *kleos* of aristocratic men and their deeds. Silence can also function as a poetic strategy. As Silvia Montiglio has shown, Pindar's silence may have a number of purposes, including a need to turn to the *laudandus* (*Nem.* 4.33–4) or a cautiousness about antagonizing the victor's home community.[71] But silence is not just a negative absence: it can also take on an active function to hide, obscure, or cover things; for Detienne, even as Pindar shrinks from Archilochean blame poetry, his silence can be equivalent to oblivion and blame.[72] The very announcement of a refusal to speak "suggests the shameful detail that it claims to conceal."[73] In regard to Heracles, Pindar gives names, places, and reasons for three instances of Heracles' theomachy in *Ol.* 9.28–42; yet he refuses to discuss them further not because they reflect badly on Heracles (as in Dione's bitter condemnation of Heracles the *theomachos* in *Iliad* 5), but because it is inappropriate to mention "war and every battle" (πόλεμον μάχαν τε πᾶσαν, 40) in the context of gods. In this case, his reference and then reticence allow him to acknowledge Heracles' potentially disruptive violence, while also avoiding blaming its excessiveness.

In the case of fr. 81, Pindar is silent because he wants to avoid Zeus' displeasure. Here Pindar implies that to criticize Heracles for his lawless aggression against Geryon would be to argue against the very will of Zeus. Perhaps this recusal functions analogously to *Pyth.* 1.27–31, in which, Race argues, Pindar recoils from a negative exemplum and prays to please Zeus.[74] But while Zeus' approval of Heracles' actions is brought within the confines of the mythic plot in *Ol.* 3, here he remains outside the frame of the narrative. Zeus' intervention occurs because he is engaged in supervising the subject of Pindar's poetry, and he approves of Heracles, specifically even when his actions are not praiseworthy. The external reality of Heracles' role as a son and favorite of Zeus can bend the poetic evaluation of his violence. In balancing speech and silence in this way,

Pindar subordinates his own judgment as poet to what he interprets to be Zeus' will, positioning himself as Zeus' poet above all.

Fragment 169a (Snell) leads with a different poetic strategy for coping with Heracles' problematic violence against Geryon. Again the poem is only partially preserved; the beginning of the fragment reads:

νόμος ὁ πάντων βασιλεύς
θνατῶν τε καὶ ἀθανάτων
ἄγει δικαιῶν τὸ βιαιότατον
ὑπερτάτᾳ χειρί. τεκμαίρομαι
ἔργοισιν Ἡρακλέος·
ἐπεὶ Γηρυόνα βόας
Κυκλώπειον ἐπὶ πρόθυρον Εὐρυσθέος
ἀνατεί τε] καὶ ἀπριάτας ἔλασεν.[75]

1–8

Nomos, the king of all, mortals and immortals, leads them in making the greatest violence just, with a superior hand. I make my case with the deeds of Heracles, for he drove the cattle of Geryon to the Cyclopean doorstep of Eurystheus [with no punishment] and without payment.

This fragment, which has occasioned lively scholarly discussion, seems to address the central question at the heart of this chapter: how can violence be considered just?[76] The poem grapples with this question by bringing in two deeds of Heracles that seem patently unjust, amplifying the agency of a personified *nomos*. In translating the participle *dikaiōn*, I follow Lloyd-Jones, who comments, "δικαιοῦν is factitive; its form suggests that it means 'make just.'"[77] The poor preservation of the papyrus makes line 8 uncertain, but a paraphrase in a speech of Callicles in Plato's *Gorgias* and by the scholiast to Aelius Aristides offers testimony to its content. Callicles asserts that Heracles obtains the Cattle, "neither purchasing nor Geryon giving" (οὔτε πριάμενος οὔτε δόντος τοῦ Γηρυόνου, *Gorgias* 484b11). The scholion, on Aristides' *On Rhetoric* 52, states that Heracles "neither asked for nor purchased" the Cattle (οὔτε αἰτήσας οὔτε πριάμενος, Dindorf vol. III, 408). Although later authors can frequently be unreliable sources, these paraphrases do at least correspond with the secure ἀπριάτας.[78] The testimonia suggest other possible means that Heracles could have employed to take possession of the Cattle: what if he had simply asked for them, and Geryon had the opportunity to willingly give them? What if Heracles had purchased them or bartered for them?[79]

This fragment thus does not question the ends of the Labor but its means, by offering alternative methods that do not rely on violence. These alternatives render

Heracles' violence a deliberate choice out of many options, a choice that looks increasingly like brutal, uncivilized force, rather than a heroic necessity, as in Hesiod. As Ostwald puts it, "the fact that the prey was seized and not acquired by way of a regular commercial transaction suggests violence on the part of Heracles over against something ordinarily described as injustice which, in this account, was sustained by Geryon."[80] Heracles does not participate in the customs developed by civil society for governing the transfer of property from one person; he thus appears to be an archaic holdover from a previous, more primitive era, a hero so devoted to violence that he is incapable of negotiating normal social relations. An even less favorable interpretation is that he is simply a murderer, an uncontrolled aggressor who turns first to illegal force when other means of exchange would easily suffice. Instead of establishing order, this Heracles seems to instigate chaos and injustice.

The poet furnishes another example of troubling Heraclean violence in the Labor of the Mares of Diomedes. In this version of the myth, Diomedes courageously fights Heracles in defense of his own rightful property:

– οὐ κό]ρῳ ἀλλ' ἀρετᾷ.
κρέσσον γ]ὰρ ἁρπαζομένων τεθνάμεν[81]
× χρη]μάτων ἢ κακὸν ἔμμεναι.
—]εσελθὼν μέγα
‿ – ν]υκτὶ βίας ὁδόν

15–19

... [not] with insolence but with excellence. For [it is better] to die while [possessions] are being carried off than to be a coward ... after entering a great (hall?) ... at night, the way of violence ...

Line 15 establishes a contrast between *koros*—a word often associated with *hybris*—and *aretē*, or the kind of heroic excellence that Heracles embodies in other Pindaric poems.[82] But any confusion about which party acts insolently and which virtuously is dispelled by the scholiast, who clarifies that Diomedes behaves courageously and Heracles, unjustly:

οὐκ ἐπὶ ὕβρει, ἀλλ' ἀρετῆς ἕνεκα. τὸ γὰρ [τὰ ἑαυτοῦ μὴ προ]ίεσθαι ἀνδρείου (ἐστίν) [ ] ἀλλ' οὐχ ὑβριστ[οῦ. Ἡρα]κλῆς δ(ὲ) ἠδί[ί]κει [ἀφελό]μενος.[83]

... not with arrogance, but for the sake of excellence. For not giving up one's own possessions is characteristic of a courageous man, but not of an arrogant man. And Heracles did wrong when he took them away.

This presentation of a courageous Diomedes in contrast with a marauding Heracles recalls Stesichorus' version of Geryon and Heracles. Indeed, the sentiment that it is preferable to die while defending one's possessions than to be proven a coward is directly in line with the decision of Stesichorus' Geryon to prioritize his family's honor over the risk of death at Heracles' hands ("Dilemma of Geryon," fr. 15 Finglass, discussed above). Pindar thus brings Diomedes into a tradition that criticizes Heracles' use of violence to accomplish his Labors.

The questioning of violence extends to other aspects of the Labor. Heracles attacks Diomedes' home at night, instead of in an open confrontation. In specifying Heracles' adoption of the "way of violence," the poet again opens up the possibility of peaceful alternatives to violence when acquiring his quarry. Pindar goes on to describe in detail the grisly death of a man, perhaps Diomedes or his servant, whom Heracles feeds to his man-eating horses (21–33). Not enough text survives for us to determine whether the man is justly consumed by his own monstrous wards, or whether he too is an innocent victim of Heraclean violence. The fact that Diomedes maintains man-eating Mares ought to give one pause, but the focus (as far as we can tell) is on the monstrosity of the Mares, not the brutality of Diomedes himself.[84] Heracles, as the aggressor, is again placed in the wrong.

This framing of the myths of Geryon's Cattle and Diomedes' Mares admits that heroic violence is not prima facie justifiable. Pindar offers instead an external justification: *nomos*, a polyvalent term which here is personified as ruling both mortals and gods with a coercive hand. The connection between *nomos* and violence is, in Gentili's view, essential: in linking them, the poem illustrates "the crux of the process of civilization," in that problematic violence is necessary for the establishment of a just order of the gods.[85] This suggests that heroic violence can be justified by its capacity to civilize the universe—even when it is unjust itself. This view mediates between Hesiod's focus on Heracles' role as a culture hero whose violence is unquestioned and Pindar's Heracles, whose violence is deeply ambivalent. Yet I am not certain that the poem supports the view that Heracles' works establish a just order by killing Geryon or Diomedes. The sympathetic depiction that positions them as victims of violence would seem to indicate that a deep injustice underlies their defeat.

The fragmentary nature of the ode has ensured that the meaning of Pindar's *nomos* remains hotly disputed. Most scholars fall into one of two basic camps, considering *nomos* as either "law" (especially the law of Zeus) or "custom" (that is, conventional beliefs).[86] I follow Kevin Crotty, who embraces the ambiguity in the term by combining the two, arguing that both aspects must be simultaneously present:

Nomos, men's esteem or hatred for the heroes, is based not only on human notions of commendable behavior but also on the gods' love for or hostility toward the hero. *Nomos* refers to men's beliefs and evaluations, but Pindar is showing how these beliefs and evaluations are grounded in the gods' activity of exalting and humbling and may even contradict men's own notions of what is praiseworthy.[87]

Crotty's interpretation appeals because it acknowledges the complex dynamics surrounding heroic violence in this myth: Hesiod can portray Heracles' violence as just and ordering, while Stesichorus can depict a virtuous Geryon under unfair attack by Heracles, a conflict which Pindar can then extend to the myth of Diomedes and his Mares. Yet the "gods' love for or hostility" towards Heracles is ultimately what leads both to his undeserved suffering and to his great glory.

Crotty's formulation of *nomos* also brings together the two approaches to Heracles' violence in fragment 81, which questions its ends, and fragment 169a, which questions its means. Fragment 169a shows that Heracles' violence against Geryon is problematic and unjustified, while fragment 81 shows that the entire poetic endeavor is guided above all by the impetus to please Zeus. Thus, if the poet wants to both acknowledge the ambivalence of heroic violence and still please the gods, he is compelled to promote Heracles' role as champion and son of Zeus over that of culture hero or monster-slayer.

More broadly speaking, the gnomic statement "*nomos* is king" became proverbial within a generation of Pindar's lifetime, perhaps even during it, and is quoted famously by Herodotus and Plato's Callicles. While a long scholarly tradition assumes that Herodotus and Callicles remove the statement from its context and use it merely as a catchphrase, recent scholarship has defended their engagement with the original Pindaric hypotext.[88] For example, Kingsley convincingly argues that Herodotus employs Pindar's complex portrayal of *nomos* and Heracles as a foil for his own depiction of Cambyses: both figures "are sanctified by *nomos*, though each transgresses the dictates of popular custom."[89] The adoption of Pindar's appeal to *nomos* for the purpose of addressing more concrete questions of violence thus illustrates how useful Heracles is for testing the limits of justifying violence, both in the ancient and modern world.

Conclusion

The myth of Geryon provides rich material for examining the instrumental nature of violence. For Hesiod, Heraclean violence is easily justified: Geryon belongs to a whole family of aberrant monsters who must be killed by early heroes. In taming the earth, Heracles functions to bolster the establishment of Zeus' ordering reign; he also acquires glory by accomplishing a challenging and dangerous task and returning with symbols of victory and wealth. But elements of the myth also lend themselves to undermining the justification for Geryon's death.

Stesichorus' *Geryoneis* highlights many elements that call into question Heracles' use of force. Heracles' journey to Erytheia demonstrates Geryon's isolation from human civilization; while it amplifies Heracles' courage and persistence in traveling beyond the known world, it also renders Geryon unthreatening to others. Moreover, the fragments depict Geryon as a beloved son, and a doomed but courageous warrior in the mold of the Homeric *agathos*. In attributing the *ethos* of an idealized fighter to a winged monster with tripled heads, arms, legs, Stesichorus challenges the Hesiodic view of monstrosity as a deviation that must be obliterated. By comparison, Heracles plays the role of violent interloper, relying on rustic, individualistic weapons to overcome him. This presentation creates tension between Heracles' roles as monster-slayer and deified hero. Where earlier Heracles' defeat of monsters served as part of the basis for his apotheosis, this particular act of killing, while impressive, seems to call that justification into question. Moreover, the negative effects of Heracles' intervention on Geryon's household draw attention to the wider costs of heroic violence.

In his engagement with the Geryon myth, Pindar puts both the ends and means of violence under scrutiny. While Heracles more often serves as the ultimate athletic victor and an exemplar worthy of imitation in Pindar's poetry, his actions against Geryon give the poet pause. In confessing a preference for Geryon over Heracles in fr. 81, Pindar seems to imply that Heracles' victory over him is inappropriate, while in fr. 169a, Pindar explicitly suggests alternative means for acquiring the Cattle, avoiding the problems of violence altogether. This renders violence a choice, rather than a necessity; Heracles' proclivity towards violence here comes closer to Benjamin's nonmediate violence. Ultimately, it is Heracles' favored status as Zeus' son—not his status as victor or his position as monster-slayer—that justifies him.

3

Heroic Competition and the Home in Sophocles' *Trachiniae*

Introduction

This chapter addresses heroic competition and its function in restraining violence in Sophocles' *Trachiniae*. Although Heracles is not the most popular of tragic heroes, the circumstances surrounding his death provide an opportunity to probe, as tragedy so often does, the intersection of heroic myth and the domestic sphere.[1] The play begins with Deianeira in exile in Trachis, in a state of ignorance and distress because Heracles has not come home in over a year. She soon receives the happy news that Heracles has successfully sacked the city of Oechalia and is sending home the slaves he has won in anticipation of his arrival. She discovers that Heracles' love for Iole, one of his prisoners of war, motivated the sack of the city, and that Heracles intends for his wife and concubine to dwell together. In hope of binding his attentions to herself, Deianeira paints a robe with an "aphrodisiac" that she received long ago from the centaur Nessus, as he lay dying from Heracles' arrow, and sends it to Heracles. The "aphrodisiac" is revealed to be the Hydra's venom, and when Heracles puts on the robe, he is reduced to writhing agonies and faces imminent death.

While the play focuses on Heracles' final days, his entire career hangs over its events. One way the play interrogates his career is through the lens of heroic competition. Heracles engages in many kinds of competition throughout his life, including athletic contests, feats of strength, and tests of endurance. In this chapter, I examine the *Trachiniae*'s treatment of two specific types of heroic competition: first, suitor competition, in which rivals, motivated by Eros, are pitted against another for the prize of a young woman; and second, the more general fight to the death against a beast or monster, from which one survives and seizes the spoils of victory from the other. I argue that the distinction between and overlap of these two categories are a critical factor driving the events that lead to Heracles' death.

Heroic competition has a dual function. First, competition serves as a mechanism for the heroic endeavor itself: an individual gains heroic status by proving himself superior to a worthy adversary through struggle, thereby displaying his *aretē*. This kind of rivalry is one aspect of a pervasive agonistic culture in ancient Greece, which is reflected from its earliest literary traditions and is one of its most familiar characteristics. For example, in the *Iliad*, Nestor recalls at a critical moment Peleus' injunction to his son Achilles to "always be the best and be superior to others" (αἰὲν ἀριστεύειν καὶ ὑπείροχον ἔμμεναι ἄλλων, 11.784; also at 6.208).[2] The result of winning the competition is becoming the victor, a role with which Heracles is closely associated. But the play pushes Heracles' status as victor to its logical extreme, revealing the consequences when victory eclipses all other concerns.

Another function of competition is to manage and constrain heroic violence. A common theme in the mythic tradition is young heroes' propensity to outbursts of deadly violence, such as Meleager's slaying of his uncle or Heracles' attack on Linus.[3] This kind of violence seems to fit within the framework of Benjamin's "nonmediate" violence, the sort that is not directed at a preconceived end, but is a manifestation of inner disorder. Competition can channel these aggressions into a context that is institutionalized and regulated by convention; violence is confined when competition operates under rules or expectations that both participants agree upon. For example, heroic convention dictates that suitable opponents include male warriors of the same social class but not women and children, and that they test each other on the basis of strength and skill.

Competition also sets an end—in terms of both a temporal conclusion and a goal—to the conflict. Typically opponents agree upon a start to the competition, and even more importantly they mutually recognize its endpoint, marking the point at which their hostility ceases. The winner acquires symbols of the victory, such as arms stripped on the battlefield, or the skinned pelt of an animal, or a woman. The rules of competition govern the means, while victory and its prizes provide an end; together they offer a way for the "nonmediate" violence of hotheaded youths to be organized within a means–ends calculus. But in the *Trachiniae*, when these conventions are overturned—for example, by displacing suitor competition into the home, where it does not belong—violence can become unbound, taking unpredictable directions and harming non-combatants.

As described in the previous chapter, Heracles' association with athletics and victory makes him a prime exemplar for epinician poetry. Easterling and Swift, among others, have explicated the play's engagement with epinician themes and conventions.[4] Yet the play actively suppresses the kind of epinician praise that promotes Heracles' victories as beneficial to mankind. Instead, the play dramatizes the catastrophic consequences of Heracles' single-minded pursuit of his own insatiable desires. The *Trachiniae* thus offers a stinging criticism of heroic victory, for while the play never denies that Heracles is a hero, he is a hero focused only on himself and his own will, without any regard for the desires of others.[5] While heroic competition ideally constrains violence to praiseworthy ends, it is also prone, as this chapter will show, to failure. This failure leads to lamentable disaster, demonstrating how even a bedrock cultural principle such as competition struggles to contain the impulse of violence, which constantly resists guidance and restraint.

Heracles and Achelous: A Paradigm of Competition

Deianeira opens the play by recounting the rivalry between Heracles and Achelous for her hand in marriage.[6] Achelous, the river god, approaches the house of her father Oeneus first; she emphasizes her fear of Achelous' strange and changeable form, a fear that turns to relief when Heracles arrives to challenge him for her hand in marriage:

χρόνῳ δ' ἐν ὑστέρῳ μέν, ἀσμένῃ δέ μοι,
ὁ κλεινὸς ἦλθε Ζηνὸς Ἀλκμήνης τε παῖς·
ὃς εἰς ἀγῶνα τῷδε συμπεσὼν μάχης
ἐκλύεταί με.

18–21

But later, to my great joy, came the famous son of Zeus and Alcmene, who released me by entering into a contest of battle with that one.

Deianeira calls the conflict between the two an *agōn*, the same term used to describe athletic competitions. But she also emphasizes its intensity, describing their competition as a battle. From the outset of the play, competition between warriors on the field of battle, athletes at an event, and suitors rivalling for a bride are shown to share much in common. Heracles defeats Achelous and claims Deianeira as his bride.

The prominence of this episode in the prologue establishes the event as the paradigm for heroic competition. Both Heracles and Achelous are worthy opponents of each other. Achelous, as a river, possesses monstrous powers of metamorphosis, and Heracles must exert himself to overcome this intimidating opponent.[7] The outcome of the struggle between the mighty river and the vigorous hero is not a foregone conclusion, and Deianeira could not bring herself to watch (21–5). Moreover, the contest between Heracles and Achelous is governed by the proper conventions. Both men traveled to Oeneus' home as suitors (μνηστήρ, 9, 15), and they engaged in open physical combat, overseen by Zeus of the Contest (Ζεὺς ἀγώνιος, 26). The competition is won without deception, ensuring the legitimacy of the victor's claim to his bride. Finally, it results in a proper marriage that produces legitimate children.

The Chorus recapitulates this competition in its first choral ode, which anticipates the successful return of Heracles.[8] That the event can serve as a subject of lyric praise emphasizes the greatness of both the combatants and the prize. The principal fight is the contest of strength between the two heroic males, as they grapple tightly and clash in hand-to-hand combat (519–23). The dramatic description captures the aural (πάταγος, 518) and visual (ἀμφίπλεκτοι κλίμακες, 520) tumult of their wrestling. Both exert themselves mightily, and the overall impression given by the ode is of a whirlwind of struggle so closely matched and intense as to be obscured by the dust cloud it raises.

Many common epinician themes emerging from the ode highlight the way competition funnels violent impulses through established channels. The wrestling contest is determined by physical strength and athletic ability; Aphrodite acts as referee, ensuring that an authority can call an official end to the contest.[9] The ode leaves implicit the conclusion of the contest; contextual clues indicate that Achelous departs in defeat and that the triumphant Heracles takes Deianeira as his bride. Strangely, Heracles is not explicitly named as victor, ceding that title to Aphrodite, who "always carries off the victories" (ἐκφέρεται νίκας / ἀεί, 497). The themes of heroic excellence (defeating a rival in a contest) and susceptibility to Eros (dependence on Aphrodite's ultimate judgment) are here closely intertwined.

Thus, at the inception of their marriage, each party seems to set and fulfill conventional expectations: the famous Heracles proves his worth to Deianeira by defeating Achelous in a display of heroic strength; she brings a reputation for physical beauty, and though that beauty must someday fade, she can offer compensation in the form of bearing heirs and managing the household with prudence and fidelity. The relationships between these figures form a competitive triangle: Deianeira is the focus and *desideratum* of both Achelous and Heracles, who compete directly with one another for the prize; the goal of each rival is to eliminate the other, which results in a collapse of the triangle into a linear relationship. When Heracles acquires Deianeira as his wife, he also acquires full control over her sexuality and affection, creating a strong and exclusive bond.

Competitions for the hand of a desirable bride are not unusual in Greek mythology, but many of the tales include some anomalous aspect in the contest.[10] For example, Pelops wins the hand of Hippodamia by defeating her father Oenomaus in a chariot race, yet his victory relies on the deceitful intervention of Myrtilus, Oenomaus' charioteer, and Pelops becomes the progenitor of a famously dysfunctional family.[11] Suitors compete with Atalanta in a footrace to earn either death or her marriage; Hippomenes defeats the fleet-footed virgin only by distracting her with golden apples. By contrast, Heracles' defeat of Achelous for Deianeira displays little irregularity.

But even as the play's early stages establish Heracles as a victor in heroic competition, they also expose the roles in which he is less successful. Heracles' life of adventure and conquest results in the neglect of his roles as husband and father—that is, the protector and maintainer of his household. That heroes should make poor husbands and fathers does not come as a surprise to any student of Greek mythology. But the *Trachiniae* goes to great effort to detail its extent in the case of Heracles and Deianeira, whose marriage, though celebrated in its beginning, has led to a troubled family life. Deianeira's simile condemns Heracles' abdication of responsibility for raising his children: "I bore children, whom he, like a farmer visiting a distant plot, looked at but once to sow and once to reap" (κἀφύσαμεν δὴ παῖδας, οὓς κεῖνός ποτε, / γῄτης ὅπως ἄρουραν ἔκτοπον λαβών, / σπείρων μόνον προσεῖδε κἀξαμῶν ἅπαξ, 31–3). In comparing herself to an out-of-the-way piece of property, Deianeira places herself on the margins, emphasizing her sense of isolation. And Heracles takes up the role of a terrible farmer, one whose crop is unlikely to turn out very well.

Encroaching on his role as protector of the household is the role of slave or servant. Deianeira describes how Heracles is not free himself, but must leave his home, "enslaved to someone or other" (λατρεύοντά τῳ, 35). She refers here to Heracles' Labors, accomplished on Eurystheus' orders and at Hera's behest.[12] While Heracles' servitude is a necessary precursor to the accomplishment of his most famous deeds, it nevertheless undermines his self-determination, with consequences that radiate outwards. Servitude in Greek myth, as Patrice Rankine has shown, is associated with ritual domination and social death.[13] These circumstances attend Heracles as well: though his physical strength is greater than Eurystheus', he nevertheless abandons home and family upon command, leading to a social estrangement revealed in Deianeira's ignorance of his whereabouts for the previous months.

His poor performance as head of the *oikos* serves to destabilize it, and his isolation is reflected in the physical displacement of his entire family. Because

Heracles murdered Iphitus, an incident integral to the unfolding of the play's events, Deianeira and the family live in exile in Trachis (38–41). Thus, Deianeira finds herself isolated from her husband, dwelling in a foreign land, far from her family by birth or marriage, as a consequence of Heracles' unlawful killing of a guest.[14] In this case, the family's exile and Deianeira's loneliness can be attributed not just to the cost of a heroic life, but specifically to Heracles' uncontrolled violence. In each of the ways that Heracles is distant from the *oikos*, he increases Deianeira's vulnerability.

As we have seen, the beginning of the play establishes the theme of heroic competition, setting Heracles against Achelous in a paradigmatic suitor competition in which violence is highly constrained. But Heracles' role as victor is in tension with his roles as head of the *oikos* and husband to Deianeira. The genre of tragedy expands the view of the role of victor beyond the scope available to epinician, allowing an exploration not only of the benefits of triumph, but also of its endemic costs. As the play explores distorted competition, violence likewise becomes unregulated, making the identity of the victor itself precarious.

Heracles and Nessus: A Distorted Suitor Competition

Shortly after Deianeira marries Heracles, she is subject to a sexual assault by the centaur Nessus. She is moved to recall the event after she discovers Iole's true identity and the threat to her status in the house.[15] In a distant and misty tone (παλαιόν . . . ἀρχαίου ποτέ, 555), she describes how, on her bridal journey from her father's house to Heracles', they came to the Evenus river; there, the centaur Nessus ferried passengers across the swift current for payment (559–63). While Nessus carries Deianeira, however, he "touches [her] with lustful hands" (ψαύει ματαίαις χερσίν, 565). In response to her cry for help, Heracles springs into action: "and immediately the son of Zeus turned and let loose a feathered arrow, which whizzed through his chest into his lungs" (χὠ Ζηνὸς εὐθὺς παῖς / ἐπιστρέψας χεροῖν / ἧκεν κομήτην ἰόν· ἐς δὲ πλεύμονας / στέρνων διερροίζησεν, 566–8).

In its outlines, the death of Nessus is another conventionally heroic feat accomplished by Heracles with his weapons. The centaur is referred to as a "beast" (θήρ, 556, 662, 680, 1162), evoking Heracles' role as a monster-slayer and tamer of animals in general, and his campaigns against the Centaurs in specific.[16] Nessus' non-human status and his attempted rape of Deianeira fully justify Heracles' violent response. The act of killing his wife's would-be rapist is a civilizing act, imposing norms of justice and order on a centaur characterized by his inability to control his own lustful and violent impulses. Furthermore, it is a demonstration of his heroic prowess in defense of his family and household. For these reasons, Heracles' use of violence is legitimate, and his status as victor confers glory upon him.

But Nessus is not only a beast who needs to be tamed. His erotic interest in Deianeira sets him up as another rival to Heracles. Like Achelous in his shape as part man, part bull, Nessus is part human and part animal in form. The centaur assaults her while she is still a virgin (παῖς ἔτ οὖσα, 557), threatening to usurp Heracles' claim as her first sexual partner. Were he to succeed, he would make her a kind of wife to him, just as Deianeira looks upon Iole not as a child (κόρη) any longer, but as a woman yoked in wedlock (ἐζευγμένη, 536). Both opponents are attracted by Deianeira's beauty and compete for the prize of sexual control over her. They form a second competitive triangle, in which Heracles again engages a rival in physical combat, triumphing this time not through his wrestling skills, but with his archery. With Nessus' defeat, Heracles has effectively resolved a suitor competition in the same way as his competition with Achelous; he continues with his bride as before.

The comparison with Achelous, however, highlights the anomalies of Nessus' competition with Heracles. Although he is fearsome and strange, Achelous is a worthy opponent for Heracles, approaching her father for Deianeira's hand and presenting himself openly as a rival when Heracles arrives. Though Achelous' physical attributes can represent the threat of unleashed male sexuality, he is nevertheless able to be contained.[17] Nessus, on the other hand, molests Deianeira on the sly, in violation of the unspoken contract between porter and passenger: Deianeira makes explicit that the Centaur "ferried mortals in his arms for payment" (βροτοὺς / μισθοῦ 'πόρευε χερσίν, 559–60). Because she is already married, his attraction to her cannot be redirected into a display of excellence that would win her. Unlike Achelous, who retreats from the couple upon his defeat, Nessus will not concede to Heracles, even in the throes of death. Without Aphrodite as referee of the lovers' contest, there is no official to declare when the contest is over.

While Heracles assumes that his conflict with Nessus has ended upon Nessus' death, Nessus does not give up the competition, instead planting the seed of a continuing struggle by appealing to Deianeira. Where Heracles views Deianeira primarily as a prize, an object to be possessed for his satisfaction, Nessus recognizes her as a person who can be influenced and can take action in her own right. Nessus therefore offers to Deianeira a "gift," accompanied by persuasive words:

> ... παῖ γέροντος Οἰνέως,
> τοσόνδ᾽ ὀνήσει τῶν ἐμῶν, ἐὰν πίθῃ,
> πορθμῶν, ὁθούνεχ᾽ ὑστάτην σ᾽ ἔπεμψ᾽ ἐγώ:
> ἐὰν γὰρ ἀμφίθρεπτον αἷμα τῶν ἐμῶν
> σφαγῶν ἐνέγκῃ χερσίν, ᾗ μελαγχόλους
> ἔβαψεν ἰοὺς θρέμμα Λερναίας ὕδρας,
> ἔσται φρενός σοι τοῦτο κηλητήριον
> τῆς Ἡρακλείας, ὥστε μήτιν᾽ εἰσιδὼν
> στέρξει γυναῖκα κεῖνος ἀντὶ σοῦ πλέον.
>
> 569–77

Child of aged Oeneus, you will benefit so much from my services, if you obey me, since you are the last of my passengers. For if you take away the clotted blood from my wounds in your hands, where the Lernaean Hydra dyed the arrows poisonous, you will have a charm for Heracles' heart, so that he will never look upon and love another woman more than you.[18]

The bestial centaur offers a token that requires great courage to accept: Deianeira must reach into the bloody wound of her would-be rapist and take for herself a portion of gore.[19] Deianeira, gullible and naïve, believes his oddly sentimental lies and follows his instructions. Her obedience reflects a deeper insecurity: even from the very beginning of their marriage, Deianeira suspected that she would have need for a powerful, almost certainly dangerous, charm to hold on to her husband, whose affection and respect for her could not be trusted.[20] Her mortal beauty succeeded in drawing him as a husband, but such beauty cannot last. Bereft of her paternal family, vulnerable now to the predations of the outside world, she is entirely reliant on Heracles for physical, financial, and social protection. Both her fear of abandonment and her need for his loyalty drive her to believe Nessus' words.

The ultimate fear for Deianeira comes in Nessus' final words to her, "love another ... *more than (instead of)* you" (ἀντὶ σοῦ πλέον, 577; emphasis mine). The doubling of *anti* and *pleon* creates a redundancy, perhaps reflecting the magnitude of Deianeira's secret fear. No doubt Heracles' reputation as a womanizer preceded him, and Deianeira does indeed overlook his many transgressions during their marriage. She tolerates Heracles' taking women *in addition to* her, but not *in replacement of* her. Her deepest fear has come to fruition with Iole's arrival in the home, and she therefore remembers Nessus' charm and decides to employ it.

Nessus' manipulation of Deianeira reveals an uncanny insight into the perils of the heroic life and the downsides of victory. Sophocles depicts Heracles in this play as a genuine heroic victor who also neglects his *oikos* spectacularly; the concurrence of the two suggests that abuse of the *oikos* is, in fact, an innate characteristic of heroism. After all, to become a hero worthy of praise and song, one must leave home and accomplish difficult, life-threatening deeds of greatness. As is demonstrated in the choice of Achilles, to live to old age with a happy and peaceful family life is antithetical to acquiring *kleos*. Just as Heracles is a supremely successful hero in glorious deeds, he is also supremely inadequate when it comes to taking care of his household. Nessus fails to overcome Heracles in terms of heroic competition, meeting immediate death after foolishly attempting to violate the new bride of Greece's greatest hero. But Nessus is clever enough to exploit Heracles' weaknesses as husband and father, threading his attack on Heracles through Deianeira and the *oikos*.

Nessus plays on Deianeira's insecurity with great effectiveness; although he does not succeed in achieving sexual gratification, he nevertheless successfully penetrates the mind and home of Deianeira with his scheme. Deianeira describes her memory as a tablet written upon by Nessus: "I preserved [Nessus' instructions], like an inscription impossible to wash from a bronze tablet" (ἀλλ' ἐσῳζόμην / χαλκῆς ὅπως δύσνιπτον ἐκ δέλτου γραφήν, 682–3). Nessus' words are as memorable as the prophecy written on an actual tablet that Heracles left behind (46–7).[21] Nessus' speech lies deep in Deianeira's mind, just as his potion is embedded in her home: she "kept the drug in the inner recesses" (ἐν μυχοῖς σῴζειν, 686), an area intended to be secured from the dangers of the outside world. The poison, kept secret and "closely locked up in the house" (δόμοις γὰρ ἦν ... ἐγκεκλῃμένον καλῶς, 578–9), compromises their marriage from its very start.[22]

Heracles at Oechalia: Another Distorted Suitor Competition

The distorted suitor competition between Heracles and Nessus lies dormant for many years, but it is activated when Lichas leads a train of captured women to Deianeira while announcing Heracles' impending return. The initial presentation of the news about Heracles by the messenger and Lichas had characterized him as the typical victorious hero. The messenger describes Heracles, who had been called a slave, as flourishing physically and in a position of power after his successful sack of Oechalia (ζῶντα ... κρατοῦντα, 182). Despite his domestic failings, Heracles can remain a praiseworthy and admirable (πολύζηλον, 185) victor. The hero of epinician has not lost his status, and moreover, he responds to victory in the proper way: by immediately offering sacrifices to the gods (κἀκ μάχης / ἄγοντ' ἀπαρχὰς θεοῖσι τοῖς ἐγχωρίοις, 182–3). Heracles' sacrifice of thanksgiving affords the gods a preeminent position in his victory and serves to reintegrate him ritually into society after killing. At this first announcement, it appears as though Heracles' *nostos* will be like the many that preceded it: the triumphant hero returns "with his victory-bearing power" (σὺν κράτει νικηφόρῳ, 186) to his household, where he will briefly enjoy his marital bed and family before departing on his next quest.

Lichas initially explains Heracles' long absence through a fairly familiar exchange of heroic aggressions and conflict. He begins *in medias res*, with the event that occupied most of Heracles' absence: his servitude to Omphale.[23] Lichas' account dwells heavily upon the humiliation of Heracles' bondage, calling him "not a free man, but bought" (οὐκ ἐλεύθερος / ἀλλ' ἐμποληθείς, 249–50). The repetition of πραθείς (252) and πρατόν (276) highlights two aspects of Heracles' powerlessness: his commodification (unthinkable for a free male, much less a famous hero), and the power of Zeus to control his son's fate. Lichas deepens Heracles' sense of injury in order to justify the scale of his response, to sack the city and enslave the family of the man who caused it. Heracles was so distraught over his "disgrace" (ὄνειδος, 254) that he swore an oath to enslave the man responsible with his wife and child (255–8). The target of Heracles' vengeance expands from the individual source, Eurytus, to his entire household and, in fact, his city.[24]

At this point, Lichas pauses to explain why Heracles calls Eurytus "alone the cause of this suffering" (μεταίτιον / μόνον βροτῶν ἔφασκε τοῦδ' εἶναι πάθους, 260–1). Despite Heracles' status as an ancestral guest friend (ξένον παλαιὸν ὄντα, 263), Eurytus offends him in three ways: Eurytus insults his skills in archery, reviles him for having served as a slave, and casts him out when he is drunk.[25] In retaliation for Eurytus' actions, Heracles kills his own guest, Iphitus, the son of Eurytus and brother of Iole, when he arrives in Tiryns in search of his lost horses.[26] Lichas describes Iphitus as distracted because of his search; Heracles seizes the opportunity to cast him headlong to his death.

This killing is a case of overt and unacceptable violence. So egregious is Heracles' act that Zeus intervenes to punish Heracles and defend the ethics of heroic conflict:

>   . . . οὐδ' ἠνέσχετο,
> ὁθούνεκ' αὐτὸν μοῦνον ἀνθρώπων δόλῳ
> ἔκτεινεν. εἰ γὰρ ἐμφανῶς ἠμύνατο,
> Ζεύς τἂν συνέγνω ξὺν δίκῃ χειρουμένῳ.
> ὕβριν γὰρ οὐ στέργουσιν οὐδὲ δαίμονες.
>
>   276–80

[Zeus] did not tolerate this, since he killed him, alone of men, by deceit. For if he had avenged himself openly, Zeus would have excused his conquering with justice. For the gods too do not love outrageous violence.

Iphitus is a full-grown man, son of a king and physically impressive, as indicated by the Homeric description Ἰφίτου βίαν (37). But Heracles does not engage him in open (ἐμφανῶς) competition as an adult male of high status; instead, he attacks him by surprise, a tactic associated with cowardice, while Iphitus is unaware and trusting in his status as a protected guest.[27] Heracles' deceptive attack is labeled an act of *hybris*, a clear indication of its reprehensible circumstances. Heracles' desire for vengeance does not receive disapproval; rather it is his surprise one-sided attack and reliance on trickery (δόλος) that draw Zeus' anger. There can be no celebration of this "victory." Moreover, Zeus proves himself *Xenios* by imposing servitude on Heracles, and his services are purchased by Omphale for a year.[28]

Lichas thus accounts for the causes of Heracles' humiliation, and quickly deals with the Oechalians' defeat: "those who were arrogant in evil speech are now inhabitants of Hades, and their city is a slave" (κεῖνοι δ' ὑπερχλίοντες ἐκ γλώσσης κακῆς / αὐτοὶ μὲν Ἅιδου πάντες εἰσ' οἰκήτορες, / πόλις δὲ δούλη, 281–3). In this framework, the sacking of Oechalia is a justified response to Eurytus' offense and Heracles' humiliation, and the arriving train of Oechalian female slaves is merely the result of a successful Heraclean expedition. They are treated as spoils of victory, a visual statement of Heracles' heroic prowess. Yet Deianeira's sympathy for the enslaved women and Iole's evident suffering direct the audience to consider the human cost of Heracles' successful revenge.

But the messenger contradicts the central claim of Lichas' speech: that Heracles sacked Oechalia out of anger at his enslavement. Rather, Heracles destroyed the city "for the sake of that maiden ... and Eros, alone of the gods, beguiled him into performing these feats of arms" (ὡς τῆς κόρης / ταύτης ἕκατι ... Ἔρως δέ νιν / μόνος θεῶν θέλξειεν αἰχμάσαι τάδε, 352–5). The messenger diminishes Heracles' outrage at his bondage in Lydia and Iphitus' unheroic murder to the status of a "thin pretense" (ἔγκλημα μικρόν, 361), and in its place promotes the role of Eros and Iole's beauty.[29] What was a regular tale of heroic punishment for a loss of status becomes a story then of the rejected suitor. Heracles has sacked the city of Eurytus because "he did not persuade the father to hand over his daughter, in order that he might obtain a secret union" (... οὐκ ἔπειθε τὸν φυτοσπόρον / τὴν παῖδα δοῦναι, κρύφιον ὡς ἔχοι λέχος, 359–60).

The motivation of love for Iole creates another distorted suitor competition, this time between Heracles and Iole's family for control over Iole. Heracles presents himself in Eurytus' home as a suitor for Iole, in a perversion of his request for Deianeira from Oeneus. But as an already-married man, he cannot be a suitable suitor, making him also a mirror of Nessus; he too is driven by unrestrained libidinous desire. Because Heracles never should have pursued Iole in the first place, convention fails to bring the competition to an appropriate close. Lichas' two tales leave the details of an archery contest rather muddied, but vase paintings and literary fragments attest to a tradition in which Heracles competes in an archery contest against Eurytus and/or his sons for Iole's hand; although he wins the contest, he is refused.[30]

I suggest that Lichas' reference to an insult to Heracles' archery "activates" this alternative version of the myth in the audience's mind, helping to frame Heracles as a suitor. Also like Nessus, he does not accept that he has lost the competition, departing from the household as Achelous did; instead, he continues to pursue revenge on the party that denies him his prize. Some details about Heracles' sack of Oechalia recall his sack of Troy, which was also provoked when a king refused to give a promised reward to Heracles. In many ways, Heracles' successful destruction of Oechalia can be similarly praised; he has avenged himself, acquired his prize, enriched himself with booty, and added another achievement to his legacy. However, he does not defeat his rivals for Iole in a conventional manner, as he did with Deianeira, so the violence that enables his victory operates outside the boundaries of competition, and his possession of her cannot lead to a legitimate marriage. Instead, it will lead to the ruin of his own *oikos*.

Iole and Deianeira Vie for Heracles

These two dysfunctional suitor competitions come together when Heracles sends Iole to take up residence at his own home. The messenger warns Deianeira about the identity of Iole and Heracles' passionate love for her:

> καὶ νῦν, ὡς ὁρᾷς, ἥκει δόμους
> ὡς τούσδε πέμπων οὐκ ἀφροντίστως, γύναι,
> οὐδ' ὥστε δούλην· μηδὲ προσδόκα τόδε·
> οὐδ' εἰκός, εἴπερ ἐντεθέρμανται πόθῳ.
>
> 365–8

And now, as you see, he arrives, sending her to this house not carelessly, Lady, and not as a slave. No, do not expect this, nor is it likely, since he has been fired by desire.

Heracles, in installing Iole within his own house as a permanent resident, betrays his selfish carelessness about his family and home. The trouble that results from housing wife and concubine under the same roof is proverbial, and Heracles' disregard of his family will seal his own doom. When the messenger forces Lichas to confess the truth, that he publicly swore "that [he] was leading that woman home as a wife for Heracles" (δάμαρτ' ἔφασκες Ἡρακλεῖ ταύτην ἄγειν, 428), Deianeira must confront Heracles' entanglement with Eros.

The arrival of a new mistress at the home of an absent warrior evokes Aeschylus' *Agamemnon*, another play that famously stages a hero's disastrous *nostos*.[31] Agamemnon returns home with Cassandra, his concubine and spoil of war, at his side; Cassandra, like Iole, is an unwilling prize of the warrior who sacked her city and destroyed her family. Upon their arrival, his unfaithful queen Clytemnestra murders them both, with the aid of her lover Aegisthus. The travails of the house of Atreus serve as the quintessential example of the demands of war and the agency of fate in Greek mythology, two themes of great importance in the *Trachiniae* as well.

But Sophocles draws a point of stark contrast between Deianeira and Clytemnestra. Clytemnestra is the most famous example of the faithless wife who betrays her husband while he fights a distant war. She deliberately plots his murder out of malevolence, desire for power, and/or grief over the sacrifice of her daughter Iphigenia; but there is no ambiguity about her responsibility or intent. In contrast, Sophocles makes Deianeira faithful and sympathetic; she is weak and passive where Clytemnestra is masculine and aggressive. By emphasizing Deianeira's innocence and love for Heracles, Sophocles places the burden of responsibility for the disaster that follows squarely on Heracles' shoulders. Deianeira has preserved her marital bed for him despite his lengthy absences, raised his children, and kept his household in order. In sending a concubine to share the same roof as his wedded wife, Heracles does unmitigated violence to his *oikos*.

Furthermore, Heracles' introduction of Iole to his home inflicts a specific sort of violence: he creates rivalry between two women, with his own affection and attention as the prize. Heracles' devotion to victory seems to make him blind to any other considerations; in sending Iole to live by his wife, he treats them both as objects, trophies installed on the same shelf. But competition in relationships, as demonstrated in the initial paradigm with Achelous, ought to exist between heroic men, with a woman as a prize, not vice versa. Now, Deianeira competes with a younger woman of royal status for the sexual attention of her own husband, though both are reluctant competitors. The locale of competition is not the battlefield or the outdoors, but the interior world of the home. The home is the site of struggle in both a physical and metaphorical sense: it is sharing the same roof that Deianeira finds truly threatening, and Iole's continuous proximity is what disturbs a fragile household already made vulnerable by exile. No convention exists for managing the hostility engendered by rivalry over the same hero for Deianeira and Iole, nor can they engage in the kind of competition available to heroic men.

But in Deianeira's response to the revelation of Iole's identity, the play seems to go out of the way to remove any trace of indignation, resentment, or hatred towards the younger woman. Despite her apparent innocence of the world, she is remarkably understanding about the caprice of desire:

> Ἔρωτι μέν νυν ὅστις ἀντανίσταται
> πύκτης ὅπως ἐς χεῖρας, οὐ καλῶς φρονεῖ·
> οὗτος γὰρ ἄρχει καὶ θεῶν ὅπως θέλει,
> κἀμοῦ γε· πῶς δ' οὐ χἀτέρας οἵας γ' ἐμοῦ;
> ὥστ' εἴ τι τὠμῷ τ' ἀνδρὶ τῇδε τῇ νόσῳ
> ληφθέντι μεμπτός εἰμι, κάρτα μαίνομαι,
> ἢ τῇδε τῇ γυναικὶ τῇ μεταιτίᾳ
> τοῦ μηδὲν αἰσχροῦ μηδ' ἐμοὶ κακοῦ τινος.
>
> 441–8

Whoever rises up against Eros, as a boxer to fisticuffs, does not think clearly: for he rules even the gods as he wishes, and me too. How then could he not rule another woman, like myself? I would be entirely mad, therefore, to blame my husband for being seized by this passion, or this woman for being accessory to an action hardly shameful nor an injury to me.

In Deianeira's view, Eros wields the highest power, even over Zeus. Thus, Heracles, who has already been described as subject to Eurystheus and enslaved to Omphale, is revealed as having yet another master. This subjection to Eros will also impinge on his ability to fulfill his role as husband.

Deianeira goes on to argue that she can receive the truth from Lichas because she will not use it to punish Iole. That Heracles has taken other lovers during their marriage is not news to her, nor has she raised objections in the past: "Hasn't Heracles, though one man, in fact bedded a host of women?" (πλείστας ἀνὴρ εἷς Ἡρακλῆς ἔγημε δή, 460). Indeed, when Deianeira looks upon Iole, she sees the fate she dreaded for herself: "her beauty destroyed her life, and the ill-fated girl has unwillingly destroyed and enslaved her fatherland" (τὸ κάλλος αὐτῆς τὸν βίον διώλεσεν, / καὶ γῆν πατρῴαν οὐχ ἑκοῦσα δύσμορος / ἔπερσε κἀδούλωσεν, 465–8).

Just as Deianeira had feared, during the contest between Heracles and Achelous for her marriage, that "my beauty may win for me sorrow at some time" (μή μοι τὸ κάλλος ἄλγος ἐξεύροι ποτέ, 25), Iole's beauty has won her overwhelming grief. The ambiguous value of κάλλος is thus clarified: Heracles' lust can save one woman (Deianeira, in her terror of Achelous) and destroy another (Iole and her family).

Despite the position that Heracles has put her in, Deianeira cannot engage in heroic competition, determined as it most often is by superiority in feats of strength or martial skill. Violence, especially of the Heraclean type, is foreign to her nature. Moreover, Deianeira recognizes that eliminating her rival will not guarantee Heracles' love or faithfulness to her, for the man who can be overtaken by "terrible desire" (ὁ δεινὸς ἵμερος, 476) has proven susceptible to its power repeatedly. She attempts a different strategy: rather than compete openly with her rival, as heroes do, she seeks to acquire her prize by directly strengthening her relationship to Heracles. For her, victory does not necessarily require the death or exile of Iole. Rather, she turns away from her rival in hope of creating an exclusive bond so strong that no triangulation with a female rival will ever be possible again.

Her attempt to solidify her connection with Heracles reflects a deeper recognition of her true position in his view: she is past her prime, a middle-aged woman and mother of many children, a wife whose tending of the house can be taken for granted. She confesses, "I see her youth blossoming, and mine withering: men's eye loves to pluck the bloom of the former, and turn their feet from the latter" (ὁρῶ γὰρ ἥβην τὴν μὲν ἕρπουσαν πρόσω, / τὴν δὲ φθίνουσαν· ὧν ἀφαρπάζειν φιλεῖ / ὀφθαλμὸς ἄνθος, τῶν δ' ὑπεκτρέπει πόδα, 547–9). Her status as wife is thus vulnerable to Iole, whose youth and beauty prove to have formidable power. Because she is unable to compete with Iole on the basis of these qualities, she chooses instead to act on Heracles, recognizing that even as the prize, he can be influenced.

As Deianeira analyzes her place in this anomalous competitive triangle, she considers her relation to her new rival, Iole. Iole is not simply a virginal, attractive serving girl, but stands to acquire the status of Heracles' actual wife, if not in name, at least in reality:

κόρην γάρ, οἶμαι δ' οὐκέτ', ἀλλ' ἐζευγμένην,
παρεισδέδεγμαι φόρτον ὥστε ναυτίλος,
λωβητὸν ἐμπόλημα τῆς ἐμῆς φρενός.
καὶ νῦν δύ' οὖσαι μίμνομεν μιᾶς ὑπὸ
χλαίνης ὑπαγκάλισμα.

536–40

For I have taken on a maiden—or dare I say, no maiden, but a married woman—
just as a sailor takes on a cargo, as merchandise baneful to my heart. And now
the two of us wait under one blanket for an embrace.

Iole has assumed Deianeira's sexual role in the household, as the yoke-mate of Heracles and a partner in his bed. It is unlikely that the male head of the *oikos* would be expected to refrain from molesting the servant girls entirely; for the audience of the *Odyssey*, it is worthy of comment that Laertes "never made love to [Eurycleia], but he shunned the anger of his wife" (*Od.* 1.433). But what Deianeira finds so appalling is that Iole will be a permanent concubine, living under the same roof: "What woman could stand dwelling together with this girl, sharing in common the same marriage?" (τὸ δ᾽ αὖ ξυνοικεῖν τῇδ᾽ ὁμοῦ τίς ἂν γυνὴ / δύναιτο, κοινωνοῦσα τῶν αὐτῶν γάμων, 545–6). Furthermore, Deianeira fears that the girl who enchants Heracles to such a degree will eventually supplant her, "that Heracles may be *called* my husband, but in reality be the younger woman's man" (φοβοῦμαι μὴ πόσις μὲν Ἡρακλῆς / ἐμὸς καλῇται, τῆς νεωτέρας δ᾽ ἀνήρ, 550–1). Deianeira therefore applies the potion to a beautiful robe and sends it with Lichas as a gift to Heracles, thus unwittingly sealing his doom.[32]

In her fear of losing her wifely status, Deianeira is not so different from another tragic heroine driven to desperate deeds, Medea. Although the relative order of the composition of the *Trachiniae* and the *Medea* remains undetermined, I argue that Deianeira's choices should be treated with the same respect as Medea's.[33] To claim, as Winnington-Ingram does, that "this is a tragedy of sex," is to limit Deianeira's perception and agency.[34] Both women, living in exile, watch their husbands enter into new relationships with younger women. Medea is physically pushed out of the household and the city, her children effectively made bastards; Deianeira faces an analogous, though more symbolic, threat. Made vulnerable by the choices of their husbands, both women turn to other means in order to protect their own interests.[35] Their responses differ greatly: Medea uses violence against their children to take revenge on oath-breaking Jason, so that he will never enjoy his life after her humiliation; Deianeira resorts to a magical charm to obtain Heracles' exclusive attention.[36] Nevertheless, the women are similar in their efforts to reassert their status in the face of a dire threat.

Deianeira's terrible recognition of the lethal nature of Nessus' ointment sets the play's *denouement* in motion. She might have expected that her love potion would weaken Heracles' self-control, by increasing his desire.[37] But the strength of the potion, now demonstrated on the tuft of wool used to apply the ointment to a robe, indicates that she will become Heracles' destroyer (ἐξαποφθερῶ, 713). And Heracles, who anticipates only open and physical combat, is therefore caught unawares by Nessus' hidden attack. He thought that he had eliminated Nessus from the competitive triangle, but in fact Nessus remains a rival through his influence on Deianeira. The play demonstrates that Nessus was unable to overcome Heracles by his own strength; rather, it took Heracles' creating an anomalous competitive triangle within his own house for Nessus to prove triumphant.

It is only through the combination of distorted competitions that Heracles finds himself defeated. Heracles' violent actions as an inappropriate suitor set the disaster in motion. But the hero who can conquer every man and beast through his strength and skill is made vulnerable because he treats Deianeira as merely a prize, while his enemy Nessus recognized long ago that she too has agency when threatened by a rival. Heracles' neglect of his role within the *oikos* not only sets the stage for his death, but triggers the weapon against himself.

The Death of a Victor

When Hyllus returns from Cape Cenaeum to report the disastrous consequences of Deianeira's gift, the play shifts its gaze, turning a critical eye on Heracles' victories in conjunction with the manner of his death.[38] Hyllus denounces his mother, wishing that she were dead, or not his, or different (734–7); he even calls *Dikē* and an Erinys upon her head, the most damning curse possible (808–9), and denies her the very name of "Mother" (817–18). If bearing legitimate children to Heracles as heirs was one of her main wifely duties, then the severing of her connection to those legitimate children undermines her position in the household in yet another way.[39] Bereft of her natal family, abandoned by Heracles, and rejected by her child, Deianeira is truly alone.

Hyllus' eyewitness account of Heracles' agonies reinforces the play's juxtaposition of Heracles' roles as victor and husband and father. Even as his home teeters on the verge of collapse in Trachis, Heracles on Cape Cenaeum appears to be the triumphant victor. As he prepares sacrifices to his father, he seems to be thriving, proving a sight for sore eyes to the anxious Hyllus (755).[40] But Heracles' tasks are interrupted by the arrival of Lichas, whose connection with the *oikos* is emphasized with "his own" (οἰκεῖος) and "from home" (ἀπ' οἴκων, 757) as he bears the poisoned robe from Deianeira. The familiar and familial origins of the messenger and his gift belie the dangerous nature of the gift itself. Heracles at first rejoices in his fine garb, until the deadly poison is activated by the heat of the sun and the flames of sacrifice. Heracles' weapon, used for his own purposes so many times, has finally been turned on him; the victorious hero is victimized by the same terrible pains that led Nessus and Cheiron to their deaths.[41]

In terrible pain, Heracles lashes out violently, as if out of a desire to see the pain he suffers reflected in those around him. Although Lichas tells the truth, that Deianeira alone was responsible for the robe, Heracles proverbially shoots the messenger, hurling him headfirst into a rock (779–83). Lichas' death resembles the unheroic murder of Iphitus, whom Heracles also tossed from the high walls of Tiryns. Verbal reminiscence draws attention to their connection: Iphitus' death is ὁ ῥιπτὸς Ἰφίτου μόρος (357); Lichas, whom Heracles ῥιπτεῖ, is δύσμορος (780, 775). Heracles' murder of Iphitus was condemned by Zeus as an unacceptable use of violence, and the allusion implies that Heracles' attack on Lichas is similarly deplorable. These are outbursts of enraged violence, unconstrained by competition or convention.[42]

In the midst of his torture, Heracles recognizes his son's face among an army of mercenaries. Though he must be grateful that a family member is present to help him, he expresses no relief; his first utterance to his son is a reminder of the depth of a son's obligation to his father: "Son, approach, do not shun my trouble, not even if you must die together with me" (ὦ παῖ, πρόσελθε, μὴ φύγῃς τοὐμὸν κακόν, / μηδ' εἴ σε χρὴ θανόντι συνθανεῖν ἐμοί, 797–8). Heracles finally realizes the value of his children: when every bystander is too terrified to come near the wild and violent man, Heracles can order his own son to obey. Hyllus, by all accounts a dutiful son, complies, and enables Heracles to avoid the shame of public collapse and the fear of dying on the island of Euboea, far from home.

As they respond to Hyllus' announcements, the Chorus helps the audience to evaluate the play's events, drawing out a comparison between Heracles and his former rival Nessus. In anticipation of Heracles' arrival, the Chorus fits the events at Cape Cenaeum together with the various prophecies recounted in the play.[43] The Chorus emphasizes Nessus' *modus operandi*: he works through guile (δολοποιὸς ἀνάγκα ... δολόμυθα ... δολίαν καὶ μεγάλαν ἄταν, 832–50). The preponderance of words built off of the root *dol-* recalls the description of Heracles' aberrant attack on Iphitus. The murder of Iphitus established that Zeus disapproves of attack "by stealth" (δόλῳ, 277); that Nessus defeats Heracles by using a similarly unheroic method thus underlines the resemblance between the two.[44] And both experience an agonized death caused by the Hydra's poison.

But Nessus' use of deception also relieves Deianeira of the burden of intent to cause Heracles' death. Misled by the Centaur, Deianeira acts only with the desire to ward off the "great ruin of a new marriage rushing upon her house" (μεγάλαν προσορῶσα δόμοισι / βλάβαν νέων ἀίσσου- / σαν γάμων, 842–4). The issue of Deianeira's intent is crucial to the play's evaluation of her character; although she possessed the various bits of information necessary to understand the substance of Nessus' charm, she nevertheless is innocent of Heracles' murder.[45] And thus the responsibility for Heracles' failure must rest, at least in large part, elsewhere. The Chorus lays the blame not only on the horrifying *nosos*, but also on the spearhead that won Iole (synecdoche for Heracles' success in warfare) and Aphrodite (associated with Heracles' uncontrollable lust). This combination of distorted competition and Eros leads to violence that spills over the channels that could ordinarily contain it.[46]

The news of Deianeira's suicide vindicates her innocence. (One can hardly imagine the victorious Clytemnestra killing herself in shame after plotting against and slaying her own husband.) Denounced by husband and son, Deianeira shows that her main concern is to bid her household farewell: "it is the *oikos* and the life she led there that she mourns."[47] Her actions are a rebuke to Heracles' neglect; she acquits herself as the proper mistress of a home, even one in exile. Her farewells culminate with the marriage bed, the symbol of her sexual bond with Heracles and the central locus of their marriage within the house. At this spot she mourns the loss of her status: "Never again will you receive me in these covers still as his wife!" (ὡς ἔμ᾽ οὔποτε / δέξεσθ᾽ ἔτ᾽ ἐν κοίταισι ταῖσδ᾽ εὐνάτριαν, 921–2). Deianeira does not yet know for a fact that Heracles is dead, but Hyllus' disavowal of her, in addition to her shame at her misdeeds, convinces her that her position in the home is permanently destroyed. Heracles has violated the sanctity of their bed by sending Iole to Trachis; Deianeira makes the pollution visible with her own blood and body. She commits suicide in a private place, but the way she kills herself is a public statement: the weapon that ends her life, the masculine and heroic sword, stands in for Heraclean violence, both in function, because it is undoubtedly Heracles' sword, and as a phallic symbol.[48]

It is only here, in the final quarter of the play, that Heracles arrives on stage. Heracles' entrance on stage is accompanied not by a triumphant song celebrating his *nostos*, but by his own agonized shouts. The contrast should be startling: Heracles' achievement in sacking Oechalia could be framed as a victory, as we assume it was in the archaic epic attributed to Creophylus of Samos; yet here there is not a word of praise for Heracles' exploit, only lament in anticipation of his death.[49] He is hardly recognizable: too weak to walk, he is borne on a litter by foreigners; his clothing lies in tatters; sleep is considered his beneficial balm, not mere respite between actions.[50] If the audience finds Heracles' appearance disconcerting, Heracles himself feels equally disoriented. When he awakens, Heracles does not recognize Trachis; perhaps he had expected to be brought by Hyllus to Thebes or Tiryns. Those cities are far from his current location, though, and it is unclear whether Heracles understands why he cannot return to Tiryns: his family is in exile because of his murder of Iphitus.

Heracles, who has dominated the narratives told by others, finally gains the opportunity to speak for himself. Heracles' first words are a rebuke against Zeus, signaling the play's narrowing focus on Zeus' wisdom and justice. Heracles expresses an acute sense of injustice at the discrepancy between his beneficial acts, which deserve reward, and the terrible suffering he experiences. In his view, he is subject to an unfair exchange, a disruption of *philia*. Although he has offered fitting sacrifices to Zeus on Mount Cenaeum, Zeus allows him to fall into ruin before the altars (993–5). Because Zeus does not appear to alleviate his pain, Heracles turns to the men nearby and begs them to put him out of his misery:

> ... πόθεν ἔστ', ὦ
> πάντων Ἑλλάνων ἀδικώτατοι ἀνέρες, οὓς δὴ
> πολλὰ μὲν ἐν πόντῳ κατά τε δρία πάντα καθαίρων
> ὠλεκόμαν ὁ τάλας, καὶ νῦν ἐπὶ τῷδε νοσοῦντι
> οὐ πῦρ, οὐκ ἔγχος τις ὀνήσιμον οὐκ ἐπιτρέψει;
>
> 1010–14

> Where are you from, most unrighteous men of all Greeks, whom I purged of pests on the sea and throughout all the forests, wearing myself out, the wretch? And now that I am ailing, will no one turn fire or a beneficial sword on me?

Heracles views the exchange of favors as purely transactional: because he has profited all men on earth with his civilizing efforts, he now demands that whoever approaches him kill him as an act of mercy. But no one approaches him to kill him, held back either by fear or scruple. Thus, Heracles is left utterly vulnerable, unable to defend himself physically or ward off his enemies. Heracles has always been a very *physical* hero, most renowned for his unmatchable strength, the power of his body. Now, the personification of youth craves nothing but freedom from a broken, burdensome body. In Segal's terms, "Heracles is defined solely in terms of his great physique. That ruined, his loss is total."[51]

Heracles goes on to deliver a great monologue that laments his humiliation at Deianeira's hands. His perspective is subjected to a form of reverse-telescoping: the events of his final days loom large, crowding out the litany of heroic successes that form the foundation of his fame. In evaluating his life more by its end than its beginning or middle, Heracles encourages the audience to view it that way as well. For the first time, the names of Eurystheus and Hera are mentioned, but only in passing (1048–9); they figure in his thoughts only inasmuch as their plots against him were not as heinous as Deianeira's.[52] In a review of his earlier accomplishments Heracles makes no mention of Iolaus, Theseus, or other male comrades. He stands alone, isolated from both friends and family.

Heracles' view of himself and his victorious life is informed by the shock of his current failure. Having never viewed Deianeira as a threat, he struggles to integrate his current debilitation at her hands with his earlier triumphs. He describes his major efforts on behalf of the gods and humankind only to elevate the humiliation he experiences at the hands of his wife:

κοὐ ταῦτα λόγχη πεδιάς, οὔθ' ὁ γηγενὴς
στρατὸς Γιγάντων οὔτε θήρειος βία,
οὔθ' Ἑλλὰς οὔτ' ἄγλωσσος οὔθ' ὅσην ἐγὼ
γαῖαν καθαίρων ἱκόμην, ἔδρασέ πω·
γυνὴ δέ, θῆλυς φῦσα κοὐκ ἀνδρὸς φύσιν,
μόνη με δὴ καθεῖλε φασγάνου δίχα.

1058–63

Not the spear of the battlefield, nor the earth-born army of Giants, nor the violence of beasts, not Greece nor a foreign place, nor any land I visited to tame, has ever done these things: but a *woman*, born female and lacking manly strength, she alone, in fact, has destroyed me, without a sword.

One of Heracles' complaints is that he is deprived of the opportunity of a heroic death in pursuit of his mission as a culture hero. In each of his previous conflicts, he has prevailed and thus proven his strength and courage through his success. Heracles laments that he is felled by an unheroic opponent, a woman, whom he could never consider a worthy adversary. His real grief stems from having fallen outside of a proper competition, and by means other than physical weapons.

Heracles addresses his own body as the locus and source of his greatness, demonstrating how he tends to conceive of his role as victor only in terms of a display of physical superiority over formidable opponents.[53] The emphasis on his physicality and the fierceness of his opponents amplifies the violence necessary to subdue them. Indeed, his catalogue is less about the achievements themselves than what was required to achieve them:

. . . ὦ χέρες χέρες,
ὦ νῶτα καὶ στέρν', ὦ φίλοι βραχίονες·

ὑμεῖς δὲ κεῖνοι δὴ καθέσταθ', οἵ ποτε
Νεμέας ἔνοικον, βουκόλων ἀλάστορα
λέοντ', ἄπλατον θρέμμα κἀπροσήγορον,
βίᾳ κατειργάσασθε, Λερναίαν θ' ὕδραν,
διφυῆ τ' ἄμικτον ἱπποβάμονα στρατὸν
θηρῶν, ὑβριστὴν ἄνομον, ὑπέροχον βίαν,
Ἐρυμάνθιόν τε θῆρα, τόν θ' ὑπὸ χθονὸς
Ἅιδου τρίκρανον σκύλακ', ἀπρόσμαχον τέρας,
δεινῆς Ἐχίδνης θρέμμα, τόν τε χρυσέων
δράκοντα μήλων φύλακ' ἐπ' ἐσχάτοις τόποις.
ἄλλων τε μόχθων μυρίων ἐγευσάμην,
κοὐδεὶς τροπαῖ' ἔστησε τῶν ἐμῶν χερῶν.

1089–102

My hands, back, and chest! Dear arms, yes, you are those famous arms, which once defeated the beast of Nemea by force, a destroyer of herds, a Lion, a terrible and unapproachable monster—and the Lernaean Hydra, and the savage army of double-natured, hoofed beasts, insolent and lawless, overbearing in force, and the Erymanthian creature, and the three-headed pup of the land of Hades, an unapproachable monster, the offspring of the fearsome Echidna, and the dragon-guard of the Golden Apples at the edge of the earth. I have tasted a thousand other toils, and no one erected a trophy over my hands.

This list functions almost as a career highlights reel for the hero, with a focus on Heracles' physical presence, appropriate for a man destroyed by a physical disease. But in emphasizing his body as the source of his strength to accomplish amazing feats, Heracles shifts the focus away from the positive aspects of heroic violence: clever strategy, unflinching courage, the desire to benefit others or protect the vulnerable. Heracles' heroism here has been distilled into its material essence, in Heracles' flesh. Heracles views his failure as primarily a physical one, that someone (his feminine wife) has brought him to a point of bodily collapse (1103–6) and that he is no longer dominant.

Even on his deathbed, Heracles seeks out victory at any cost. Just as he introduced competition into his relationship with Deianeira by installing Iole under the same roof, he also introduces competition with Deianeira into his relationship with Hyllus. Heracles, who had never before viewed Deianeira as a rival, now feels compelled to challenge her: he demands that Hyllus declare his allegiance to his father alone and repudiate his mother. And just as he took no thought for his *oikos* before sending Iole home, he now shows no concern that his competition will tear apart his family.

ὦ παῖ, γενοῦ μοι παῖς ἐτήτυμος γεγώς,
καὶ μὴ τὸ μητρὸς ὄνομα πρεσβεύσῃς πλέον.
δός μοι χεροῖν σαῖν αὐτὸς ἐξ οἴκου λαβὼν
ἐς χεῖρα τὴν τεκοῦσαν, ὡς εἰδῶ σάφα
εἰ τοὐμὸν ἀλγεῖς μᾶλλον ἢ κείνης ὁρῶν
λωβητὸν εἶδος ἐν δίκῃ κακούμενον.

1064–8

Son, become my true-born son, and do not honor your mother's name more [than mine]. Remove your mother from the house with your own hands and hand her over to me yourself, so that I might know clearly whether it pains you more to look upon my outraged body or hers, justly injured.

Heracles cruelly co-opts Hyllus for his plan of revenge against his wife, viewing his compliance as a test of his very paternity. He demands this despite the fact that Heracles as a father had been compared by Deianeira to a distant farmer, neglectful of his crop (31–3). Heracles now expects the cooperation of his son, without having committed properly to the role and responsibilities of that paternity. Moreover, Heracles requires that Hyllus *enjoy* participating in his mother's punishment. But Hyllus has already displayed his loyalty to Heracles when he confronted Deianeira earlier, by rejecting her as mother in defense of his father (734–820). What Heracles seeks is too much satisfaction, obliterating any concern for others involved in the situation.

Thus, though Heracles and Deianeira are both parents to Hyllus, Heracles attempts to eliminate his rival and take the role of sole progenitor; Hyllus' affection and allegiance are the prize. In this way, Heracles will be able to declare a double victory over his wife: he intends to inflict the same physical tortures on her, despite his weakness, and destroy her mother's heart, by lording Hyllus' disavowal over her. He proclaims:

ἀλλ᾽ εὖ γέ τοι τόδ᾽ ἴστε, κἂν τὸ μηδὲν ὦ
κἂν μηδὲν ἕρπω, τήν γε δράσασαν τάδε
χειρώσομαι κἀκ τῶνδε· προσμόλοι μόνον,
ἵν᾽ ἐκδιδαχθῇ πᾶσιν ἀγγέλλειν ὅτι
καὶ ζῶν κακούς γε καὶ θανὼν ἐτισάμην.

1107–11

But know this well: even if I am nothing, even if I cannot move, I will subdue the woman who did this to me, even in my current state: may she only approach, so that she may be taught to proclaim to all that I, both living and dead, make the guilty pay!

Heracles, even as he recognizes that he will die, refuses to let his enemy enjoy a long triumph. The declaration of his intent to kill Deianeira, even θανών, places him again in parallel to Nessus: just as Nessus planted the seeds in Deianeira's mind that would ultimately destroy Heracles as he lay dying, so Heracles intends to destroy Deianeira despite his physical incapacitation. There is no end to a competition until he wins. But the play deflates Heracles' show of bravado, since Deianeira does not need to be taught the meaning of honor; her shame has already driven her to her death. Heracles' vaunting over her self-slain body becomes a parody of his heroism, for just when he calls upon the last reserves of his legendary strength, he no longer needs it.

In a rare ray of light in this play, Hyllus refuses to continue his family's cycle of dysfunctional competition. He neither supports his father nor rebels against him; instead, he relies on the expression of truth. Hyllus' rhetorical skill reflects his maturation; gently, respectfully, Hyllus acknowledges both his father's physical pain (νοσῶν, 1115) and his mental anguish (δάκνῃ / θυμῷ, 1117–18), while defending his mother's innocent intentions and legitimizing her fear of the new marriage being introduced into the home (1136–9).[54] Moreover, Hyllus succinctly lays out the entire backstory: "The Centaur Nessus long ago persuaded her to excite your desire with this potion" (Νέσσος πάλαι Κένταυρος ἐξέπεισέ νιν / τοιῷδε φίλτρῳ τὸν σὸν ἐκμῆναι πόθον, 1139–40). Upon hearing this, Heracles immediately pivots from his threats of vengeance on Deianeira to the dispensation of his legacy, for he recognizes that he is dying, and dying in accordance with previous prophecy.[55] Thus, the final words concerning Deianeira exonerate her and reveal that her deeds were integral to the fulfillment of Heracles' prophecies. She has died, heartbroken and disgraced, but in the service of Zeus' will.

Heracles' newfound understanding may shift his attention, but it does not alter his relationship with his household. As he comes nearer to death, his failures as a father and husband only grow more prominent. He immediately calls his family to attend him as witness to his final transmission of knowledge (1147–50), but no one is available.[56] This moment of grand solemnity—Heracles' recognition of his impending death—is immediately undercut by the reality of his scattered *oikos*. For the assembly he envisions, of his mother, his descendants, and those most affected by his life and death, is simply unattainable. It falls to Hyllus to explain to his father why his command cannot be fulfilled:

ἀλλ' οὔτε μήτηρ ἐνθάδ', ἀλλ' ἐπακτίᾳ
Τίρυνθι συμβέβηκεν ὥστ' ἔχειν ἕδραν.

παίδων δὲ τοὺς μὲν ξυλλαβοῦσ᾽ αὐτὴ τρέφει,
τοὺς δ᾽ ἂν τὸ Θήβης ἄστυ ναίοντας μάθοις.

1151–4

But your mother is not here; it happens that she keeps her home in Tiryns, by the sea. But she has taken some your children with her and raises them there. The others, you will learn, inhabit the city of Thebes.

Heracles is still clueless about his family, which leads to this rather embarrassing moment. His mistaken assumption that his family is ready at his beck and call at the moment that he shows interest in them, just as he called Hyllus to help him on Cenaeum, demonstrates his egoism.

Furthermore, this particular reference to Tiryns and Thebes also reminds the audience of the two locations where Heracles can no longer reside, due to his inability to control his violence. In Thebes, he murdered his wife Megara and his children, an example of heroic violence gone terribly awry. And in Tiryns, as the play attests, Heracles murdered his ancestral guest-friend, Iphitus, which prompted his entire family to be exiled to Trachis. These two *loci* of his legendary tales are the places where he *ought* to be when he dies. Yet they are precisely where Heracles *cannot* be, as a result of his own blameworthy actions. Thus, this exchange highlights not only Heracles' exclusion from domestic knowledge, but also the unstable nature of his engagement with violence.

With past oracles fully explicated, the play can look towards the future.[57] But Heracles cannot change. Heracles extracts an oath of obedience from the reluctant Hyllus by framing his compliance as his highest duty: "but (you must) agree to cooperate, observing the best of laws, obeying your father" (ἀλλ᾽ αὐτὸν εἰκαθόντα συμπράσσειν, νόμον / κάλλιστον ἐξευρόντα, πειθαρχεῖν πατρί, 1177–8). By specifying "father" instead of "parents" (as in Aesch. *Supp.* 707-9), Heracles privileges his authority over Deianeira's—a moot point, given that Deianeira is already dead.[58] He then makes two demands of Hyllus, both of which offend the younger man's scruples. The play offers no explanation of Heracles' motivation for commanding Hyllus to build a pyre for him on Mount Oeta and set it alight, such as another oracle or previous instruction from Zeus. Hyllus refuses to become his father's murderer, having already taken responsibility for his mother's death earlier in the day (932–3). Hyllus only accepts after Heracles has threatened to curse him from the underworld and suggests disowning him (1200–5). Just as Heracles undermined Deianeira's position in the household, so he now threatens to put Hyllus' role in jeopardy as well.[59]

Heracles' second request is even more appalling: Hyllus must take Iole, whose presence has precipitated the utter destruction of his family, as his own bride.[60] Heracles bases his order on the demands of heroic status: "let no other mortal take her, who has lain by my side, except you. You yourself, son, join your bed to hers" (μηδ' ἄλλος ἀνδρῶν τοῖς ἐμοῖς πλευροῖς ὁμοῦ / κλιθεῖσαν αὐτὴν ἀντὶ σοῦ λάβῃ ποτέ, / ἀλλ' αὐτός, ὦ παῖ, τοῦτο κήδευσον λέχος, 1225–7). Heracles has thus demanded two horrifying transgressions of his son: to kill his father, and then to marry his "mother," like Oedipus.[61] What is striking is that Heracles acts to limit Iole's sexuality after his death, an atypical concern for a dying hero.[62] The play thus uses Heracles' disturbing demands to draw attention to the mismatch between Hyllus and Iole, a pairing demanded by the mythological tradition. Strangely, Iole never bears children to Heracles, though he usually impregnates every woman with whom he has intercourse, while it is her children by Hyllus that occupy the attention of the mythical tradition.

Heracles' instructions about the pyre call to mind the unusual circumstances of Heracles' death and afterlife: does the play imply that Heracles will be deified? Or does it deliberately exclude mention of that particular branch of Heraclean mythology? Does Heracles himself expect to go to Hades or Olympus? Scholars such as Holt and Hahnemann have established that, by the time of Sophocles, Athenian audiences were familiar with the tradition of Heracles' apotheosis, and thus could well have expected the *Trachiniae* to represent that story.[63] The fact that Sophocles does not make the apotheosis explicit, though, could suggest that the playwright purposely suppressed its occurrence.[64]

A dramaturgical perspective on these debates may offer insight into the play's treatment of Heracles' fate: I suggest that Sophocles dimly forecasts Heracles' apotheosis by giving him superhuman authority to direct the final outcomes of the plot.[65] In wrenching the play into shape so that it aligns with major traditions, Heracles takes on the role of a *deus ex machina*, while still acting as a living character within the framework of the play. This point marks a movement from mortal hero, dying on the stage, to a god who possesses knowledge of the future. His requests then may be in part a reflection of Heracles' innate distance from ordinary human people, but also in part a reflection of his transition to deity.[66] At the point in the play when Heracles reveals his final oracles and the entire plot becomes coherent to all involved, the play is positioned to end. Heracles' final instructions thus ensure that the actions of the play ultimately conform to the demands of the mythological tradition.[67] By employing a protracted back-and-forth between Heracles and Hyllus about the pyre, Sophocles raises the possibility that Heracles could die in the "wrong" location—Trachis, of all places, a city full of strangers and lacking significance to Heracles. Before Heracles makes Hyllus swear obedience, it is unclear how Heracles would make it to Mount Oeta, the "proper" site for his expiration. Heracles imposes his will on Hyllus, through the mechanism of a forced oath; Hyllus' pain makes clear that the pyre is not a natural, organic outcome of the play's actions.[68] Heracles' enforcement of his own mysterious will recalls his role in a later play of Sophocles, the *Philoctetes*. There Heracles actually appears as a *deus ex machina* and overrules the decision that Neoptolemus and Philoctetes spent the whole play deliberating, compelling them to obey him because of his special knowledge of their fate. In the same way, the *Trachiniae*'s Heracles can be seen as anticipating this role in his coercion of Hyllus into fulfilling the requirements of Zeus' will.

Likewise, the marriage of Hyllus and Iole is a major aspect of the mythical tradition, for their descendants become the Heracleidae, who base their ancestral claim to rule of the Peloponnese on Heracles' origins in the area.[69] Yet the grieving Hyllus is rightly offended by the suggestion of cohabiting with the young woman: "who could choose these things, unless infected by fiends? Better for me to die, father, than to dwell together with my greatest enemy" (τίς ταῦτ' ἄν, ὅστις μὴ 'ξ ἀλαστόρων νοσοῖ, / ἕλοιτο; κρεῖσσον κἀμέ γ', ὦ πάτερ, θανεῖν / ἢ τοῖσιν ἐχθίστοισι συνναίειν ὁμοῦ, 1235–7). Moreover, Heracles' demand flies in the face of established custom. In the mythological world, at least, it was expressly forbidden for a son to have sexual relations with his father's concubine.[70]

Thus, the play draws attention to the many reasons for both Hyllus and the audience to find Heracles' request repulsive. But in response to Hyllus' resistance, Heracles becomes even more dominating. His coercive pairing of Hyllus to Iole is not so different from Apollo's commands at the conclusion of Euripides' *Orestes*, when the god appears and orders Orestes to marry Hermione at the very moment that he takes her hostage and threatens to burn down the palace. Apollo's *deus ex machina* appearance interrupts this ludicrous scene, and he resolves it simply: "Orestes, against whose neck you hold your sword, Hermione, it is your destiny to marry" (ἐφ' ἧς δ' ἔχεις, Ὀρέστα, φάσγανον δέρῃ, / γῆμαι πέπρωταί σ' Ἑρμιόνην, 1654–5). Orestes responds promptly, and seemingly, happily: "Look, I am releasing Hermione from slaughter and approve our marriage, whenever her father gives her" (ἰδού, μεθίημ' Ἑρμιόνην ἀπὸ σφαγῆς, / καὶ λέκτρ' ἐπῄνεσ', ἡνίκ' ἂν διδῷ πατήρ, 1671–2). The entire scene, including Apollo's interruption and Orestes' abrupt change of heart, smacks of parody; perhaps Euripides even had in mind scenes like ours in the *Trachiniae*.

In demanding that his son suffer in order to fulfill his will, Heracles imitates his own father Zeus; for Heracles, too, is subject to the inscrutable will of his father.⁷¹ This does not cast Zeus in a favorable light. The prominence of the name of Zeus, combined with a variety of epithets, points towards his control over the actions of the play.⁷² The final words of the play, whether spoken by the Chorus or Hyllus,⁷³ lay full responsibility on Zeus:

> λείπου μηδὲ σύ, παρθέν᾽, ἀπ᾽ οἴκων,
> μεγάλους μὲν ἰδοῦσα νέους θανάτους,
> πολλὰ δὲ πήματα καὶ καινοπαθῆ,
> κοὐδὲν τούτων ὅ τι μὴ Ζεύς.
>
> 1275–8

Do not be left, maiden, at the house, either, for you have seen terrible recent deaths, and many trials and unheard-of sufferings. And there is nothing in them that is not Zeus.

The play's events have been relentlessly dark, and their attribution to Zeus emphasizes his power rather than his beneficence. Zeus' justice is effective, though not necessarily human.⁷⁴ The foreshadowing of Heracles' apotheosis brings to mind his role as the favored son of Zeus. But the associations that usually accompany this role—Heracles' Labors, his service of his father's agenda, Hera's endless hatred—do not appear prominently in this play. What we have is apotheosis without the usual justification, that life on Olympus is the reward he receives as compensation for his suffering for mortals. But if Zeus is both powerful and capable of cruelty, as the Chorus suggests, then perhaps Heracles' deification is equally arbitrary.

Conclusion

The action of Sophocles' play demonstrates what Heracles' role as victor can accomplish and also its limitations. In each of the competitions, he triumphs: he defeats Achelous to win Deianeira, he kills Nessus, he sacks Oechalia, and he seizes Iole for his own. Yet he dies an unheroic death, felled by poison rather than an edged weapon, far from the battlefield, conquered not by a warrior but by his own timid wife. Defeating opponents in competition thus proves to be insufficient: because Heracles' understanding of heroic action is focused on his own physical power, he makes no distinction between proper and improper heroic competition, or between prizes that are valuable objects and prizes that are beautiful women with independent emotional landscapes and their own agency. This blindness leads him to create competition for his affection between women in his own *oikos*, a choice that will ultimately destroy him. And even to the end, Heracles feels compelled to display his dominance over others.

Repeated, anomalous competitions fail to regulate violence through convention, allowing it to course through and destroy the household, reaching even beyond the competitors themselves. As violence becomes unbound, it radiates outwards to touch not only Heracles, but also Iole's family, Deianeira, and Hyllus. Heracles' violence is a manifestation of his excessive power and distance from human relations, and thus resists an means-ends calculus that allows violence to be justified. Heracles' path to victory requires not only the suffering of his defeated enemies, but also the sacrifices of Deianeira and Hyllus, those ostensibly on his side. Yet their sorrows have meaning only in so far as they advance the predetermined plans of Zeus: the family is nothing but collateral damage in the path of Heracles' ascent to Olympus. By condemning Heracles' heroism and its devastating effects on those near (his family) and far (Oechalia) at the same time as foreshadowing his eternal reward, the play stresses the seeming arbitrariness of the gods. Though the play begins with a statement of the uncertainty of mortal fate (1–3), it ends with an assertion of Zeus' rule.[75] Heracles does not receive what he deserves. Thus, in the world of the *Trachiniae*, Zeus' will is inescapable, but not praiseworthy—just like Heracles' heroic violence, which is denied epinician glorification in the play, but still leads to apotheosis.

4

Coping with Violence

Victory and Friendship in Euripides' *Heracles*

Introduction

Euripides' *Heracles* presents the furthest extremes of Heracles' mythical tradition: in the warm and devoted father who uses violence to rescue his family from persecution is an admirable savior; in the maddened Heracles who uses brutal violence to murder that same family is the most unstable and dangerous Heracles. Compared to the ending of Sophocles' *Trachiniae*, in which Heracles takes little responsibility for his destruction of the household, the ending of Euripides' play may come as a surprise: Heracles is so broken by his actions that he wishes to kill himself, but is rehabilitated and ultimately decides to live. The play engages directly with questions of the justification of violence and its nature as an instrument and/or a manifestation. Furthermore, it addresses the conundrum of coping with heroic violence when it resists constraint. In this way, Euripides' *Heracles* provides an almost ideal "laboratory" for experimenting with the dynamics and effects of heroic violence.

The play falls into three parts. It opens with a suppliant drama in which a nearly idealized Heracles returns in the nick of time to save his family from an evil tyrant; his violence is constrained, I argue, by two roles, the *kallinikos* victor of epinician poetry, a symbol of individual excellence, and *philos*, a communal role that sets him in relationship with others. These roles also establish the ends—victory, protection of friends, and harm to enemies—that justify the means of heroic force. The second part of the play dramatizes Heracles' most horrific act of violence, the murder of his wife and children. His madness is explicitly externally instigated by Lyssa and Iris, but the method is all too familiar: in a terrible reversal, Heracles murders his closest *philoi* in the very same manner in which he completed his Labors and distinguished himself as an athletic champion. In the third part of the play, Heracles considers suicide—violence against the self—but is restrained from that violence and rehabilitated when Theseus offers him the kind of *philia* that allows him to regain his status as *kallinikos*.

In tracking the constraint and release of heroic violence, my argument engages in a long-running scholarly debate over the unity and themes of the play.[1] While some critics see a fundamentally disjointed work, many other scholars have seen the presentation of *aretē* (excellence) as a central problem.[2] In relating the conclusion of the play to its opening, Chalk argues, like Arrowsmith and Wilamowitz before him, that Heracles demonstrates a *new* form of courage in choosing life over suicide in the conclusion of the play.[3] Several others have followed Chalk's lead, emphasizing that Heracles' rejection of suicide entails a repudiation of an outdated system of heroism embraced by the first action of the play.[4] In following the thread of heroic violence from beginning to end, my approach to the text presumes that the play can be interpreted as a whole. But while Arrowsmith argues that the play demonstrates a "conversion" from old to new values, I argue that Euripides explores how the rather traditional roles of *philos* and *kallinikos* constrain violence in the first part, and how the very same roles facilitate Heracles' recovery, even after unspeakable disaster.

Philia, or friendship, is the relationship that exists between *philoi*, a term that in tragedy can include blood relatives, spouses, community members, *xenoi*, and suppliants.[5] While the relationship between *philoi* can be characterized by affection and goodwill, its basis is rooted in a reciprocal relationship based on favors (*charis*), the action "to help friends and harm enemies."[6] In the mythical tradition, Heracles occupies extremes on the spectrum of *philia*: he notoriously violates *xenia* by killing his guest-friend Iphitus, an act condemned as early as the *Odyssey*, but his commitment as a magnificent *philos* sits at the heart of Euripides' earlier play *Alcestis*.

The cult epithet *kallinikos* ("gloriously conquering," καλλίνικος) appears eight times in this play. The term is associated with Heracles' feats of strength accomplished in the famous Labors, as well as with his status as a "patron of war and athletic contests."[7] Furthermore, in his role as Heracles *kallinikos*, Heracles serves as the victor par excellence in epinician poetry, as demonstrated in the victory song attributed to Archilochus in Pindar's ninth Olympian ode: "*Tenella* gloriously-conquering one, hail, lord Heracles!" (τήνελλα καλλίνικε / χαῖρε ἄναξ Ἡράκλεις, fr. 324.1–2 West). Its use in our play is varied—it occurs as an epithet, an adjective, and a noun with both masculine and feminine definite articles—but its connection to the epinician genre is clear.[8] In a close reading of the play, Laura Swift shows how epinician language and themes suffuse not only the play's three main choral odes, but also the messenger speech and Heracles' *nostos*.[9] My interest is in how the role of *kallinikos* serves (and also fails) to delimit the use of violence: athletic contests channel the physical skills useful in both sport and war into displays of excellence in ritualized competition, a popular theme in heroic poetry.[10] Epinician poetry also participates in this project, as Leslie Kurke has demonstrated, by carefully integrating the flourishing victor in his community and in relationship to the gods.[11] As the play engages with Heracles' most appalling act of violence, we will observe how it tests the boundaries and resilience of these roles.

Violence against Enemies

The first action of the play presents Heracles through a framework that privileges his roles as *philos* and *kallinikos*, strenuously justifying his use of heroic violence. Amphitryon's prologue provides the setting for the opening of the play: Heracles has not returned from his final Labor for Eurystheus, the capture of Cerberus from Hades, while his family in Thebes is under the threat of death by the new tyrant, Lycus. Heracles' Labors and his legacy of heroic success are centered in this first speech: Amphitryon uses the terms μοχθέω and πόνος to describe Heracles' toiling and his Labors (22), terms that repeatedly recur throughout the play.[12] He also calls his son "that famous Heracles" (ὁ κλεινὸς Ἡρακλῆς, 12) to emphasize his pan-Hellenic reputation.

By reversing the traditional order of the murder of Heracles' family and the penance of enslavement to Eurystheus, Euripides enables Amphitryon to frame the Labors as a voluntary endeavor, mentioning the roles of Hera and necessity only in passing (20–1). He attributes to the Labors instead an important social function by emphasizing the parties that benefit from his actions. First, Heracles proves *philos* to his father, undertaking the Labors to enable Amphitryon's return to Argos from exile (15–17). This is no easy feat (μισθὸν μέγαν, 19), but nevertheless Heracles exerts himself in honor of his father, to "lighten [his] misfortune" (συμφορὰς δὲ τὰς ἐμὰς / ἐξευμαρίζων, 17), proving himself a particularly filial son. Second, the Labors provide a safer environment for all humankind by "clearing the earth" of uncivilized threats (ἐξημερῶσαι, 20). Third, Heracles has been a *philos* to the Thebans by defeating the Minyans of Orchomenos, its main rival city (50), establishing an expanding sphere of *philoi* from Heracles' own blood-kin to his adopted city of Thebes to all of humankind.

Heracles' defeat of the Minyans both establishes Heracles as *kallinikos* and initiates a relationship of *philia* with the Thebans: in dedication to Zeus Soter after his victory, Heracles established an altar magnifying his "gloriously conquering spear" (καλλινίκου δορός, 49), where his family now sits suppliant. The play thus associates the epithet *kallinikos* not just with athletic victories in a festival context, but also specifically with acts that define Heracles as a *philos*, channeling Heracles' strength, physical prowess, and martial skill towards communal ends. But although Thebans now owe a return favor to Heracles, the protection of his family, they have abandoned them to Lycus. Amphitryon laments the state of his personal friends: some are unreliable in his time of need (οὐ σαφεῖς ὁρῶ φίλους, 55), while those who are loyal are unable to help (ἀδύνατοι προσωφελεῖν, 56).

The failure of the Thebans' *philia* and Heracles' absence throw Heracles' status as *philos* and *kallinikos* into doubt. As Lycus threatens to eliminate Heracles' family (166–9), Heracles is nowhere to be found, presumed dead by many. A failure to return successfully from Hades would be the ultimate defeat, and his *philia* towards his family will be rendered futile if he allows them to be killed by an enemy. Pressed on both sides by a hopeless situation and the plaintive questions of her innocent children, Megara is forced to invent lies: "I put them off with stories, making up fiction" (διαφέρω / λόγοισι μυθεύουσα, 76–7). That Megara, the wife of the great man himself, resorts to telling false stories about him raises doubts about the traditional accounts of his glorious deeds. Megara's desperation, in juxtaposition with Amphitryon's prologue of praise, makes evident the tensions between Heracles' domestic and heroic responsibilities. Euripides raises the possibility that his Heracles will be like Sophocles': a negligent husband and father whose life of heroism undermines his *oikos*. As the moment of execution comes nearer, this tension grows ever more pressing.

The tyrant Lycus cements his role as villain by insulting Heracles' status as *kallinikos*. According to Lycus, he is certainly dead, already lying in Hades like a corpse (παρ' Ἅιδηι . . . κείμενον, 145).[13] The well-known deeds of famous Heracles are easily diminished; the Lernaean Hydra is but a marsh snake, and Heracles defeated the Nemean Lion by capturing it in nets, not with his bare hands (152–4). Moreover, Lycus denigrates Heracles' other roles, calling Heracles' claim to be a son of Zeus "empty boasts" (κόμπους κενούς, 148) and reducing his entire heroic legacy to mere animal-taming: "he held a reputation for courage (though being a nothing after all) in fighting beasts, but was not brave in any other respect" (ὁ δ' ἔσχε δόξαν οὐδὲν ὢν εὐψυχίας / θηρῶν ἐν αἰχμῆι, τἄλλα δ' οὐδὲν ἄλκιμος, 157–8).[14]

At the heart of Lycus' radical reevaluation of Heracles' glorious courage is a debate over the role of the archer.[15] Although the club is frequently depicted as

Heracles' weapon of choice, here the bow serves as the symbol of his earth-taming exploits and his value as a hero.[16] Lycus flatly denies that the bow is "proof of the courage of a man" (ἀνδρὸς δ' ἔλεγχος οὐχὶ τόξ' εὐψυχίας, 162), and instead elevates the courage of the ordinary hoplite, who must maintain his position in the battle line in the face of great danger (163-4). Lycus' praise is for the man who joins and maintains a community of soldiers, not for the individual actor, always prepared to run away (τῇ φυγῇ πρόχειρος ἦν, 161). Lycus' speech thus demonstrates the vulnerability of Heracles' legacy; for just as his deeds can be praised by the Chorus, they can also be denigrated and insulted by his enemies. Heracles' status as *kallinikos* is thus made contestable.

Amphitryon will not permit Heracles to be slandered, emphasizing the necessity of protecting Heracles' reputation (173). He provides several scenarios in which the mobility and resources of archery prove most advantageous, emphasizing the archer's ability to take advantage of "the most prudent thing in battle, harming his enemies while preserving his own body" (ἐν μάχῃ / σοφὸν μάλιστα, δρῶντα πολεμίους κακῶς / σῴζειν τὸ σῶμα, 201-3). This is another expression of traditional *philia*: the archer is perfectly capable of benefiting his *philos* (himself) and harming his enemies.[17] In defense against the charge of cowardice, Amphitryon cites two major battles: Heracles' battle against the Giants as an ally of the Olympian gods, and his conflict with the Centaurs. After Heracles helped to defeat the Giants, "he celebrated the glorious victory with the gods" (τὸν καλλίνικον μετὰ θεῶν ἐκώμασεν, 180), where the term *kallinikos* stands for the victory hymn and dance.[18] Heracles' *philia* thus extends beyond the human race to the gods themselves. These particular exploits are associated with his function as a monster-slayer and civilizer of the universe, the sort of role for which he is praised in Hesiod's *Theogony*. Nevertheless, Zeus fails to save his *philoi* (σῴζειν δὲ τοὺς σοὺς οὐκ ἐπίστασαι φίλους, 346), causing Amphitryon to lament that he himself surpasses the father of the gods in *aretē* (ἀρετῆι σε νικῶ θνητὸς ὢν θεὸν μέγαν, 342).[19]

As the family prepares to die at Lycus' hands, the first choral ode intervenes.[20] At 93 lines, it is lengthy and generically complex, functioning both as a lament for the dead (a *thrēnos*) and a hymn of praise.[21] Laura Swift, among others, has established how the ode describes Heracles' Labors in a manner characteristic of epinician and encomiastic poetry.[22] My reading here has two aims: to demonstrate how the ode 1) intertwines Heracles' roles as *kallinikos* and *philos* in his use of violence; and 2) establishes a specific vocabulary of praise for the Labors through images and terms that will be unfortunately echoed in Heracles' disaster and later recovery.

The focus of the ode is on twelve of his Labors, stories which would have been familiar to Euripides' audience: the Nemean Lion, the battle with the Centaurs, the Hind of Artemis, the Mares of Diomedes, Cycnus, the Apples of the Hesperides, the calming of the sea, Atlas, the Girdle of Hippolyta, the Lernaean Hydra, Geryon, and finally Cerberus (359–429). The ode displays the various facets of Heracles' victorious conquests, each of which requires the use of heroic violence: there are the animal Labors, which rid the earth of dangers to man from the world of beasts (Lion, Hind, Mares, Hydra). Also featured is the punishment of monsters and evildoers—Cycnus, Geryon—through which Heracles imposes order upon corrupt customs. Lastly, there are the Labors associated with conquering death and achieving immortality.[23] His Labors lead him beyond the Peloponnese to the very ends of the known world, from the far west of the Garden of the Hesperides to the far east of the Amazons, making him a hero for all of Greece and the known world.

Though most of his Labors require the use of fatal violence, they are celebrated as displays of excellence that yield glorious trophies: the skin of the Nemean Lion continues to protect Heracles, and the Girdle of Hippolyta can still be viewed at Mycenae. The glory of Heracles *kallinikos* is linked explicitly with his work as a benefactor of a similarly expanding sphere of *philoi*: the death of the Nemean Lion makes Zeus' grove safer; his battle with the Centaurs frees the people of Thessaly from their chaos; Heracles kills the Hind to protect farmers and sets it up as a trophy in Artemis' honor; he protects travelers by defeating Cycnus; and he makes the sea safe for mortal sailors.[24] These beneficial results serve to justify his use of violence.

The ode also highlights specific skills and language that define the praiseworthy Heracles. The Chorus extols the "bloody bow" (τόξοις φονίοις, 367) and "winged arrows" (πτανοῖς βέλεσιν, 367) that lay low the Centaurs, Cycnus, the Lernaean Hydra, and Geryon; their praise serves as a rebuke to Lycus' accusations about the bow. In order to tame the man-eating Mares of Diomedes, he climbs on a chariot (τεθρίππων τ' ἐπέβα, 380), marking himself as a superior charioteer. The Chorus makes the hand of Heracles the locus of his power, singing that he "plucks with his hand the gold fruit" of the Hesperides (χρύσεον . . . χερὶ καρπὸν ἀμέρξων, 396-7) and "drives his hands" (ἐλαύνει χέρας, 404) to uphold the weight of heaven at Atlas' home. The Chorus calls his Labors *ponoi*, but also likens his acts to *dromoi* ("races," 425), an important conflation of athletic competition and heroic activity.

When Heracles arrives at last, he demonstrates his commitment to acting as a *philos* and *kallinikos*, confirming the idealized portrait presented by the family and the Chorus. Megara's greeting emphasizes both her affection for her husband (ὦ φίλτατ' ἀνδρῶν, 531) and his obligatory *philia* towards his family, "Were you saved to come to the aid of your *philoi* in the nick of time?" (ἐσώθης εἰς ἀκμὴν ἐλθὼν φίλοις; 532). Revealing his own adherence to the code of exchange, Heracles expresses disbelief at the false *philia* of the Thebans:

Ηρ. οὕτω δ' ἀπόντες ἐσπανίζομεν φίλων;
Με. φίλοι γάρ εἰσιν ἀνδρὶ δυστυχεῖ τίνες;
Ηρ. μάχας δὲ Μινυῶν ἃς ἔτλην ἀπέπτυσαν;
Με. ἄφιλον, ἵν' αὖθίς σοι λέγω, τὸ δυστυχές.

558–62

Heracles Was I so lacking in *philoi* while I was away?
Megara Who are *philoi* to an unfortunate man?
Heracles And they disdained the battles against the Minyans which I endured?
Megara Poor luck is friendless, I say again.

In his first significant speech in the play, Heracles frames the defense of his family against their enemies as another Labor.[25] He calls his vengeance against Lycus "the work of my hand" (τῆς ἐμῆς ἔργον χερός, 565), a phrase that recalls the Labors in the choral ode. He will punish the cowardly Thebans with his "gloriously conquering weapon" (τῷ καλλινίκῳ τῷδ' ὅπλῳ, 570), a statement that unifies the imperatives of the victor with the punishment of a failure of *philia*.[26] He eagerly takes responsibility for protecting his wife, children, and father (574–5), recognizing that the ties of *philia* demand he use his warrior's skills to defend his close relatives and spouse.

With the trouble in his domestic sphere made clear, Heracles releases his former adventures: "farewell, Labors!" (χαιρόντων πόνοι, 575). Bond's translation takes it even further: "I disown my labors," as though he "must for shame give up his title καλλίνικος."[27] If he wants to remain known as "Heracles the glorious conqueror" (Ἡρακλῆς / ὁ καλλίνικος, 581–2), he must "exert [himself] over the death" of his children (ἐκπονήσω θάνατον, 581).[28] This Heracles is diametrically opposed to the self-aggrandizing Heracles of the *Trachiniae*. Euripides' Heracles prizes his children above all, characterizing this as a common human trait: "man's affairs are all alike: both the rich and the poor love their children" (πάντα τἀνθρώπων ἴσα· / φιλοῦσι παῖδας οἵ τ' ἀμείνονες βροτῶν / οἵ τ' οὐδὲν ὄντες, 633–5). Far from the untamed hero of the wild, this Heracles is thoroughly domesticated, gladly submitting himself to the bonds of family and *oikos*.

Just as protecting his family confirms his heroism, it also reaffirms his *aretē* as *philos*. Amphitryon notes approvingly of Heracles' intent: "it is just like you, son, to be a friend to your friends, and to hate your enemies" (πρὸς σοῦ μέν, ὦ παῖ, τοῖς φίλοις <τ'> εἶναι φίλον / τά τ' ἐχθρὰ μισεῖν, 585–6).[29] This very traditional formulation of *philia*, when applied to Heracles, banishes the doubts aired earlier about his devotion to his *philoi*. Furthermore, Amphitryon's curious querying about Heracles' long absence further establishes his success: Heracles indeed captured and retrieved the terrifying Cerberus (610–11), successfully completing what had been called his final Labor (23, 427). Furthermore, he continues to demonstrate his *philia* by rescuing Theseus from the Underworld, a benefaction that has made the young man "joyful" (ἄσμενος, 621).

The second choral ode celebrates Heracles' return and the apparent change in the family's fortune from disaster to salvation. Although they do not speak the name of Heracles until the third stanza, the song nevertheless serves as fitting praise for the hero. The Chorus seems to begin by expressing regret for their own lost youth. The topic of youth is particularly appropriate in a song of praise for Heracles, for he is the "personification of *neotas*," which is "in agonistic contexts a common prerequisite or concomitant of *arete*."[30] Indeed, the Chorus wishes that a second youth could serve as a "clear stamp of excellence" (φανερὸν χαρακτῆρ' ἀρετᾶς, 659) of a man's good character, a contrafactual wish that is actually fulfilled in the tradition of Heracles' apotheosis and marriage to Hebe. Athletic imagery dominates the song, with this "second youth" (δίδυμον ἥβαν, 657) envisioned as "doubled racecourses" (δισσοὺς διαύλους, 662), which Bond explicates as a race of four legs (κῶλα): from Hades (the start) to the light (the turning post) and back to Hades, then repeated again.[31] In this metaphorical framework, Heracles, who has just captured Cerberus in Hades and returned to the light, is running the third *kōlon* of his life. That is, he has already achieved the longed-for second youth, and fulfills the wish of the Chorus.[32] In obtaining this second youth and proving clearly his *aretē*, Heracles acquires the glory of an athletic victor.

Despite the Chorus's grousing about the difficulty of discerning true virtue, Heracles emerges as a clear example of a man of excellence by their standards. In the next stanza, the Chorus responds by clearly reaffirming his status: "still I sing the glorious victory song of Heracles" (ἔτι τὰν Ἡρακλέους / καλλίνικον ἀείδω, 680-1).[33] The *kallinikos* song of the Chorus is realized in the final stanza, which praises Heracles in traditionally encomiastic terms.[34] The Chorus celebrates three aspects of the hero: his divine lineage, his *aretē* that surpasses his birth, and the peace he has established through the destruction of fearsome beasts (696–700). Each of these responds to doubts or accusations raised earlier: Amphitryon's remonstrations with Zeus (339–47); Lycus' accusations about the cowardly nature of the bow (157-64); and Lycus' denigration of Heracles' beast Labors (151-5). Heracles' effort in his Labors does not go unrecognized: he has toiled for the benefit of mankind, and the reward for his efforts is the hymn of praise.

To some scholars, the hymnic tone of the ode and the one that follows is foreboding.[35] For example, Parry notes "the absence of the frequent Pindaric warning that mortal victors are *not* gods" and argues that Heracles is elevated "to so dangerous a height that his fall becomes almost inevitable."[36] The problems of praise are indeed real: excessive praise can generate envy (*phthonos*) in the hearts of men, posing a challenge to integrating a returning victor into his community and in relation to the gods.[37] Nevertheless, the claim that over-praise of Heracles commits the play to his downfall may not be taking into account the way that tragedy uses the lyric genre. I follow Chris Carey, who argues that "what tragedy extracts is for the most part the celebratory dimension" of epinician; tragedy's reductivist treatment of epinician means that we need not expect an actual Pindaric ode.[38] The celebration here, I suggest, serves rather to emphasize the relief surrounding Heracles' return and set up a truly shocking reversal.

As Heracles prepares an ambush for Lycus, the Chorus rejoices in a world in which wrong has been made right and order has been restored. All would seem to be well: Heracles has completed his Labors for Eurystheus, and the death of Lycus, an enemy (ἐχθρός, 734) of the house, has been assured. In fact, full confidence in the justice of the gods is required here in order for the *peripeteia* to have its full effect. The ruin of the unjust tyrant proves that "there are gods, who care for men," the Chorus' positive theodicy and a rebuke of the hopeless skepticism expressed earlier by Amphitryon and Megara.[39] The joyful song also follows the conventions of epinician: the Chorus commands the landscape to praise Heracles, an example of "the encomiastic use of geography," following Pindaric convention.[40] The personified landscape and Nymphs join to sing of the "gloriously won contest of Heracles" (τὸν Ἡρακλέους / καλλίνικον ἀγῶνα, 787-9).[41] The language of athletic victory is thus applied to Heracles' work within the house, the slaughter of the unjust king Lycus.[42]

The third choral ode thus reaffirms the living Heracles as friend and conqueror.[43] Though he arrives at the last possible moment, he nevertheless rescues his dearest *philoi* at the moment when they were truly on the "knife's edge" of danger (ὧδ' ἔβητ' ἐπὶ ξυροῦ, 630). He has proven himself *philos* to his family by saving them from death (helping friends) and eagerly undertaking vengeance against their persecutor Lycus (harming an enemy). Moreover, his violence against Lycus is fully warranted: Lycus is an interloper from Euboea and not a native Theban (26-34); he seized power by exploiting civil unrest (588-94);

and he is willing to burn Heracles' suppliant family alive at an altar (247–51), a deeply sacrilegious act. The ends of Heracles' violence thus fully justify the means.

Violence against Friends

The second part of the play presents the episode of Heracles' madness and murder of his family. At the center of his madness is a case of mistaken identity: under the illusion that he travels to Mycenae and kills Eurystheus and his children, he instead wanders within his home at Thebes and murders his own wife and children. He kills his closest kin whom he had aimed to protect and violates the code that governs suppliancy, both obvious violations of *philia*. Even more disturbingly, the mad Heracles, Foley writes, "is represented in the language of the text as a perversion of the hero of encomiastic poetry."[44] The episode thus decouples the union of *kallinikos* and *philos* that had previously constrained and justified Heracles' violence. Here he uses his renowned physical valor and his martial skills to harm rather than help his friends. Moreover, killing Eursytheus and his children is an act to depose the reigning king and eliminate his heirs, a reenactment of the same unlawful killing Lycus had intended for Heracles' family. The familiarity of Heracles' violence, even when used to the wrong ends, highlights the ambivalence of heroic violence and its essential threat: that even in the person of the most lauded hero, violence can never be fully constrained.

The Chorus's restored confidence in the gods is immediately contradicted by the unusual mid-play epiphany of Lyssa and Iris, Hera's lackeys. Their appearance is wholly unanticipated, and the irrationality of Heracles' fall in the midst of celebration emphasizes the amorality of the gods.[45] Iris orders Lyssa to make Heracles "ferry across the river of death his crown of beautiful children" (πορεύσας δι' Ἀχερούσιον πόρον / τὸν καλλίπαιδα στέφανον, 838–9), a metaphor that frames Heracles as a *kallinikos* victor even as the crown is dashed from his head. But Lyssa initially refuses Iris' orders to make Heracles mad, arguing that he is not a proper object of her madness because of his record of benefactions to others and his great fame: he is famous among mortals and gods (849–50); for humankind he has "tamed the uncrossable land and the wild sea" (ἄβατον δὲ χώραν καὶ θάλασσαν ἀγρίαν / ἐξημερώσας, 851-2), and for the gods, he "alone upheld honors falling at the hands of unholy men" (ἀνέστησεν μόνος / τιμὰς πιτνούσας ἀνοσίων ἀνδρῶν ὕπο, 852-3). Lyssa is thus made to articulate the audience's complaint: Heracles has been depicted thus far as the embodiment of heroic success, in all of its glory, not only for Heracles as an individual, but for his family and community at large.

Iris nevertheless overrules Lyssa, and the madness Lyssa inflicts expresses itself in a very specific way: though insane, Heracles acts much like the *kallinikos* hero of epinician poetry. The work of Swift, among others, has identified the many epinician motifs in the messenger's account of Heracles' madness.[46] My interest is in the way that Heracles distorts several familiar roles—athlete, victor, monster-slayer, civilizer, *philos*—by directing his violence against the wrong parties. His excellence at athletics is reflected in Lyssa's intention to "run races into Heracles' heart" (στάδια δραμοῦμαι στέρνον εἰς Ἡρακλέους, 863); Heracles responds fittingly as the madness takes over, and "tosses his head at the start of the race" (τινάσσει κρᾶτα βαλβίδων ἄπο, 867). Amphitryon's cries of alarm reveal the devastation from within the house: the master hunter of the Erymanthian Boar or the Cretan Bull becomes again a "huntsman" (κυνηγέτῃ, 860) who "hunts down a chase of children" (κυναγετεῖ τέκνων διωγμόν, 896), a bizarre jumbling of the proper categories, in which an activity for the wild (hunting) occurs in the domestic space of the house, and children are treated as prey.

The messenger speech presents Heracles' delusional pursuit of Eurystheus as a parody of specific famous acts in his mythical tradition, almost a twisted reenactment of the Labors described in the first choral ode, among others. Even at his point of greatest distance from reality, Heracles nevertheless acts in a way that is oddly familiar, and the "mad Heracles repeats patterns of behavior known from his heroic past."[47] As delusions overtake Heracles' mind, he decides to put off the purificatory sacrifice until he has killed Eurystheus, the commander of his Labors, so as not to create "double the labor" (πόνους διπλούς, 937) for himself.[48] He ascribes the accomplishment of his vengeance to his strong hand, "Arranging these affairs well is the work of my single hand" (ἔργον μιᾶς μοι χειρός, 938), an obvious echo of 565, when Heracles proclaims the defense of his home and destruction of Lycus "now the work of my hand" (νῦν γὰρ τῆς ἐμῆς ἔργον χερός). Thus, Heracles establishes the murder of Eurystheus as an extension of his work in taking vengeance on Lycus, itself a new kind of Labor attached to the legendary ones.

Yet this "new Labor" of vengeance against Eurystheus is only a caricature of his famous deeds. As Heracles prepares his weapons for the journey to Mycenae, the audience witnesses an imaginary journey to the Peloponnese, an inversion of the encomiastic use of geography displayed in the previous choral ode. Heracles' plan to destroy the Cyclopean walls of Mycenae with levers and picks is reminiscent of his Labor at the Stables of Augeas, especially as depicted in a metope on the Temple of Zeus at Olympia (Figure 4.1). The missing implement

Figure 4.1 Heracles' Labor at the Stables of Augeas. Metope from the Temple of Zeus at Olympia, c. 475 BCE. Archaeological Museum, Olympia, Greece. Credit: Alinari/Art Resource, NY.

has been variously described as a shovel or even a crowbar.⁴⁹ The action of levering the foundations of the famous walls (μοχλοὺς δικέλλας . . . Κυκλώπων βάθρα, 944) is not so far off from that of digging a large trench.

Heracles, believing that he has mounted a chariot, whips the empty air (948–9), an imitation of his taming of Diomedes' Mares as charioteer (380). The itinerary he purports to establish imitates his previous well-known journeys on his Labors: he pauses for feasts among friends and pursues athletic competitions in the midst of his assignments.⁵⁰ His servants, bewildered by his behavior, can only stare as Heracles "moved up and down the palace" (ὁ δ' εἷρπ' ἄνω τε καὶ κάτω κατὰ στέγας, 953), transforming his own home into an imaginary map of Greece. Upon reaching the banqueting hall, he declares that he has reached the city of Megara. He engages in a parody of *xenia*: as though received by a proper host, he reclines (on the floor) and enjoys a feast (prepared by and for himself) (κλιθεὶς ἐς οὖδας ὡς ἔχει σκευάζεται / θοίνην, 955-6). These actions draw upon Heracles' reputation as a difficult guest and a hungry glutton on the comic stage; however, the familiarity of the comic character of Heracles, set in this inappropriate context, only deepens the sense of dread building through the speech.[51]

After a brief respite, he arrives mentally at the Isthmus, where he pauses to compete in "fantasy athletics."[52] That he finds an athletic festival in his delusions should come as no surprise: surely his "participation" in these games recalls to mind his establishment of the Olympic Games, a frequent Pindaric theme. The messenger pays special attention to the details of Heracles' bizarre behavior: he strips naked and wrestles against an invisible opponent (γυμνὸν σῶμα θεὶς πορπαμάτων / πρὸς οὐδέν' ἡμιλλᾶτο, 959-60). Heracles' hallucinations do not end with his competition in the event; he also performs the role of herald. For, "having commanded a hearing, he proclaimed himself gloriously victorious to no one at all" (κἀκηρύσσετο / αὐτὸς πρὸς αὑτοῦ καλλίνικος οὐδενός, / ἀκοὴν ὑπειπών, 960-2). Heracles here awards himself the cult epithet *kallinikos*, used in glorification and praise so many times in this play. He is aping his *aretē* of glorious victory at the very moment when his heroic skills lead him to his greatest defeat at the hands of Hera. The juxtaposition is both pointed and painful.

The tension increases as Heracles believes he reaches Mycenae and the palace of Eurystheus. In fear, Amphitryon reaches out and touches "his mighty hand" (θιγὼν κραταιᾶς χειρός, 964), an attempt by his human father to reach him through the source of his power. Heracles recognizes it as a gesture of supplication (968-9) and thrusts him away. In refusing the supplication of his father, Heracles also refuses the *philia* relationship that binds the *agathos* who accepts a *hiketēs*.[53] The violation of this convention is a stunning reversal for the hero praised earlier for his *philia*. Heracles instead prepares his bow and arrows, as though to kill Eurystheus' children.

As he begins the attack, the maddened Heracles enacts the same crime that Lycus intended: to eliminate the threat posed by an enemy's sons. Iris and Lyssa's exchange establishes the outcome of Heracles' hallucination, but not its substance. The fact that mad Heracles seems to adopt Lycus' plan for himself reveals an unsettling likeness between villain and hero.[54] This, combined with Heracles' confusion of friend for enemy, undermines our confidence in the justifiability of instrumental violence. For how can violence be evaluated within a means-ends calculus when its result is not intended in the first place?

He hunts his children with bow and arrows, like birds, an analogy the messenger makes explicit (ἄλλος δὲ βωμὸν ὄρνις ὣς ἔπτηξ' ὕπο, 974). The analogy recalls Megara's despair in Part I, when she compares herself to a mother bird who nestles her young under her wing (71–2); Amphitryon uses the comparison again to heighten the Thebans' betrayal in not protecting "these nestlings" (νεοσσοῖς τοῖσδε, 224–5). The repetition adds emphasis to the family's protectiveness of their vulnerable children, a natural paternal feeling bizarrely missing in Heracles' maddened state. Heracles' prowess as an archer has already been extolled by the Chorus, and his success now is in no doubt. The Chorus, in its eulogistic praise of Heracles, specifically connects his archery skills to his conquest of the Centaurs (366–7), Cycnus (392), and Geryon (422).[55] His actions here recall yet another Labor, the Labor of the Stymphalian Birds. Though in the earliest testimony Heracles defeated the destructive Birds by frightening them away, an Attic black-figure lekythos in Vienna depicts Heracles bringing down the flying Birds with his bow, with two already wounded (Figure 4.2).

In the play Heracles flushes his children from their hiding places (ἐξελίσσων παῖδα κίονος κύκλῳ, 977), and then targets them with his arrows. But where his

Figure 4.2 Heracles and the Stymphalian Birds. Attic black-figure lekythos, c. 500–480 BCE. Kunsthistorisches Museum ANSA IV 1841, Vienna. Photo Credit: KHM-Museumsverband.

Labor to remove the Stymphalian Birds was a genuine struggle against a troublesome enemy, Heracles softens the analogy and makes it pathetic. As his son lies dying, Heracles crows, "This nestling, one of Eurystheus', dead, has fallen and paid back his father's hatred of me" (Εἷς μὲν νεοσσὸς ὅδε θανὼν Εὐρυσθέως / ἔχθραν πατρῴαν ἐκτίνων πέπτωκέ μοι, 982–3). The contrast between the formidable Stymphalian Birds and his helpless children undermines Heracles' victorious vaunting.

Heracles' second son approaches him in full suppliant pose, kneeling and grasping his father's chin (986–7). He begs for mercy and affectionately appeals to the *philia* between fathers and children, addressing Heracles as "dearest father" (ὦ φίλτατε πάτερ, 983). Heracles, just earlier proven a loyal *philos*, completely ignores his obligation to spare the kneeling suppliant and protect his heirs.[56] Heracles fails in *philia*, but succeeds as a warrior: because his suppliant son is too close to shoot, he clubs him on the head. Heracles completes the debacle by pursuing his last son and Megara, who have taken refuge in the house and locked the doors. Heracles is undeterred, and tears apart the doors to reach them. His actions remind the messenger of his earlier threat to uproot and overturn the Cyclopean walls of Mycenae (943–6), and the messenger sees the threat symbolically fulfilled as Heracles attacks his own house: "he, as though at the Cyclopean walls themselves, digs, levers up the door flaps and breaks down the door posts" (ὁ δ' ὡς ἐπ' αὐτοῖς δὴ Κυκλωπίοισιν ὤν / σκάπτει μοχλεύει θύρετρα κἀκβαλὼν σταθμά, 998–9). Here, Heracles actually reenacts the earlier allusion made to his Labor for Augeas (see Figure 4.1). The messenger describes Heracles' attack: "he laid them low with a single missile" (ἑνὶ κατέστρωσεν βέλει, 1000), in diction that specifically parallels the Chorus's praise for Heracles' battle against the Centaurs (ἔστρωσεν τόξοις φονίοις, 366).

Finally, one Olympian deity, Athena, materializes to bring a halt to the carnage instigated by another Olympian, Hera. Although she appears as a phantom, she wields her favored weapon, the spear. She appears, then, as she is pictured on three of the metopes of the Temple of Zeus at Olympia, standing alert with her spear in aid of her favorite. Here she actively intervenes, knocking Heracles into a coma to spare him the *miasma* of patricide.[57] The goddess who presided over his legendary exploits then disappears, leaving the hero to grapple with the consequences of his actions on his own.

Swift concludes that the juxtaposition of athletics and murders "highlights the amoral nature of physical *aretē* ... whereas the traditional values of *epinikion* celebrate physical *aretē* as a morally praiseworthy quality, *Heracles* uses the same language to undermine this value system, demonstrating how dangerous athletic strength can be if misapplied."⁵⁸ This episode reveals the delicacy of the line that separates praiseworthy violence from complete disaster, highlighting both the importance of the communal *philia* in constraining the ends of violence and its susceptibility to failure. Not only does Heracles kill his own *philoi*, but the gods, whom he has benefited significantly, fail him as well. And by using the violence of the *kallinikos* to produce a victory that cannot be celebrated, Heracles brings about a collapse of the epinician endeavor. Heracles' fall "silences this poetry of praise, for if the gods are irrational and unjust and the hero cannot be celebrated, choral poetry loses its function."⁵⁹ The man praised for his *aretē* can, at the inscrutable turn of a god's will, bring lasting disgrace upon himself, his family, and his city.

The whole of Heracles' exploits that this scene draws upon leads us to take a step further: this devastating catalogue calls into question the entire means-ends logic of Hannah Arendt's assessment of violence, that it is instrumental in nature and that its justification relies on its end.⁶⁰ Walter Benjamin's rejection of means-ends logic suggests other views on Heracles' actions. On the one hand, Heracles' madness is explicitly externally imposed by unjust gods, and the epiphany of Iris and Lyssa perhaps evokes Benjamin's "mythic violence," which he defines as "a manifestation of the existence of the gods."⁶¹ He illustrates this phenomenon with the myth of Niobe, another story of a mortal who challenges "fate" and loses her children as a result. But in Euripides' play, violence, though motivated by Hera's hatred, flows directly through Heracles himself, and ironically in his specific role as *kallinikos* athlete and warrior. In the repetition of epinician motifs, we can see how Euripides has made, in Burnett's terms, "the god-imposed crime of madness … like Herakles' own willed acts of violence."⁶² The play's insistence on the consistency of Heracles' violence brings us closer to Benjamin's example from "every day experience," that of a man whose most visible outburst of violence is not a means to a preconceived end but a manifestation of his inner state.⁶³

The episode of Heracles' madness thus shows how illusory the constraints on heroic violence, which were so effective in the first part of the play, can be. Hera's involvement proves the frailty of the assumption that violence can be justified by its ends; rather, it is vulnerable to being nothing more than a manifestation, a phenomenon in and of itself. But the consequences of this manifestation of violence are permanent; his wife and children are dead. The question remains: after such a disaster, can Heracles ever reclaim his roles as *philos* and *kallinikos*? In the third part of the play, Euripides works towards an answer.

Violence against the Self

As Heracles is revealed to the Chorus on stage, in a coma and bound to a broken column from his own ruined home, his collapse is made clear. In dismay at the tableau, the Chorus laments Amphitryon, the children, and "the gloriously conquering head," as if mourning the end of his claim to that epithet (τὸ καλλίνικον κάρα, 1046). When Amphitryon reveals what he has done, Heracles instinctively decides to take his own life. I propose to view Heracles' threat of suicide as a threat of self-inflicted violence, generating the same questions we have been asking—is this use of violence instrumental or a manifestation of inner disorder? If it is instrumental, is it justified by its end? And how can it be constrained? In what follows, I trace the play's debate about the means, ends, and significance of suicide, showing how *philia* becomes a mechanism through which Heracles *kallinikos* is revived.

Heracles' immediate response to the revelation of the murders articulates both potential means of suicide and their ends.

οἴμοι· τί δῆτα φείδομαι ψυχῆς ἐμῆς
τῶν φιλτάτων μοι γενόμενος παίδων φονεύς;
οὐκ εἶμι πέτρας λισσάδος πρὸς ἅλματα
ἢ φάσγανον πρὸς ἧπαρ ἐξακοντίσας
τέκνοις δικαστὴς αἵματος γενήσομαι,
ἢ σάρκα †τὴν ἐμὴν† ἐμπρήσας πυρὶ
δύσκλειαν ἢ μένει μ' ἀπώσομαι βίου;

1146–52

Alas! Why then do I spare my own life when I have become the murderer of my dearest children? Won't I leap into the sea from a sheer rock, or, by striking a sword into my heart, extract justice for my children for their blood? Or by burning the flesh, won't I reject the ill-fame of life which awaits me?

The juxtaposition of *philtatoi* with *phoneus* highlights how he has become an enemy, an agent of force, against his own *philoi*. This leads to the first end of suicide: Heracles could prove himself a *philos* once more by killing his children's murderer, that is, himself. The means he suggests are either to leap from a cliff or to stab himself with his sword.[64] The verb he employs for "stabbing," *exakontizō*, has strong overtones of the javelin throw; even now Heracles conceives of violence in athletic terms.[65] Wrapped up in these suggestions is another method— he proposes burning himself, a method that recalls Lycus' threat to burn Heracles' family at the altar (240–5)—and another end, the escape of disgrace and the shame it entails. The piling up of methods and the intertwining of the demands for vengeance and the escape from disgrace reveal a mind in turmoil. At first his inclination to direct violence towards himself is a gut reaction; he will offer a more reasoned defense later in a debate with Theseus.

Amphitryon's response signals one way to read his declaration: that the act of self-directed violence would be another manifestation of madness. When Heracles first awakens, Amphitryon hesitates to unbind him, fearing a recurrence of madness that would lead to patricide. Now Amphitryon supplicates him and begs that he restrain his "spirit of a wild lion" (λέοντος ἀγρίου θυμόν, 1211), implying that his intention is part of an uncivilized impulse to slaughter. Furthermore, Amphitryon labels his course "murderous" and "unholy" (φόνιον ἀνόσιον, 1212), suggesting that a self-inflicted death would not avenge his children, but would be a polluted act itself, extending rather than curtailing the series of blood crimes. The fact that Heracles does not raise this particular end again suggests that he is persuaded on this point.

But the problem of disgrace (*dyskleia*) is more stubborn, and its solution arrives in the person of Theseus, whose appearance serves as a living reminder of Heracles' previous success as *philos* and *kallinikos*. Heracles recognizes him when he enters the stage as both friend and kinsman (συγγενὴς φίλος τ' ἐμός, 1154), but it is his role as *philos* that will prove instrumental in saving Heracles. Having heard the news of Lycus' usurpation, he brings an Athenian army with him to defend Heracles' rule. This is not unmotivated benevolence; Theseus explicitly reciprocates the favor Heracles bestowed on him in Hades: "I come to pay back in exchange the favors which Heracles began, when he saved me from the underworld" (τίνων δ' ἀμοιβὰς ὧν ὑπῆρξεν Ἡρακλῆς / σώσας με νέρθεν ἦλθον, 1169–70). Theseus' arrival, then, follows the traditional code of *philia*, as Amphitryon had expressed it earlier, to help friends and hate enemies (585–6). Just as Heracles delayed his return from the Underworld in order to free Theseus, using his superhuman strength to aid him, Theseus now offers the aid of his own hand along with an army (χειρὸς ὑμᾶς τῆς ἐμῆς ἢ συμμάχων, 1171).[66] His steadfast aid stands in direct contrast to the Thebans, the gods, and especially Zeus, who have abandoned Heracles.[67]

Heracles' rehabilitation rests on a continuing exchange of favors with Theseus; the first step involves removing the veil with which he covered his head when Theseus entered. When Theseus bids him unveil himself, Heracles acquiesces, "Since I helped you, I do not refuse you" (εὖ δράσας δέ σ' οὐκ ἀναίνομαι, 1235). Theseus, too, understands that his presence is fulfilling an obligation incurred in the Underworld: "And I, being well treated then (by you), pity you now" (ἐγὼ δὲ πάσχων εὖ τότ' οἰκτίρω σε νῦν, 1236).⁶⁸ In this almost mechanical exchange, both refer to Heracles' past rescue of Theseus, which, because it ensured Theseus' return to the light, functions almost as another form of "unveiling." This demonstration of the functioning of *philia* grounded in the past actions of Heracles *kallinikos* establishes the framework in which their debate over suicide can unfold.

Initially, Theseus, like Amphitryon, views self-inflicted violence as a consequence of rage (θυμούμενος, 1246) or a lack of reasoning (ἀμαθία, 1254), suggesting an underlying anxiety about Heracles' control over his mind and emotions. When Heracles insists on the necessity of his death, Theseus tries to discourage him by framing the act as uncharacteristic of someone of his status. Theseus dismisses Heracles' desire for suicide as "the speech of a mere ordinary man" (ἐπιτυχόντος ἀνθρώπου λόγους, 1248), behavior unsuitable for the extraordinary breed of heroes. Moreover, Theseus "deliberately gives Heracles a heroic title, πολύτλας," in an attempt to discourage him from acting like a common person.⁶⁹ Finally, Theseus resorts to reminding Heracles of his heroic reputation as a great benefactor and friend to mortals (εὐεργέτης βροτοῖσι καὶ μέγας φίλος, 1252). His speech appeals "almost to the *duty* of heroism incumbent on such a famous hero."⁷⁰ By casting suicide in a shameful and cowardly light, Theseus hopes to provoke Heracles *kallinikos* to reject it. Theseus' repudiation of suicide seems to support Loraux's argument that the only honorable death for a warrior is at the hand of an enemy on the battlefield.⁷¹

Heracles rejects this reasoning, however; his intent may have begun as a gut instinct, but he now defends it as if in a debate. He argues that his life is unlivable by giving the play's third recapitulation of the Labors, but this time he shifts the focus away from the victims and beneficiaries of his violence. His view of the Labors thus reduces the importance of the violence's ends or results in favor of an emphasis on its compulsory nature and attendant suffering. The very things for which he was praised earlier are now reasons for despair. He laments the bad behavior of his two "fathers" and traces Hera's enmity from infancy. But he reserves his greatest disgust and weariness for his Labors:

... μόχθους οὓς ἔτλην τί δεῖ λέγειν;
ποίους ποτ' ἢ λέοντας ἢ τρισωμάτους
Τυφῶνας ἢ Γίγαντας ἢ τετρασκελῆ
κενταυροπληθῆ πόλεμον οὐκ ἐξήνυσα;
τήν τ' ἀμφίκρανον καὶ παλιμβλαστῆ κύνα
ὕδραν φονεύσας μυρίων τ' ἄλλων πόνων
διῆλθον ἀγέλας κἀς νεκροὺς ἀφικόμην,

Ἅιδου πυλωρὸν κύνα τρίκρανον ἐς φάος
ὅπως πορεύσαιμ' ἐντολαῖς Εὐρυσθέως.

1270–8

...Why must I discuss the labors I endured? What lions or triple-bodied Typhons or Giants or war with four-legged Centaurs did I not dispatch? After I killed the Hydra, a beast with heads budding again all around, I went through herds of a thousand other Labors until I arrived among the dead, in order that I might bring the gate-guarding, triple-headed dog of Hades to the light, on Eurystheus' orders.

Heracles' own recounting of his Labors stands in stark contrast to the hymnic tone of the Chorus's first stasimon about his deeds. Barlow argues that, in the first ode, Euripides creates "a glossy ornamental romantic atmosphere" in contrast to the messenger speech;[72] I would go further to suggest that the Chorus's praise of Heracles' deeds is meant to stand in juxtaposition with Heracles' own assessment of his toils in this passage. Indeed, the lack of horror, pain, and moral weight that Barlow criticizes in the ode is more than amply supplied here, and, most compellingly, in the voice of the one who suffered it all. Heracles emphasizes the chronological length of his toils from before his conception until that very day; the sheer number of labors; and the monstrosity of the beasts he battled. Where the Chorus saw deeds worthy of praise and glory, Heracles only sees a useless life worthy of lament (βίον γ' ἀχρεῖον ἀνόσιον, 1302). Heracles explicitly incorporates his latest act of violence into his list of Labors, adding the murder of the family as his final labor (*ponos*). Where before he had thought he had completed his Labors with the capture of Cerberus, he now realizes that the suffering imposed by Hera has no end.

Furthermore, his speech suppresses the socially beneficial aspects of his violence entirely. Without the ends of protection for the Greeks and glory for the gods, his heroic violence becomes merely a desperate response to Hera's hatred. Without a communal justification or the impetus to excellence in competition, Heracles' violence is reduced to a mechanism for survival. His existential despair is compounded by fears about practical living. The pollution of kin-killing is a real problem, as demonstrated in the myths about Heracles' struggle to be purified after his murder of Iphitus.[73] In exile from both Thebes and Argos, deprived of divine and human company, he fears that he will be recognized and mocked, his reputation reduced to one fact, that he killed his wife and children (1287–90). In an aria of despair, he even imagines that the earth, sea, and river will reject him (1295–8), realms that he had once tamed and made safe for men.

Finally, Heracles concedes that Hera is victorious, and he is defeated. His life is wholly destroyed, and she can dance for joy. Where previously Hera's role in the Labors had been downplayed by Amphitryon, she now dominates. Heracles criticizes Hera for selfishly destroying him for her own gain; once himself κλεινός (12), he now sarcastically calls her "celebrated" (κλεινή, 1303). She has reduced the "best man of Greece" and "innocent benefactor of Greece" to nothing (ἄνδρ' Ἑλλάδος τὸν πρῶτον, 1306; τοὺς εὐεργέτας / Ἑλλάδος ἀπώλεσ' οὐδὲν' ὄντας αἰτίους, 1309–10). His previous greatness increases the magnitude of her triumph, and Heracles, now destroyed, indeed serves as the "glory of Hera."

Theseus counters with a theological argument: while he agrees that Hera has won the contest or *agōn*, he universalizes the experiences of mortals and gods, claiming that all are subject to *tyche*. But more effectively, he ameliorates the practical drawbacks of exile with a litany of practical favors. He offers a new home in Athens, where Heracles can take refuge in his exile.[74] The problem of Heracles' pollution is easily remedied by Theseus' plan to "purify [his] hands of *miasma*" there (ἐκεῖ χέρας σὰς ἁγνίσας μιάσματος, 1324). Theseus compensates for Heracles' lost status and alleviates humiliating poverty by sharing his wealth, "houses and a portion of my possessions" (δόμους τε δώσω χρημάτων τ' ἐμῶν μέρος, 1325), as well as the prizes the Athenian citizenry gave him for killing the Minotaur (1326). He offers a counterexample to the aphorism of Megara, who, friendless and abandoned by her own city, had observed, "they say the faces of hosts look fondly upon exiled friends for one day alone" (ὡς τὰ ξένων πρόσωπα φεύγουσιν φίλοις / ἓν ἦμαρ ἡδὺ βλέμμ' ἔχειν φασὶν μόνον, 305–6).

Theseus' actions promise to renew Heracles' legacy in subsequent times. He offers to rename the plots of land called Theseia after Heracles; in the future, they will be Heracleia (1330–1). Heracles' heroism will continue to be recognized, even after his death: "the whole city of Athens will honor you with sacrifices and stone memorials" (θυσίαισι λαΐνοισί τ' ἐξογκώμασιν / τίμιον ἀνάξει πᾶσ' Ἀθηναίων πόλις, 1332–3).[75] Thus, though exiled, Heracles will be restored at least in part to his heroic stature, receiving wealth and honors while living, and sacrifices when dead. With these status markers, Heracles will not have to endure the shameful, disgraced life he had been imagining for himself.

Theseus does not conceive of his offers, generous as they are, as a mere favor. As always, his benefaction receives a reciprocal *charis* from the *philos*. Heracles' *dyskleia* will be converted into *eukleia* for Athens, which will gain like a victor a "noble crown" (καλὸς γὰρ ἀστοῖς στέφανος, 1334). And in providing for a defeated Heracles, Theseus sees the fulfillment of his prior obligation: "I will repay to you this favor for my salvation" (κἀγὼ χάριν σοι τῆς ἐμῆς σωτηρίας /

τήνδ' ἀντιδώσω, 1336–7). When Theseus was in desperate straits, Heracles benefitted him; now, when Heracles is in need of friends (1337), Theseus can provide a worthy recompense, a return to the light and a new life.

Heracles' initial response indicates that he rejects Theseus' offer.[76] He dismisses Theseus' aid as subordinate, *parerga*, to his sorrows (πάρεργα < > τάδ' ἔστ' ἐμῶν κακῶν, 1340) and refutes his characterization of the gods' subjection to *tyche*.[77] But clearly his thinking has changed, and the timing here, as pointed out by Yoshitake, is significant.[78] With the threat of shame of exile and loss of status averted, Heracles comes to view his choices in a different light: where before he had thought of death as an escape from his suffering, he now considers that in dying he might incur the charge of cowardice, *deilia* (μὴ δειλίαν ὄφλω τιν' ἐκλιπὼν φάος, 1348).[79] Theseus' material *philia* enables Heracles to view suicide not as an honorable response to shame but as a cowardly act of escape and an inappropriate use of violence. That is, by rehabilitating Heracles as *philos*, Theseus enables him to reemerge as *kallinikos*.

Many scholars have commented on the play's presentation of endurance as an admirable trait in his turn to life. But Heracles does not seem to advocate for endurance *qua* endurance. Rather, he can only conceive of endurance in a specific way: he assimilates the qualities of endurance specifically to the courage required in battle. As he begins to think of self-directed violence as a cowardly act, he says, "whoever does not withstand misfortunes would not be able to withstand the weapon of a man" (ταῖς συμφοραῖς γὰρ ὅστις οὐχ ὑφίσταται / οὐδ' ἀνδρὸς ἂν δύναιθ' ὑποστῆναι βέλος, 1350–1).[80] By drawing a parallel between sustaining life's disasters and standing up to an enemy in armed combat, Heracles converts a passive endurance into active resistance. His decision to live is thus incorporated into his earlier role, before the madness, as an avatar of heroic success in physical conflict.

Heracles deals similarly with the conundrum of his weapons. If he keeps them, they will constantly reproach him with their use against his children. But he hesitates to throw them away:

> ... ἀλλὰ γυμνωθεὶς ὅπλων
> ξὺν οἷς τὰ κάλλιστ' ἐξέπραξ' ἐν Ἑλλάδι
> ἐχθροῖς ἐμαυτὸν ὑποβαλὼν αἰσχρῶς θάνω;
>
> 1382–4

But stripped of the weapons with which I accomplished the finest acts in Greece, am I to subject myself to my enemies and die shamefully?

Here the priorities of his *kallinikos* role reassert themselves: he calls his Labors *ta kallista* instead of *mochthoi* (1270), and his fear is no longer of pollution and exile, but of being defeated in armed struggle. His violence is constrained—the weapons will not be turned against himself, but, turned outwards against *echthroi*, they become suited again to accomplish *kallista* acts. In choosing to keep the weapons and resuming the task to lead Cerberus to Mycenae, we see a Heracles who, although forever changed, nevertheless retains a commitment to victory.

This is not to say that Heracles is not thoroughly humbled. Theseus must help him to a standing position, offering, "Give your hand to your helper and friend" (δίδου δὲ χεῖρ' ὑπηρέτηι φίλωι, 1403). The mighty hand of Heracles, which provided the power to accomplish famous deeds, now relies on the proffered aid of another. And the language of *philia* dominates their conversation: Heracles instructs his father, "one must have this sort of man as a friend" (τοιόνδ' ἄνδρα χρὴ κτᾶσθαι φίλον, 1404). Their relationship is not all comfort, however. When Heracles, overcome with grief, weeps, Theseus chides him with a reminder of his extraordinary Labors and accuses him of being no longer "the famous Heracles" (ὁ κλεινὸς Ἡρακλῆς οὐκ εἶ νοσῶν, 1414). Heracles retorts that this trial is his worst (1411), and repays the favor by reminding Theseus of the time when he too was weak and broken (1415–16). Heracles, though crushed, begins rising back to his status as a noble man through a demonstration of his freedom of speech.

Euripides thus presents a path forward for reckoning with the unpredictability and ambivalence of heroic violence—a problem that plagues heroes beyond Heracles. While the first part of the play demonstrates how *philia* constrains the violent acts of a *kallinikos* hero to socially beneficial ends, the murder of Heracles' family reveals the awful results of epinician violence turned against one's *philoi*. The debates of the final part of the play show how self-directed violence can be averted by Theseus' friendship, which becomes the mechanism for Heracles' reemergence on the path to becoming a *kallinikos* hero once more. Ultimately it is the communal value of *philia* that, although vulnerable to divine interference, stops the cycle of violence and saves Heracles' life.

Conclusion

Let us assess the results of Euripides' experiment in coping with and recovering from heroic violence. While his solution to Heracles' explosion of unconstrained violence enables Heracles to live, it is nevertheless costly. Heracles' rehabilitation occurs without recourse to the gods, their guidance, or approval. When Theseus invites Heracles to Athens, he offers only hero cult, not divine worship; after death, Heracles would receive sacrifices at his tomb, like any other hero (1331–3). In exchange for a return to life, it seems, Heracles gives up his apotheosis. Furthermore, in dismissing the exploits of Olympians as mere "wretched tales of poets" (ἀοιδῶν οἵδε δύστηνοι λόγοι, 1346), Heracles also rejects any intimation that he will (or would want to) join them.[81] This runs against what had become the dominant tradition of the time, that Heracles is introduced to Olympus as a reward for his Labors and his suffering; there he is married to Hebe, the personification of youth, and reconciled with his enemy Hera.

The texts that celebrate his apotheosis tend to elide his blameworthy acts of violence—especially his kin-killing—emphasizing instead the Labors associated with a defeat of death, such as the acquisition of Geryon's Cattle in the far west and the Apples of the Hesperides or his return with Cerberus from the Underworld. Of special concern to us is Pindar's epinicians, in which Heracles' status as a *hērōs theos* is a critical part of his exemplary function. In *Isthmian* 4, Pindar describes Heracles' afterlife in Olympus as his reward for his civilizing exploits. However, when he addresses the death of Heracles' sons, he alters its circumstances: the sons are described as "bronze-clad" (χαλκοάρας, 4.63) and receiving burnt offerings. By using an adjective suitable for adult warriors and alluding to hero cult, Pindar implies that the sons died as adults, suppressing Heracles' involvement entirely. For this poet and this genre, then, the apotheosis myth seems almost to require a disavowal of Heracles' murder of his children.

But Euripides, in centering his play around the death of the family, must directly confront the challenge the myth poses to his deification. By placing it after Heracles' Labors, the play also forecloses the possibility of Heracles' working out his penance towards future glory. In losing his apotheosis, Heracles also loses unique compensation for his extraordinary benefit to others. His great downfall seems to have had a flattening effect, preventing him from ascending to the greatest of heights. By insisting on Heracles' use of epinician violence against his family, Euripides seems to suggest that even the roles of *philos* and *kallinikos* are limited in what they can accomplish. Although they may constrain self-directed violence, they are human roles that cannot make one a god. Thus, the hero who had served the gods, then became their victim, remains outside their circle in the end. This suggests that coping with violence and finding a way forward, may be, for better or worse, a distinctly human endeavor.

5

Heracles the Fool

Laughing at Violence

Introduction

Comedy has a special tool to cope with both the triumphs and the disasters caused by heroic violence: laughter. I turn now to the comic Heracles, whom I define broadly as the Heracles that provokes laughter. Comic Heracles appears, naturally, in comedy, but also in satyr play; he crosses dramatic genres, but also serves to link them through an emphasis on humor. In the first section of the chapter, I focus on two roles that frequently emerge in comic fragments related to Heracles: the voracious glutton and, once again, the victor. Drawing on Mikhail Bakhtin's ideas about grotesque realism and ambivalent laughter, I argue that laughter at Heracles' exaggerated appetites debases him, yet in these plays in which he always leaves the victor, he is "recrowned" and his use of violence is likewise renewed. I then examine Euripides' handling of the comic Heracles in the "pro-satyric" *Alcestis*, arguing that the play's resolution requires the reconciliation of the comic and epinician Heracles. The chapter concludes with a discussion of the multiplicity of Heracleses in Aristophanes' *Frogs*. Following Bakthin's work on polyphony and dialogism, I argue that Aristophanes sets the comic, tragic, epic, and lyric Heracles in dialogue with one another, revealing the underlying ambivalence of this very polyphonal figure.

The majority of Heracles' comic appearances occur in mythological travesties or parodies; while their plots remain mostly mysterious, many are related to defeats of villains or adventures related to his Labors. In these plays, Heracles is placed in a world that, while still retaining a fantastic mythological setting, nevertheless comes into contact with some realities of everyday life. Heracles' excessiveness easily lends itself to parody, and by bringing him closer to the real world, comedy brings the most ridiculous aspects of Heracles to the fore. As the most athletic of heroes, Heracles' tremendous body is often at the center of his exploits; in the logic of travesty, the attention paid to his incredible physical exertions inevitably leads to a preoccupation with his equally outsized bodily needs. So it is no surprise that the comic Heracles is defined by his physical appetites for food, alcohol, and sex. Often, his subjection to these enormous appetites renders him stupid and grotesque, making him the preeminent buffoon of the Greek stage.

The comic manifestation of Heracles was ubiquitous and enduringly popular, dwarfing the representation of Heracles in tragedy, for example. Audiences laughed at Heracles on stages from Sicily to Athens, from a time preceding the establishment of comic competitions in Athens and into Middle Comedy. The prominence of the comic Heracles may seem to create tension with the more "serious" Heracles, who was the object of cult worship, appeared prominently on religious and civic architecture, and was the subject of "high" literary genres such as epic, lyric, and tragedy. As I have argued, these genres examine the difficulties generated by Heracles' violence, which, on the one hand, is a means to acclaimed victories, and on the other, is destructive.

In this chapter, I argue that mockery of Heracles serves to mediate between these two extremes. In terms of the larger theoretical framework for this study, the comic Heracles' propensity to excessive violence is just one of the many physical impulses that drive his behavior. In a figure lacking entirely in self-moderation and beholden to his appetites, his violence threatens to manifest itself at any time as a form of Benjamin's "nonmediate" violence. But Heracles' degraded state blunts its menace. Laughter serves to negate the fear engendered by his violence, thereby leaving his use of force "cleansed," as it were, of its dangerous aspects. And in comic plots that end with Heracles' defeat of villains, Heracles' triumph serves to restore an acceptable end for the means of violence, allowing his victories to be celebrated.

In my investigation of humor's mediating effects, I draw on ideas about the carnivalesque as developed in the works of Bakhtin.[1] The comic Heracles is dominated by associations with the "material bodily lower stratum," which Bakhtin defines as the parts of the body associated with defecation and copulation, but also conception, pregnancy, and birth. In the Rabelaisian folk culture Bakhtin describes, contact with the material bodily lower stratum yields a two-fold result: degradation—an "uncrowning" of that which is high and serious—but also carnival or ambivalent laughter, which revives and renews through its association with fertility and super-abundance.[2] While the majority of the comic fragments related to Heracles come from Attic dramatic festivals, an official and state-controlled event, the ubiquity of the gluttonous Heracles outside of Athenian political comedy suggests that Bakhtin's understanding of carnival's effects can help us understand the comic Heracles as well.[3]

In the introduction to *Aristophanes and the Carnival of Genres*, Charles Platter identifies two ways of understanding carnival: first, as a historical folk-cultural phenomenon that is anthropological in nature, as described above; second, as a more specifically literary phenomenon that "*always* happens within language as the inevitable result of a (public) critical discourse that problematizes the official categories of everyday life."[4] Platter goes on to show how Aristophanes' literary carnivalization is related to Bakhtin's observations about literary polyphony and dialogism, as developed in *Problems of Dostoevsky's Poetics* and "Epic vs. Novel." Following on Platter's work, I explore how the *Frogs* (and to some extent Euripides' *Alcestis*) puts the comic Heracles into conversation with the Heracles of other genres, such as epic, epinician, and tragedy. The dialogue between these manifestations of Heracles comes to its most cacophonous point at the gate of the Underworld, where the figure of Heracles undergoes a ludicrous destabilization. As a single figure capable of representing both the "high" and "serious" of official culture and the "low" and "comic" of folk culture, Heracles readily reflects comedy's polyphony and openness to centrifugal forces. This results in a kind of carnivalization of Heracles, one in which laughter cleanses and renews both his violence and his victories.

Victory and the Flesh: Renewing Violence through Laughter

Heracles appears to have featured across a wide range of comic productions, from Epicharmus' plays in Sicily, to Athenian satyr play, and Old and Middle Comedy. Unfortunately, aside from the eleven full plays of Aristophanes, our evidence for comic productions is unfortunately fragmentary: while some material has survived on papyrus scraps excavated at Oxyrhynchus, the majority of our fragments derive from later writers who quote short snippets of text as an illustration. For Heracles, the most important of these later writers is Athenaeus, whose detailed discussions of types of seafood in *Deipnosophistae* include numerous citations of feasts in which Heracles participated.[5] The nature of our evidence, then, is particularly limited: we may know only the titles of plays, or we may be forced to extrapolate a play's themes or plot based on a short excerpt that was not chosen to exemplify them.[6] Yet despite these limitations, two themes consistently emerge in fragments about Heracles: his exaggerated physical appetites and the achievement of victory.

Gluttony is the central characteristic of the comic Heracles. Over and over and over again, Heracles' exaggerated, enormous appetites for food, drink, and sex provoke laughter. Instead of looking at the external effects of his extraordinary body and his use of force on the world, comedy looks at the internal demands of that body. His body is viewed less as an object of admiration and more as a bottomless pit. Audiences laugh at the hungry, dimwitted Heracles, allowing for the common person's "self-assertion," that is, the "opportunity to assert himself by ridiculing the ruler."[7] In Heracles' gluttony we see two sides: the first side emphasizes absence—Heracles is depicted as starving, driven to lunacy or reduced to animal-like behavior because of hunger. The other side emphasizes abundance, with scenes of Heracles' feasting on an endless parade of dishes in a celebratory atmosphere. These are two sides of the same coin, and, I suggest, they correspond with the material bodily lower stratum that demands and swallows, but also excretes and renews. Alongside his gluttony is his love of drinking and the resulting drunkenness, and lust for sex.

In mythological travesties, Heracles' appetite is often featured in plots that climax with a victory over villains. These victory plots are common in Sicilian comedy and satyr play, and mythological plots continue to be developed in Old Comedy and Middle Comedy. Myths about Heracles' Labors and his defeats of ogres, monsters, and criminals, reaching back to Hesiod's presentation of Heracles as a culture hero, provide a large variety of tales from which to draw. By meting out punishment on villains like Busiris or Syleus or the Centaurs, our comic hero gives the audience reasons to cheer, elevating him once again in a re-ordered universe. These themes are rooted in Heracles' earlier traditions: as Casolari points out, Heracles is primarily a strong man in the folktale tradition, and in cult he is worshiped as *alexikakos*; he is also closely associated in cult with eating and the feasting rituals of *theoxenia*.[8] The traditions she identifies belong more to popular tales and common religious rituals than higher genres of poetry, suggesting that the comic Heracles at least belongs more "to the people" than to the ruling classes, making him an appropriate figure of carnival culture. In the following section, I survey the varied and fragmentary evidence in search of the defining qualities of Heracles' roles as a buffoon and comic victor. As these roles become clearer, we will observe how their carnivalesque traits serve to deflate the threat of the manifestation of violence, while Heracles' "recrowning" provides a satisfactory goal for his use of force.

Epicharmus

The work of the Sicilian poet Epicharmus provides our oldest literary evidence for the gluttonous Heracles, and how he may have been treated in one of these victory plots.⁹ His play *Busiris* presumably portrays Heracles' defeat of Busiris, a king of Egypt who captures and sacrifices foreigners, until Heracles breaks free and kills him (Ps.-Apoll. 2.5.11). In killing the inhospitable Egyptian, Heracles enforces Greek norms of *xenia* and brings justice upon the unjust. But the sole surviving fragment of *Busiris* tells us only about his appalling eating habits:

πρᾶτον μὲν αἰκ ἔσθοντ' ἴδοις νιν, ἀποθάνοις·
βρέμει μὲν ὁ φάρυγξ ἔνδοθ', ἀραβεῖ δ' ἁ γνάθος,
ψοφεῖ δ' ὁ γομφίος, τέτριγε δ' ὁ κυνόδων,
σίζει δὲ ταῖς ῥίνεσσι, κινεῖ δ' οὔατα.

fr. 18

First, if you saw him eating, you would die! His throat rumbles within, and his jaw rattles, and his molars clack, his canines grind, he snorts through his nostrils, and he waggles his ears.

This fragment, which Athenaeus provides as evidence that Heracles is "gluttonous" (ἀδηφάγος, 10.411A), illustrates well the "starving Heracles." Apparently spoken by a dumbfounded and disgusted servant, the description of Heracles' eating degrades him from hero to beast. The speaker emphasizes the cacophony of sounds Heracles emits, more suitable to barnyard feeding than royal banquets. The elaborate survey of Heracles' head and neck lends him an alien quality, as of a beast which Heracles might otherwise be tasked with killing himself.¹⁰ This description fits well with Bakhtin's grotesque realism, in which the focus of the body is on the open mouth, the gullet, the teeth, and the tongue.¹¹ But this same noisy eater presumably faces off in a physical struggle with the evil Busiris and emerges triumphant. Laughter at Heracles' gluttony, then, only temporarily debases him, for he is revived as victor; this process demonstrates how contact with the material body and its bodily phenomena can be converted into a positive renewal.

The celebratory side of gluttonous Heracles appears in other works of Epicharmus, centered around the feast, where the "shrove" principles of food, drink, procreative force, and merriment are on full display.¹² We have about two dozen fragments of the *Wedding of Hebe*, all drawn from Athenaeus, which indicate that an enormous feast of all sorts of obscure seafood marks the occasion (fr. 40–63). In a carnivalesque context, such banqueting associates Heracles with another sort of victory: as Bakhtin writes in *Rabelais and his World*, "Man's encounter with the world in the act of eating is joyful, triumphant; he triumphs over the world, devours it without being devoured himself."¹³ The endless and endlessly inventive catalogue of foods suggests a mood of joy and abundance, connecting Heracles' merrymaking with the enjoyment of life itself.

Furthermore, his appetite for food is matched by his appetite for drink, which is likely highlighted in *Heracles at the House of Pholus* (fr. 66). As recounted in Ps.-Apollodorus (2.5.4), Heracles badgers his host, the centaur Pholus, to open a jar of fragrant wine, the scent of which attracts other centaurs and leads to a brawl in which Heracles kills many of them. Heracles' success as a sexual hero could easily have figured into the depiction of his interactions with Hippolyta in *Heracles' Quest for the Belt* (fr. 65), as well as in the conclusion of the *Wedding of Hebe*. Thus many elements of the buffoonish Heracles that emerge in Attic drama can already be observed in Epicharmus' performances in Sicily.

Satyr play

The carnivalesque themes identified in early Sicilian comedy about Heracles can also be found in Athenian satyr play, where fragments and titles indicate that Heracles figured often and prominently.[14] Heracles' connections with satyrs precedes the development of satyr play, as Lissarrague argues from a survey of vase paintings depicting them together.[15] While Heracles sometimes has the civilizing task of putting the unruly satyrs in their place, the visual motif of the satyrs stealing Heracles' weapons acts as an inversion of the arming of a hero, resulting in "the negation of heroism."[16] The early relationship between satyrs and Heracles thus embraces both the crowning and the uncrowning of the victor. The famous Pronomos Vase of approximately 400 BCE is overtly theatrical, depicting an actor dressed as Heracles alongside two other actors, musicians, actors costumed as a chorus of satyrs and Silenus, and Dionysus and Ariadne themselves (Figure 5.1). If Griffith is right in arguing that the painting represents a generalized performance, rather than a specific play, then Heracles' presence suggests his centrality to the genre.[17] One wonders whether he serves here to identify the genre of satyr play almost as much as Silenus and his band of satyrs do.

With only one complete satyr play surviving (Euripides' *Cyclops*), much about the genre remains mysterious.[18] A typical satyr play, which followed each trilogy of tragedies at the City Dionysia, seems to have dramatized a heroic myth and featured a *thiasos* of cowardly, drunken, horny satyrs as its chorus, creating a performance genre that is separate from but in some ways related to comedy.[19] While formally more like tragedy in structure, meter, and diction, satyr play involved humorous elements. According to Seaford, important themes include: defeating a persecutor of mankind, emergence from the underworld, the marriage of a hero, and athletics; Sutton adds to this list hospitality and its abuse, bondage and escape, folktale elements, and happy endings.[20] The tension between

Figure 5.1 Heracles among satyr performers. Pronomos Vase, Attic red-figure volute crater, c. 400 BCE. Naples 81673. Reproduced by permission of the Ministero per i Beni e le Attività Culturali e per il Turismo—Museo Archeologico Nazionale di Napoli.

the low, vulgar satyrs and the high heroism of heroic myth produces "the comedy of incongruity," resulting in an absurdity that leads to laughter.[21] Even in this reductive list of common themes, Heracles' myths have obvious potential as source material for the genre.

A brief survey of the "big three" tragedians' satyr plays reveals the aptness of Heracles' Labors and *parerga*, especially his symbolic conquering of death with his capture of Cerberus, for satyr plots.[22] Aeschylus' *Kerykes* may depict Heracles' mutilating the heralds of Erginus of Orchomenos, before defeating the king himself and freeing Thebes from its subjugation to Orchomenos, while *Leon* seems likely to be about Heracles' pursuit of the Nemean Lion (fr. 123).[23] Four titles of satyr plays by Sophocles relating to Heracles have survived: *Heracliscus, Epitaenarii* or *Epi Taenario, Cerberus,* and *Heracles*. Whether these four titles refer to four separate plays, or three, or two, or one, remains unclear.²⁴ But it seems quite possible for at least one play to have focused on Heracles' retrieval of Cerberus from Hades, one entrance of which is identified as Cape Taenarum, and another play to have featured baby Heracles' defeat of Hera's snakes (treated seriously in Pindar *Nem.* 1). Euripides' *Busiris* likely treated the same tale as Epicharmus, which became a popular theme on Attic red-figure vases, while his *Eurystheus* is a burlesque of the Labor of Cerberus, which caps his Labors and ensures his freedom from the tyranny of Eurystheus (frr. 371–80).²⁵ Heracles' persona in satyr play thus parallels his presentation in Epicharmus' comedies: as Sutton observes, "Heracles appears especially in two capacities, as monster-subduing hero and Gargantuan eater and drinker."²⁶

The somewhat more substantial remains of Euripides' *Syleus* offer insight into how one of Heracles' myths can be translated into satyr drama: in this case, Heracles demonstrates his excellence in a drinking contest, which may even serve as the main competition between hero and villain. In the course of discussing the nature of satyr play, Tzetzes provides a summary of the play's plot (*Prolegomena* Xia II Koster). While overcoming and punishing the wicked Syleus, Heracles also sates his appetite for food, wine, and sex:

Ἡρακλῆς πραθεὶς τῷ Συλεῖ ὡς γεωργὸς δοῦλος ἐστάλη εἰς τὸν ἀγρὸν τὸν ἀμπελῶνα ἐργάσασθαι, ἀνεσπακὼς δὲ δικέλλῃ προρρίζους τὰς ἀμπέλους ἁπάσας νωτοφορήσας τε αὐτὰς εἰς τὸ οἴκημα τοῦ ἀγροῦ θωμοὺς μεγάλους ἐποίησε καὶ τὸν κρείττω τε τῶν βοῶν θύσας κατεθοινᾶτο καὶ τὸν πιθεῶνα διαρρήξας καὶ τὸν κάλλιστον πίθον ἀποπωμάσας τὰς θύρας τε ὡς τράπεζαν θεὶς "ἦσθε καὶ ἔπινεν" ᾄδων, καὶ τῷ προεστῶτι δὲ τοῦ ἀγροῦ δριμὺ ἐνορῶν φέρειν ἐκέλευεν ὡραῖά τε καὶ πλακοῦντας· καὶ τέλος ὅλον ποταμὸν πρὸς τὴν ἔπαυλιν τρέψας τὰ πάντα κατέκλυσεν ὁ δοῦλος ἐκεῖνος ὁ τεχνικώτατος γεωργός. τοιαῦτα τὰ σατυρικὰ δράματα . . .

Heracles, after he was sold to Syleus as a farm slave, was sent to the field to labor in the vineyard. But he ripped up all the vines from the roots with a doubled fork and carried them on his back to the farmhouse, forming huge piles. After he sacrificed the stronger of the cattle, he feasted; he broke open the cellar and, removing the lid from the best jar and setting the doors as a table, he "ate and drank"²⁷ while singing. And glaring sharply at the overseer of the field, he ordered him to bring seasonal fruits and flatcakes. Finally, he diverted the whole river towards the farmhouse and washed everything out—the slave, that most skillful farmer. Such are satyr plays . . .

Tzetzes' summary helps to refine Griffith's schema of a split between the childish-slavish satyrs and the high hero: we do not simply see the grand hero Heracles interacting with silly, distractible satyrs, though that may certainly have occurred throughout the play.[28] Rather, in this outline of plot, we see high and low versions of Heracles himself, in a representation of tonal extremes. He does the serious work of a culture hero in destroying Syleus' property, presumably including his vineyards, the scene of his transgression; he diverts a nearby river, recreating his Labor to clean the Stables of Augeus, which demonstrates his superhuman strength and endurance. Yet Tzetzes' wry application of "that most skillful farmer" to the slave who utterly destroys the vineyards perhaps signals the buffoonish qualities of the protagonist as well. Heracles' greatest priority seems to be sating his enormous appetite, and clearly a significant portion of the play is devoted to Heracles' feasting, drinking, and carousing.

Heracles challenges Syleus to a drinking contest, prior to—or perhaps instead of—attacking him with physical violence: "Recline and let's drink! And make a trial of me in this right away, to see if you will surpass me" (κλίθητι καὶ πίωμεν· ἐν τούτῳ δέ μου / τὴν πεῖραν εὐθὺς λάμβαν' εἰ κρείσσων ἔσῃ, fr. 691). The challenge is reminiscent of a competition at a local bar that inevitably devolves into a fight. Heracles' preeminence is no longer defined by strength, skill in battle, or strategy; he wins through his capacity to hold his liquor. The appetites of the grotesque body seem to supplant his use of violence as the means by which he establishes his superiority. For this contest, the roles of glutton and victor are entirely assimilated to one another.

Moreover, his victory over Syleus is crowned with sexual conquest. He is said in a fragmentary hypothesis to have "saved" or "rescued" Syleus' daughter Xenodoce (*P. Oxy.* 2455 fr. 8, l. 107), and he urges her: "Let's go inside and go to bed! Wipe away your tears!" (βαυβῶμεν εἰσελθόντες· ἀπόμορξαι σέθεν / τὰ δάκρυα, fr. 694). Xenodoce's tears may indicate grief over the defeat of her father and loss of her home, suggesting that Heracles rapes her (not that the matter of her consent would have any bearing on the play's ostensibly happy ending). Or, if he instead prevents a satyr attack upon her (the satyr chorus fantasizes about a gang rape of Helen in *Cyclops* 179–87), perhaps she is relieved by her rescue and her tears of fright can be soothed. Heracles the former slave triumphs over Syleus the master by razing his property and probably depriving him of life, regaining his freedom and enjoying a triumphal ending. His acts of violence are no doubt praised by the chorus of satyrs who are freed alongside him. Moreover, his buffoonery in this play does not disqualify him later from serving as an example of a free and virtuous man for Philo, the first-century BCE Hellenistic Jewish philosopher (*Every Good Man is Free* 98–104).

Ion of Chios' *Omphale* provides another example of a satyr play in which a test of endurance of consumption of food may have replaced the physical toils of the Labors or of violent conflict. The play depicts Heracles' period of servitude (perhaps one or three years) to the Lydian queen Omphale, a punishment stemming from his murder of Iphitus. In a judicious review, Easterling cautions us that much of the plot cannot be reconstructed from the surviving fragments.[29] Yet the episode plays an important but tangential role in Sophocles' *Trachiniae*, as discussed in Chapter 3, and Maitland tentatively offers an attractive suggestion—that Ion's play was written with the *Trachiniae* in mind.[30] Even if the specific connection must remain speculative, the satyric *Omphale* provides a happier take on an episode that is easily treated as an unspeakable humiliation and source of shame.[31] Omphale may have punished Heracles with the task of feasting; as Heracles states, "I must celebrate the feast for a year" (ἐνιαυσίαν γὰρ δεῖ με τὴν ὁρτὴν ἄγειν, fr. 21). Surviving fragments indicate festive music, drinking, and eating, and perhaps even cross-dressing on the part of the satyrs and Heracles himself. Following Loraux's explication of Heracles' feminine qualities, Uhlig draws attention to the play's eastern, Lydian setting, arguing that even eastern dress—that may not be marked overtly as women's clothing—transgresses normative gender presentation, perhaps even tipping over into drag.[32] Later tradition, especially among the Romans, takes a lighthearted approach to making them lovers, with Heracles playing a feminized role and Omphale "wearing the pants" in the relationship; perhaps this tradition has its roots in satyr play.[33]

The gender dynamics of *Omphale*, although hazy to us, may reflect some of the underlying functions of satyr drama. Heracles arrives in distant Lydia on Boreas' horse (fr. 17a), an appropriately serious steed for the still-masculine hero. But as he and the satyrs become subordinated to a woman, they dabble in the feminine. This humiliation, as much as Heracles' eating and drinking, must have been a source of humor. Edith Hall has written persuasively that the genre "was characterized by an unapologetic obsession with male sexuality, visually represented in the satyrs' [ithyphallic] costumes, and a masculine, *homosocial* consciousness manifested in and articulated by its chorus of satyrs."[34] Satyr drama's masculinity, Hall argues, answers to the preceding tragedies' "femininity," with its choruses of women, female lead characters, and emotions of grief and pity, reaffirming the masculine self-conception of Athenian male citizens as they depart the theater.[35] Heracles and the satyrs' state of emasculation is temporary: presumably Heracles overcomes a challenge (a year-long eating contest?) and he and the satyrs, removing their makeup and perfumes, return to a more "natural" state of freedom for Heracles, and reunion with Dionysus for the satyrs. This suggests that *Omphale* accomplishes on the level of an individual play the phenomenon Hall describes occurring over the unit of the tetralogy.

The examples of Euripides' *Syleus* and Ion of Chios' *Omphale* together attest to the effects of satyr drama's conventions on the figure of Heracles and his violence: Heracles' violence remains necessary to effect a happy ending, but it is reshaped, and sometimes even displaced, as a contest of physical or athletic supremacy is replaced by a drinking or eating contest. Heracles' enormous appetites, and his subjection to them, provide a kind of release in laughter; yet he still wins the day and retains his status as the strong and victorious hero. In a parallel manner, the horny satyrs often discuss sexual violence, but their desires are never consummated; the audience's mirth at their frustration also deflates the threat of sexual assault. Sutton traces the roots of this phenomenon to basic human psychology, "that we laugh at that which we fear in an effort to reduce the anxiety produced, and a good deal of humor is explicable in this fashion."[36] Yet the laughter that reduces anxiety leads only to a brief diminishment from which Heracles can easily recover.

Relative to tragedy, the ethical scheme of satyr drama is greatly simplified, permitting the audience to set aside the complexity of heroic violence temporarily. Heracles' opponents—such as Syleus or Sositheos' Lityerses—exhibit no redeeming qualities or complexity. The plays thus allow their audience to cheer the defeat of the ogre, while enjoying a laugh at the expense of the protagonist and the satyr chorus. Heracles is thus not reduced entirely to the buffoon, and the required happy ending restores him by giving his violence an acceptable objective. As Griffith says, "These characters [the heroes] are seen to come from, and return to, positions of honor and authority within a legitimate kind of social structure, once this brief interlude in the wilds is concluded."[37] In this sense, the humor of satyr drama participates in the phenomenon of carnival laughter, liberating its audiences from the seriousness of heroic myth.

Old and Middle Comedy

Sicilian comedy and satyr play, each in its own way, unite Heracles' victories over villains and his tremendous appetites for food, drink, and sex. Indeed, these themes continue to resonate throughout Heracles' characterization in Athenian comedy.[38] Judging from fragments and titles, mythological plays were common in Old Comedy, and rose to prominence again in the last two decades of the fifth century and throughout the fourth century BCE.[39] Unsurprisingly, Heracles is one of the most popular heroes to figure in these plays.[40] As in earlier iterations of the laughable Heracles, a number of plays seem to show Heracles defeating a villain (Cratinus' *Busiris*, Hermippus' *Cercopes*).[41] His penchant for feasting is well represented among the fragments, preserved largely by Athenaeus (Archippus' and Nicochares' *Heracles Marrying*, Philyllius' *Auge*, Strattis' *Callipides*).

So prevalent was the comic Heracles that by the time of *Wasps* in 422 BCE, Aristophanes could dismiss "Heracles cheated of his dinner" (Ἡρακλῆς τὸ δεῖπνον ἐξαπατώμενος, 60) as a cliché of "vulgar comedy" (κωμῳδίας φορτικῆς, 66). But even Aristophanes cannot resist riffing on the stock Heracles, who appears in the *Birds* as a particularly stupid and hungry ambassador, easily swayed by the prospect of a roasted bird for lunch. (Aristophanes' much richer engagement with Heracles in the *Frogs* will be addressed at the end of this chapter.) Nevertheless, although the adventures of Heracles are not as prominent in Aristophanes' comedy, focused as it tends to be on contemporary political and intellectual issues facing the *polis*, we can still find traces of them in the fragments of Old Comedy that survive from other poets.

But the comic Heracles was not restricted to mythological burlesques that followed traditional plots. In *Zeus Abused* by Plato Comicus, a comic poet who straddles what scholars call Old and Middle Comedy, Heracles engages in the symposiastic drinking game of *cottabus*. The scenes trade on Heracles' role as athletic victor but place him in a context closer to everyday life. The object of the game is to toss the wine lees from the bottom of one's cup into smaller vessels floating in a basin of water, causing them to sink—a task made increasingly difficult the more one drinks.[42] The play seems unlikely to be pure mythological travesty, given that Heracles engages in a form of entertainment contemporary to aristocratic fifth- and fourth-century Athens. But in the following conversation, which involves presumably a hetaera and her pimp (Speaker A), Heracles draws on his reputation as an athlete:

A. πρὸς κότταβον παίζειν, ἕως ἂν σφῷν ἐγὼ
τὸ δεῖπνον ἔνδον σκευάσω. **ΗΡΑΚΛΗΣ.** πάνυ βούλομαι.
ἀγὼν ἐμός ἔστ'. **A.** ἀλλ' εἰς θυῖαν παιστέον.
ΗΡ. φέρε τὴν θυῖαν, αἶρ' ὕδωρ, τὰ ποτήρια
παράθετε. παίζωμεν δὲ περὶ φιλημάτων. (5)
A. . . . . . ἀγεννῶς οὐκ ἐῶ
παίζειν. τίθημι κοττάβεια σφῷν ἐγὼ
τασδί τε τὰς κρηπῖδας ἃς αὕτη φορεῖ,
καὶ τὸν κότυλον τὸν σόν. **ΗΡ.** βαβαιάξ, οὑτοσὶ
μείζων ἀγὼν τῆς Ἰσθμιάδος ἐπέρχεται.

fr. 46

A. ... To play *cottabus*, while I prepare the dinner inside for you two.

Heracles I am very willing—for the contest is mine!

A. But you must play with a mortar.

Heracles Bring the mortar, draw water, set out the cups. Let's play for kisses!

A. ... I will not allow you to play for low stakes. I set as the *cottabus* prizes for you two these platform shoes, which she is wearing, and your cup.

Heracles Oy! This contest is turning up bigger than the Isthmian games!

This scene juxtaposes what Rosen describes as a "banal, domestic setting" with references to Heracles' athletic background.[43] Kaibel's emendation in line 3 (ἀγὼν ἐμός ἔστ᾽ for the manuscript's ἀλλα νεμος ἐστ) restores the language of competition earlier in the conversation, highlighting Heracles' status as a *kallinikos* victor. The joking comparison of this game—played against a hetaera, in a private setting, with rules reminiscent of strip poker—to the competitions held at the panhellenic Isthmian games exploits the distance between the high heroics of epinician competition/victory and the domestic flirtation between Heracles and a woman who is not his wife.

We have already seen a tragic exploitation of the distance between epinician and domestic space in Euripides' *Heracles* in Chapter 4. In the prelude to murdering his children and wife, the maddened Heracles hallucinates that he arrives and competes at the Isthmian games, though he in reality remains within the halls of his own home: "he announced that he was arriving at the wooded plains of the Isthmus. And there, after he had stripped his body naked of garments, he began to compete against no one" (Ἰσθμοῦ ναπαίας ἔλεγε προσβαίνειν πλάκας / κἀνταῦθα γυμνὸν σῶμα θεὶς πορπαμάτων / πρὸς οὐδέν᾽ ἡμιλλᾶτο, 958–60). Heracles' imagined competition at the Isthmian games, enacted within the inappropriate space of the *oikos*, anticipates the crime of his fatal use of weapons against his own family. I make reference to Euripides' tragic scene not to suggest that Plato's is directly parodying it, but to highlight how Plato's comic exploitation of a similar incongruity functions. The athletic "event," a toss requiring a smooth flick of the wrist (as described in fr. 47) and eye-hand coordination, can only be enacted after the wine cup has been drained dry. Since a prize is set should the hetaera win, it seems that Heracles and a young woman compete on equal terms; his strength and size offer no real advantage. But the ability to hold one's liquor is an advantage, an area in which Heracles presumably excels through frequent practice and long experience. Moreover, the discussion over the contest's prizes shows off Heracles' lusty enthusiasm; though initially content with kisses from the young woman, the stakes are ratcheted higher by the possibility of winning her shoes, perhaps a prelude to sexual intercourse. Here, victory means pleasurable sexual conquest, not a crown or eternal *kleos*. This scene thus reduces Heracles' many athletic strengths to his ability to drink and his motivation to bed a woman; his victory is fueled by drink and crowned by the procreative act. Thus, even in a non-mythological play, Heracles remains connected to his gluttony and the material bodily lower stratum.

The functions of the lower body are prominently on display in a fragment from Eubulus' *Cercopes* (fr. 53). Heracles is the likely speaker, describing the customs in Thebes: they feast all day and night, and they locate the outhouse right near door, so that the celebrants only have to take a short walk to relieve themselves.[44] The cyclical nature of the material bodily lower stratum, with its association of eating and drinking with defecation and urination, is here made explicit. Heracles speaks approvingly of the Thebans' practice, thus positioning himself within a cycle of gaiety, of fertility and renewal.[45] The title *Cercopes* implies that the play is concerned with Heracles' capture of the mischievous Cercopes while in Lydia, providing another opportunity to unite his roles as glutton and victor.

The theme of Heracles' extraordinary youth also allows for incidents that deflate the acts of the heroic Heracles with laughter. Tales of exceptional youth tend to sprout up around heroes with exceptional adult careers, and Heracles' youth and education serve as subjects both in "serious" literature and comic literature.[46] He famously strangles twin snakes sent by Hera to kill him as a young infant, an episode that Pindar celebrates at the center of his first *Nemean* ode—and that may have been the subject of Sophocles' satyr play *Heracliscus*. Another influential episode from Heracles' youth is Prodicus' allegorical tale known today as "the Choice of Heracles," in which an adolescent Heracles sits at a crossroads and must decide whether to take the path of life recommended by seductive Vice or by admirable Virtue.[47]

The *Linus* of Alexis, a playwright who straddles Middle and New Comedy, offers a comic take on Heracles' relationship with his teacher Linus, whom in other sources Heracles kills in an angry outburst of fatal violence. Here, a contemporizing scene presents a conversation between a sophisticated teacher and stupid pupil:[48]

ΛΙΝ. . . . βιβλίον
ἐντεῦθεν ὅ τι βούλει προσελθὼν γὰρ λαβέ,
ἔπειτ' ἀναγνώσει— **ΗΡ.** πάνυ γε.[49] **ΛΙΝ.** διασκοπῶν
ἀπὸ τῶν ἐπιγραμμάτων ἀτρέμα τε καὶ σχολῇ.
Ὀρφεὺς ἔνεστιν, Ἡσίοδος, τραγῳδίαι, (5)
Ἐπίχαρμος, Ὅμηρος, Χοιρίλος συγγράμματα
παντοδαπά. δηλώσεις γὰρ οὕτω τὴν φύσιν,
ἐπὶ τί μάλισθ' ὥρμηκε. **ΗΡ.** τουτὶ λαμβάνω.

ΛΙΝ. δεῖξον τί ἐστι πρῶτον. **ΗΡ.** ὀψαρτυσία,
ὥς φησι τοὐπίγραμμα. **ΛΙΝ.** φιλόσοφός τις εἶ, (10)
εὔδηλον, ὃς παρεὶς τοσαῦτα γράμματα
Σίμου τέχνην ἔλαβες. **ΗΡ.** ὁ Σῖμος δ᾽ ἐστὶ τίς;
ΛΙΝ. μάλ᾽ εὐφυὴς ἄνθρωπος. ἐπὶ τραγῳδίαν
ὥρμηκε νῦν, καὶ τῶν μὲν ὑποκριτῶν πολὺ
κράτιστός ἐστιν ὀψοποιός, ὡς δοκεῖ (15)
τοῖς χρωμένοις, τῶν δ᾽ ὀψοποιῶν ὑποκριτής.
. . . .
ΛΙΝ. βούλιμός ἐσθ᾽ ἄνθρωπος. **ΗΡ.** ὅ τι βούλει λέγε.
πεινῶ γάρ, εὖ τοῦτ᾽ ἴσθι.

fr. 140

Linus Go over and take from there whatever book you want; then read . . .
Heracles Right away!
Linus . . . after carefully examining the titles, quietly and leisurely. There's Orpheus, Hesiod, tragedies, Epicharmus, Homer, Choerilus, all kinds of prose. In this way you will make clear your nature, according to what you're bent on.
Heracles I take this one!
Linus Show first what it is.
Heracles A cookbook, so the title says.
Linus You are some philosopher, clearly, since you passed over so many treatises and chose the art of Simus.
Heracles Who is Simus?
Linus A very clever person—now he's set on tragedy, and of all the actors, he is by far the best cook, so it seems to his associates, and of cooks, he's the finest actor . . .
<lacuna?>
Linus The man is starving!
Heracles Say whatever you will: I'm hungry, you can count on that!

This silly exchange finds Heracles' famous music teacher attempting to give him a literary education; Linus predicts that Heracles' first choice of a book will reveal his nature, and in this, he is not wrong. Heracles selects a cookbook, but has no interest in its author (who comes in for some ribbing as well). While some editors posit a lacuna after line 16 to explain Linus' startled comment at the beginning of 17, I believe that Rusten is absolutely right to suggest that perhaps "we are to imagine some sudden action on Heracles' part—such as eating the papyrus book roll!"[50]

Devouring non-edibles in a fit of hunger is a trait of the gluttonous Heracles that emphasizes absence, instead of abundance. In Aristophanes' *Frogs*, Plathane the innkeeper complains about how Heracles "ate up the fresh cheese, the wretch, with the baskets and all!" (τὸν τυρόν γε τὸν χλωρόν, τάλαν / ὃν οὗτος αὐτοῖς τοῖς ταλάροις κατήσθιεν, 559–60). In the *Frogs*, at least Heracles manages to include actual foodstuffs in his frenzy; in a satyr play(?) of Ion, he devours the cooking materials for roasted meat, but possibly not even the meat itself. In the short fragment, Heracles is unable to wait for a communal meal to begin; instead "during the religious silence, he gobbled down both the kindling and the charcoal!" (ὑπὸ δὲ τῆς εὐφημίας / κατέπινε καὶ τὰ κᾶλα καὶ τοὺς ἄνθρακας, fr. 29).

Heracles' habit of eating household objects is both humorous and degrading. In the structuralist schema that divides humans from animals based on whether they consume their meat cooked or raw, where do books, baskets, logs, and coal fit in? Heracles seems to slot in somewhere between goat and garbage can. His laughable inability to control his hunger, much to Linus' consternation, is a welcome lapse of control in comparison to the episode in which Heracles murders Linus. As recounted in Pseudo-Apollodorus (2.4.9) and Diodorus (3.67.2), when Linus criticizes Heracles' singing or slowness in learning, Heracles loses his temper and beats his teacher to death with a kithara.[51] This frightening episode is depicted on several Attic red figure vases from the first half of the fifth century BCE; in these images, Heracles kills Linus with a stool.[52] Alexis' comic take on Heracles' education retains the same dynamic of bad pupil disappointing his teacher, but transforms Heracles' propensity to fatal violence into degrading gluttony. As we laugh at his disinterest in a literary education, we also deflate the threat that he will respond to his failure by killing the authorities.

This survey of Heracles' appearance in the rather scanty remains of Sicilian comedy, satyr play, and Old and Middle Comedy reveals some of the ways that the buffoonish Heracles can deflate heroic violence. In some examples, his gluttony makes him an object of mockery by subjecting him to physical appetites; but after this "uncrowning," he is restored to the role of victor by his triumph over a simplistic villain or ogre or release of an enslaved satyr chorus, leading to celebrations and abundance. In other cases, the kind of violence and skill required to win competitions in athletics or Labors against monsters is supplemented or supplanted by Heracles' superior ability to eat, drink, and feast. Overall, comic Heracles' contact with the material bodily lower stratum aligns with Bakhtin's process of degradation through grotesque consumption, followed by joyful renewal in victory.

The Comic Heracles in Euripides' *Alcestis*

The peculiar power of the carnivalesque Heracles—that is, the connection between his buffoonery and his victory—is illustrated by his role in Euripides' *Alcestis*. In this play, I argue, both the buffoonish Heracles and the epinician Heracles are required to bring about a happy ending, and the emphasis on the material bodily lower stratum brings these two roles together. In the larger mythical tradition of Alcestis' voluntary death in Admetus' place, Heracles does not always participate: his presence in Phrynichus' version remains undetermined, and in Lesky's compilation of folk sources, the myth does not even necessarily end with the couple's happy reunion.[53] Yet in Euripides' drama, the plot's resolution relies entirely on Heracles, who arrives at Admetus' palace just as it is plunged into grief by Alcestis' long-awaited death. At Admetus' insistence, Heracles is received as a guest and enjoys a solitary but drunken feast; horrified when he discovers his friend's desolation, Heracles wrestles Death himself and returns Alcestis to her husband.[54] Heracles' successful rescue of Alcestis is revealed in the opening of the play, eliminating any suspense about the resolution of the plot. In his debate with Death, Apollo predicts that Heracles, "after being received as a guest in these halls of Admetus, will snatch this woman from you by force" (… ξενωθεὶς τοῖσδ' ἐν Ἀδμήτου δόμοις / βίᾳ γυναῖκα τήνδε σ' ἐξαιρήσεται, 68–9). Heracles' characteristic method "by force" or "with violence" (*bia*) is specified here.

The main interest in the play is therefore not *whether* Alcestis is saved, but *how* the rescue is to unfold. Heracles' intervention arrests a cycle of extended life and unintended consequences that is reiterated throughout the play: Apollo's son Asclepius was killed by Zeus for daring to raise the dead, in return for which Apollo killed Zeus' sons, the Cyclopes; Zeus in turn sentenced Apollo to a period of servitude to Admetus. In return for Admetus' kindness and generosity, Apollo tricked (δολώσας, 12) the Moirai into allowing Admetus to delay his death by providing a substitute. Yet Apollo's gift is revealed to be no boon at all, resulting in the loss of a beloved mother, mistress, and wife, the fracturing of Admetus' relationship with his parents, and the loss of Admetus' reputation. Goldfarb convincingly argues that much of the play's tension results from the conflicting obligations of *philia* and *xenia*.[55] The play pits these values against one another until Admetus and his family are all tied up in a terrible knot.

Against this background, Heracles' introduction comes like a thunderclap. I argue that Heracles' comic presentation allows for the emergence of the epinician victor who conquers death and saves the day. Unlike nearly everyone else in the play, who rushes to avoid death, Heracles is willing to confront Death head-on. His attitude is startling in a narrative dominated by the desire to escape from death, to achieve (even if temporarily) immortality.[56] As revealed in his drunken philosophizing, his embrace of the carnivalesque, which celebrates the cyclical nature of birth and death, facilitates an acceptance of the possibility of death. In leaping to face off against Death in a wrestling match, Heracles' role as epinician victor can take precedence, leading to inevitable success.[57] I argue that it is precisely this combination of carousing and courage that enables *Alcestis*' Heracles to become the "superhero" that Admetus and Alcestis need.

The play offers—and then rejects—other possible saviors who are capable of bringing back the dead: Asclepius, the son of Apollo who raised the dead contrary to Zeus' will, and Orpheus, the famous singer who charmed the king and the queen of the Underworld with his song in an ultimately failed attempt to resurrect his wife. In the parodos, the Chorus sings of Asclepius:

> μόνος δ' ἄν, εἰ φῶς τόδ' ἦν
> ὄμμασιν δεδορκώς
> Φοίβου παῖς, προλιπεῖν
> ἦνεν ἕδρας σκοτίους Ἄιδα τε πύλας.
>
> 122–5

> The son of Phoebus alone, if he still looked upon this light with his eyes, could cause her to leave behind the dark seats and gates of Hades . . .

The Chorus's portrait of Asclepius is mixed. On the one hand, he possessed the extraordinary power to return the dead to life. On the other, his misuse of this same power has led not only to his own death—and thus his inability to help at this juncture—but also eventually to the death of Alcestis herself.[58] Thus, even if he still lived, his use of medicine to rob Death of the life owed to him would again violate Zeus' law and incur punishment. Medicine, then, fails as a route for saving Alcestis, a failure that is reflected in the limited effectiveness of the *paian*, as Swift has shown.[59]

Orpheus also figures as a potential savior in two different guises. In his grief, Admetus wishes to have Orpheus' melodious voice and song to retrieve his wife from Persephone and Hades. While medicine is applied to the physical body, music possesses the power to influence the authorities who control the souls of the dead.

> εἰ δ' Ὀρφέως μοι γλῶσσα καὶ μέλος παρῆν,
> ὥστ' ἢ κόρην Δήμητρος ἢ κείνης πόσιν
> ὕμνοισι κηλήσαντά σ' ἐξ Ἅιδου λαβεῖν,
> κατῆλθον ἄν . . .
>
> 357–60

> But if I had the tongue and tune of Orpheus, such that I could charm the daughter of Demeter or her husband with songs and seize you from Hades, I would have gone down . . .

But two factors undermine Admetus' sentiment: while Orpheus persuades the rulers of the Underworld to release Eurydice, he does not succeed in restoring her to life; furthermore, Admetus' wish is expressed in a contrafactual conditional statement, an admission from the start that his wish can never be fulfilled. If Orphic music is not able to save Alcestis, neither is the knowledge transmitted through Orphic writings.

The Chorus later treats Orphic wisdom and Asclepiadean medicine together as forces insufficient to overcome Necessity. With both of these methods failing as cures or remedies, the Chorus goes on to urge Admetus to accept Alcestis' death as an inevitability:

ηὗρον οὐδέ τι φάρμακον
Θρήσσαις ἐν σανίσιν, τὰς
Ὀρφεία κατέγραψεν
γῆρυς, οὐδ' ὅσα Φοῖβος Ἀ-
σκληπιάδαις ἔδωκε
φάρμακα πολυπόνοις
ἀντιτεμὼν βροτοῖσιν.

966-72

I have found no cure on Thracian tablets, which the Orphic voice inscribed, nor did Phoebus give such drugs to the sons of Asclepius, having cut them as a remedy for much-belabored mortals.

The Orphic writings described above may refer to alternative medical therapies, or even eschatological bliss found through induction into the Orphic mysteries.[60] Yet even a method associated with cult mysteries does not have the potential to overcome Necessity or Death. Apollo has no healing knowledge to pass along through the Asclepiadae, and his technique of relying on a trick to deceive the Moirai cannot be employed again—though the Chorus begs him to find "some contrivance" (ἔξευρε μηχανάν τιν' Ἀδμήτῳ κακῶν, 221).

Music, medicine, and trickery all fail as means to the end of saving Alcestis and, by extension, Admetus. Instead, what will succeed is Heraclean violence (*bia*), as Apollo prophesies in his first mention of Heracles (69). But this is not the violence of Euripides' *Heracles*, which is improperly aimed at family members, or the violence Heracles directs against his own household in Sophocles' *Trachiniae*. Here his violence is constrained by his roles as buffoon and epinician victor. Where previously in this play violence had led only to death, Heracles' force is put in service of life.

Heracles' introduction in the play interrupts a stream of nearly unmitigated grief over the death of the virtuous Alcestis. From the start, he does not share the other characters' attitude towards death. Over and over again, various characters have asked whether Alcestis' death can be put off any longer, and the resounding answer is no, no longer. So it is startling when Heracles treats the possibility of his own death with equanimity. He comes to Admetus' palace on his way to capture the Mares of Diomedes. Strikingly, Heracles seems to accept the terrible burden of his Labors without complaint or resentment. When the Chorus reacts with alarm over how he must confront Diomedes and seize his man-eating Horses, Heracles replies calmly, "At any rate, it is not possible for me to renounce these toils" (ἀλλ' οὐδ' ἀπειπεῖν μὴν πόνους οἷόν τ' ἐμοί, 487). The Chorus points out "Either you will come back after killing him or you will die and remain there" (κτανὼν ἄρ' ἥξεις ἢ θανὼν αὐτοῦ μενεῖς, 488), to which Heracles again calmly responds, "This is not the first race that I would run" (οὐ τόνδ' ἀγῶνα πρῶτον ἂν δράμοιμ' ἐγώ, 489). His statement is akin to our modern slang, "This ain't my first rodeo," a casual statement of confidence.

But his casualness is paired with resoluteness. This conversation between Heracles and the Chorus establishes the ethos of the particular Heracles that is needed in this play. Heracles does not kick against the pricks; instead, he declares:

> καὶ τόνδε τοὐμοῦ δαίμονος πόνον λέγεις
> σκληρὸς γὰρ αἰεὶ καὶ πρὸς αἶπος ἔρχεται ... (499–500)
> ἀλλ' οὔτις ἔστιν ὃς τὸν Ἀλκμήνης γόνον (505)
> τρέσαντα χεῖρα πολεμίαν ποτ' ὄψεται.
>
> 499–500, 505–6

This labor you describe is in accordance with my destiny, which is always difficult and steep ... but no one will ever look upon the son of Alcmene trembling at an enemy's hand.

His ready acceptance of his *daimōn* or destiny stands in contrast with Admetus' evasion of his own death and Alcestis' mourning of hers. His greatest commitment is to the display of courage against an enemy and a renunciation of cowardice, even in the face of death. His bravado is thus linked to the values associated with the *kallinikos* victor as expressed at the end of Euripides' later play *Heracles*.[61] His devotion to courage here foreshadows the importance that his role as epinician victor will play in the rescue of Alcestis.

Before Heracles can emerge as savior and victor, though, he displays his buffoonish side. The servant's account of his drunkenness provokes a sudden shift in tone after extended scenes of mourning and a bruising argument between Admetus and his father Pheres. While everyone else has been grappling with the loss of Alcestis, Heracles, it turns out, has been feasting within the halls. His celebratory actions conflict boorishly and painfully with the mood of the household. The speech presents themes associated with Heracles' comic manifestations:

... ἀλλὰ τοῦδ' οὔπω ξένου
κακίον' ἐς τήνδ' ἑστίαν ἐδεξάμην ... (750)
ἔπειτα δ' οὔτι σωφρόνως ἐδέξατο (753)
τὰ προστυχόντα ξένια, συμφορὰν μαθών,
ἀλλ', εἴ τι μὴ φέροιμεν, ὤτρυνεν φέρειν.
ποτῆρα δ' ἐν χερσὶ κίσσινον λαβὼν
πίνει μελαίνης μητρὸς εὔζωρον μέθυ,
ἕως ἐθέρμην' αὐτὸν ἀμφιβᾶσα φλὸξ
οἴνου. στέφει δὲ κρᾶτα μυρσίνης κλάδοις,
ἄμουσ' ὑλακτῶν· δισσὰ δ' ἦν μέλη κλύειν·
ὁ μὲν γὰρ ᾖδε, τῶν ἐν Ἀδμήτου κακῶν
οὐδὲν προτιμῶν, οἰκέται δ' ἐκλαίομεν
δέσποιναν ... (763)
καὶ νῦν ἐγὼ μὲν ἐν δόμοισιν ἑστιῶ (765)
ξένον, πανοῦργον κλῶπα καὶ λῃστήν τινα.

749–50, 753–63, 765–6

But I have never welcomed a worse guest than this one at this hearth ... Then, he did not accept the hospitality on offer, although he knew our misfortune, but if we did not bring him something, he ordered us to bring it. And taking the drinking cup of ivy in his hands, he drinks the wine from the dark grape unmixed, until the flame of wine embraced and warmed him. He wreathes his head with myrtle branches, howling off-key. There were two types of song to hear: this man was singing, taking no notice of the troubles of Admetus' house, while we servants were lamenting our mistress ... and now I entertain a stranger in the home, some wicked thief or bandit.

The aggrieved servant's complaint recalls the fragment of Epicharmus' *Busiris* described above.[62] This servant uses more elevated language to describe how appalled he is at Heracles' greed and his ill-mannered behavior. Heracles' appetite for food and drink, typical comic fare, is totally excessive: he demands a huge feast; he drinks unmixed wine; he sings badly. These actions are bad enough, but they are particularly offensive in a household plunged into mourning and seemingly in the grips of foolishly made, intractable bargains. The tension is made clear in the two kinds of songs which ought to exist in mutually exclusive environments: the drinking song of the symposium and the funeral lament.

One result of this clash is to frame Heracles' comic role as inappropriate and ill-suited for a play about such serious themes. This is comedy intruding on tragedy, a category error. The prevailing mood is so somber that Heracles' actions provoke discomfort, rather than hilarity. The audience receives the servant's perspective *first*, before seeing Heracles' carousing for themselves; he offers the perspective of the household, which is critical and unsympathetic. Heracles' engagement with the carnivalesque is solipsistic, hardly the popular form of a communal phenomenon. Moreover, even as he receives the hospitality of Admetus, out of Admetus' regard for their long friendship, his inopportune feasting threatens to disrupt the bonds of *philia* and *xenia*.

Heracles' buffoonish behavior culminates in a speech that is equally ill-suited to the context. He emerges onto the stage and launches into a fit of drunk, somewhat sophomoric philosophizing, perhaps reminiscent of when the symposium runs a little too long.[63] This is a hero who turns the encounter with the material bodily lower stratum into a life philosophy:

> βροτοῖς ἅπασι κατθανεῖν ὀφείλεται,
> κοὐκ ἔστι θνητῶν ὅστις ἐξεπίσταται
> τὴν αὔριον μέλλουσαν εἰ βιώσεται·
> τὸ τῆς τύχης γὰρ ἀφανὲς οἷ προβήσεται,
> κἄστ' οὐ διδακτὸν οὐδ' ἁλίσκεται τέχνηι.
> ταῦτ' οὖν ἀκούσας καὶ μαθὼν ἐμοῦ πάρα
> εὔφραινε σαυτόν, πῖνε, τὸν καθ' ἡμέραν
> βίον λογίζου σόν, τὰ δ' ἄλλα τῆς τύχης.
> τίμα δὲ καὶ τὴν πλεῖστον ἡδίστην θεῶν
> Κύπριν βροτοῖσιν· εὐμενὴς γὰρ ἡ θεός.
> τὰ δ' ἄλλ' ἔασον πάντα καὶ πιθοῦ λόγοις
> ἐμοῖσιν, εἴπερ ὀρθά σοι δοκῶ λέγειν.
> οἶμαι μέν. οὔκουν τὴν ἄγαν λύπην ἀφεὶς
> πίηι μεθ' ἡμῶν [τάσδ' ὑπερβαλὼν τύχας,
> στεφάνοις πυκασθείς]; καὶ σάφ' οἶδ' ὁθούνεκα
> τοῦ νῦν σκυθρωποῦ καὶ ξυνεστῶτος φρενῶν
> μεθορμιεῖ σε πίτυλος ἐμπεσὼν σκύφου.
> ὄντας δὲ θνητοὺς θνητὰ καὶ φρονεῖν χρεών.
>
> 782–99

All mortals are obligated to die, and there is no one of mortals who knows whether he will live to see the following day. Where the outcome of fortune leads is hidden; it cannot be taught, or grasped by means of skill. Therefore, since you have heard and learned these things from me, cheer up! Drink, and consider today's life yours, but the rest, fortune's. Honor Cypris, the sweetest of all the gods to mortals, for this goddess is kindly. But let go of all the rest and trust my sentiments, if indeed you think that I speak correctly, which I think you do. Well then, won't you send away your extreme grief and drink with me [surpassing these misfortunes and crowned with wreaths]? And I know clearly that when the force of the wine cup falls on you, it will release you from your current gloom and clotted mind. For as mortals, we must also consider mortal thoughts.

Heracles' outlook is informed by a life of unpredictability of the most extreme kind: he constantly confronts death and undertakes Labors with the highest risks, forcing him to admit that he has no purchase on what his fortune holds. In response, he turns to the pleasures of the lower body: drink and sex. There is some freedom in this realization; by surrendering to *tychē*, Heracles also releases fear, and he can experience gladness and cheer in a way totally absent otherwise from the play.

But Heracles' philosophy is also completely isolated from the events of the play thus far. The message is "no one knows the day he will die," but for Alcestis the day of her death *is* appointed and has been long and carefully anticipated. As Apollo announces as the play opens, "On this day, it has been fated for her to die" (τῇδε γάρ σφ' ἐν ἡμέρᾳ / θανεῖν πέπρωται, 20–1), and the fact that this is the "fated day" is reiterated throughout.[64] Admetus too states that he has been worn down by his foreknowledge of her impending doom (420–1). Moreover, Heracles himself proves his own philosophy wrong. Through his efforts, Admetus and Alcestis manage to outwit fate and fortune, extending their lives beyond their appointed days.

Nevertheless, Heracles' attitude is part of what enables him to disrupt the dynamics of the play. Comic Heracles' carnivalesque characteristics are wrapped up in a more honest confrontation with death, in part because carnival's celebration of life, fecundity, and generation is one part of a cycle that by nature includes death. As Heracles savors the pleasures of living, he also acknowledges the necessity of death for all mortals, illustrating the essential connection between death and renewal.[65] And because the nature of life and death is cyclical, Heracles' acceptance of death—expressed in the transactional language of obligation—leads to victory over fear of death, leading further to renewal and a new life for Alcestis.

Even as the comic role of Heracles establishes a foundation for his decision to take on Death, it also leads temporarily to humiliation. The servant's disapproval is justified when Heracles comes to recognize the inappropriateness of his own behavior in the house of mourning. He had crowned himself for the banquet, but ironically his untimeliness causes him to be "uncrowned"; this process is symbolized by his removal of his crown when he comes to realize the error of his ways. This decrowning is necessary, however, because it will enable him to be recrowned as the victor over Death. Once he recognizes that Admetus deceived him—something he suspected anyway—he quickly sobers up and determines to return an equally generous favor to his friend. The comic undertones of Heracles' speech are replaced with serious, "high" language:

> ὦ πολλὰ τλᾶσα καρδία καὶ χεὶρ ἐμή,
> νῦν δεῖξον οἷον παῖδά σ' ἡ Τιρυνθία
> ἐγείνατ' Ἠλεκτρύωνος Ἀλκμήνη Διί.
> δεῖ γάρ με σῶσαι τὴν θανοῦσαν ἀρτίως
> γυναῖκα κἀς τόνδ' αὖθις ἱδρῦσαι δόμον
> Ἄλκηστιν Ἀδμήτωι θ' ὑπουργῆσαι χάριν.
> ἐλθὼν δ' ἄνακτα τὸν μελάμπτερον νεκρῶν
> Θάνατον φυλάξω, καί νιν εὑρήσειν δοκῶ
> πίνοντα τύμβου πλησίον προσφαγμάτων.
> κἄνπερ λοχαίας αὐτὸν ἐξ ἕδρας συθεὶς
> μάρψω, κύκλον γε περιβαλὼν χεροῖν ἐμαῖν,
> οὐκ ἔστιν ὅστις αὐτὸν ἐξαιρήσεται
> μογοῦντα πλευρά, πρὶν γυναῖκ' ἐμοὶ μεθῆι.

837–49

O heart that has endured so much, and my hand, now reveal what sort of son Tirynthian Alcmene, daughter of Electryon, bore to Zeus! I must rescue the woman who just died and settle Alcestis again in this house, returning a favor to Admetus. I will go and lie in wait for the black-winged lord of the dead, Death. I think that I will find him drinking from the sacrifices near the tomb. And if I rush out from a hidden spot and take hold of him, encircling him with my arms, no one will take him away from me as he suffers pain at his sides, until he gives the woman up to me.

With his elevated diction and heroic stance, Heracles regains his stature, which had been so degraded in the previous comic scene. His focus shifts from the lower stratum of the body to its upper parts, his heart and arms.[66] The glorification of his appetites is eclipsed by his serious intention to return Alcestis to Admetus. Heracles proposes a wrestling contest with Death, drawing upon his reputation as an athlete and re-engaging with his role as conqueror of the Labors. He goes on to suggest that if he fails to overcome Death, he will go to the Underworld himself to negotiate with Persephone and Hades, returning with Alcestis as a successful Orpheus.[67] This possibility becomes unnecessary; Heracles' force succeeds on the first try. As Garner and Swift have shown, Heracles' language evokes the themes of epinician poetry.[68] In this way, Heracles also reapproaches the role of an epinician victor whose triumph benefits not only himself, but also his larger community of *philoi*.

The epinician undertones of Heracles' declaration come to full fruition in his deceptive explanation for how he acquires the veiled young woman.[69] He explains that she is one of the victory prizes for a public athletics competition:

πολλῶι δὲ μόχθωι χεῖρας ἦλθεν εἰς ἐμάς·
ἀγῶνα γὰρ πάνδημον εὑρίσκω τινὰς
τιθέντας, ἀθληταῖσιν ἄξιον πόνον,
ὅθεν κομίζω τήνδε νικητήρια
λαβών. τὰ μὲν γὰρ κοῦφα τοῖς νικῶσιν ἦν
ἵππους ἄγεσθαι, τοῖσι δ' αὖ τὰ μείζονα
νικῶσι, πυγμὴν καὶ πάλην, βουφόρβια·
γυνὴ δ' ἐπ' αὐτοῖς εἵπετ'· ἐντυχόντι δὲ
αἰσχρὸν παρεῖναι κέρδος ἦν τόδ' εὐκλεές.
ἀλλ', ὥσπερ εἶπον, σοὶ μέλειν γυναῖκα χρή·
οὐ γὰρ κλοπαίαν ἀλλὰ σὺν πόνωι λαβὼν
ἥκω ...

1025–36

She came into my hands by great effort: for I found some people setting a public competition, a challenge worthy for champions, from which I carried off this woman as a prize of victory. The winners of the lighter contests won horses, while those conquering the greater events, boxing and wrestling, herds of oxen. The woman followed on these. It would have been shameful for me, since I happened upon it, to pass by this glorious profit. But just as I said, you must take care of this woman. For I did not take her by theft, but with labor ...

Heracles' fabricated competition is all the more believable because of its proximity to truth. In using terms frequently associated with his Labors (*mochthos, ponos*), he assimilates this competition to acts he undertakes because of his fate. His acquisition of a woman as a prize in a match aligns with his frequent association with heroic competition, as explored in Sophocles' *Trachiniae*. Moreover, this fantasy can be understood as a happy version of the mad Heracles' delusions that he competes in athletics in Euripides' later *Heracles*. Here Heracles presents himself as an athletic victor as a kind of ruse, but the reality that he has triumphed in a variation of a wrestling match is soon revealed.

Heracles overcomes Death by the sheer force of his bare hands. As he reveals to Admetus, he accosts Death by Alcestis' tomb, eliminating the need to travel to the Underworld. His return marks him truly as a victor; although he no longer wears a physical crown from the feast, Alcestis serves as the ultimate prize. He is thus "recrowned" after his comic humiliation, becoming the savior Admetus requires:

Ηρ.	μάχην συνάψας δαιμόνων τῶι κυρίωι.
Αδ.	ποῦ τόνδε Θανάτωι φὴις ἀγῶνα συμβαλεῖν;
Ηρ.	τύμβον παρ' αὐτόν, ἐκ λόχου μάρψας χεροῖν.

1140–2

Heracles I joined in battle against the lord of the spirits.
Admetus Where do you say you contended in this contest with Death?
Heracles By the tomb itself, when I ambushed him and seized him in my hands.

Their hand-to-hand combat is described as a battle (*machē*) and a contest (*agōn*), recalling the specific diction used earlier in anticipation of Heracles' conflict with Diomedes (486, 489). In Heracles' triumph we see the fulfillment of his role as epinician victor: the prize of Alcestis proves his excellence while serving to make her household whole again. Heracles' violence is channeled into a competition of physical superiority against a worthy adversary and harnessed to bring about a tremendous benefit to his *philoi*. The excessiveness he demonstrated in his boozing is transformed into an exceptional deed of extraordinary *philia*.

Alcestis' Heracles is a figure of carnival ideas and carnival laughter, who represents the material bodily lower stratum and is degraded, but who in celebrating life also accepts its ultimate end, death. While much of the play is predicated on the avoidance of Death, Heracles is the only one who lies in wait for *him*. He temporarily overcomes Death, mastering him in the role of athlete, which foreshadows his later apotheosis. The reconciliation of the laughable comic Heracles with the epinician Heracles reveals two things: first, the play shows how the same violence and excessiveness that aggravate his obnoxious and drunken behavior can also be yoked to bring about the magnanimous salvation of his friends; second, it demonstrates how the comic Heracles' engagement with the carnivalesque's cyclical nature can lead to recrowning and victory.

A Polyphony of Genres in Aristophanes' *Frogs*

The first half of Aristophanes' *Frogs* puts Heracles on the stage in multiple guises. Dionysus intends to embark on a *katabasis* to retrieve Euripides from the Underworld, and though several heroes in Greek mythology accomplish such a journey, he explicitly mimics Heracles' tradition. The play first directly portrays Heracles on stage in conversation with his brother Dionysus. Then, during Dionysus and his slave Xanthias' journey, they take turns donning the costume of Heracles, each embracing the role of a mock Heracles in different ways; as Dionysus competes with the chorus of frog-swans, he imitates Heracles' engagement with fantastic beasts. Finally, several inhabitants of the Underworld remember Heracles, revealing both the good fun he brought with him and the destruction he left in his wake. These varying views of Heracles allow for a juxtaposition of his roles in different poetic genres, and the significance of this particular myth makes it an ideal platform for exploring Heracles' multifaceted literary roles.

Aristophanes' adaptation of Heracles' journey to the Underworld positions the play within a broad tradition of *katabasis* narratives. A number of other mythological precedents were available to Aristophanes, from Theseus and Peirithous' failed attempt to kidnap Persephone, to Orpheus' fruitless retrieval of Eurydice, to the journey Dionysus himself took to rescue Semele and introduce her to Olympus.[70] In relying on Heracles as the model narrative of a successful *Hadesfahrt*, the play engages predecessors from other genres. An archaic epic *katabasis* of Heracles has been hypothesized as a shared source for a number of authors from Bacchylides to Virgil, and Panyassis' *Heraclea* may have included Heracles' descent to the Underworld.[71] Stesichorus wrote a *Cerberus* (fr. 165 Finglass), and Pindar composed a dithyramb (2) entitled "Heracles' Katabasis or Cerberus" (fr. 70b), showing that the task can be featured in the lyric tradition as well. The *katabasis* myth appears as a theme in satyr play, where, as discussed above, Heracles' physical appetites and role as victor feature prominently. Sophocles wrote an *Epi Tainario* (fr. 198) and a *Cerberus* (fr. 327),[72] and Euripides wrote a satyric *Eurystheus* about the expedition to the Underworld (frr. 371–80).[73]

But Heracles' descent to the Underworld is perhaps best represented for us in the genre of tragedy. As Matthew Farmer has shown, Aristophanes' comedies regularly engage with the genre of tragedy, creating a "culture of tragedy" in their comic Athens; he distinguishes tragic culture from tragic parody, both of which appear in the *Frogs*.[74] More specifically, Gregory Dobrov has established how Aristophanes' *Frogs* functions as a "sustained mimesis" of the *Peirithous* of Euripides (or perhaps of Critias), a tragedy that also stages an exchange between Aeacus and Heracles at the gate to the Underworld (fr. 1).[75] Although the *Frogs* does not explicitly parody Euripides' *Heracles*, a conversation from *Heracles* provides a brief glimpse into how Heracles' return from Hades is treated in a "high" genre. Amphitryon asks his son about the feat with reverent wonder:

Αμ. ἦλθες γὰρ ὄντως δώματ' εἰς Ἅιδου, τέκνον;
Ηρ. καὶ θῆρά γ' ἐς φῶς τὸν τρίκρανον ἤγαγον.

> **Αμ.** μάχηι κρατήσας ἢ θεᾶς δωρήμασιν;
> **Ηρ.** μάχηι· τὰ μυστῶν δ' ὄργι' εὐτύχησ' ἰδών.
>
> 610–13
>
> **Amphitryon** Did you really go to the house of Hades, son?
> **Heracles** I did, and I brought the three-headed beast into the light.
> **Amphitryon** Did you defeat him in a fight, or by the gifts of the goddess?
> **Heracles** In a fight; because I observed the rites of the initiates, I succeeded.

Even for a hero as accomplished as Heracles, a safe return from Hades is difficult to fathom. His journey requires not only courage and persistence, but also the successful use of violence in mastering the three-headed dog. Heracles attributes the success of his attack to his initiation into the mysteries at Eleusis, a reference that not only acknowledges Attic religious rituals to an audience of Athenians, but also invokes his role in cult and anticipates his apotheosis.[76]

The story, then, is ripe for a literary carnivalization that puts various manifestations of Heracles into conversation with each other.[77] In contrast with the "serious" genres of epic, tragedy, and lyric, comedy tends to bring its gods, demigods, and heroes low, on a plane equal with contemporary life, short-circuiting epic distance.[78] In the *Frogs*, the comic strategies of parody, caricature, and deflation are applied to Heracles' various roles in the "higher" genres. Charles Platter's study *Aristophanes and the Carnival of Genres* shows how "the techniques Bakhtin developed to describe the interaction of different genres within the modern novel are effective tools for describing the myriad juxtapositions of language levels that make up Aristophanic comedy and their tendency to undermine with laughter even aspects of Athenian cultural life of which the poet might have approved."[79]

In this section, I extend Platter's analysis by investigating how Aristophanes uses a multiplicity of Heracleses to create a carnivalizing comic discourse. This display of centrifugal forces makes explicit a destabilization of the central defining characteristics of Heracles. The radical ambivalence of carnivalized discourse leads to the disintegration of "Heracles" at the gate of the Underworld, as his costume gets passed back and forth between Dionysus and Xanthias until it disappears altogether. The breakdown of the unity of Heracles as a coherent figure has further implications for the treatment of heroic violence. As the many Heracleses collide, their incompatibilities become more pronounced, suggesting an analogous conflict between the different strategies employed by the various genres to constrain and justify Heracles' violence. In the fragmentation of Heracles then is also the breakdown of the project to tame Heracles, illustrating his resistance to reform.

Heracles in Retirement

The first view of Heracles puts him directly on the stage, now retired from his Labors and deified. The play's initial representation of the real Heracles may have surprised: this is not the buffoon of other comic plays, who is reduced to the behavior of a mindless animal in pursuit of food or who wields violence against exaggerated villains.[80] Instead, Aristophanes rather counterintuitively gives us a more civilized hero, one who is less ridiculous than the play's main character, Dionysus. His elevation undercuts Dionysus, who plays the role of goofy little brother. Their similarities invite comparison: they are both sons of Zeus by mortal mothers, recipients of cult worship, and relative latecomers to Olympus. Yet in other ways, they could hardly be more different. Heracles' life of toil and suffering stands in stark contrast to Dionysus' reputation for dissolution and sacred revelry. Even their comic personae differ: Heracles' is primarily preoccupied with food and drink (and women, to a lesser extent), while Dionysus' tends toward drink and sensuality.

The contrast serves to make Heracles the straight man, Dionysus the fool, and Xanthias the comic relief. The play opens with Dionysus in an unusual costume: in addition to his typical comic garb of a long saffron robe and buskins, he wears Heracles' attributes—a lion skin paired with a giant club.[81] Dionysus' assumption of Heracles' identity highlights an incongruity. Like a child wearing a parent's over-large clothes in order to project an aura of authority, Dionysus' apparel only emphasizes how ill-suited he is to "play" Heracles as a theatrical role.[82] His attempts to make his capabilities more convincing with external signs only prime him to be deflated. When Dionysus rattles Heracles' door with his club, Heracles calls out, "Who knocked on the door? He came at it like a centaur, whoever . . . Tell me, what is this?" (τίς τὴν θύραν ἐπάταξεν; ὡς κενταυρικῶς / ἐνήλαθ' ὅστις· εἰπέ μοι τουτὶ τί ἦν; 38–9). Upon seeing Dionysus in his ridiculous get-up, Heracles bursts out in uncontrollable laughter: "But I'm not able to scare off the laughter when I see a lion-skin worn over the saffron robe! What is the purpose? Why have the boot and the club joined forces?" (ἀλλ' οὐχ οἷός τ' εἴμ' ἀποσοβῆσαι τὸν γέλων, / ὁρῶν λεοντῆν ἐπὶ κροκωτῷ κειμένην. / τίς ὁ νοῦς; τί κόθορνος καὶ ῥόπαλον ξυνηλθέτην; 45–7). In these lines, Heracles articulates the heart of the joke that will run on for the next six hundred lines: the strange juxtaposition of Dionysus' aspirations to the high-heroic (represented by the club) against the reality of his low-comic absurdity (represented in the actor's boot). When Heracles laughs at Dionysus' get-up, he is articulating the inconcinnity for the audience as well; for once we laugh with, not at, Heracles.

Heracles' opening lines comparing the intensity of Dionysus' knock to a Centaur's charge quickly activate an array of associations with his roles as monster-slayer, victor, and Eleusinian initiate. The joke shows that Dionysus is incompetent at "playing a hero," for in announcing his presence the way he imagines Heracles would, he completely overdoes it; instead of the authoritative knock of a confident hero, he overcompensates, sounding more like a wild, uncontrollable half-beast. In contrast, by raising the possibility that Centaurs are attacking his house, Heracles immediately reminds the audience of his previous involvement in defeating them in epic and tragedy. Heracles' battle with the Centaurs was associated with his capture of the Erymanthian Boar, and was possibly described in the now-lost epics by Pisander and Panyassis.[83] Though not considered among his twelve canonical Labors, the Centauromachy is praised by the Chorus in Euripides' *Heracles*:

> τάν τ' ὀρεινόμον ἀγρίων
> Κενταύρων ποτὲ γένναν
> ἔστρωσεν τόξοις φονίοις,
> ἐναίρων πτανοῖς βέλεσιν.
>
> 364–7

He once laid low the hill-dwelling race of wild Centaurs with his deadly bow, slaying them with his winged arrows.

Yet in exaggerating Dionysus' knock, Heracles too may have drawn a laugh. This Heracles has now retired from the life of battles and victories, and perhaps his eagerness to remember his heroic past suggests that he is itching for a little action.

Furthermore, Heracles' battle against the Centaurs is part of the sequence of events that precedes his *katabasis*, Heracles' signal act for the *Frogs*. According to Diodorus Siculus and Ps.-Apollodorus, Heracles required initiation in the rites of Eleusis in order to approach the Underworld.[84] He could not be initiated, however, until the pollution of his slaughter of the Centaurs was purified.[85] The significance of the theme of the Eleusinian mysteries and Dionysus' relationship to them have been persuasively explicated by scholars such as Segal, Bowie, and Lada-Richards.[86] In reenacting many elements of the Eleusinian rituals in the course of his *katabasis*, Dionysus imitates Heracles, the most famous of initiates.[87]

But as their conversation continues, Heracles' comic appetites join his other traits as the epic hero and religious initiate. In reference to Euripides, Dionysus claims he is motivated by a "desire" (πόθος, 53), and "such a longing" (τοιοῦτος ἵμερος, 59), terms frequently used in erotic contexts.[88] But Dionysus' desire for Euripides is too powerful to be compared to lust, even Heracles', the famous sexual athlete.[89] Dionysus insists that the only way in which Heracles can comprehend the intensity of his longing is by comparing it to Heracles' appetite, thus introducing the stock comic motif of Heracles' hunger. Dionysus asks, "Have you sometime, in the past, experienced a sudden craving for pea soup?" (ἤδη ποτ' ἐπεθύμησας ἐξαίφνης ἔτνους; 62). Heracles affirms with great enthusiasm, now fully able to relate to Dionysus' urge. While Heracles' lust can be an element in a tragic narrative (e.g., Sophocles' *Trachiniae* or Euripides' *Auge*), his physical hunger can only be a comic trait. This view of Heracles thus runs quite the gamut, from references to his beast-taming to his gluttony.

Just as Dionysus proposes to take Heracles' role as hero and savior, Heracles challenges Dionysus as the proper judge of tragedy. Surprisingly, he is something of a literary critic, in contrast with his presentation in the *Birds* (where he is a dunce) and in Alexis' *Linus* (where he is only interested in a cookbook). This discussion reveals the spirit of competition between them, a spirit that will also animate Dionysus' mimicry of Heracles in the Underworld. Heracles counters Dionysus' assertion that all the skillful poets have died, offering living examples of decent poets, and suggesting to Dionysus that he bring up Sophocles instead: "Then will you not lead up Sophocles, since he is superior to Euripides, if you must bring someone back from there?" (εἶτ' οὐ Σοφοκλέα πρότερον ὄντ' Εὐριπίδου / μέλλεις ἀναγαγεῖν, εἴπερ ἐκεῖθεν δεῖ σ' ἄγειν; 76–7). The play will confirm Heracles' evaluation when, with the exception of Euripides, all the characters living and dead accept the greatness of Sophocles.[90]

Aristophanes uses Heracles to express the "common sense opinion" in counterpoint to Dionysus' declarations about Euripides' poetry. When Dionysus confidently recites mangled lines of Euripides with gusto, Heracles protests, "Surely that is hogwash, even you must agree" (ἦ μὴν κόβαλά γ' ἐστίν, ὡς καὶ σοὶ δοκεῖ, 100). Dionysus' botched delivery is indeed more entertaining than enlightening, and no doubt Heracles' evaluation of the mangling is shared by the audience. So when Dionysus counters Heracles with pure insult alone—"Teach me to dine!" (δειπνεῖν με δίδασκε, 106)—as appropriate as the insult may be, we are left with the strange sense that Heracles' critical opinion is, somehow, the superior one.[91]

After bickering with Heracles, Dionysus reveals the real motivation for his arrival: he is on a fact-finding mission in preparation for a trip to the Underworld. Dionysus' comic conception of a *katabasis* emphasizes the pleasures of travel and suppresses the courage and violence required for a successful journey:

ἀλλ' ὧνπερ ἕνεκα τήνδε τὴν σκευὴν ἔχων
ἦλθον κατὰ σὴν μίμησιν, ἵνα μοι τοὺς ξένους
τοὺς σοὺς φράσειας, εἰ δεοίμην, οἷσι σὺ
ἐχρῶ τόθ', ἡνίκ' ἦλθες ἐπὶ τὸν Κέρβερον,
τούτους φράσον μοι, λιμένας, ἀρτοπώλια,
πορνεῖ', ἀναπαύλας, ἐκτροπάς, κρήνας, ὁδούς,
πόλεις, διαίτας, πανδοκευτρίας ὅπου
κόρεις ὀλίγιστοι.

108–15

But the reason I came in this get-up in imitation of you, was so that you might tell me about your hosts, in case I need them, whose reception you enjoyed when you went for Cerberus. Tell me about these, the harbors, bakeries, brothels, inns, forks in the road, springs, streets, cities, accommodations, innkeepers with the fewest bedbugs.

Dionysus treats Heracles as a knowledgeable travel agent, and his places of interest indicate that he intends to enjoy the most pleasant sojourn possible. His assumption that the trip could be congenial diminishes the difficulty of the attempt; one can almost hear in Dionysus' lines the swagger of a rivalrous brother: "if you could do it, surely it can't be all that hard." The diminishment of Heracles' most impressive Labor shifts the focus from the exertion of the upper body to the celebration of the lower body, diminishing the fear of death itself.

Heracles' guidance proves to be largely accurate, but ironically Dionysus' line of questioning will also be vindicated. For the innkeepers and the food-purveyors of the Underworld do know Heracles in a variety of guises: they suffered from his violence, feared his instability, and enjoyed his merry-making. Dionysus seems to anticipate that he can follow in the footsteps of the comic Heracles, with his physical appetites and crowning as victor; but he does not realize that in donning the costume of Heracles, he may also become a representative of the negative traits associated with heroic violence. In introducing the other roles of Heracles, the play thus subjects the whole of Heracles' legacy to scrutiny.

The Mock Heracles

The adventures of Dionysus and Xanthias in the Underworld function as a parody of Heracles' Labors. They offer a comic take on his struggles with strange beasts, and the courage and physical pain they require. Dionysus' first conflict begins at the entrance to the Underworld, when he finds himself engaging in a battle with a band of singing Frogs.[92] My reading suggests that viewing Dionysus' competition with the Frogs as a parody of a Heracles' role as monster-slayer helps to explain the presence of this initial chorus.[93] The animals Heracles confronted in life were distinctive—the Hydra's many heads, the Lion's impenetrable skin, Diomedes' Mares' unusual appetite, and so on. The Frogs here too are distinctive, for they are hybrid Frog-Swans (βατράχων κύκνων, 207) according to Charon. Charon thus prepares the audience for Frogs that do not croak like their brethren, but are "melodious singers," as swans were assumed to be in antiquity, at least at their death.[94] It is against these strange and unexpected creatures that Dionysus must battle.

I suggest that the Frogs are reminiscent of the Lernaean Hydra, leading to a contest heroic in concept, but comic in form. Again in Euripides' *Heracles*, Lycus refers dismissively to the Hydra as "a snake from the marsh" (ὕδραν ἕλειον, 152). The tyrant's aim is to de-heroize Heracles' achievement by belittling the stature of the animal he conquered—in some ways, a parallel diminution to what we see in comedy. The Chorus of Frogs describe themselves as "children from the marsh, of streams" (λιμναῖα κρηνῶν τέκνα, 211). As Moorton has observed, the Frogs are amphibians; by definition, they are liminal creatures that can cross between land and water, above and below.[95] Heracles fights at the boundaries of civilization and the wild;[96] likewise, Dionysus encounters this conflict as he crosses from upper to lower world.[97]

The actual substance of the contest between Dionysus and the Frogs remains in dispute. The contest, in a Heraclean touch, is related in some way to physical exertion and strength. Dionysus complains about their singing because he is in physical agony; perhaps the song sets the rhythm for his rowing, and their swift cadence requires that he row faster and faster—something this weak and lazy god is both unwilling and incapable of doing. Wills argues that the competition is based on aesthetics, and Dionysus defeats the gurgling Frogs with his massive flatulence;[98] MacDowell and Campbell see the contest as one of persistence;[99] Habash suggests that Dionysus triumphs by being loudest.[100] Without performance cues, the subject of the contest remains unfortunately obscure. Perhaps even the original audience was unsure about what exactly silences the Frogs, and they laughed at the sight of Dionysus' distress more than anything. I wonder whether the solution could be as simple as the Frogs singing mainly in a stationary location, so as Dionysus continues to row, he eventually rows past them and leaves them behind, their voices fading into the distance. This scenario likely requires that the Chorus playing the Frogs remain hidden behind the *skene*.[101]

But regardless of whether Dionysus shouts *brekekekex koax koax* more or less quickly, loudly, slowly, or beautifully than the Frogs, he is focused on assuming the role of victor. He defiantly shouts, "You will not prevail in this" (τούτῳ γὰρ οὐ νικήσετε, 261) and is determined to prove himself superior (ἐπικρατήσω, 266). His triumph in this parodic contest is a deflated version of Heracles' victories. Dionysus wins without great strength, skill, strategy, nor do the Frogs appear to be dangerous monsters whose elimination will create a more ordered universe. Though they encumber Dionysus with physical discomfort—ass-soreness, primarily—they do not appear to threaten the larger community; at least Charon seems perfectly accustomed to them. Dionysus' "Labor" is appropriate for a fat, incompetent, and cowardly kind of hero. Nevertheless, he, like Heracles, is "master of the animals" when he arrives at the other end of the bottomless lake.

Flush from his triumph over the Frogs, Dionysus is raring to confront the challenges of Hades. Dionysus, in imitating Heracles' endeavor, is in effect attempting to write his own epic *katabasis*. He wishes to repeat Heracles' journey—and even surpass it. In a moment of foolish bravado, Dionysus defies the "fearsome beasts" (278–9) that may lurk ahead:

ἠλαζονεύεθ᾽ ἵνα φοβηθείην ἐγώ,
εἰδώς με μάχιμον ὄντα, φιλοτιμούμενος.
οὐδὲν γὰρ οὕτω γαῦρόν ἐσθ᾽ ὡς Ἡρακλῆς.
ἐγὼ δέ γ᾽ εὐξαίμην ἂν ἐντυχεῖν τινι
λαβεῖν τ᾽ ἀγώνισμ᾽ ἄξιόν τι τῆς ὁδοῦ.

280–4

[Heracles] was just bragging so that I would be frightened, jealous when he saw that I'm in fighting shape. For nothing is as boastful as Heracles! I could even pray to encounter something and to achieve some feat worthy of the journey.

Even as he dismisses Heracles for his envy, Dionysus expresses his own desire to be just like Heracles. Aristophanes has demoted Dionysus from god to aspiring hero, allowing his audience to laugh at his humiliation.[102] He is getting puffed up, just in time for another comic deflation: just as Dionysus starts to feel confident, the possibility of an encounter with a shape-shifting Empusa reveals his cowardice (289–305).

The hybrid nature of Empusa associates her with other strange creatures of a mixed nature, the type of antagonist that Heracles tames in his role as a culture hero. But Dionysus falls into trembling, helpless fear, a clear trait of the Aristophanic "hero."[103] Henderson regards this Empusa as imaginary, invented by Xanthias to tease his master.[104] Regardless, the encounter ends with the comic revelation of Dionysus' lower body through a degrading act of defecation, rather than a display of physical excellence. Thus, whether Dionysus is conquering a band of singing Frogs or fleeing an imaginary shapeshifter, his efforts to engage in a Heraclean Labor only draw attention to his inability to measure up. Yet in provoking the audience's laughter with his cowardice and grotesque body, he succeeds in diminishing the threatening nature of violence which the role of monster-slayer seeks to constrain.

Heracles Remembered

As Dionysus and Xanthias arrive at the gatekeeper's door, a fuller picture of Heracles' previous journey to Hades comes into view. In tragedy, Heracles' violence is framed within the concerns of the *oikos*; here, Heracles' violence is presented through the comic perspective of the working-class community directly impacted by his visit. The duo discover that the legacy of Heracles' victory is more mixed than they had anticipated: through their interactions with Aeacus, Persephone's maid, and two angry innkeepers, the aftermath of the epic, tragic, and comic Heracles comes to light. The epinician tradition mostly neglects these aspects of Heracles' successes, but in Aristophanic comedy the tension between glorious victory and destructive consequences can be exploited by taking Heracles out of the realm of myth and putting him in contact with people like the audience. Through the humorous costume-shifting of Dionysus and Xanthias, the double-edged nature of "playing Heracles" is revealed: when Dionysus most wants to partake in Heracles' success, he must contend with the impact of Heracles' violence, lack of control, and destruction; meanwhile, the festival nature of comic Heracles seems only to benefit Xanthias.[105]

Dionysus discovers Heracles' troubled history once he arrives at the gatekeeper's door. For the dreaded doorkeeper Aeacus, Heracles' successful capture of Cerberus makes him *persona non grata* in the house of Hades. He is the first to establish the social disruption caused by Heracles' past achievements, a disruption mirrored in the chaos and disorder released by his threats.[106] When Dionysus announces himself as "Heracles the Strong" (Ἡρακλῆς ὁ καρτερός, 464), he clearly expects to intimidate the doorkeeper, assuming that Heracles' victory would have left the populace in fear. But Aeacus does not live in fear of Heracles' return; rather, he has been awaiting his opportunity for revenge. It is as if Aeacus' door opens to reveal a "Wanted" sign with an image of Heracles in lion skin with club. As Moorton phrases it, Dionysus has unwittingly assumed the identity of "a known felon."[107] Aeacus "recognizes" Dionysus in costume and excitedly lambasts him:

> ὦ βδελυρὲ κἀναίσχυντε καὶ τολμηρὲ σὺ
> καὶ μιαρὲ καὶ παμμίαρε καὶ μιαρώτατε,
> ὃς τὸν κύν' ἡμῶν ἐξελάσας τὸν Κέρβερον
> ἀπῇξας ἄγχων κἀποδρὰς ᾤχου λαβών,
> ὃν ἐγὼ 'φύλαττον. ἀλλὰ νῦν ἔχει μέσος.
>
> 465–70

You loathsome, shameless, daring man, abominable, totally abominable, most abominable! You drove away my dog, Cerberus, whom I used keep. Throttling him, you dashed away, and when you left, you took him with you in flight. But now I've got you!

Aeacus goes on to threaten Dionysus with physical harm in a parody of high-falutin' tragic language.[108] As Dobrov has shown, this exchange is a clear instance of tragic parody, in this case of the *Peirithous* (fr. 1), variously attributed to Euripides or Critias.[109] The comic Aeacus' memory of Heracles is dominated by the violence with which Heracles subdued Cerberus. Aeacus accuses Heracles of nearly strangling the dog, as if it were merely a beloved sheepdog.[110] By diminishing the Hound of Hades to a cherished pet, Aeacus likewise turns Heracles' heroic effort into a petty dognapping, and Aeacus becomes the primary victim of the act.

Heracles' great exploit becomes the act of a disruptive hooligan, a comic diminution of the twelfth Labor that signifies Heracles' triumph over death itself. The joke undercuts the goal for Heracles' role as a tamer of the universe, since his violence creates more chaos than order. The parody recalls some of the tropes that made Stesichorus' *Geryoneis* so interesting. I have argued that the *Geryoneis* destabilizes the means-ends calculus that justifies Heracles' slaying of monsters: when Geryon is humanized and Heracles' actions are not obviously civilizing, the killing of Geryon becomes more troubling. Aeacus' complaint accomplishes similar work in a comic vein: Heracles becomes a villain, and Cerberus and his keepers, the victims of a marauder. The capture of Cerberus has no value other than to prove his mastery; no other party benefits from this act. Heracles is reduced from victor to a common "dog thief" (κυνοκλόπος, 605), one who deserves punishment and must pay a penalty.

In contrast, the maid of Persephone reveals the positive side of the comic Heracles, the carnival feaster and celebrator of abundance. Apparently, on his previous visit he became a guest-friend dear to the queen of the Underworld,

Persephone.[111] While Aeacus prepares his revenge against Heracles, Persephone's maid issues Xanthias-Heracles a warm invitation for a feast:

ἡ γὰρ θεός σ' ὡς ἐπύθεθ' ἥκοντ', εὐθέως
ἔπεττεν ἄρτους, ἧψε κατερικτῶν χύτρας
ἔτνους δύ' ἢ τρεῖς, βοῦν ἀπηνθράκιζ' ὅλον,
πλακοῦντας ὤπτα κολλάβους <τ'>. ἀλλ' εἴσιθι.

504–7

When the goddess heard that you had arrived, she immediately began baking bread, heating up pots of ground pea-soup—two or three—she was roasting a whole ox and baking flat cakes and rolls. Come in!

Xanthias demurs, but the maid continues to entice him with offers of poultry, sweetmeats, and sweet wine. Xanthias, apparently not hungry, again refuses, until the maid advertises the presence of a beautiful flute-girl and dancers. Heracles' love for pea-soup was established in his earlier conversation with Dionysus, and so great is his appetite for women that Persephone has brought in the musical entertainment before the feast has even begun.[112] The stereotypical traits of the comic Heracles that were less obvious in his direct representation in the beginning of the play—his capacity for a tremendous amount and variety of food, his enjoyment of drink, his lustiness—are now here in full display.

Persephone's reception emphasizes the jovial, convivial side of the buffoonish Heracles. The interaction with the maid makes no acknowledgment of Heracles' weariness after a dangerous journey or the courage and violence that enabled his living presence in the halls of Hades.[113] Instead, we see the festival aspects of the hero's material bodily lower stratum, which links his famous appetite with abundance, fertility, and renewal, even as he consumes and swallows. Through the emphasis on his lower parts, a sense of warmth and life comes into a place of death.

But the approach of an innkeeper and her maid Plathane reveals the other side of comic Heracles, one that emphasizes his unruly ravenousness. It turns out that Dionysus' superficial questions to Heracles earlier about the inns and hostels of the Underworld were more pointed that they initially appeared, since Heracles did indeed patronize the local establishments of Hades. The story that the innkeeper tells provides yet another perspective on Heracles' excessiveness: he bolted down sixteen loaves of bread, twenty portions of meat, garlic, salt-fish, and fresh cheese with the baskets, stock, and sausages (549–60). Apparently his Labor to subdue Cerberus stimulated his hunger and thirst; but his appetites lead not to feasting and abundance, but a famished insatiability. Plathane's added detail of Heracles' consuming the baskets right along with the actual food stuff, as described above, pushes him almost into the category of animal.[114]

At the heart of the innkeeper's lament is not the measure of Heracles' hunger, but his antisocial behavior. One of the play's running jokes is the persistence of a monetary economy in the Underworld. A recent corpse refuses to carry Dionysus' luggage for the price he offers; Charon requires two obols as fare for passage across the bottomless lake; and now the audience finds that Heracles' greatest crime was to dine and dash. The innkeeper and Plathane represent the same values that are held by contemporary marketwomen of Athens. They are incensed that Heracles depleted their stock and damaged their property without appropriate recompense. As the innkeeper recounts, "And then, when I began to ask for payment, he gave me a fierce look and bellowed... and he drew his sword, like a madman!" (κἄπειτ' ἐπειδὴ τἀργύριον ἐπραττόμην, / ἔβλεψεν εἴς με δριμὺ κἀμυκᾶτό γε...καὶ τὸ ξίφος γ' ἐσπᾶτο, μαίνεσθαι δοκῶν, 561–2, 564).

This description of Heracles pivots to yet another Heraclean identity: the tragic madman. The innkeeper's diction invites a comparison between Heracles' behavior in the inn and Heracles' madness in Euripides' *Heracles*.[115] At Hera's behest, Lyssa casts madness into Heracles' mind, causing him to murder his wife and children. As Lyssa begins to infect his mind, she narrates, "he silently rolls his distorted, fierce-eyed pupils ... and bellows fearsomely" (καὶ διαστρόφους ἑλίσσει σῖγα γοργωποὺς κόρας...δεινὰ μυκᾶται δέ, 868–70). The ferocity of Heracles' look and his beast-like roar (both Aristophanes and Euripides use the verb μυκάω) characterize him as out of control—and life-threatening. The innkeeper and her maid thus associate the hungry glutton with his most dangerous violence, revealing how Heracles' buffoonery cannot always contain his dark side. In a comic touch, the innkeeper notes that when Heracles "rushed out, he took the mattresses with him" (ὁ δ' ᾤχετ' ἐξᾴξας γε τὰς ψιάθους λαβών, 567). Fortunately, Heracles' destruction here is reparable. Yet what use could Heracles possibly have for the mattresses? The point is that he has no purpose in mind: this is not the violence of a monster-slayer, but the inner disorder of an unstable madman.

By providing the perspective of middle-class contemporary Athenians on Heracles' *katabasis*, Aristophanes punctures an inflated view of Heraclean victory. Aeacus' indignant desire for vengeance against the thief of his pet and the innkeeper's outrage at Heracles' barbarity, though light-hearted in nature, nevertheless point out a troubling contradiction in the traditions about Heracles. Aeacus—and by extension, Cerberus—are the innocent victims of Heracles' ambush; the landladies just want to run their business. The suppression of reasons for praise of Heracles and the emphasis on reasons for criticism, while part of the comic project of ridiculing prominent figures, cast doubt on the strategies employed to constrain Heraclean violence.

As the play pits different versions of the remembered Heracles against each other, Dionysus and Xanthias exchange the Heracles costume between themselves. In the eyes of the two characters, Heracles' attributes have the potential to transfer his heroic qualities to their wearer. When Dionysus hesitates to knock on the gate to the Underworld, Xanthias urges him to imitate Heracles: "Stop wasting time and try the door, in the form and spirit of Heracles!" (οὐ μὴ διατρίψεις, ἀλλὰ γεύσει τῆς θύρας, / καθ' Ἡρακλέα τὸ σχῆμα καὶ τὸ λῆμ' ἔχων, 462–3). Xanthias thus recommends that Dionysus internalize his outer disguise and unite his actions with his appearance. As Habash writes, "The theatrical illusion that one playing a role is transformed into the portrayed character through theatrical props and garb is created by the actors. Aristophanes brilliantly puts a spin on this technique by having his own actor fooled, as is the audience, or at least feign belief, and therefore create comedy through the parodying of this technique."[116] These metatheatrical ideas playfully contribute to the jumbling of Heracles' identities that runs throughout the play; their uncrowning and recrowning, and the disruption of hierarchy this represents, bring the carnivalesque into this exchange.

But the Heracles costume also evokes different reactions from different audiences. Each time they put on and take off the Heracles costume is coordinated with a shift in how Heracles is perceived by others. When Dionysus wants to avoid Aeacus' vengeful anger, he persuades Xanthias to exchange identities with him (494–7), only to watch in dismay as Xanthias is invited to a party, rather than threatened with a beating. The topsy-turvy world of comedy is on full display, as the god-dressed-as-a-god becomes a slave, and the slave takes on the trappings of a god. Their conversation assumes a correspondence between one's internal qualities and his outward appearance; the contrast in reactions to the costume thus also brings out the contradictions of Heracles himself.

Dionysus' transformation into a slave, followed by the resumption of his former identity, recalls Heracles' subjection as slave to Omphale after his murder of Iphitus, a common theme for the comic Heracles.[117] From the evidence found in vase painting, already by the sixth century Omphale assumed Heracles' attributes; according to Lucian's later account, Heracles wore a saffron gown.[118] In Aristophanes' play, then, as Dionysus takes off the attributes of Heracles and stands in his *krokotos*, he mimics precisely the events in Heracles' life. Aristophanes treats the parallels playfully: Dionysus "becomes" a slave in order to avoid punishment; Heracles became a slave to Omphale as a form of punishment itself. By the Roman period, Heracles' servitude to Omphale is distinctly sexual in nature. But in Aristophanes, by taking on the role of slave, Dionysus is denied sexual opportunity.

The fluidity of identity in the play reflects the multiplicity of Heracles himself. Dionysus can become Heracles, but so can Xanthias, while Dionysus can also become a slave. The inhabitants of the Underworld accept Dionysus and Xanthias in Heracles' costume at face value; no one seems to notice what must have been obvious distinctions among the three figures. So prominent is Dionysus' actorly costume that the innkeeper notes that his boots do *not* deceive her into not recognizing "Heracles"! Moreover, Dionysus, in his fear, occasionally longs to be neither Dionysus nor Heracles (298–300); he would prefer to remain nameless than be known to hostile parties in the Underworld. The arbitrariness of identity—that one can try it on, discard it, adopt nothing at all—plays into the *Frogs'* juxtaposition of Heracles' many roles. Heracles can be comic and epic, heroic and buffoonish, friend and enemy. So Dionysus and Xanthias display on stage the versatility of the figure of Heracles himself; the alternation between Dionysus-Heracles and Xanthias-Heracles mimics the alternation in the play between high-heroic Heracles and low-buffoonish Heracles.

As the rate of costume changes accelerates, the various roles of Heracles collide, producing a destabilization of the very figure of Heracles. When Aeacus returns to punish the thief, Dionysus and Xanthias manage to get themselves into a whipping contest to prove their true identities. In preparation, Aeacus orders them both to strip (ἀποδύεσθε δή, 641). Xanthias removes his Heracles costume, and Dionysus removes the trappings of a slave. The contest proves inconclusive after several rounds, and Aeacus, that great judge of the Underworld, sends them both inside to Hades and Persephone (668–71). The parabasis intervenes, and when the plot resumes, the focus has shifted to Dionysus' adjudication of a poetry contest between Aeschylus and Euripides; Heracles is largely forgotten.

Aristophanes' play has juxtaposed many roles of Heracles, from the relaxed hero in retirement, to the wrangler of animals and monsters, to the thief, welcome guest, and brigand. The decentralizing of a single authoritative Heracles illustrates the "centrifugal style" of Aristophanic comedy, an insight drawn by Platter from Bakhtin's portrayal of the novel.[119] Against a background of the hero's signal accomplishment, the collapse of the Heracles disguise in the *Frogs* highlights the incongruities of Heracles' roles: how can the god-like conqueror of death be the same madman of threatening violence as well as the starving glutton and the life of the party? The tension that arises from the jumbling of Heracleses is never resolved; Heracles is not *changed* by being put into a carnival of genres. Instead, we are left to understand that the incongruities are a byproduct of the dialogical nature of Heracles himself.

Heracles thus proves an ideal figure for literary carnivalization in Aristophanic comedy, which "cannibalizes other genres to create a type of literature that bills itself as capable of passing judgment on the genres it recycles."[120] The *Frogs* is a particularly fine example of this phenomenon, given its preoccupation with judging between competing tragedians. Just as Heracles serves the play's generic agenda, the play allows us in turn to examine the divisions and continuities between Heracles' roles, a sort of compressed version of this book. Heracles is not transformed by being put into the carnival of genres; instead, the limitations of each role in controlling and justifying violence rise to the surface. While Dionysus' imitation of the beast Labors diminishes their prestige through parody, Heracles' function as a monster-slayer is subjected to greater scrutiny in the Underworld; his capture of Cerberus is revealed to be not just a source of glory for himself, but also a crime against Aeacus. While his feasting endears him to Persephone, his insatiable gluttony results in damage to the innkeepers. Laughter is threaded through each of these episodes, but in this case the uncrowning of the figure of Heracles is not followed by recrowning and victory. In this way, the polyphony of Aristophanes' comedy allows even the limitations of Heracles' role as comic buffoon role to come into the light.

Conclusion

I have drawn on a Bakhtinian reading of the lower body to argue that carnival laughter directed at the comic Heracles diminishes the ever-present fear of his violence. On the one hand, he is debased by his gluttony, which reduces him to a starving belly; on the other, his association with outlandish abundance makes him a welcome guest and symbol of the feast's plenty. The cyclical nature of the carnivalesque means that even as Heracles is dominated by his appetites, his physical excesses can be harnessed towards triumph over villains; the hero who is uncrowned by laughter is renewed as a victor. Euripides' *Alcestis* shows how Heracles' carnival philosophy can enable a direct confrontation with Death, which leads to renewed life for his friends. In this way, the comic Heracles shows how Benjamin's "nonmediate" violence—that is, violence as a manifestation—can be brought into a means-ends calculus that enables heroic violence to be justified.

But the *Frogs*, in bringing the comic Heracles into a dialogue with his traits in other genres, negates the fear of violence with laughter but does not restore him as a victor. The result of the juxtaposition of Heracles' roles shows that laughter does not always negate the violence itself; the various constraints of different genres and different roles can only offer partial solutions to violence's negative effects. Thus the centrifugal forces of Aristophanic comedy point to the limitations of laughter, which does not resolve the injuries Heracles leaves in his wake, and the ultimate ambivalence of Heracles himself. In Heracles' persistent resistance to reform is a challenge that demands recognition and requires continual confrontation.

Conclusion

Which Path Did Heracles Choose?

The ambivalence and incompatibility of Heracles' roles—so powerfully presented in Aristophanic comedy—undergird Prodicus' famous didactic allegory, commonly referred to as the "Choice of Heracles." The anecdote, as recounted by Socrates in Xenophon's *Memorabilia*, centers around a youthful Heracles deliberating about the future direction of his life. As he sits at a crossroads, down each path approaches a tall and striking woman, a study in contrasts. His preference between the women is significant because, like Paris' choice of Olympian goddesses, it not only dictates the course of his life's events, but also reveals the nature of his moral and ethical character.

In brief: the first woman to approach is dolled up, vain, and alluring. She promises Heracles:

> ἐὰν οὖν ἐμὲ φίλην ποιησάμενος, ἐπὶ τὴν ἡδίστην τε καὶ ῥᾴστην ὁδὸν ἄξω σε, καὶ τῶν μὲν τερπνῶν οὐδενὸς ἄγευστος ἔσει, τῶν δὲ χαλεπῶν ἄπειρος διαβιώσῃ.
>
> 2.1.23

> If you make me your friend, I will lead you on the most pleasurable and easy road, and of pleasures, not one will be untasted, and you will conduct your life free of toils.

When Heracles inquires as to her name, she admits that she has two: she is *Eudaimonia* (or Happiness) to her friends; *Kakia* (or Vice) to her detractors.

The other woman, *Aretē*, is distinguished by her restrained beauty and modest manner. She first appeals to Heracles' parentage and training, and then makes her pitch: an alliance with her demands hard work and discipline—travel along a steep road—but results in honor and glory. She claims,

τῶν γὰρ ὄντων ἀγαθῶν καὶ καλῶν οὐδὲν ἄνευ πόνου καὶ ἐπιμελείας θεοὶ
διδόασιν ἀνθρώποις, ἀλλ' εἴτε τοὺς θεοὺς ἵλεως εἶναί σοι βούλει, θεραπευτέον
τοὺς θεούς, εἴτε ὑπὸ φίλων ἐθέλεις ἀγαπᾶσθαι, τοὺς φίλους εὐεργετητέον.

2.1.28

The gods give none of the real benefits and honors to men without toil and diligence; if you want the gods to favor you, serve the gods; if you wish to be beloved by friends, benefit your friends.

When *Eudaimonia/Kakia* points out that *Aretē*'s way of life is unpleasant, *Aretē* defends herself by mocking *Kakia*'s offerings and boasting of her own honors among the gods and men. Furthermore, her rewards last beyond mortal life:

ὅταν δ' ἔλθῃ τὸ πεπρωμένον τέλος, οὐ μετὰ λήθης ἄτιμοι κεῖνται, ἀλλὰ μετὰ
μνήμης τὸν ἀεὶ χρόνον ὑμνούμενοι θάλλουσι. τοιαῦτά σοι, ὦ παῖ τοκέων
ἀγαθῶν Ἡράκλεις, ἔξεστι διαπονησαμένῳ τὴν μακαριστοτάτην εὐδαιμονίαν
κεκτῆσθαι.

2.1.33

When the fated end comes [to my friends], they do not lie forgotten and unhonored, but they flourish, sung and remembered forever. Such things are yours, Heracles, son of noble parents, if you labor to acquire the most enviable happiness.

With this, Socrates concludes his retelling, and a conversation with a new interlocutor is introduced.[1]

On first glance, the casting of Heracles in the role of the paradigmatic decider at the crossroads is a bit surprising.[2] As Mary Kuntz has shown, against the background of the complex mythical tradition treated in this book, Prodicus' allegory relies on a reductionist approach to the figure of Heracles.[3] The narrative assumes that Heracles is a blank slate at this moment of transition between childhood and young adulthood (ἐπεὶ ἐκ παίδων εἰς ἥβην ὡρμᾶτο, 2.1.21). This approach elides the tales of extraordinary youth that foreshadow his extraordinary adult career, whether his celebrated strangling of two snakes as an infant (Pindar, *Nem.* 1) or the murder of his music teacher Linus as a student, as discussed in Chapter 5. Moreover, Socrates offers the allegory in the context of a larger discussion about the importance of self-control (*enkrateia*), yet Heracles famously struggles to control his impulses both laughable and threatening.[4] Even the fundamental conceit that personal choice can determine one's destiny has no foothold in Heracles' mythology.[5] He is persecuted by Hera and subordinated to Eurystheus from birth, aspects of his myth already legendary in the *Iliad*

(19.74–144). The attribution of independent free will to Heracles thus pushes this Heracles into new territory.

While the allegory suppresses certain aspects of Heracles' myths, it also highlights the traits that make him suitable as the central subject for this story. When *Eudaimonia/Kakia* addresses Heracles, she appeals to the pleasures of the material bodily lower stratum: food and drink, the enjoyment of the senses, sex, and general abundance.[6] Her doubled name reflects the doubled nature of the lower body, which I argue in Chapter 5 is fundamental to the buffoonish Heracles. *Eudaimonia* can be associated with the comic Heracles who revels in abundant feasts and whose celebrations are life-affirming; *Kakia*, on the other hand, better describes the debased Heracles whose buffoonery makes him the object of derision rather than celebration. But *Eudaimonia/Kakia* offers a life that neglects a critical component of the comic Heracles, the context of the victory plot. Without a victory over villains that recrowns the debased hero, the Heracles who chooses her may remain degraded, arrested in only one half of the cyclical carnivalesque.

If *Eudaimonia/Kakia* aims to appeal to Heracles' comic persona, *Aretē* draws on his roles as epinician hero and friend. She emphasizes the importance of directing his efforts towards the benefit of others—whether the gods, his friends, or his city—describing an exchange of favors that fits traditional notions of *philia*. She thus echoes the kind of constraints that Pindar puts on Heraclean violence in his third Olympian ode, as discussed in Chapter 2: Heracles serves the gods by honoring Artemis and Zeus, refrains from using force against the Hyperboreans, and brings shady olive trees to Olympia for the equal benefit of all attendees. *Aretē*'s speech also recalls the *philia* of Euripides' Heracles in the first section of the *Heracles*, in which he aims to return his father from exile to his home city, protects the city of Thebes against the Minyans, and honors the gods, as I argue in Chapter 4.

Aretē's mode of life constrains Heracles' violence and directs it towards specific ends, giving an instrumental justification for the use of force. Violence in the service of others is framed primarily as toil and effort (*ponos, epimeleia*), diction that suggests that his subsequent Labors (*ponoi*) make him the ideal judge at this crossroads. Yet the deemphasis on violence leads in unexpected directions: *Aretē*'s recommendations culminate in the odd vision of Heracles as a particularly productive farmer, whose efforts result in abundant harvests and rich flocks (2.1.28).[7] Furthermore, Heraclean violence as a manifestation of inner disorder seems not to have a place in this dichotomy between *Eudaimonia/Kakia* and *Aretē*. Nowhere in Prodicus' presentation is there room for "effort gone awry," which characterizes so much of Heraclean indignity. Typically, Heracles' problem is not that he is "lazy," exactly, but that whatever he does, he does to an exaggerated degree. When thirsty, he drinks dry a river; when hungry, he devours even the charcoal for cooking the meat; and when angry, he razes an entire city.

As in the now-familiar process of changing mythological representations, the "Choice of Heracles" engages with previous tropes from comedy, epinician, and tragedy, even as it promotes a transformed Heracles, now an avatar for young, contemplative philosophers. But just as Aristophanes' *Frogs* destabilizes the figure of Heracles by juxtaposing incompatible roles, so Prodicus' allegory struggles to reconcile the Heracles who belongs to the way of both vice and virtue. Xenophon's Socrates concludes the tale without describing Heracles' actual choice, his only function in the allegory. The end is not in doubt: *Aretē* gets the last word, Socrates titles the narrative "the education of Heracles by *Aretē*" (τὴν ὑπ' Ἀρετῆς Ἡρακλέους παίδευσιν, 2.1.34), and in its influential afterlife, its didactic purpose clearly lies in Heracles' alliance with *Aretē*.[8] Nevertheless, I argue that Socrates stops short of describing the judgment because we are meant to hesitate, as perhaps Heracles does. In this moment, the audience wonders, "Well, which path *did* Heracles choose?"

The question arises because Xenophon's audience knows that both paths characterize Heracles over the course of his career. In the lower literary/performance genres of satyr play and comedy, audiences delighted in laughing at the buffoonish, lustful Heracles; and we have observed the efforts in the higher-register genres of epic, epinician, and tragedy to direct Heracles' force towards communally beneficial ends. In the pause between the conclusion of *Aretē*'s speech and Socrates' resumption of the discussion with Aristippus, the audience must reckon with the comic Heracles who obviously sides with *Eudaimonia/Kakia*! Even when made into an archetype of sagacious youth for didactic purposes, Heracles resists a single meaning. The tension underlying Heracles' choice thus mirrors the existing tensions between the genres this book has explored: even when transformed through the genre of philosophical prose, Heracles' ambivalence inevitably follows.

This brief reading of Prodicus' allegory reveals how my analysis of Heracles as a violent hero can help us to understand how mythic narrative functions as exemplary material more generally. The various Heracleses of epic, lyric, tragic, and comic poetry demonstrate different approaches to violence, a component of heroism both necessary and increasingly problematic as Heracles becomes a god. The interplay between genre, Heracles' roles, and the constraint or release of his violence allows for an engagement with the complex nature of individual violence, whether understood as a means to an end or as a manifestation. In investigating Heracles' roles in early epic—as monster-slayer, *theomachos*, sacker of cities—the first chapter develops the fundamental elements of episodes of heroic violence. The mechanics of those elements can also be manipulated to present, for example, an act of theomachy as justified by the approval of a goddess, or condemned as a reckless act. Episodes of violence thus prove to be an indispensable tool in constructing a Heracles who can be praiseworthy, deplorable, or even simply entertaining in turn: in the poets' hands, violence becomes as malleable as mythic material itself.

But while heroic violence is versatile, it is not neutral: its potential for tremendous damage continually prompts narrative efforts to control it. One fundamental method is to constrain violence to justifiable ends. In the case of Hesiod's *Theogony*, Heracles plays the role of monster-slayer, and the means of violence is justified by its end, the promotion of order in Zeus' universe. But this justification is complicated in Stesichorus' *Geryoneis*: because this Geryon is explicitly humanized and endowed with the qualities of an admirable Homeric hero, Heracles' role as killer of monsters and tamer of a savage and disorderly world is diminished. If the ends of Heracles' violence are questioned in this presentation, the means of violence itself is scrutinized in Pindar. In fr. 169a, Pindar undermines the means–ends calculus of instrumental violence by opening up the possibility of other means apart from violence, suggesting that Heracles simply could have asked for or purchased the Cattle.

Pindar's transformation of Heracles into an epinician victor, as exemplified in his third Olympian ode, proves both problematic and challenging. This role draws upon Heracles' record as a vanquisher of beasts and villains and a hero of physical excellence. So dominant is Heracles that he could be viewed almost as the embodiment of victory itself, his success a form of justification for violence. But where Heracles' role as victor makes him worthy of imitation for Pindar's patrons, its limitations are revealed in Sophocles' *Trachiniae*: Heracles is seemingly never defeated in competition, yet the play ends with his physical agony and impending death. I argue that the play shows how the decoupling of conventional heroic competition from victory allows violence to become unbound. The practice of heroic competition, which ordinarily constrains violence by pitting two heroic male opponents against one another for a prize, becomes distorted in a series of transgressive competitions, between Heracles and Nessus, Heracles and Iole's family, and Iole and Deianeira. The disastrous end of Heracles' life demonstrates the difficulty of restraining violence with rules and conventions, suggesting that force is less a tool for triumph and more a barely controlled impulse.

The role of the victor again comes under scrutiny in Euripides' *Heracles*, which brings the furthest extremes of Heraclean violence onto the same stage. The play shows how the roles of victor and friend undergird Heracles' praiseworthy exploits; yet when he falls into a fit of Hera-imposed madness, he commits violence of the same sort that brings him victory, but this time against his closest *philoi*. The reunion of the values of the glorious victor and *philos* allows him to recover, an indication that victory—the goal of individual agonistic encounters—must be informed by social and communal priorities. Thus, in tragedy, underneath instrumental restraints on heroic violence lies the constant threat of unbound violence; furthermore, the social conventions or communal prerogatives that typically govern conflict are vulnerable to failure, allowing violence to destroy even the most celebrated of heroes.

While tragedy explores the limitations of the victor, the genre of comedy applies a different strategy for coping with the dark side of heroic violence: laughter functions to diminish the threat of violence, leaving it cleansed of its dangers even as it leads to a victory that yields celebration. The role of buffoon brings to light a Heracles—always the most physical of heroes—characterized by his connection with the material bodily lower stratum, as defined in the works of Mikhail Bakhtin. Through carnivalesque laughter, the gluttonous, stupid, and lustful Heracles is degraded but then renewed as he defeats villains and partakes in festive abundance. The popularity of the comic Heracles attests to the desirability of this form of control. As the violent hero is demeaned by ridicule, the audience experiences a joyful superiority; in this moment of self-assertion, one could believe that Heracles has temporarily been tamed.

In examining the struggle to constrain heroic violence, this book also underlines a pervasive anxiety around victory itself, ostensibly the desideratum of the agonistic strain of ancient Greek culture. Even in a culture that personifies *nikē* as a goddess, winning requires restraint—a precept already familiar from the depiction of Achilles' excessive punishment of Hector's corpse in *Iliad* 22. In the myths of Heracles, victory alone is insufficient for his city, home, or even himself; his violence cannot be justified solely by supremacy and the display of power. For Heracles, his role as successful monster-slayer in the *Theogony* is connected to the human community that benefits; his capture of the Ceryneian Hind in Pindar's epinicians is paired with persuasion and philanthropy; a commitment to *philia* can also curb victory's latent perils. The way that victory is construed reflects directly on the violence required to obtain it.

Furthermore, the analysis in this book illuminates how the treatment of heroic violence differs between genres—whether epic, lyric, tragedy, or comedy—and how specific approaches to violence can serve to delineate generic boundaries. For example, in investigating the effects of Heraclean violence on the *oikos*, tragedy also interrogates Heracles' status as athlete and victorious hero in epinician poetry. By the end of the fifth century BCE, the establishment of these generic manifestations of Heracles can be put to use in the work of Aristophanes and Prodicus. In Aristophanic comedy, which relies on a carnivalization of genres, the conflict between the madman of tragedy and the comic glutton leads to amusement, but also highlights the incompleteness of each genre's handling of violence. In his philosophical allegory, Prodicus embodies the tension between the sensual Heracles of the lower body and the toiling hero whose acts benefit other people in the figures of *Eudaimonia/Kakia* and *Aretē*. But in Xenophon's retelling, Socrates leaves his audience suspended, highlighting Heracles' difficulty in choosing between two aspects so deeply embedded in his mythological tradition.

In the conflict between these various personas lies the reason for Heracles' continued productivity as a lens for the role of the violent hero within a community. To offer but a brief illustration: even when Heracles adopts a novel role as the devoted lover of Hylas in Hellenistic poetry, concerns about his violence and varied generic strategies for addressing it remain at the fore.[9] Both Theocritus and Apollonius of Rhodes present the story of Hylas' kidnapping by nymphs on Mysia during the expedition for the Golden Fleece; Heracles becomes extremely distraught at the loss and is left behind by Jason and the Argonauts.[10] An extension of this book's analysis shows how these presentations—Theocritus in the bucolic genre of the idyll and Apollonius in his epic *Argonautica*—draw on different generic approaches to Heracles to address heroic violence. In Theocritus' *Idyll* 13, Heracles is a laughable figure. He is maddened by passionate heartbreak, as driven as a lion towards prey; but he is also foolish, as his anguish is expressed primarily by the great extent of his wandering through the area.[11] The threat of violence is avoided because he is alone, and no one gets in his way. Moreover, his emotional distress is described with the same verb associated with his toiling at the Labors (ἐμόγησεν, 66), diminishing his glorious exploits with its association with private emotional pain. The comic nature of the episode is made explicit when the Argonauts "taunt Heracles as a deserter" (Ἡρακλέην δ' ἥρωες ἐκερτόμεον λιποναύταν, 73). Their mockery gives permission to the poem's audience to laugh alongside them, and when Heracles follows his comrades on foot and rejoins them in Colchis, he recovers from his degradation and his status appears to be restored. In Theocritus' vision, Heracles the lover can be a comic figure.

In his epic, Apollonius shows us how Heracles the lover can be tragic: as in Theocritus' version, when Heracles discovers that Hylas has gone missing, he charges mindlessly through the forest.[12] But the poem also compares him to a maddened bull who sends forth a "bellow" (ἵησιν μύκημα, 1.1269), alluding to Lyssa's narration of madness descending upon Heracles in Euripides' *Heracles*, where Heracles too is described as a bull who "bellows" (δεινὰ μυκᾶται, 870) at the moment that the carnage against his family begins. Apollonius' Heracles also commits violence against *philoi* in relation to this episode: he later kills the two sons of Boreas, his former allies, because they had prevented the Argonauts from returning to retrieve Heracles. The poem attributes this act to hateful vengeance (στυγερὴ τίσις, 1.1302) arising from Heracles' heartbreak and abandonment.[13] This act of violence has no communal concern or social benefit to justify it; indeed Glaucus' epiphany and prophecy provide the authoritative reason not to return and search for Heracles, rendering the intervention and death of the Boreads superfluous. Instead, it is a smaller-scale act akin to the kind of tragic violence Heracles wields in the sack of Oechalia in Sophocles' *Trachiniae*, another assault in response to erotic loss and humiliation. Thus, even as Heracles' myths develop new roles (that of lover) and enter new literary genres (that of bucolic poetry) over time, the comic and tragic approaches to heroic violence remain with and continue to shape his presentation.

From the beginning, this study proposed to explore shifting and overlapping conceptions of violence, whether it is treated as an instrument or as a manifestation. As we have seen, when violence is treated as an instrument, a means–ends calculus can be applied, providing a framework in which a test of the ends can justify the means of violence. Justified ends for Heracles' violence often take the form of a defense of justice (the punishment of villains) and protection for vulnerable parties (the killing of dangerous beasts); at best, Heracles' violence serves the purpose of enforcing order and civilization over disorder. Under these circumstances, the hero is in a position of control: violence is one tool among many, and it is utilized at his will. When violence is not justifiable, however, it tends to be presented as a manifestation, a force that remains a constant threat and is ever difficult to control. In this case, violence becomes something of a character trait inherent to the hero, and its outburst must be constrained by social conventions such as *philia* or defanged by laughter.

These two approaches to violence are not mutually exclusive, sometimes appearing even in the same text about the same myth. But violence as a manifestation nevertheless proves far more problematic, imposing costs on innocent bystanders, leaving a trail of collateral damage in its wake, and even destroying the hero himself. Ultimately, these attempts to restrain heroic violence—whether by instrumental justification, communal pressures, or deflation—fall short. They are limited in scope, temporary, and incomplete, inevitably allowing the hero to wreak lamentable damage. Yet the heroic endeavor relies upon violence. The ambivalent violence of Heracles' myths, then, reflects more broadly the ambiguous position of the extraordinary hero in the Greek imagination, a figure whose status remains eternally unstable.

Notes

Introduction

1 Pinker 2011.
2 Riess 2012: 2. Riess's definition includes his translation of the definition of violence in Fuchs-Heinritz et al. 1994: 247. This kind of violence is distinct from forms of violence such as state violence, structural violence, or economic violence (see Arendt 1970; Butler 2004; Žižek 2008).
3 For a full exploration of the lexical range of *bia*, see F. D'Agostino 1983.
4 To name just a few studies: see van Wees 1992 on violence as the result of status rivalry for prestige; Dover 1974 on violence and aggression in the context of the Greek moral viewpoint of the world; D. Cohen 1995 on the development of legal regulation of violence at Athens; Allen 2000 on punishment as a socially authorized deployment of violence within Athenian political and legal frameworks; Herman 2006 on the Athenians' turn away from private revenge towards public punishment; Trundle 2020 is a recent overview.
5 On violence against women, see, e.g., Deacy and Pierce 1997; Foxhall and Salmon 1998; Omitowoju 2002; Deacy and McHardy forthcoming. On violence against slaves, see, e.g., DuBois 1991; Klees 1998; Akrigg and Tordoff 2013; Hunt 2016.
6 Foraboschi 2018.
7 Riess and Fagan 2016; Xydopoulos, Vlassopoulos, and Tounta 2017. On late antiquity, see Drake 2006.
8 Shay 1994, 2002.
9 See, e.g., Meineck 2012; Meineck and Konstan 2014; Doerries 2015 (pp. 211–58 on Heracles); Torrance 2017.
10 For an exploration of contemporary representations of violence, see Matthews and Goodman 2013. The ethical complications of representing violence, and the violence inherent in any representation itself, are addressed in the volume's first essay, Noys 2013.
11 See de Romilly 2000 for an argument that Greek literature, especially tragedy, depicts violence in order to condemn it in favor of values like justice, gentleness, and solidarity. I am not convinced that Greek literature is so univocal on the topic.
12 Bushman and Huesmann 2010: 834–5.
13 Arendt 1970: 51.
14 Benjamin 1986: 277.

15 Ibid.: 294.
16 Riess 2012: 7. See especially the charts summarizing his findings on pp. 101 and 139. His historical approach is situated within performance and ritual studies and bridges the gap between the use of "actual" violence in fourth-century Athens and its performance within ritual contexts of the courts, curse tablets, and comic drama.
17 See, e.g., Recke 2002; Fischer and Moraw 2005; Seidensticker and Vöhler 2006; Muth 2008. See also van Wees 2008's review.
18 See, e.g., Hoff 2005; Borg 2006.
19 Muth 2008.
20 On the oral-formulaic technique of oral poets, see Lord 1965.
21 For example, see Montiglio 2011 on the shifting depictions of Odysseus from trickster to sage.
22 On Heracles as a prehistoric figure of "Master of the Animals," see Burkert 1979: 78–98. Nilsson 1932: 8: 187–220 is outdated, but nevertheless usefully speculates on the origins of Heracles' myths in the exploits of a local strongman.
23 As defined in Hardwick 2003: 10, 14.
24 Jauss 1982a: 22–4.
25 Ibid.: 25. For a fuller exposition of the dialogicity of the horizon structure, see Jauss 1989. Effe 1980 applies Jauss's framework for heroes from Jauss 1977 (in English: Jauss 1982b) to Heracles, arguing that the audience relates to Heracles in Greek literature through four main modes of identification: *admirativer Identifikation, sympathetischer Identifikation, kathartische Identifikation,* and *ironischer Identifikation.*
26 Bär 2019: 4. See also Bär 2018: 26–9; De Temmerman and van Emde Boas 2018: 4–5.
27 For an influential understanding of (especially Homeric) heroes, see Nagy 1999.
28 See Currie 2005, especially pp. 60–70, on the different uses of the word *hērōs*, beginning with the Bronze Age. For more on the open-ended nature of the religious cult hero, see Jones 2010.
29 See Ekroth 2002.
30 For a study of the political aspects of the heroization of athletes, see Currie 2005: 120–57.
31 Fontenrose 1968: 76–9; see more recently, Lunt 2009.
32 For a survey of violence as entertainment in the Western tradition, see Schechter 2005.
33 Martindale 1993: 22.
34 The loss of the epic *Thebais*, which depicts the attack of the Seven against Thebes, deprives us of the most important archaic literary source for this incident. Tydeus' role in the assault on Thebes is described in the *Iliad* (4.376–98); Pherecydes (3F97) provides the vivid details of Tydeus' final meal. See Gantz 1993: 510–19.

35 Segal 1981: 39–40. The modern obsession with brain-eating zombies reflects similar preoccupations.
36 On the nature of the scattered evidence, see Holt 1992.
37 See Boardman 1990.
38 Boardman 1972, 1975a, 1989.
39 C. 600 BCE, from Necropoli dell'Oseteria, Vulci. See *LIMC* V, Herakles 3331; and discussion in B. D'Agostino 2016: 247–50.
40 See, e.g., Shapiro 1983; Ekroth 2002; Verbanck-Piérard 1989 argues that Heracles received mostly divine cult, rather than dual cult.
41 *Histories* 2.44. This polarization should be treated with caution.
42 For an overview of the evidence, see Stafford 2012: 171–97; she discusses the rituals related to Heracles both in and outside of Athens in Stafford 2005. See also Farnell 1921: 95–174; Woodford 1966: 8–53, 1971; Berguist 1973; Bonnet 1988; Verbanck-Piérard 1989; Jourdain-Annequin 1992.
43 See Holt 1989.
44 Heroic success often requires not just violence, but also strategy, cleverness, alliances, etc. Heracles demonstrates many of these other traits, but they will not be the focus of this study.
45 On the depiction of Heracles in Apollonius, Callimachus, and Theocritus, and the metapoetical relationship between them, see Heerink 2012, 2015: 3–82.
46 For application in Homer and Classics more generally, see de Jong 1987, 2014.
47 On genre mixing and dynamic play as a feature of Greek poetry from even the archaic period, see Foster, Kurke, and Weiss 2019: 10–19.
48 Des Essarts 1871; Schweitzer 1922; Flacelière and Devambez 1966.
49 Galinsky 1972; Stanford 1954. For a similarly comprehensive look at Heracles in visual images, see Uhlenbrock and Galinsky 1986. For an analysis of the Heracles myths divided into diachronic and synchronic approaches, see Padilla 1998.
50 Kirk 1974: 176–212.
51 Stafford 2012.
52 Student interest in learning more about Heracles is indicative of a broader general interest in the hero. Blanshard 2005 provides an overview of Hercules' life for a non-specialist audience.
53 Bonnet and Jourdain-Annequin 1992; Jourdain-Annequin and Bonnet 1996; Bonnet, Jourdain-Annequin, and Pirenne-Delforge 1998; Rawlings and Bowden 2005.
54 Allan, Anagnostou-Laoutides, and Stafford 2020; Blanshard and Stafford 2021.
55 Ogden forthcoming.
56 See Murray 1946; Kirk 1977; Philips 1978; Effe 1980; Fuqua 1980.
57 Papadopoulou 2005.
58 Other such treatments of mythological heroes include King 1991; Montiglio 2011; Fantuzzi 2012.

1. Heraclean Force and the Representation of Violence

1 Riess 2012; see especially the charts on pp. 101 and 139.
2 On the Mycenaean roots of this expression, see Burkert 1972: 81; Ruijgh 1995: 82–3, 2011: 283–4.
3 See vv. 289, 315, 332, 943, 982.
4 For citations especially of archaic and classical poetry, see *LSJ*, s.v.
5 Hainsworth 1985: 3: 300 *ad* 690 observes that *biē* is modified by a masculine participle at *Il.* 11.690, "a useful certification that the formula is indeed the equivalent of a name-epithet phrase."
6 For an overview of these early fragmentary epics, see Huxley 1969: 99–112.
7 Fr. 1 Bernabé.
8 Theocritus, Epigr. 22 (Test. 2 Bernabé). See frr. 1–12 Bernabé.
9 *Suda*, s.v. (Test. 1 Bernabé). See frr. 1–26 Bernabé; see also the summary at Huxley 1969: 177–86.
10 Two Hesiodic poems concerned with Heracles, *The Wedding of Ceyx* and *Aigimios*, are not addressed in this chapter, due to their fragmentary state (see especially Huxley 1969: 106–10).
11 On the relatively positive presentation of Heracles in the *Theogony*, especially in comparison with his Homeric predecessors, see Bär 2018: 54–62.
12 All translations, unless otherwise indicated, are the author's own.
13 Likewise, the geographic localization of the Hydra at Lerna draws attention to the danger it poses to nearby settlements. The poem describes the Hydra as "evil-minded" (λυγρὰ ἰδυῖαν, 313), suggesting an active threat.
14 See Clay 1993: 112.
15 The son of Amphitryon at 317 alone, but the son of Zeus elsewhere; see especially 943–4, which clearly states that Zeus fathered Heracles with Alcmene.
16 On the relationship between Prometheus' punishment, mortality, and Heracles' *kleos*, see Mueller 2016.
17 On vv. 950–5, which I take to be an interpolation, see my discussion of *Odyssey* 11 below.
18 "Le vrai héros, le vrai sujet, le centre de l'Iliade, c'est la force. La force qui est maniée par les hommes, la force qui soumet les hommes, la force devant quoi la chair des hommes se rétracte." Translation by James Holoka from Weil 2003: 45.
19 See Grethlein 2012: 15; Bär 2019: 7–9.
20 See 2.658, 2.666, 5.638, 11.601, 11.690, 15.640, 18.117, 19.98.
21 Narratological terms are drawn from their usage in de Jong 1987.
22 I follow de Jong's basic definition of focalization: "the seeing or recalling of events, their emotional filtering and temporal ordering, and the fleshing out of space into scenery and persons into characters" (2014: 47).

23 Heracles is called "the son of Amphitryon" once, at 5.392.
24 Davidson 1980 argues that Agamemnon ironically compares himself to Eurystheus and Achilles to Heracles in this analogy. See also de Jong 1987: 172–3.
25 In narratological terms, Athena functions as an internal secondary narrator-focalizer, and Hera is an internal secondary narratee-focalizee (see de Jong 1987: 37). This embedding allows for a distinct spin on Heracles to be brought out, one that is rarely represented elsewhere in Greek literature.
26 Lang 1983: 152; see also pp. 149–53.
27 For Heracles' adventures on Cos, see Pherecydes 3F78, in which Heracles sacks the city of the king Eurypylos; Heracles' sack of the city is also mentioned in Hes. fr. 43a M–W. See also the fragments of the epic *Meropis* (frr. 1–6 Bernabé), in which Heracles fails to penetrate the skin of the invulnerable Asteros with his arrows; Athena rescues him, kills and flays Asteros, and wears Asteros' skin for her own protection. Though Lloyd-Jones and Parsons printed the text in *Supplementum Hellenisticum* (1983), Lloyd-Jones later suggests a date in the second half of the sixth century (reprinted in Lloyd-Jones 1990a), in agreement with Koenen and Merkelbach 1976.
28 See Yasumura 2011: 45–54 on the "cosmic strife" underlying this episode.
29 See Stamatopoulou 2017: 921–30.
30 A rare instance in the *Iliad* of Heracles' focalization through an internal secondary narratee: de Jong 2014: 22–3.
31 See discussion in Janko 1992: 4: 191–3. For a full discussion of the scattered evidence in poetry and art of Heracles' aid to the gods in their battle with the Giants, see Gantz 1993: 445–54.
32 So strange is this incident that Willcock suspects (following Fränkel) that the story is an invention of the Homeric poet (Willcock 1964: 145–6).
33 For the Olympian gods' reinforcing the boundary between immortal and mortal, see Apollo's protection of Aeneas against Diomedes (5.431–4).
34 Allen-Hornblower 2014 shows how the wounds of the gods at the hands of mortals in Book 5 brings gods and men closer together while paradoxically underlining their inescapable differences.
35 See also the accounts in Pausanias (10.13.8) and Hyginus (*Fab.* 32).
36 Servitude to humans is not restricted to mortals alone; even Apollo spent a period in servitude to Admetus (see Euripides' *Alcestis*, in which Heracles also plays a prominent role). Yet Admetus allowed Apollo to complete his servitude with dignity, at least in Euripides' version, while Heracles' servitude to Omphale is marked in the Roman period by suspicions of effeminate licentiousness and the adoption of women's actions and roles.
37 For assessments of the varying traditions and a full catalogue of images, see Luce 1930; Brommer 1956: 38–46.

38 Parke and Boardman 1957: 278–81.
39 See, e.g., Luce 1930: 317–18; Guillon 1963; Shapiro 1984a; Janko 1986.
40 Parke and Boardman 1957 argues that Heracles and Apollo represent opposing sides of the First Sacred War. Boardman 1972 argues that Heracles' introduction to Olympus served as a symbol for Peisistratus' return to Athens and effected a change from Heracles' approaching Olympus on foot to approaching on a chariot, by Athena's side. Boardman 1975a sees a reflection of the Athenian assumption of power over the Lesser Mysteries at Eleusis behind the iconographical shift to a less violent approach in Heracles' capture of Cerberus in the Underworld. Boardman 1978 addresses objections to his 1957 article with Parke.
41 Pindar alludes to a struggle between Heracles and Apollo (*Ol.* 9.43–7); though the exact context is unclear, it seems likely that he refers to this conflict. See also *Ol.* 9.32–3, which mentions in addition a conflict between Heracles and Poseidon, and Heracles and Hades.
42 On the shaping of these stories as myth, see Sourvinou-Inwood 1988.
43 Lloyd-Jones 1993: 207–8.
44 Pindar fr. 55 also depicts Apollo's takeover of Delphi as violent, for which Gē wanted to send him to Tartarus. See discussion in Rutherford 2001: 395–97.
45 In Euripides' presentation of this procession from chthonic to Olympian powers, the chthonic deities do not appear to require much civilization. See Kyriakou 2006: 401.
46 As Sommerstein 1989: 80–1 has shown, the insistence on a peaceful transfer anticipates the reconciliation at the climax of the play.
47 Plutarch is the only author who suggests that Heracles managed to hold on to the tripod; apparently, he brought it to Pheneus (*De sera numinis vindicta*, 12).
48 For a reading of the *Shield* as a reception of Diomedes' *theomachia* in *Iliad* 5, see Stamatopoulou 2017. Stamatopoulou compares Diomedes and Heracles and finds that Diomedes is defined by his piety and understanding of mortal limits, while Heracles is self-sufficient and acts independently of, but in line with, Olympian motivation. My argument falls more in line with Galinsky 1972: 17–19.
49 For a thorough overview of the myth through its material, visual, and literary evidence, see Zardini 2009. Her updated database of 166 vase paintings depicting Heracles and Cycnus (though 56 may have alternate interpretations) is of particular importance.
50 Russo 1965: 191–2 casts doubt on the authenticity of the final lines, but for their defense, see Janko 1986: 44–5.
51 While this analysis focuses on the conflict between Heracles and Ares, it is the battle between Heracles and Cycnus that becomes a very popular scene in Attic vase painting of the archaic period, with over 100 representations surviving. For a close analysis of the shifting iconography of the fight, see Muth 2008: 28–64. Muth maps the representation of the Gewalt-Ausübung and the Gewalt-Auswirkung onto

Heracles and Cycnus, revealing the vase painters' various methods for communicating both Heracles' courage in a perilous fight and his dominating victory over a lesser victim. Few of the vases directly depict the duel between Heracles and Ares, the focus of this analysis, but see discussion on p. 62 of images of Ares approaching Heracles with weapon raised, just behind the falling Cycnus.

52 Shapiro 1984a examines the political associations and Delphic connections between the myths of Heracles and Apollo's struggle for the tripod and Heracles' defeat of Cycnus in archaic Attic vase painting.

53 Cf. Achilles' instructions to Patroclus to defend only the Trojan ships and not press on to Ilium (*Il.* 16.87–96). Patroclus, roused by Zeus, ignores Achilles' order, and meets his death (16.684–91).

54 The reference to an attack on Ares at Pylos draws on Heracles' acts of theomachy in the *Iliad*. Janko 1986: 49 points to this passage as an example of the poet's innovation: inspired by *Iliad* 5, the poet adapts the wounding of Hades to the Olympian opponent at hand, Ares. The shift in focalization from Dione to Heracles demonstrates how theomachy can fluctuate between a dangerous subversion of established order and a source of heroic glory.

55 Shapiro 1984b: 526–7 attributes the appearance of Athena *between* Heracles and Ares on a Euphronius calyx-crater, among others, to this portion of the *Shield*.

56 On an unusual black-figure oenochoe (575–525 BCE), Lydos depicts the fight between Ares and Heracles over the dead body of Cycnus (Berlin 1732, *ABV* 110, 37). Shapiro 1984b: 525–6 argues that Lydos' iconography demonstrates an "unparalleled familiarity" with the *Shield*. Muth 2008: 38–9 addresses two other works of Lydos depicting Heracles against Cycnus; her overall analysis of the heterogeneity of the Heracles–Cycnus iconography rejects the premise that scholars can detect a direct dependence of a particular iconography on a literary work (see esp. pp. 30–1).

57 Cf. Ps.-Apollod. 2.5.11, in which Ares and Heracles struggle hand-to-hand, and Zeus breaks them apart with a blast of lightning.

58 Galinsky 1972: 19 takes this even further, arguing that the *Shield* "discards the negative heritage of the hero and establishes him as the resplendent victor, the *kallinikos*, and as a man of high morality, the saving *alexikakos*. These were his most famous titles in cult, and they called for and found a literary expression."

59 Though see 15.638–40 for a brief mention of the herald who serves as a go-between for Eurystheus and Heracles.

60 Kelly 2010: 273; see also Alden 2000: 160.

61 See Willcock 1964; Lang 1983. See also Bär 2018: 40–43, 2019: 8–9 on Heracles as an exemplum for Achilles.

62 On how Tlepolemus and Sarpedon both fail to match their use of the past with current circumstances, see Kelly 2010.

63 The sack of Elis—a myth first attested in the fifth century—follows the same general outline. Augeas withholds the pay promised to Heracles for cleaning the stables; after defeating the fearsome defenders, the Moliones, Heracles sacks Elis and with the spoils establishes the sanctuary of Zeus nearby and the Olympic games. See Gantz 1993: 392–4, 424–6.

64 Barker and Christensen 2014: 264–5.

65 Another city that Heracles sacks, Pylos, becomes an important locus of Heracles' adventures, if we follow the D-scholia in placing the wounding of Ares and Hera in the same series of incidents with the fight against Neleus and his sons (Hainsworth 1985: 3: 300 *ad* 690). The episode is mentioned obliquely by Nestor, when he explains that the Pylians were at a disadvantage to the Epeians because "mighty Heracles came and afflicted us during years past, and so many of our best died. For there were twelve sons of blameless Neleus of which I alone was left, and all the rest perished" (ἐλθὼν γάρ ῥ' ἐκάκωσε βίη Ἡρακληείη / τῶν προτέρων ἐτέων, κατὰ δ' ἔκταθεν ὅσσοι ἄριστοι. / δώδεκα γὰρ Νηλῆος ἀμύμονος υἱέες ἦμεν: / τῶν οἶος λιπόμην, οἳ δ' ἄλλοι πάντες ὄλοντο, 11.689–93). Nestor provides no motive for Heracles' destruction of the city and his own brothers, perhaps preferring to emphasize instead his own contributions to rebuilding Pylos' glory. The relevant fragments from the *Catalogue of Women*—fr. 33(a) and 35 (M–W)—seem to focus on Heracles' defeat of the shape-shifting son of Neleus, Periclymenus. According to Ps.-Apollodorus 2.6.2, Heracles is angered at Neleus because Neleus refuses to purify him from the pollution incurred by his murder of Iphitus, so he sacks Pylos before heading to Delphi, where he wrestles Apollo for the tripod. In this version, Heracles' theomachic tendencies and his propensity towards city-sacking are brought into alignment. Heracles is also known to have sacked Sparta and killed its ruler Hippocoon along with his sons; see Gantz 1993: 427–8.

66 See discussion in Gantz 1993: 434–7.

67 For a detailed analysis of Heracles' appearance in the *Odyssey* and his comparison with Odysseus, see Crissy 1997. On the parallel function of archery and the bow in Heracles and Odysseus' narratives, see Anderson 2012.

68 See Bär 2019: 11. While Odysseus' slaughter of the suitors can likewise be criticized as poor hospitality, I view the poem as strenuously justifying the slaughter based both on the suitors' behavior and the demands of the gods.

69 Though Odysseus too enacts this "slaughter at the feast" motif in his murder of the suitors, the narrative strenuously justifies his revenge. See Hankey 1990.

70 On Heracles as a model and counter-model for Achilles, see Barker and Christensen 2014: 269–77.

71 For a detailed investigation of the implications of mortality for the heroes of the *Iliad*, see Schein 1984.

72 See Rabel 1997: 163–9 on the implications of Achilles' taking Heracles as a model for himself. Note especially Rabel's discussion of Heracles' aggression, which positions him against his enemy as predator to prey and promotes killing as the goal of combat, rather than simply victory.
73 Nagy 1999: 318–21.
74 Laurens 1990; for a brief overview, see Stafford 2012: 173–5.
75 For the full catalogue, see Brommer 1973.
76 Scholars have connected the popularity of Heracles' introduction to Olympus to the development of Heracles' initiation at Eleusis and the artistic program of Peisistratus in the last third of the sixth century. See Boardman 1975a; Holt 1992.
77 See, e.g., the *Homeric Hymn to Heracles*, which contrasts Heracles' life of servitude to Eurystheus, inflicting and experiencing suffering, with his pleasant afterlife on Olympus.
78 See Bär 2018: 46–8, 2019: 9–10 on how Odysseus and Heracles' encounter suggests that Heracles no longer belongs in the "here and now" and should no longer remain within epic memory.
79 Dindorf 1855: *ad* 11.604; see also E. D'Agostino 2007. On the identity of the scholiast, West writes "it was presumably a Pergamene who dreamed up this ascription" (West 2014: 223, n. 131).
80 E.g., a brief summary of the reasons for doubt can be found in Stanford 1947: 1: 403. West 1966: 417 assesses ancient critical opinion of these lines in the *Odyssey* and similar passages in Hesiod's *Theogony* (947–55) and *Catalogue of Women* (frr. 25.26–33 and 229), concluding that "the deification of Heracles is indeed an indication of lateness." Heubeck and Hoekstra suggest that lines 602–4 may be genuine if the poet here is attempting a compromise between popular belief and narrative purpose; they admit, however, that such a compromise is "illogical" (Heubeck and Hoekstra 1990: 2: 114). For an argument that the whole episode, including the *eidolon*, is genuine, see Hooker 1980.
81 For a discussion of the dynamics of Odysseus' interaction with Heracles in context, see Karanika 2011.
82 Perhaps the symbolism would be too broad in a context where Odysseus too travels to the Underworld and back while still living, but entertains no hopes of immortality.
83 Fontenrose 1968; see also Currie 2005: 120–57; Lunt 2009.
84 Both of these poles are encompassed in the fragments of the Hesiodic *Catalogue of Women*. For a perceptive analysis of Heracles as a transitional figure in the poem, see Haubold 2005 and, building on Haubold, Ormand 2014. Haubold persuasively argues, "Looking ahead from the formation of the cosmos, as Hesiodic poetry does in the *Theogony*, Heracles appears as an indispensable pillar of Zeus' emerging order. Looking back in time from the more civilised era of the Trojan War (essentially the

Homeric perspective), he becomes himself an outsider and comes into conflict with the norms of a civilised human existence" (95). My one reservation about Haubold's argument pertains to his framing of city-sacking as inherently negative, which my reading of *Il.* 5 shows is not always the case. See also Bär 2018: 62–8.

2. Hero or Monster? Justifying Violence against Geryon

1 For speculation on Stesichorus' inclusion of adventures in Sicily on Heracles' return, see Sjoqvist 1962. On Heracles as a role model for Greek colonists and the long legacy of his journey from Spain to Greece, see Kajava 1997: 67–9.
2 Arendt 1970: 51.
3 Burkert 1979: 97.
4 Clay 1993: 106.
5 See Clay 1993, 2003: 150–74 on how both monsters and heroes are anomalous hybrids; heroes (positive, controlled) kill monsters (destructive, disordered) to reinforce the boundaries demarcating gods, humans, and beasts.
6 Clay 1993: 112. On the importance of the "superlative cap" in Hesiodic catalogues, see Faraone 2013.
7 Clay 1993: 109–10.
8 Ibid.: 112.
9 Lada-Richards 1998: 52.
10 For an anthropological survey of cattle raiding in the Greek heroic tradition, see Walcot 1979: 326–51.
11 His Labor to bring the Cattle of Geryon to the world of mortals marks Heracles as "the Master of Animals." Burkert 1979: 78–98 argues that Heracles' animal Labors share a common basis with shamanistic hunting rituals: Heracles "transfers the mastership of animals to man, animals difficult to get, dangerous, and cared for by superhuman owners" (95).
12 See Beaulieu 2015: 42–53. For more on the influence of the apotheosis myth on Stesichorus' *Geryoneis*, see Eisenfeld 2018.
13 Beaulieu 2015: 49.
14 Davies 1988: 279.
15 Aeschylus, *Heraclidae* F74 *TrGF*.
16 For the initial publication of the fragments, see Lobel 1967.
17 Davies and Finglass 2014: 36–7.
18 Tsitsibakou-Vasalos 1990: 28. On Stesichorus' use of Homer, see Kelly 2015: 39: "Stesichorus consistently us[es] images from the *Iliad* that are (1) unique to that poem, and (2) applied there to the Trojans, in order to flesh out the characterization of Geryon and his situation."

19 See Lada-Richards 1998: 46–8.
20 Eisenfeld 2018 takes a different approach, arguing that the poem positions Geryon as a hero, but Heracles as a god.
21 See fr. 84–9 Finglass.
22 Janko 1986.
23 5 Finglass = *SLG* 87; Di Gregorio 1975: 57.4–7.
24 Robertson 1969 uses the unusual detail of the wings to establish a relationship between Stesichorus' poem and this and certain other vases.
25 See the vase paintings depicting this episode in *LIMC* Herakles 2551, 2552. Panyassis and Apollodorus give varying explanations for how Heracles came to borrow the Sun's cup. Panyassis asserts that the sea god Nereus aided Heracles in acquiring the Sun's cup (fr. 9 Bernabé); in Apollodorus' version (2.5.10), an overheated Heracles threatens the Sun by drawing his bow against him; impressed, the Sun offers him the use of his cup.
26 Franzen 2009.
27 Curtis 2011: 21.
28 Castellaneta 2005 argues that the allusion to Hecuba anticipates Geryon's death, framing Callirhoe as a mother in mourning in addition to a mother in supplication.
29 I cite the Greek text as printed in Davies and Finglass 2014. For the possible identification of a grieving woman as Callirhoe on the vases, see Robertson 1969: 217.
30 The breast-baring gesture can be deceptive and manipulative as well, as Aeschylus' Clytemnestra later demonstrates (*Choephoroi* 896–8). Despite the incongruity of Clytemnestra's calling for "a man-killing axe" (ἀνδροκμῆτα πέλεκυν, 888) immediately before baring her breast to her son, her gesture nevertheless forces Orestes to hesitate.
31 Eisenfeld 2018: 93 detects a reference to Thetis as well, which would identify Geryon with both Hector and Achilles, excluding Heracles from the heroic conflict and proleptically framing him as a divinity.
32 Barrett suggested this context for the fragment, based on the account in Ps.-Apollodorus (Barrett 2007a: 13). Alternatively, Gentili 1977: 301 suggests Heracles as the interlocutor. See also Carmignani 1981: 34–5.
33 Jenny Strauss Clay remarks on this passage, "Geryon's dilemma is that of every offspring of a divine/human union" (Clay 1993: 109). Cf. discussion in Mann 1994: 317–20, on Peleus' hope that Achilles might prove immortal.
34 Tsitsibakou-Vasalos 1991: 259–60.
35 See discussion below on Pindar's fr. 169a.
36 See Page 1973; Tsitsibakou-Vasalos 1991; Barrett 2007a, 2007b; Lazzeri 2008: 117–19; Rozokoki 2008.
37 Page 1973. But Kelly 2015: 41–2 argues that "formularity pushes this parallel below the evidence bar."

38 Davies and Finglass print ἐ]λέγχεα (noun = reproaches) in the text and the papyrus' reading, ἐ]λεγχέα (adjective = cowardly), in the app. crit., but they print ἐ]λεγχέα in the commentary and defend the papyrus' use of the adjective there.
39 Barrett 2007b: 28. See Davies and Finglass 2014: 270–4 for a comparison of the supplements and the conclusion that Barrett's both "fits the traces, and makes sense." See also Page 1973: 149–50. Curtis 2011: 119 throws up his hands over these lines, declaring "the original sense of this fragment is probably lost forever." He also rejects similarities between this fragment and Sarpedon's speech to Glaucus and "the belief that this fragment portrays Geryon with a noble heart."
40 Frame 1971 argues that an association between cattle and immortality is a mythological archetype, suggesting that Geryon is fated to die upon the loss of his cattle.
41 Eisenfeld 2018: 85.
42 Ibid.: 86–7.
43 Some modern scholars even rely on the clarity of Geryon as the victim and Heracles as the aggressor to evaluate proposed supplements to the text. See the discussion of *P.Oxy.* 2617 fr. 1.2 in Curtis 2011: 106, where Curtis argues, "As Geryon looks to be legitimate in his defence of the cattle it seems unlikely that the Moirai would be pursuing him for transgression."
44 As far as I know, we have no evidence from the archaic period that indicates that Heracles was aware of his eventual apotheosis. In poetry, Sophocles' *Trachiniae* comes closest to revealing what one version of Heracles knew about his death: Heracles is in possession of oracles from Zeus, which he promptly misunderstands (in the vein of Sophoclean heroes like Oedipus). The philosophical Heracles, as represented in Prodicus' tale, deliberately chooses a difficult life full of suffering, with the promise of attaining Virtue at the end, but literal immortality is not considered the main prize.
45 Page 1973: 150 suggests that Athena exhorts Poseidon, "Remembering your promise to Geryon, go ahead and save him if you can; I will make certain that Heracles kills him nevertheless" ([ἄγ' ὑποσχέσιο]ς μεμναμένος ἅ[ν]|[περ ὑπέστας]|[Γαρυ]όναν θ[αν]άτου, ll. 6-8). Barrett 2007a: 17 proposes an addition, [ἄγ' ὑποσχέσιο]ς μεμναμένος ἅ[ν|περ ὑπέστας]|[μὴ βούλεο Γαρυ]όναν θ[αν]άτου, with the sense, "remember your promise (to me) and *do not* try to save Geryon from death." But Curtis 2011: 133 points out a major flaw in both suggestions: "Promises in Homer precede fulfilment, not (as possibly here) non-fulfilment," suggesting instead that "Athena challenges Poseidon to let Geryon confront Herakles: 'Come, let him, being noble, take thought as he fights with (my) man'" ([ὧδ' ὢν ἀγαθὸ]ς μεμναμένος ἀ[ν]|[δρὶ μαχέσθω]). Curtis's supplement is modeled on *Il.* 19.153, ὧδέ τις ὑμείων μεμνημένος ἀνδρὶ μαχέσθω.
46 See, e.g., Boardman 1975b: fig. 26.

47 This cup from Vulci, now lost, is known from drawings. See Beazley 1963: 62, no. 84; Robertson 1969: 210, 214.
48 See discussion at Lazzeri 2008: 175–80.
49 The involvement of another set of deities may be reflected in fr. 19.18–19 Finglass = SLG S21.1-2:

–]ν μεγ[⏑ –]. ρ̣ονες, ὠκυπέτα[
⏑ – ⏑ – ⏑]. ν ἐχοισαι

Suggested supplements have included unnamed [δαί]μονες ὠκυπέτα[ι] (Lerza 1978: 86-7); the Moirai (Lazzeri 1995: 93-9, with suggested [δολιό]φρονες ὠκυπέτα[ι] | [τόκα Μοῖραι πότμ]ον ἐχοίσαι); and the Keres (Irvine 1997: 38). The presence of the Moirai or Keres would indicate that this fragment belongs to the description of Geryon's death, and Davies-Finglass combine this fragment with SLG S15 to form a single fr. 19. Irvine 1997: 44 goes as far as to argue, based on Iliadic parallels, that Stesichorus may have depicted a *kerostasia* in the poem; for further analysis of the role of *kerostasia* in the *Iliad*, see Morrison 1997. Ercoles 2011 proposes a different restoration, in which "the Keres cower on the earth near Geryon ready to bring him to Hades at the proper time of the duel." Curtis 2011: 105 goes his own way, asserting that "the most obvious choice is Helios' horses" for ὠκυπέτα[.

50 Tsitsibakou-Vasalos 1990: 9.
51 For the collected fragments of Megaclides, see Janko 2000: 138–43. Based on the development of visual evidence, Robertson 1969: 213 judges that "the appearance of club and lion-skin in works of art is quite compatible with their being the invention of Stesichorus."
52 Though perhaps Stesichorus was the first to arm Heracles with all three weapons at once; see Davies and Finglass 2014: 568–70.
53 See Maingon 1980. On Stesichorus and Homer, see Kelly 2015.
54 Later, in Euripides' *Heracles*, the evil tyrant Lycus insults Heracles' reliance on archery and accuses him of cowardice: "in all else he wasn't at all brave, who never held a shield on his left arm nor approached the spear. But with his bow, the most cowardly weapon, he was prepared for flight" (... τἆλλα δ' οὐδὲν ἄλκιμος, / ὃς οὔποτ' ἀσπίδ' ἔσχε πρὸς λαιᾷ χερὶ /οὐδ' ἦλθε λόγχης ἐγγύς, ἀλλὰ τόξ' ἔχων, / κάκιστον ὅπλον, τῇ φυγῇ πρόχειρος ἦν, 158-62). Lycus denigrates archery in comparison with the demands on the hoplite soldier. Amphitryon, in response, mounts an able defense of Heracles' archery by arguing that his skills enable him to protect his *philoi* (including himself). Though Euripides' Lycus will be proven wrong in the play, he nevertheless expresses an attitude with a well-established history.
55 Kirk 1990: 2: 253.
56 For catalogue, see Brize 1980: 133–44, and further discussions and commentary in Brize 1988, 1990.

57 See Robertson 1969.
58 "Die Kunstler waren vor allem an die für die jeweilige Gattung spezifischen Traditionen gebunden" (Brize 1980: 65).
59 Muth 2008: 65–92; she warns us to avoid reading these images of violence as representations of historical attitudes towards violence.
60 The poisonous nature of the Hydra's venom and its application to the arrow may be Stesichorus' innovation (Davies and Finglass 2014: 286).
61 See Eisenfeld 2018: 90 on how the introduction of the Hydra's poison activates a "payload of mythological tradition that not only looks back to the Hydra's death, but also ahead to the end of Herakles' mortal life." In Hesiod's *Theogony*, as discussed above, the Hydra is a member of Geryon's extended family. The distinction between the human-like Geryon and the snake-like Hydra is even clearer in this poem.
62 For a further examination of the Homeric resonances of this scene, see Maingon 1980: 103–7. Cf. also *Iliad* 14.499.
63 Page 1973: 153.
64 Maingon 1980: 107.
65 D. Fowler 1987: 189.
66 For an overview of Heracles in Pindar, see Hernandez 1993.
67 See, e.g., Shapiro 1983; Stafford 2005.
68 See Robbins 1982; Köhnken 1983.
69 On the later reception of Heracles as an eloquent, persuasive orator among French kings, see Stafford 2012: 215–18.
70 The peaceful nature of this interaction may be Pindar's innovation; see Robbins 1982: 300.
71 Montiglio 2000: 82–115.
72 On lack of praise as a form of blame, see Detienne 1996: 47–9. On the "σιγά motive" in Pindar's epinicians, see Bundy 1962: 73–6. On contrast between Pindar and Archilochus, see Montiglio 2000: 88–91.
73 Montiglio 2000: 111.
74 Race 1989: 190–1.
75 I print the text as it appears in Maehler and Snell 1989.
76 See Kingsley 2018 for a recent summary of the bibliography.
77 Lloyd-Jones 1972: 49. Though he had argued in 1968 that δικαιῶν means "bringing violence to justice," Pavese comes to accept Lloyd-Jones' approach, suggesting "deem or claim as a right" (Pavese 1993: 146). Kyriakou 2002 follows this formulation, arguing that the participle means "claiming as its right" or prerogative; *nomos* thus becomes a "sovereign, amoral power" that uses Heracles' injustice to accomplish its will (Kyriakou 2002: 200).
78 But on the possibility of deliberate misquotation in Plato, see Dodds 1959: 270–2; Demos 1994; Grote 1994.

79 Mythological characters' involvement in a money economy is more often associated with comedy; see, e.g., the innkeepers of the Underworld in Aristophanes' *Frogs*.
80 Ostwald 1965: 118.
81 Line 15's supplement belongs to Snell; line 16's to Lobel.
82 *LSJ* s.v. κόρος. Pindar closely associates Heracles and *aretē* in *Nem*. 1.33–4.
83 For supplement and discussion, see Lobel 1961: 149–50.
84 Compare with the presentation in Euripides' *Alcestis* of Diomedes (481–506).
85 Gentili 1977: 305.
86 For a neat summary of the opposing camps, see discussion in Lloyd-Jones 1972: 55–6. Gigante's thorough survey of ideas ultimately supports the idea of divine law, concluding that *nomos* is the absolute principle of divinity, which has force as one of its attributes (1956: 1: 92). On the other hand, Ostwald represents the "custom" category, defining *nomos* as "a traditional attitude which implies certain deep-seated convictions and beliefs" (1965: 124). Pike 1984: 20 offers a third interpretation, that there is one *nomos* for gods, another for humans, and another for heroes, and "any act committed by a person is just—so long as it falls within the limits imposed by the νόμος of the class to which that person belongs." In the context of the *Gorgias*, Payne 2006: 170 further refines this claim by suggesting that "the manner in which [Heracles] fulfills his tasks is entirely his own, the fulfillment of his own specific nature and being."
87 Crotty 1982: 106.
88 After discussing Cambyses' madness and Darius' test of funerary *nomoi*, Herodotus cites Pindar approvingly, "Correctly Pindar seems to me to compose, saying '*Nomos* is king of all'" (ὀρθῶς μοι δοκέει Πίνδαρος ποιῆσαι, «νόμον πάντων βασιλέα» φήσας εἶναι, 3.38). In Plato's *Gorgias* (484b), Callicles refers to Pindar and argues that *nomos* is the law of nature, i.e., "might makes right," an interpretation that Payne 2006 defends.
89 Kingsley 2018: 53.

3. Heroic Competition and the Home in Sophocles' *Trachiniae*

1 For speculation on why tragedy features Heracles infrequently, see Galinsky 1972: 40–2; Silk 1985.
2 For a general overview of competition or athletics in archaic Greek culture with bibliography, see Fisher 2009; see also Poliakoff 1987; Knox 1999; Hawhee 2002; Kyle 2014: 53–90.
3 See Weiler 1974.
4 Easterling 1982: 133; Swift 2011.
5 Effe 1980: 154.

6 Earlier traditional accounts may have characterized Deianeira as an Amazon-like warrior. In addition to the evidence of her name ("man-slayer"), further evidence for a warlike Deianeira is presented in March 1987: 49–59. Just as a clever Penelope proves a fitting wife for wily Odysseus, a bold-hearted and violent Deianeira would seem to suit Heracles. But Sophocles' Deianeira is radically different from Heracles, and he desires her as a partner not in combat, but in bed.
7 See Isler 1970.
8 On tragedy's treatment of the same material in both iambic trimeters and lyric, see Davies 1991: 136–8.
9 On this contest as "an athletic competition," see Swift 2011: 394–7.
10 See Nilsson 1941: vol. 1, 19; Thompson 1955: H 310, 326 ll. 2, 335. On bridal competitions and matrilineal succession, see Finkelberg 1991.
11 On the darker tradition of Myrtilos' involvement in the race, see Gantz 1993: 541–3. Pelops' son Thyestes commits adultery with the wife of his brother Atreus, who has his revenge when he murders Thyestes' sons and feeds them to him. Atreus' sons, Agamemnon and Menelaus, hardly find happiness in their families.
12 Though Deianeira is not yet aware of Heracles' servitude to Omphale, the audience may already have the Lydian woman in mind.
13 Rankine 2011.
14 For a comparison of the *Odyssey*'s treatment of this episode, see Liapis 2006, which suggests that Sophocles frames his own Eurytus as a Homeric Heracles. See also discussion of the death of Iphitus, as it relates to Heracles' role as sacker of cities, in Chapter 1.
15 On the importance of narrative story-telling in interpreting the play, see Kraus 1991.
16 See Stafford 2012: 68–70.
17 See Wender 1974: 4–5.
18 Lines 573–4 pose a notorious textual problem. See discussion in Easterling 1982: 144–5; I follow her second interpretation and take μελαγχόλους as proleptic, though the phrase remains difficult.
19 Though Nessus instructs Deianeira to touch his blood with her (presumably bare) hands, the poison of the Hydra does not seem to affect her.
20 Faraone 1994: 115–23 argues that Deianeria already knew that the "charm" was a dangerous poison, and her mistake is in underestimating the power of this particular poison.
21 Bowman 1999 argues that one of Deianeira's mistakes was to ascribe the authority that belongs only to Zeus to Nessus' pronouncements.
22 A comparison to Odysseus' household in the *Odyssey* is instructive. The epic depicts in great detail the suffering of Odysseus' *oikos* in his absence during the war: his son Telemachus watches their wealth disappear into the guts of the suitors who plague his faithful wife, Penelope; even his servants and the productivity of his land suffer

decline. Yet the marital bed, constructed by Odysseus' own hands and literally rooted in the center of the household, remains an undefiled symbol of their marriage; despite the deterioration of the household, the uncorrupted inner sanctum reflects an inner strength of Odysseus and Penelope's union. That strength will prove critical to Odysseus' successful *nostos* and resumption of power. In contrast, Sophocles reveals that a dangerous poison lies within Heracles and Deianiera's physical household, a weakness that will be reflected externally in the actions of the play. For a longer comparative analysis of the two texts, see Davidson 2003, itself an elaboration on Fowler 1999: 161–5.

23 On satyric representations of this myth, see Chapter 5.
24 Most of the "Sack of Oechalia" (Οἰχαλίας ἅλωσις), an archaic epic, has been lost. See discussion in Davies 1991: xxii–xxvi.
25 Lichas' reference to a "judgment of the bow with his children" (τῶν ὧν τέκνων λείποιτο πρὸς τόξου κρίσιν, 266) alludes to a tradition that Heracles, in pursuit of Iole's hand in marriage from Eurytus, competed in an archery contest with Iole's brothers, an example of proper heroic competition. When Eurytus denied Heracles despite his victory, Heracles sacked Oechalia. The story falls into the same narrative pattern as Poseidon's sack of Troy, after he helped to build the walls for Laomedon but was deprived of payment.
26 See my discussion of the *Odyssey*'s use of this incident in Chapter 1.
27 Halleran 1986 argues that the emphasis on the stealthy nature of Heracles' murder is a Sophoclean innovation for the purpose of drawing a comparison to Deianeira's stealthy use of the love potion.
28 The situation is analogous to Apollo's servitude to Admetus, described in the prologue of Euripides' *Alcestis*.
29 For a survey of the treatment of Iole in epic and tragedy, see Pralon 1996, which argues that the conflicting accounts of Lichas and the messenger represent a transition from epic narrative to tragic enactment (see especially 69–72).
30 See Gantz 1993: 434–7.
31 As many have noted, the phrase Ἐρινύων ὑφαντὸν ἀμφίβληστρον (1051–2) alludes to Aeschylus, *Agamemnon,* 1382 (ἄπειρον ἀμφίβληστρον) and 1580 (ὑφαντοῖς ἐν πέπλοις Ἐρινύων). See Easterling 1982: 206.
32 On Deianeira's hasty decision making (the opposite of late-learning), see E. Hall 2009.
33 Faraone 1994 recognizes Deianeira's concern for dynastic status. Wender 1974: 1 makes a similar observation.
34 Winnington-Ingram 1980: 75.
35 In Ode 16, Bacchylides attributes Heracles' destruction to *phthonos* (v. 31). This "envy" or "jealousy" is typically taken to refer to Deianeira's jealousy of the younger and more beautiful Iole, but Platter argues that *phthonos* should be understood as

"resentment" or "blame," and thus refers to Nessus' attitude towards Heracles (Platter 1994: 346). But Deianeira too is entitled to feel resentment regarding Heracles' actions; it is her lack of ill-will towards Iole that is truly extraordinary.

36 That Deianeira can act in defense of her status without adopting harsh masculine qualities at the same time has confused many critics. See Kirkwood 1994: 115, n. 17.
37 Faraone 1994: 126.
38 In this sense, the *Trachiniae* resembles another play of Sophocles', the *Ajax*. For the *Ajax* stages the great conflict between Teucer and the sons of Atreus over the heroic status of Ajax, newly dead by his own hand. The Atreidae insist that Ajax's body remain unburied, a fitting punishment for a traitor who attempted to assassinate the leaders of the Greek expedition; in contrast, Teucer defends his half-brother by relying on his displays of heroic valor—his defense of the ships from Hector's attack, his single-champion fight with Hector—and attacking the Atreidae's own claim to superiority. Odysseus arrives belatedly to referee the dispute. In a surprising turn, Odysseus, whose deep enmity towards Ajax was established in the opening of the play, defends Ajax and insists on a proper burial. Odysseus, in fact, overrules Agamemnon and assists Teucer, because Ajax was γενναῖος (1355) and because of his ἀρετή (1357). Thus, the play can be read as argument for overlooking Ajax's great fall at the end of his career as an aberration, and privileging his heroic service over his shameful end. This argument takes place in the army's camp, however, a far cry from the domestic scene of the *Trachiniae*. The relationship between Ajax and Tecmessa is likewise very different from Heracles and Deianeira. Despite the harshness of Ajax's spirit, they still share a warm affection (Stanford 1963: xxvii–xxxiii).
39 In Euripides' *Medea*, Medea offers one reason why a man might take a new marriage: "For if you were still childless, it would be excusable for you to crave another marriage" (εἰ γὰρ ἦσθ' ἄπαις ἔτι, / συγγνώστ' ἂν ἦν σοι τοῦδ' ἐρασθῆναι λέχους, 490–1).
40 For a wider study of forms of Zeus as related to cult ritual and sacrifice, see Ellinger 2005.
41 He is a victim of the Hydra's poison, but also framed as a victim of a perverted sacrifice: see Calame 1998.
42 Heracles also curses his "poorly-mated marriage with wretched [Deianeira] and the alliance of Oeneus" (τὸ δυσπάρευνον λέκτρον ἐνδατούμενος / σοῦ τῆς ταλαίνης καὶ τὸν Οἰνέως γάμον, 791–2). Heracles instinctively sees in his connection to Deianeira a relationship with her father. His first thought seems to be of the *other* marital alliances he could have more profitably made instead. See the discussion of these dynamics in terms of homosocial relationships in Wohl 1998: 17–29 and Ormand 1999: 36–59.
43 Segal 2000 resolves the ostensibly conflicting accounts provided by various prophecies. The theme of knowledge recurs throughout the play. On knowledge,

truth, falsehood, and ignorance, see Lawrence 1978. On late-learning in this play and the uncertainty of knowledge, see Whitman 1951: 103–21.
44 For Heracles as a quasi-bestial creature, see Segal 1977: 109.
45 Carawan 2000 argues, contrary to the *communis opinio,* that Deianeira is "burdened with guilty knowledge," and though she did not *intend* to kill Heracles, she would be considered guilty in a legal context. Bowra 1944: 127–8 calls Deianeira's act to subject her husband to her own will "an intolerable act of arrogance," not a single error of judgment in an otherwise sympathetic life.
46 On the similarity between Heracles' disease and lust, see Biggs 1966: 228. Compare the language of Iole's capture (ἰὼ κελαινὰ λόγχα προμάχου δορός, 856) with the language of Deianeira's destruction (τίς θυμός, ἢ τίνες νόσοι, / τάνδ' αἰχμᾷ βέλεος κακοῦ / ξυνεῖλε, 882–4).
47 Carawan 2000: 218.
48 Wender 1974: 13.
49 On Creophylus, see discussion in Huxley 1969: 105–6.
50 Many have seen a feminized Heracles in this scene. Loraux 1990: 28 asserts "Herakles suffers like a woman before resolving to die like a man."
51 Segal 1977: 115.
52 Indeed, the play's actions reveal how "many of his adventures were caused entirely by his own character," not the imposition of the gods (Ehrenberg 1946: 153).
53 Heiden 1989: 141 calls Heracles' attention to his body "vanity."
54 See Pozzi 1999. It also reflects the kind of change produced by a character who has at last acquired full knowledge. Hyllus has discovered the meaning behind his mother's actions and the solution to his father's fate and can thus act with deliberate wisdom, while Heracles is the only figure on stage who does not yet understand the origins of his fatal robe and the meaning of his life's oracles. Carawan 2000: 220–9 argues that Hyllus acquits Deianeira under the rules of the "sympathetic *oikos,*" as opposed to the rules of the polis, agora, or assembly.
55 On the inability of Deianeira, Heracles, and Hyllus to attain self-knowledge, see Lefèvre 2001: 11–39.
56 Easterling 1982: 217 suggests that this exchange emphasizes the significance of the moment without the distraction of introducing new family members to the stage.
57 Segal 2000 is right to assert that the *Trachiniae*'s oracles "converge." As Kirkwood 1994 argued, the audience was unlikely to have been distracted by their minor inconsistencies (79). Whitman 1951: 108 calls the multiple oracles "deliberately confusing" in order to illustrate the impossibility of knowing the future. According to Schwinge 1962: 101–3, the gap between men's understanding of differing oracles and the gods' intention to bring them to fruition in the same action only emphasizes the remoteness and overwhelming power of the gods.
58 Easterling 1982: 220.

59 Varying traditions allowed Philoctetes or his father Poeas to kindle the flame. See Lloyd-Jones 1971: 127–8.
60 Whether Iole is to be a concubine or wife is not of great importance here. MacKinnon 1971 argues that Iole is only intended to be a concubine; Segal 1994 disagrees, seeing her as wife of full status.
61 Richard Janko suggested this formulation to me.
62 Ruth Scodel suggests the comparison to Ajax and Tecmessa in Sophocles' *Ajax*: Ajax sees to it to that Teucer takes responsibility for his concubine's physical and financial protection, but he does not forbid a future remarriage.
63 Holt 1989; Hahnemann 1999. See also Finkelberg 1996.
64 Stinton 1990 denies that Sophocles alludes to the tradition of apotheosis; he builds his argument on Easterling 1981, which suggests that the play incorporates an ironic allusion to apotheosis, but leaves it open-ended. For full bibliography on this debate, see Liapis 2006: 56–9 with notes. On Sophocles' tendency to conclude by referencing future events while leaving them open, see Roberts 1988.
65 Sophocles' interest in innovative dramatic technique in general has been long recognized. See Aristotle, *Poetics* 1449a13; Kirkwood 1994: 94–7.
66 Segal 1977: 138–41.
67 I am not asserting that Sophocles was compelled to allude to Heracles' apotheosis; as discussed in Chapter 1, earlier tradition indicates that Heracles simply became an inhabitant of the underworld, and that tradition was certainly available to Sophocles and his audience. But I do believe that, in insisting on a pyre on Mount Oeta, Sophocles draws attention to and allows for the possibility of apotheosis, thus choosing to privilege the more recent legend.
68 On Heracles' insistent demands, see Kirkwood 1994: 118: "There is something more than human in this aspect of Heracles' personality"; and Bowra 1944: 135–8, which emphasizes Heracles' unique status and power, enabling him to stand apart from the typical judgment rendered on mortals.
69 See J. M. Hall 1997: 67–107 on the political significance of claims to ancestry from Heracles, especially in the Argolid.
70 A comparison with Phoenix's tale in *Il.* 9.448–57 is instructive. Phoenix's story makes clear that his father's concubine is off-limits; whatever the effects of Phoenix's sexual prowess on the young woman, the result of his action is to insult his father by claiming his sexual partner for himself. Amyntor calls upon the Furies, "because they are the guardians of the natural order and punish those whose unnatural acts (whether speech by a horse or disrespect for parents) have breached it" (Hainsworth 1985: 3: 122). Phoenix's infertility serves as a sign and confirmation of his father's curse.
71 In Segal's words, "Heracles' failure toward his own house is only a lesser reflection of Zeus's failure toward his" (Segal 1981: 81).

72 See vv. 19, 26, 128, 139, 200, 238, 251, 275, 287, 303, 437, 751, 826, 959, 995, 1002, 1022, 1041, 1048, 1086, 1106, 1149, 1159, 1185, 1188, 1191, 1278. Mikalson 1986 argues that in Euripides' *Heracles*, Zeus mainly appears in the role of *Sōtēr*, whereas in the *Trachiniae*, Sophocles introduces a wide range of Zeuses.
73 See discussion in Easterling 1982: 231–2.
74 Lloyd-Jones 1971: 104–28 also concludes that the end of the *Trachiniae* develops a notion of divine justice, but is overly confident about the possibility of divining Sophocles' personal opinion on the justice of the gods.
75 Versnel 2011 offers a thorough discussion of divine justice versus divine arbitrariness, and "the persistent and pervasive *lack of consistency* in expressions concerning divine causation of good and evil in archaic and early classical literature" (162).

4. Coping with Violence: Victory and Friendship in Euripides' *Heracles*

1 For a succinct summary of scholarly opinions on the play's structure, see Foley 1985: 200–4.
2 Swinburne most memorably denigrates the *Heracles* as a fractured tragedy, calling it a "grotesque abortion" (quoted in Verrall 1905: 136). For studies that argue for unity, see, e.g., Arrowsmith 1954; Conacher 1955; Kamerbeek 1966; Silk 1985; Papadopoulou 2005. Seminal studies on the question of *aretē* are Sheppard 1916 and Chalk 1962; more recently, Papadopoulou 2005 writes, "the question of Heracles' prowess ... is problematized throughout the play" (137).
3 Arrowsmith 1954: 14; Wilamowitz-Moellendorff 1895: 127–8. Wilamowitz's argument is based on his conception of Heracles as a "Dorian hero," who, after suffering an attack of megalomania (128), is left passive (109–11) and in need of Athenian rescue in the person of Theseus.
4 See, e.g., de Romilly 1980; Barlow 1981; Furley 1986. For a contrarian reading, see Adkins 1966: 218–19.
5 Belfiore 2000: 7.
6 Schein 1990: 58. The role of *philia* in Euripides' works has generated significant discussion: Scully 1973; Scodel 1979; Schein 1988; McDonald 1990; Goldfarb 1992; Belfiore 2000; Johnson 2002.
7 Farnell 1921: 148.
8 Perhaps Euripides' composition of an epinician song for Alcibiades indicates a deeper interest in the genre (Plutarch, *Life of Alcibiades*). On the role of epinician in tragedies beyond the *Heracles*, see Steiner 2010; Swift 2010; Carey 2012.

9 Swift 2010: 121–56. See also Foley 1985: 177–8 on how the first half of the play presents Heracles as an epinician hero.
10 On Greek athletics in literary contexts, see Golden 1998: 74–103; Kyle 2014: 54–71.
11 Kurke 1991.
12 For μοχθέω and πόνος, see 355, 356, 388, 427, 575, 578–81, 698, 725, 830, 937, 1190, 1197, 1251, 1270, 1275, 1279, 1353, 1369, 1410, 1411. The pan-Hellenic character of Heracles' fame belies Wilamowitz's emphasis on Heracles as a Dorian figure: see Wilamowitz-Moellendorff 1895: 128; Bond 1981: xxxii; Papadopoulou 2005: 83.
13 Bond 1981: 103. Even the sympathetic Chorus calls him "the husband in the halls of Hades" (117–18), as though he resides there permanently.
14 The question of Heracles' double paternity runs throughout the play. In part III, a bitter Heracles even considers Amphitryon as his true father instead of Zeus (1263–5).
15 Some scholars have linked this debate to the presence or absence of Athenian archers during the battles at Pylos and Delium in 425/4 (see Bond 1981: 109).
16 B. Cohen 1994 argues that in the fifth century, the bow became associated with the barbarian Persian army; as a result, Heracles wields a club instead on the metopes of the Temple of Zeus at Olympia.
17 For the self as "a person's closest *philos*," see Belfiore 2000: 101–16 in the context of Sophocles' *Ajax*.
18 Bond 1981: 115.
19 Megara's response to their extremity marks her as a suitable spouse for Heracles, unlike the timid and fearful Deianeira of the *Trachiniae* (see Michelini 1987: 247; contra Burnett 1971: 160–3). Just as Heracles toiled at his Labors (ἐξεμόχθησεν πόνους, 23), so Megara toiled at women's task, the bearing of children (ἀμόχθησα, 281). Despite his absence, she proclaims that her "husband, even unwitnessed, is glorious" (οὑμὸς δ' ἀμαρτύρητος εὐκλεὴς πόσις, 290), gently rebuking Amphitryon's earlier call to the gods and locales of Heracles' deeds as witnesses of his prowess (174ff.; see Bond 1981: 106). But her decision to accept death at Lycus' hands as a way of preserving public reputation is distinct from Heracles' consideration of suicide in part III of the play: Megara has no ability to constrain Lycus' violence, while Heracles has the choice to direct violence towards himself or not.
20 Pindar is fond of envisioning song as a precious object (Kurke 1991: 105). Cf. *Ol.* 11.13–14, *Nem.* 7.77–9. Its syntax and imagery of praise "are firmly Pindaric in inspiration" (Carey 2012: 28).
21 Bond 1981: 146–50; Hose 1991: 121; Carey 2012: 28–9.
22 Swift 2010: 124–9. See also Michelini 1987: 255.
23 Although the play conspicuously makes no mention of the tradition of Heracles' apotheosis, the theme of the defeat of death is of obvious concern in the play (see the second stasimon, esp. vv. 655–72, and Iris's motivation in 838–42).

24 For evidence of Heracles' role as a protector of travelers, including sailors, see the Roman Imperial inscription discussed in Kajava 1997.
25 Where Wilamowitz saw the seed of madness and heroic bombast in this speech, I see a fully justified response to Lycus' brutal villainy. Indeed, as Chalk puts it, to look for signs of emerging insanity earlier in the play is to "dilute the responsibility of Hera and so blur the point of the play" (1962: 15). Heracles' madness is externally imposed; the appearance of Iris and Lyssa and their conversation make this explicit. For the external nature of his insanity, see Hartigan 1987.
26 Bond 1981: 208.
27 Ibid.: 209.
28 Here I follow Bond (1981: 210), who argues that "labour to avert" is contrary to Euripidean usage.
29 For Heracles as *aristos* at this moment, see Hartigan 1987: 127.
30 Parry 1965: 365–6. Parry's article remains the definitive study of epinician language in the second stasimon. See also Swift 2010: 130.
31 Bond 1981: 233–4.
32 For a spatial analysis of this metaphor, see Kratzer 2010: 59–93.
33 Here, the substantive καλλίνικον is paired with a feminine definite article; in 180, the masculine article appears.
34 Parry 1965: 373.
35 According to Desch's psychological (and idiosyncratic) reading, the celebrations of the first two stasima reveal the unreasonable mental stress that the heroic life and the Chorus's high expectations must have placed on Heracles; part II thus dramatizes the consequences of Heracles' mental breakdown (1986: 13–14). In this ode, Weiss identifies an "extreme mixing of genres" that "undercuts the chorus' celebratory festivity," leading eventually to lament and then to choral silence (2019: 171).
36 Parry 1965: 364. See also Burnett 1971: 178 on the emotional responses of Heracles' family, who, desperately in need of a savior, believed that "Heracles was wholly mortal and yet (here is the danger) they began to treat this 'mortal' as if he were a god"; Swift 2010: 148–9.
37 See Pindar's *Pyth.*1.81–4 on the importance of brevity in praise. For a study of the poetics of envy, see Most 2003.
38 Carey 2012: 27.
39 Bond 1981: 267.
40 Ibid.: 272.
41 On epinician's use of local places and mythology, see Swift 2010: 131–3.
42 See also the framing of the conflict as an *agōn* in 812.
43 Critics have also found fault in the celebratory tone of the ode; see Sheppard 1916: 77; Foley 1985: 185. For a defense of the tone, see Bond 1981: 263–4 and the analysis of epinician in tragedy in Carey 2012.

44 Foley 1985: 176.
45 Chalk 1962: 15; Wildberg 2002: 170. So striking is the lack of justification for Lyssa's intervention that Wildberg must classify the epiphany in the *Heracles* apart from the other Euripidean dramas (2002: 127, n. 41; 170–1). Bartosiewiczova 1987, baffled by Heracles' madness, compares the play to "das moderne absurde Drama" (4).
46 See Swift 2010: 143–7 on athletic imagery in the messenger speech; Papadopoulou 2005: 70.
47 Papadopoulou 2005: 70. See also Burnett 1971: 171; Holmes 2008.
48 For an analysis of the importance of the disordered sacrifice here, see Foley 1985: 147–75.
49 Brommer 1986: 30 describes Heracles, in the metope on the Temple of Zeus at Olympia that represents this Labor, as grasping a stick, perhaps the handle of a shovel or hoe. Ashmole and Yalouris 1967: 29 call it a "crowbar."
50 For example, see Euripides' dramatization of Heracles as *xenos* in the *Alcestis* (especially 477–506), and Pindar's account of the foundation of the Olympic Games in *Olympian* 10.
51 See, e.g., Aristophanes' *Birds*, especially 1565–693. I discuss the comic character of Heracles in Chapter 5.
52 Swift 2010: 144.
53 Adkins 1972: 17.
54 As Chalk 1962: 16 writes, Heracles is "affected by the very βία that possessed Lycus," displaying "what actions good and bad alike have in common—violence."
55 Papadopoulou explains the inappropriateness of the use of the bow within Thebes, since "the bow belongs to the wild world of the labours" (2005: 146–7).
56 Belfiore 2000: 127.
57 Her actions prompt the question: why is murdering one's wife and children permissible, but one's father beyond the pale? Here Euripides perhaps trades on the characterization of Athena in Aeschylus' *Eumenides* (see especially 734–43), where the motherless and virginal Athena prioritizes paternity over every other family relationship.
58 Swift 2010: 144.
59 Foley 1985: 150.
60 Arendt 1970: 51.
61 Benjamin 1986: 294.
62 Burnett 1971: 171, n. 20.
63 Benjamin 1986: 294.
64 On the flight of the suicidal wife in tragedy, see Loraux 1987: 17–21. On Ajax's stabbing of himself with Hector's sword, see Belfiore 2000: 110.
65 The basic verb ἀκοντίζω was used to describe hurling a javelin as early as *Iliad* 14.402. The compound verb is frequent in Euripides (s.v., *LSJ*).

66 Mette 1983 argues that Euripides' lost *Peirithous* preceded our *Heracles*.
67 Note Theseus' denigration of "aging" friendship in 1223-5, which implicitly values its opposite, a friendship that stays youthful, as Heracles (the personification of *neotas*) does. Theseus thus demonstrates the most traditional form of *philia* which depends "not only on sentiments and intentions but on deeds: what counts is what one does for a friend, for that is the surest evidence of devotion" (Konstan 1997: 56).
68 See discussion in Johnson 2002: 118 on compassion as a reciprocal response to beneficial action.
69 Bond 1981: 380.
70 Conacher 1955: 149.
71 Loraux 1987: 11. On Ajax's suicide as self-caused death, see Belfiore 2000: 101-16; on suicide as a means to avoid shame and maintain honor, see Garrison 1995: 45-79. On suicide in the ancient world more generally, see van Hooff 1990.
72 Barlow 1982: 119.
73 See Chapter 1.
74 In Heracles' exile, we see another demonstration of the failure of epinician. For if Kurke 1991: 7 is correct in formulating the ultimate goal of epinician as "the successful integration of the athlete into a harmonious community," then the poetic genre fails utterly here. Heracles overturns his own *oikos* and is exiled from his city, prevented from burying his own sons, never to see his father alive again. That he finds refuge in Athens has less to do with the triumph of a victorious return than it does with the positive representation of Athenian values in this play. On Athens as a refuge in Greek tragedy, see Tzanetou 2012.
75 In the establishment of hero cult, Swift sees an aetiology for epinician in general, a genre that connects the praise of an exceptional person with posthumous cult (2010: 155).
76 Yoshitake 1994: 141.
77 The term *parerga* recalls the heroic deeds Heracles accomplished while pursuing the canonical Labors ordered by Eurystheus (a categorization that probably occurred with the late mythographers). The rescue of Theseus, in fact, might be termed a *parergon*: Heracles' main goal in Hades was the capture of Cerberus, but he delayed his return in order to release Theseus as well (619). Thus, in denigrating the honors Theseus offers, Heracles also rejects the positive associations of his legendary exploits and glorious reputation.
78 Yoshitake 1994: 142.
79 Conacher 1955: 150 calls this decision "Heracles' final victory."
80 One is reminded of Shakespeare's union of the two ideas in Hamlet's soliloquy, "to suffer the slings and arrows of outrageous fortune" (Act III, scene i).
81 Hose 2008: 114. For his broader view of the play as transforming Heracles from an aristocratic into a democratic hero, see Hose 2008: 101-14.

5. Heracles the Fool: Laughing at Violence

1. Classicists have long been using Bakhtin, who trained as a classicist, to think about Greek texts. Other works on Bakhtin in Classics include: Stevens 1958; Nightingale 1995; Branham 2002; Platter 2007.
2. Bakhtin 1984a.
3. For example, Heracles appears in Epicharmus' works in Sicily, where dramatic performance culture remains a bit hazy; we also see him in art and prose mimes. On the limitations of applying Bakhtin's analysis of carnival to Greek Old Comedy, see Edwards 2002.
4. Platter 2007: 8–9.
5. It is possible that the proportion of food fragments in the surviving corpus distorts the importance of feasting for the comic Heracles, but the evidence provided by Euripides' *Alcestis* demonstrates its centrality.
6. Due to the nature of our evidence, I am particularly aware of the risks of 1) making overly broad claim about Heracles in comedy, and 2) eliding the significant geographic, historical/chronological, and generic differences between various kinds of dramatic performances. In the following treatment, my focus is more on teasing out the threads of continuity that help to bring out a fuller picture of the relationship of comic Heracles to violence.
7. Dover 1972: 32.
8. Casolari 2003: 227–95. See also Galinsky 1972; Stafford 2012: 105–17. On Heracles *alexikakos* and his use of the poison of the Hydra, see Janko 2013.
9. Mythological narratives appear to occupy a significant part of his *oeuvre* (twenty-four of about forty-one plays), with Heracles taking a preeminent place. At least six titles refer to Heracles myths: *Alcyoneus*, *Busiris*, *Wedding of Hebe* (or in its revised form, *Muses*), *Heracles at the House of Pholus*, *Heracles' Quest for the Belt*, and *Heracles the <>*, and perhaps *Dexamenos*.
10. See Olson 2007: 40–2.
11. Bakhtin 1984a: 338.
12. Ibid.: 294. The tradition of mocking Heracles continues in Sicily in the form of Sophron's mimes, short humorous sketches in prose, and the so-called phlyax plays, including a *Heracles* (fr. 3) of Rhinton of Taras. On the relevant fragments of Sophron (frr. 59, 68, 72, 134), see Hordern 2004. While the influence of Epicharmus on Athenian drama remains the subject of lively scholarly debate, these themes stand out persistently in later representations of the humorous Heracles.
13. Bakhtin 1984a: 281.
14. The influence of Sicilian comedy on Athenian satyr play remains a subject of scholarly discussion. One can reasonably suppose that Aeschylus may have watched

Epicharmus' productions during his visit in Sicily, perhaps importing them to Athens when he returned.
15 Lissarrague 1995.
16 "La négation de l'héroïsme," Lissarrague 1995: 176.
17 Griffith 2015a.
18 The monumental edition of satyr play fragments compiled, edited, translated, and discussed by Krumeich, Pechstein, and Seidensticker brings the remnants of the genre into welcome light, though it equally stirs regret over how much remains unknown (Krumeich, Pechstein, and Seidensticker 1999).
19 Shaw 2014 argues for essential connections to comedy while Griffith 2015b sees closer connections with tragedy.
20 Seaford 1988: 33–44; Sutton 1980: 145–57.
21 Sutton 1980: 159–61.
22 Other satyr plays related to Heracles include: Achaeus' *Omphale* and *Linus*; Demetrius' *Hesione*; Astydamas II's *Heracles*; Dionysius I's *Limus*; Sositheos' *Daphnis or Reapers*; and an anonymous *Atlas*.
23 Van Groningen 1930; Podlecki 2005: 5. Sutton thinks Aeschylus' *Theoroi* may also involve Heracles (1980: 32–33).
24 See discussion in Krumeich, Pechstein, and Seidensticker 1999: 259–60.
25 *Sisyphus* fr. 673 may also refer to Heracles.
26 Sutton 1980: 154.
27 A common Homeric phrase (O'Sullivan and Collard 2013: 407, n. 1).
28 Griffith 2015c: 48–50.
29 Easterling 2007.
30 Maitland 2007.
31 See *Trachiniae* 252–7, where Lichas embeds Heracles' enslavement in a dishonest report explaining his absence, but the core deception is about Heracles' attraction to Iole, not Omphale.
32 For Heracles' femininity, sexual appetites, and transvestism, see Loraux 1990 and Uhlig forthcoming.
33 Achaeus also wrote an *Omphale*, but too little survives for us to assess it. On the post-Ion tradition, see Easterling 2007.
34 Hall 2006: 160–1.
35 Zeitlin 1990 established the essential argument for the femininity of tragedy. For an earlier version of Hall's argument, see Hall 1998.
36 Sutton 1980: 164.
37 Griffith 2015c: 24.
38 The relationship between Sicilian comedy, satyr play, and Athenian Old Comedy remains controversial. While Dobrov 2007 argues for a "firewall" between comedy and satyr play, other scholars differ: Storey 2005 shines a light on the satyr choruses

of Old Comedy; Bakola 2010: 81–117 reveals the cross-fertilization of comedy and satyr play in Cratinus' *Dionysalexandros*; and Shaw 2014 draws out essential continuities from Epicharmus, among other Sicilian comic poets, through satyr play, and from there, to the mythological travesties of Middle Comedy (Shaw 2014: 56–77, 106–22); see also Lämmle 2013: 35–50. Rusten and Henderson (2011: 60) concur: "These [Athenian] tragedians all wrote satyr plays, and the similarities with Epicharmus are too many to dismiss as coincidence."

39 Casolari 2003.
40 See Bowie 2000: 319–25.
41 Antiphanes, Ephippus, and Mnesimachus also wrote a *Busiris*; Cratinus' *Archilochoi* makes mention of the Cercopes (fr. 13). On the Cercopes as comic figures with a potential connection to Euripides' *Heracles*, see Kirkpatrick and Dunn 2002.
42 Olson 2007: 313.
43 Rosen 1995: 125. See also Nesselrath 1990: 234.
44 See Hunter 1983: 140–1.
45 Bakhtin 1984a: 368–436.
46 See Casolari 2003: 262–9. Sutton 1980: 153 identifies "birth, childhood, and upbringing of gods and heroes" as common theme of satyr play, especially for Sophocles.
47 Xenophon, *Mem.* 2.1. See discussion in Conclusion.
48 As Arnott says, "Alexis transports characters and ambience from the heroic past to the Athens of his own day, and this involves him, like other Greek writers of mythical comedy from Epicharmus onwards, in amusing anachronisms" (1996: 407). Achaeus also wrote a *cottabus* scene in his satyr play *Linus* (fr. 26), which anticipates the *Realien* of Middle Comedy (Shaw 2014: 114).
49 I follow Arnott's edition in reading πάνυ γε as an interjection by Heracles.
50 Rusten and Henderson 2011: 544, n. 16. Arnott 1996: 414, n. 1 cautions, however, that "non-textual indications (e.g. visual stage-business by Heracles, revealing a desire for food) should normally be ruled out for ancient drama unless they are endorsed by the text."
51 Nesselrath 1990: 227–9 finds the story of Heracles' murder of Linus "so untragisch und skurril" that the tragic poets could only have used it for satyr play; he follows Kock (1880: vol. 2, 345) in positing that the story has its origins in comedy.
52 See *LIMC* Herakles 1666–73. There is nothing in these images that suggests comic or satyric overtones, however, undermining Nesselrath and Kock's interpretation of the episode.
53 Lesky 1925.
54 The question of the play's genre is vexed, performed as it was following a trilogy of tragedies, but lacking a satyr chorus. Clearly the play draws on attributes of the comic Heracles, but that role is not the only one present. Perhaps the simplest

approach is Buxton's: "But when all is said and done, *Alkestis* is not a tragedy, it is a non-satyric fourth play" (Buxton 2013: 204).
55 Goldfarb 1992.
56 The scholarship on the themes of the play is vast. See, e.g., Scodel 1979; Garner 1988; Schein 1988; Padilla 2000.
57 For another famous example of Heracles' success as a wrestler, see discussion in Chapter 3 on Heracles' defeat of Achelous.
58 On the irony of Asclepius' causing Alcestis' death, see Swift 2012: 156.
59 Swift 2012.
60 See Parker 2007: 246–7; de Jáuregui 2016: 217–19.
61 See discussion in Chapter 4.
62 This later becomes a motif in comedy; see Dale 1978: 108; Parker 2007: 201.
63 Perhaps a foreshadowing of the role Heracles plays in the symposiastic philosophizing of Prodicus' "Choice of Heracles" in Xenophon's *Memorabilia* 2.
64 See, e.g., vv. 105, 147, 158, 320–1.
65 See Bakhtin 1984b: 124–6.
66 Cf. Heracles' address in the *Trachiniae* to his arms, back, and chest (1089–90).
67 Perhaps this is a reference to Heracles' initiation into the Eleusinian mysteries. See de Jáuregui 2016: 221–3.
68 Garner 1988; Swift 2012.
69 On the wrestling theme, see Kratzer 2015.
70 As far as we can tell, Aristophanes ignores Dionysus' own *katabasis*; the ancient accounts of this journey are late (Ps.-Apoll. 3.5.3 and Diod. Sic. 4.25.4). On Dionysus' and Orpheus' journeys to the Underworld, see Clark 1979: 95–124.
71 See Lloyd-Jones 1990b. Robertson 1980 argues that the epic should be identified with the *Aegimius* by Cercops of Miletus. The epic *Minyas* by Prodicus of Phocaea (frr. 1–8 Bernabé) described the *katabasis* of Theseus and Peirithous; see also Janko 2000: 336, n. 1; West 2003: 268–75.
72 These titles might refer to the same play; see Krumeich, Pechstein, and Seidensticker 1999: 259–60.
73 See discussion in O'Sullivan and Collard 2013: 392–7.
74 Farmer 2017. In *Frogs*, we observe characters discussing tragedy explicitly on stage (tragic culture), and the play directly imitates tragedies for an audience accustomed to seeing them performed with more gravity (tragic parody).
75 Dobrov 2001: 133–56.
76 See Lloyd-Jones 1990b.
77 For an analogous study of how Apollonius' *Argonautica* exploits the contradictions of Heracles' character, creating a "narrative palimpsest," see Bär 2018: 73–99, 2019: 11–19.
78 Platter 2007: 25.

79 Ibid.: 73.
80 Aristophanes gives us the stereotypical comic Heracles in other places. Although his Chorus in *Peace* denigrates other poets' productions by praising him, "and he was the first to disdain and drive off those Heracleses, always chomping and starving" (τούς θ' Ἡρακλέας τοὺς μάττοντας καὶ τοὺς πεινῶντας ἐκείνους / ἐξήλασ' ἀτιμώσας πρῶτος, 741–2), one should not take Aristophanes at face value here. He uses a gluttonous and buffoonish Heracles as a running joke in the *Birds*: Heracles, Poseidon, and a Triballian god serve as emissaries from the gods, charged with making a settlement with the leaders of Cloudcuckooland (1565–91), but Heracles' initial aggression ("I want to strangle the guy," τὸν ἄνθρωπον ἄγχειν βούλομαι, 1575) is quickly neutralized by the prospect of a feast on roasted fowl. The possibility of a delicious meal outweighs Heracles' consideration of his own mission, his father's kingdom, or his personal inheritance.
81 See the lost Apulian bell-krater (Berlin Staatliche Museen F3046) reproduced in line drawing at Taplin 1993: 46–7, where Taplin argues that the painting of a Herakles-figure at the door accompanied by a slave on donkey is "more probably than not inspired by Aristophanes' *Frogs*."
82 On Dionysus' shifting theatrical roles, see Padilla 1992.
83 See Huxley 1969: 102, 104, 183.
84 The connections between the defeat of the Centaurs, Heracles' initiation in the Eleusinian rites, and his descent to Hades are attested in Diod. Sic. 4.14.3, 4.25.1; Ps.-Apoll. 2.5.12.
85 Clark 1979: 79–94 argues that the "Eleusinianization" of Heracles in the sixth century and the accompanying absence of the wounding of Hades represents a move away from his archaic reputation for violence.
86 Segal 1961; Bowie 1993: 228–53; Lada-Richards 1999. Bowie emphasizes the possible Orphic associations in addition to the Dionysiac.
87 For an earlier discussion of Heracles as Eleusinian initiate and Dionysus as Eleusinian god, see Lapalus 1934. See also Lloyd-Jones 1990b.
88 The erotic language of Dionysus' wish recalls Orpheus' longing for his dead wife, Eurydice, for whom he also embarked on a journey to the Underworld.
89 Cf. the myth of Heracles' sleeping with Thespius' fifty daughter (Herodoros 31F20; Pausanias 9.27.6–7; Diod. Sic. 4.29.2–3; Ps.-Apoll. 2.4.10).
90 On how this passage reflects a last-minute insertion upon Sophocles' recent death, see Sommerstein 1996: 20–1.
91 For those scholars who see Aeschylus as a "Heraclean" figure, it is fitting that Heracles dismisses Euripides (or at least, Dionysus' memory of Euripides) from the beginning: see Padilla 1992.
92 For frogs as a hostile party in a battle, see the Hellenistic poem *Batrachomyomachia*, which describes a fight between frogs and mice in an epic style.

93 Confusion well expressed in the title of Wills's 1969 article "Why Are the Frogs in the *Frogs*?"
94 Sommerstein 1996: 176.
95 Moorton 1989: 312.
96 See Segal 1995: 47–9, 58–9; Liapis 2006: 52–4.
97 Dover 1993: 119 identifies the species of our Frogs as *Rana ridibunda*, the most populous marsh frog in southern Europe; it is considered harmless.
98 Wills 1969.
99 MacDowell 1972: 3–5; Campbell 1984.
100 Habash 2002.
101 For arguments for an unseen Chorus, see Wills 1969; Higgins 1977; Allison 1983. For arguments for a visible Chorus, see MacDowell 1972; Campbell 1984.
102 On the disparity between Dionysus' aspirations and actual antics, see Kratzer 2010: 28–58.
103 Dover 1993: 32.
104 Henderson 1991: 193.
105 See Edmonds 2003: 190–1.
106 Apte 1985: 160–1.
107 Moorton 1989: 318.
108 Dover 1993: 253–4.
109 Dobrov 2001: 133–56.
110 Euripides gives the dog three heads; Hesiod, fifty (*Th.* 310–12). For a survey of the variations, see Gantz 1993: 413–16.
111 Dover 1993: 143 raises the possibility that this private dinner for two may reflect "that in vulgar belief Persephone fancied Herakles."
112 Ibid.: 144.
113 One variation on the myth claims that Persephone offered Cerberus to Heracles as a goodwill gesture because he had been initiated into the Eleusinian rites (see Diod. Sic. 4.26.1). Aristophanes clearly does not follow this version, as the audience hears from Aeacus how Heracles obtained Cerberus in combat.
114 Lada-Richards 1999: 175 remarks, "his gulping down the wooden baskets would certainly appear to Greek eyes as the peak of brutishness." See also Segal 1981: 13–42.
115 Another moment of paratragedy, as defined in Farmer 2017.
116 Habash 2002: 3.
117 Segal 1961: 213 calls this "the fullest possible execution of the *mimesis* of Heracles."
118 See ibid.: 232, n. 18; Gantz 1993: 439.
119 Platter 2007: 22–3.
120 Ibid.: 23.

Conclusion: Which Path Did Heracles Choose?

1. On the folktale roots of the narrative, see Davies 2013.
2. Socrates introduces Prodicus' allegory by referring to Hesiod's model of the hard and easy roads in *Works and Days* 287–92, which became the most quoted Hesiodic passage in antiquity (Koning 2010: 145); on Hesiod's influence, see also Hunter 2014: 141–5. But it is worth noting that Hesiod's presentation lacks an individualized judge.
3. Kuntz 1993. On the reshaping of Heracles as a representative for the improvement of young men, see Alpers 1912. Galinsky argues that Prodicus chose Heracles "because the most popular hero of Greece ... most suggested himself as Everyman" (1972: 102); but Heracles is in fact *exceptional* in every way.
4. See Dorion 2009 on the necessity of *enkrateia* for Xenophon's Socrates.
5. On the importance of "free decision" in Prodicus' ethic, see Untersteiner 1954: 220.
6. On the characterizations of *Aretē* and *Eudaimonia/Kakia*, see Wolfsdorf 2008.
7. The agricultural theme connects nicely with the larger context of Prodicus' *Hōrai*, the treatise from which the "Choice of Heracles" was excerpted, and the context of Hesiod's *Works and Days*. See Nestle 1936: 153–63 on the suggestion that Prodicus theorized that all human civilization derived originally from the practice of agriculture. But the farming motif hardly matches what the mythological tradition suggests for Heracles' future path to glory.
8. Furthermore, Philostratus reports that Prodicus wrote a "very long epilogue" after the allegory (*VS* 1.482–83). On the reception of the "Choice of Heracles," see Panofsky 1930.
9. See Heerink 2015.
10. The question of priority has generated much scholarly criticism. For an overview of the two poles of the debate, see Köhnken 1965 and Effe 1992.
11. On the contrast between the heroic and the erotic, see, e.g., Mastronarde 1968; Gutzwiller 1981: 19–29.
12. For a narratological approach to how the *Argonautica* exploits the multifaceted and contradictory aspects of Heracles, see Bär 2018: 73–99, 2019: 11–19.
13. On the varied mythological tradition surrounding Heracles' killing of the Boreads, see Jackson 2003.

References

Adkins, A. W. H. 1966. "Basic Greek Values in Euripides' *Hecuba* and *Hercules Furens*." *The Classical Quarterly* 16 (2): 193–219.
Adkins, A. W. H. 1972. *Moral Values and Political Behaviour in Ancient Greece: From Homer to the End of the Fifth Century*. Ancient Culture and Society. New York: Norton.
Akrigg, B., and Tordoff, R., eds. 2013. *Slaves and Slavery in Ancient Greek Comic Drama*. Cambridge: Cambridge University Press.
Alden, M. 2000. *Homer Beside Himself: Para-Narratives in the Iliad*. New York: Oxford University Press.
Allan, A., Anagnostou-Laoutides, E., and Stafford, E., eds. 2020. *Herakles Inside and Outside the Church: From the First Apologists to the End of the Quattrocento*. Leiden: Brill.
Allen, D. S. 2000. *The World of Prometheus: The Politics of Punishing in Democratic Athens*. Princeton, NJ: Princeton University Press.
Allen-Hornblower, E. 2014. "Gods in Pain: Walking the Line between Divine and Mortal in *Iliad* 5." *Lexis: Rivista di poetica, retorica e comunicazione nella tradizione classica* 32: 27–57.
Allison, R. H. 1983. "Amphibian Ambiguities: Aristophanes and His Frogs." *Greece & Rome* 30 (1): 8–20.
Alpers, J. 1912. "Hercules in bivio." Dissertation, Göttingen.
Anderson, Ø. 2012. "Older Heroes and Earlier Poems: The Case of Heracles in the Odyssey." In Anderson, Ø. and Haug, D. T. T. eds. *Relative Chronology in Early Greek Epic Poetry*. Cambridge: Cambridge University Press. 138–51.
Apte, M. L. 1985. *Humor and Laughter: An Anthropological Approach*. Ithaca, NY: Cornell University Press.
Arendt, H. 1970. *On Violence*. New York: Harcourt Brace Jovanovich.
Arnott, W. G. 1996. *Alexis – the Fragments: A Commentary*. Cambridge Classical Texts and Commentaries; 31. Cambridge: Cambridge University Press.
Arrowsmith, W. 1954. "The Conversion of Herakles: An Essay in Euripidean Tragic Structure." Dissertation, Princeton, NJ: Princeton University.
Ashmole, B., and Yalouris, N. 1967. *Olympia: The Sculptures of the Temple of Zeus*. London: Phaidon.
Bakhtin, M. M. 1984a. *Rabelais and His World*. Translated by Hélène Iswolsky. Bloomington, IN: Indiana University Press.
Bakhtin, M. M. 1984b. *Problems of Dostoevsky's Poetics*. Translated by Caryl Emerson. Minneapolis, MN: University of Minnesota Press.

Bakola, E. 2010. *Cratinus and the Art of Comedy*. Oxford: Oxford University Press.

Bär, S. 2018. *Herakles im griechischen Epos: Studien zur Narrativität und Poetizität eines Helden*. Stuttgart: Franz Steiner Verlag.

Bär, S. 2019. "Heracles in Homer and Apollonius: Narratological Character Analysis in a Diachronic Perspective." *Symbolae Osloenses*: 1–26.

Barker, E., and Christensen, J. 2014. "Even Heracles Had to Die: Homeric 'Heroism', Mortality and the Epic Tradition." *Trends in Classics* 6 (2): 249–77.

Barlow, S. A. 1981. "Sophocles' *Ajax* and Euripides' *Heracles*." *Ramus* 10: 112–28.

Barlow, S. A. 1982. "Structure and Dramatic Realism in Euripides' 'Heracles.'" *Greece & Rome* 29 (2): 115–25.

Barrett, W. S. 2007a. "Stesichoros and the Story of Geryon." In West, M. L., ed. *Greek Lyric, Tragedy, and Textual Criticism: Collected Papers*. Oxford: Oxford University Press. 1–24.

Barrett, W. S. 2007b. "Stesichorus, Geryoneis, *SLG* 11." In West, M. L., ed. *Greek Lyric, Tragedy, and Textual Criticism: Collected Papers*. Oxford: Oxford University Press. 25–37.

Bartosiewiczova, J. 1987. "Zum *Herakles* des Euripides: ein Beitrag zur Interpretation." *Graecolatina et Orientalia* 19–20: 3–11.

Beaulieu, M.-C. 2015. *The Sea in the Greek Imagination*. Philadelphia: University of Pennsylvania Press.

Beazley, J. D. 1963. *Attic Red-Figure Vase-Painters*. Oxford: Clarendon Press.

Belfiore, E. S. 2000. *Murder among Friends: Violations of Philia in Greek Tragedy*. New York: Oxford University Press.

Benjamin, W. 1986. "Critique of Violence." In *Reflections: Essays, Aphorisms, and Autobiographical Writings*. Translated by Edmund Jephcott. New York: Schocken Books. 277–300.

Berguist, B. 1973. *Herakles on Thasos: The Archaeological, Literary and Epigraphic Evidence for His Sanctuary, Status and Cult Reconsidered*. Uppsala: University of Uppsala.

Bernabé, A., ed. 1996. *Poetae Epici Graeci. Testimonia et Fragmenta. Pars I*. 2nd ed. Stuttgart: De Gruyter.

Biggs, P. 1966. "The Disease Theme in Sophocles' *Ajax*, *Philoctetes* and *Trachiniae*." *Classical Philology* 61 (4): 223–35.

Blanshard, A. 2005. *Hercules: A Heroic Life*. London: Granta.

Blanshard, A., and Stafford, E., eds. 2021. *The Modern Hercules: Images of the Hero from the Nineteenth to the Early Twenty-First Century*. Leiden: Brill.

Boardman, J. 1972. "Herakles, Peisistratos and Sons." *Revue Archéologique Paris* 1: 57–72.

Boardman, J. 1975a. "Herakles, Peisistratos and Eleusis." *The Journal of Hellenic Studies* 95: 1–12.

Boardman, J. 1975b. *Athenian Red Figure Vases: The Archaic Period*. London: Thames & Hudson.

Boardman, J. 1978. "Herakles, Delphi and Kleisthenes of Sikyon." *Revue Archéologique Paris* (2): 227–34.

Boardman, J. 1989. "Herakles, Peisistratos and the Unconvinced." *The Journal of Hellenic Studies* 109: 158–9.
Boardman, J. 1990. "VIII. Herakles' Death and Apotheosis." In *LIMC*. V.2: 121–32.
Bond, G. W. 1981. *Heracles*. Oxford: Clarendon Press.
Bonnet, C. 1988. *Melqart: cultes et mythes de l'Héraclès tyrien en Méditerrannée*. Leuven: Uitgeverij Peeters.
Bonnet, C., and Jourdain-Annequin, C., eds. 1992. *Héraclès: d'une rive à l'autre de la Méditerranée: bilan et perspectives: actes de la Table Ronde de Rome, Academi a Belgica-Ecole française de Rome, 15–16 septembre 1989*. Vol. 28. Etudes de philologie, d'archéologie et d'histoire anciennes. Bruxelles: Institut Historique Belge de Rome.
Bonnet, C., Jourdain-Annequin, C., and Pirenne-Delforge, V., eds. 1998. *Le bestiaire d'Héraclès: IIIe Rencontre héracléenne: actes du colloque organisé à l'Université de Liège et aux Facultés universitaires Notre-Dame de la Paix de Namur, du 14 au 16 novembre 1996*. Vol. 7. Kernos Supplément. Liège: Centre internationale d'étude de la religion grecque antique.
Borg, B. 2006. "Gefährliche Bilder? Gewalt und Leidenschaft in der archaischen und klassischen Kunst." In Seidensticker, B. and Vöhler, M., eds. *Gewalt und Ästhetik zur Gewalt und ihrer Darstellung in der griechischen Klassik*. Berlin: De Gruyter. 223–57.
Bowie, A. M. 1993. *Aristophanes: Myth, Ritual, and Comedy*. Cambridge: Cambridge University Press.
Bowie, A. M. 2000. "Myth and Ritual in the Rivals of Aristophanes." In Harvey, D. and Wilkins, J., eds. *The Rivals of Aristophanes: Studies in Athenian Old Comedy*. Swansea: Classical Press of Wales. 317–40.
Bowman, L. 1999. "Prophecy and Authority in the 'Trachiniai.'" *The American Journal of Philology* 120 (3): 335–50.
Bowra, C. M. 1944. *Sophoclean Tragedy*. Oxford: Clarendon Press.
Branham, R. B., ed. 2002. *Bakhtin and the Classics*. Evanston, IL: Northwestern University Press.
Brize, P. 1980. *Die Geryoneis des Stesichoros und die frühe griechische Kunst*. Würzburg: Triltsch.
Brize, P. 1988. "Geryoneus." In *LIMC*. IV.1: 186–90.
Brize, P. 1990. "IV.L Herakles and Geryon (Labour X)." In *LIMC*. V.2: 73–84.
Brommer, F. 1956. *Vasenlisten zur griechischen Heldensage; Herakles, Theseus, Aigeus, Erechteus, Erichthonios, Kekrops, Kodros, Perseus, Bellerophon, Meleager, Peleus*. Marburg/Lahn: N. G. Elwert.
Brommer, F. 1973. *Vasenlisten zur griechischen Heldensage*. Marburg: Elwert.
Brommer, F. 1986. *Heracles: The Twelve Labors of the Hero in Ancient Art and Literature*. New Rochelle, NY: A.D. Caratzas.
Bundy, E. L. 1962. *Studia Pindarica*. Berkeley, CA: University of California Press.
Burkert, W. 1972. "Die Leistung eines Kreophylos: Kreophyleer, Homeriden und die archaische Heraklesepik." *Museum Helveticum* 29 (2): 74–85.

Burkert, W. 1979. *Structure and History in Greek Mythology and Ritual*. Berkeley, CA: University of California Press.

Burnett, A. P. 1971. *Catastrophe Survived: Euripides' Plays of Mixed Reversal*. Oxford: Clarendon Press.

Bushman, B. J., and Huesmann, L. R. 2010. "Aggression." In *Handbook of Social Psychology*, 5th ed. Hoboken, NJ: John Wiley & Sons, Inc. 833–63.

Butler, J. 2004. *Precarious Life: The Powers of Mourning and Violence*. New York: Verso.

Buxton, R. 2013. *Myths and Tragedies in Their Ancient Greek Contexts*. Oxford University Press.

Calame, C. 1998. "Héraclès, animal et victime sacrificielle dans les *Trachiniennes* de Sophocle?" In Bonnet, C., Jourdain-Annequin, C., and Pirenne-Delforge, V., eds. *Le bestiaire d'Héraclès: IIIe Rencontre héracléenne: actes du colloque organisé à l'Université de Liège et aux Facultés universitaires Notre-Dame de la Paix de Namur, du 14 au 16 novembre 1996*. Kernos Supplément. Liège: Centre internationale d'étude de la religion grecque antique. 7: 197–215.

Campbell, D. A. 1984. "The Frogs in the *Frogs*." *The Journal of Hellenic Studies* 104: 163–5.

Carawan, E. 2000. "Deianira's Guilt." *Transactions of the American Philological Association* 130: 189–237.

Carey, C. 2012. "The Victory Ode in the Theatre." In Agocs, P., Carey, C., and Rawles, R., eds. *Receiving the Komos: Ancient and Modern Receptions of the Victory Ode*. London: Institute of Classical Studies. 17–36.

Carmignani, L. 1981. "Stile e tecnica narrativa di Stesicoro." In *Studi di Letteratura Greca*. Richerche di Filologia Classica. Pisa: Giardini. I: 25–60.

Casolari, F. 2003. *Die Mythentravestie in der griechischen Komödie*. Münster: Aschendorff.

Castellaneta, S. 2005. "Note alla 'Gerioneide' di Stesicoro." *Zeitschrift für Papyrologie und Epigraphik* 153: 21–42.

Chalk, H. H. O. 1962. "Arete and Bia in Euripides' *Herakles*." *The Journal of Hellenic Studies* 82: 7–18.

Clark, R. J. 1979. *Catabasis: Vergil and the Wisdom-Tradition*. Amsterdam: Grüner.

Clay, J. S. 1993. "The Generation of Monsters in Hesiod." *Classical Philology* 88 (2): 105–16.

Clay, J. S. 2003. *Hesiod's Cosmos*. Cambridge: Cambridge University Press.

Cohen, B. 1994. "From Bowman to Clubman: Herakles and Olympia." *The Art Bulletin* 76 (4): 695–715.

Cohen, D. 1995. *Law, Violence, and Community in Classical Athens*. Key Themes in Ancient History. Cambridge: Cambridge University Press.

Conacher, D. J. 1955. "Theme, Plot, and Technique in the 'Heracles' of Euripides." *Phoenix* 9 (4): 139–52.

Crissy, K. 1997. "Herakles, Odysseus, and the Bow: 'Odyssey' 21.11–41." *The Classical Journal* 93 (1): 41–53.

Crotty, K. 1982. *Song and Action: The Victory Odes of Pindar*. Baltimore, MD: Johns Hopkins University Press.

Currie, B. 2005. *Pindar and the Cult of Heroes*. Oxford Classical Monographs. Oxford: Oxford University Press.

Curtis, P. 2011. *Stesichoros's Geryoneis*. Mnemosyne Supplements. Leiden: Brill.

D'Agostino, B. 2016. "Potters and Painters in Archaic Corinth: Schemata and Images." In Colesanti, G., Lulli, L., and Nicolai, R., eds. *Submerged Literature in Ancient Greek Culture 2: Case Studies*. Berlin: De Gruyter. 243–57.

D'Agostino, E. 2007. *Onomacriti: Testimonia et fragmenta*. AION. Sezione filologico-letteraria Quaderni 10. Pisa: Istituti editoriali e poligrafici internazionali.

D'Agostino, F. 1983. *Bia: violenza e giustizia nella filosofia e nella letteratura della Grecia antica: sondaggi lessicali*. Milano: Giuffrè.

Dale, A. M. 1978. *Euripides: Alcestis*. New York: Clarendon Press.

Davidson, J. 2003. "Sophocles' *Trachiniae* and the *Odyssey*." *Athenaeum* 91 (2): 517–23.

Davidson, O. M. 1980. "Indo-European Dimension of Herakles in 'Iliad' 19.95–133." *Arethusa* 13 (2): 197–202.

Davies, M. 1988. "Stesichorus' *Geryoneis* and Its Folk-Tale Origins." *The Classical Quarterly* 38 (2): 277–90.

Davies, M. 1991. *Sophocles: Trachiniae*. New York: Oxford University Press.

Davies, M. 2013. "The Hero at the Crossroads: Prodicus and the Choice of Heracles." *Prometheus* 39: 3–17.

Davies, M., and Finglass, P. 2014. *Stesichorus: The Poems*. Cambridge: Cambridge University Press.

Deacy, S., and McHardy, F. forthcoming. *Gender Violence in Ancient Greece*. London: Bloomsbury Academic.

Deacy, S., and Pierce, K., eds. 1997. *Rape in Antiquity: Sexual Violence in the Greek and Roman World*. London: Duckworth.

Demos, M. 1994. "Callicles' Quotation of Pindar in the *Gorgias*." *Harvard Studies in Classical Philology* 96: 85–107.

Des Essarts, E. 1871. *Du type d'Hercule dans la littérature grecque depuis les origines jusqu'au siècle des Antonins*. Paris: Thorin.

Desch, W. 1986. "Der 'Herakles' des Euripides und die Götter." *Philologus* 130 (1): 8–23.

Detienne, M. 1996. *The Masters of Truth in Archaic Greece*. Translated by J. Lloyd. New York: Zone Books.

Di Gregorio, L. 1975. *Scholia vetera in Hesiodi Theogoniam*. Milan: Università Cattolica del Sacro Cuore.

Dindorf, W. 1855. *Scholia Graeca in Homeri Odysseam*. Oxford: E. Typographeo Academico.

Dobrov, G. W. 2001. *Figures of Play: Greek Drama and Metafictional Poetics*. New York: Oxford University Press.

Dobrov, G. W. 2007. "Comedy and the Satyr-Chorus." *Classical World* 100 (3): 251–65.

Dodds, E. R. 1959. *Plato: Gorgias*. Oxford: Clarendon Press.

Doerries, B. 2015. *The Theater of War: What Ancient Greek Tragedies Can Teach Us Today*. New York: Alfred A. Knopf.

Dorion, L.-A. 2009. "Xenophon's Socrates." In Ahbel-Rappe, S. and Kamtekar, R., eds. *A Companion to Socrates*. Malden, MA: Wiley-Blackwell. 93–109.

Dover, K. J. 1972. *Aristophanic Comedy*. Berkeley, CA: University of California Press.

Dover, K. J. 1974. *Greek Popular Morality in the Time of Plato and Aristotle*. Berkeley, CA: University of California Press.

Dover, K. J. 1993. *Aristophanes: Frogs*. Oxford: Clarendon Press.

Drake, H. A., ed. 2006. *Violence in Late Antiquity: Perceptions and Practices*. Aldershot, UK: Ashgate.

DuBois, P. 1991. *Torture and Truth*. New York: Routledge.

Easterling, P. E. 1981. "The End of the *Trachiniae*." *Illinois Classical Studies* 6: 56–74.

Easterling, P. E. 1982. *Trachiniae*. Cambridge Greek and Latin Classics. Cambridge: Cambridge University Press.

Easterling, P. E. 2007. "Looking for Omphale." In Jennings, V. and Katsaros, A., eds. *The World of Ion of Chios*. Leiden: Brill. 282–92.

Edmonds, R. 2003. "Who in Hell Is Heracles? Dionysos' Disastrous Disguise in Aristophanes' *Frogs*." In Dodds, D. and Faraone, C., eds. *Initiation in Ancient Greek Rituals and Narratives: New Critical Perspectives*. London: Routledge. 181–200.

Edwards, A. 2002. "Historicizing the Popular Grotesque: Bakhtin's *Rabelais and His World* and Attic Old Comedy." In Branham, R. B., ed. *Bakhtin and the Classics*. Evanston, IL: Northwestern University Press. 27–55.

Effe, B. 1980. "Der Funktionswandel des Herakles-Mythos in der griechischen Literatur." *Poetica* 12: 145–66.

Effe, B. 1992. "Die Hylas-Geschichte bei Theokrit und Apollonios Rhodios: Bemerkungen zur Prioritätsfrage." *Hermes* 120 (3): 299–309.

Ehrenberg, V. 1946. "Tragic Heracles." In *Aspects of the Ancient World*. New York: W. Salloch. 144–66.

Eisenfeld, H. 2018. "Geryon the Hero, Herakles the God." *Journal of Hellenic Studies* 138: 80–99.

Ekroth, G. 2002. *The Sacrificial Rituals of Greek Hero-Cults in the Archaic to the Early Hellenistic Periods*. Vol. 12. Kernos Supplément. Liège: Centre international d'étude de la religion grecque antique.

Ellinger, P. 2005. "Zeus et les limites de la répression." In Bertrand, J.-M., ed. *La violence dans les mondes grec et romain: actes du colloque international, Paris, 2–4 mai 2002*. Paris: Publications de la Sorbonne.

Ercoles, M. 2011. "Stesichorus *PMGF* S21.1–3 (Geryoneis): A Textual Proposal." *Greek, Roman, and Byzantine Studies* 51 (3): 350–62.

Fantuzzi, M. 2012. *Achilles in Love: Intertextual Studies*. Oxford: Oxford University Press.

Faraone, C. 1994. "Deianeira's Mistake and the Demise of Heracles: Erotic Magic in Sophocles' *Trachiniae*." *Helios* 21: 115–35.

Faraone, C. 2013. "The Poetics of the Catalogue in the Hesiodic *Theogony*." *Transactions of the American Philological Association* 143 (2): 293-323.
Farmer, M. C. 2017. *Tragedy on the Comic Stage*. New York: Oxford University Press.
Farnell, L. R. 1921. *Greek Hero Cults and Ideas of Immortality*. Gifford Lectures. Oxford: Clarendon Press.
Finkelberg, M. 1991. "Royal Succession in Heroic Greece." *The Classical Quarterly* 41 (2): 303-16.
Finkelberg, M. 1996. "The Second Stasimon of the 'Trachiniae' and Heracles' Festival on Mount Oeta." *Mnemosyne* 49 (2): 129-43.
Fischer, G., and Moraw, S., eds. 2005. *Die andere Seite der Klassik: Gewalt im 5. und 4. Jahrhundert v. Chr.: kulturwissenschaftliches Kolloquium Bonn, Kunst- und Ausstellungshalle der Bundesrepublik Deutschland, 11.-13. Juli 2002*. Stuttgart: Steiner.
Fisher, N. 2009. "The Culture of Competition." In *A Companion to Archaic Greece*. Malden, MA: Wiley-Blackwell. 524-41.
Flacelière, R., and Devambez, P. 1966. *Héraclès: Images et Récits*. Paris: E. de Boccard.
Foley, H. P. 1985. *Ritual Irony: Poetry and Sacrifice in Euripides*. Ithaca, NY: Cornell University Press.
Fontenrose, J. 1968. "The Hero as Athlete." *California Studies in Classical Antiquity* 1: 73-104.
Foraboschi, D. 2018. *Violenze Antiche: Testo pubblicato postumo a cura di Silvia Bussi*. Wiesbaden: Harrassowitz Verlag.
Foster, M., Kurke, L., and Weiss, N. 2019. "Introduction." In Foster, M., Kurke, L., and Weiss, N., eds. *The Genres of Archaic and Classical Greek Poetry: Theories and Models*. Boston: Brill. 1-28.
Fowler, D. 1987. "Vergil on Killing Virgins." In Whitby, M., Hardie, P., and Whitby, M., eds. *Homo Viator: Classical Essays for John Bramble*. Bristol: Bristol Classical Press. 185-98.
Fowler, R. 1999. "Three Places of the *Trachiniae*." In *Sophocles Revisited*. New York: Oxford University Press. 161-75.
Foxhall, L., and Salmon, J., eds. 1998. *When Men Were Men: Masculinity, Power, and Identity in Classical Antiquity*. London: Routledge.
Frame, D. 1971. "The Origins of Greek ΝΟΥΣ." Unpublished dissertation, Cambridge, MA: Harvard University.
Franzen, C. 2009. "Sympathizing with the Monster: Making Sense of Colonization in Stesichorus' *Geryoneis*." *Quaderni urbinati di cultura classica* 92 (2): 55-72.
Fuchs-Heinritz, W., Lautmann, R., Rammstedt, O., and Wienold, H., eds. 1994. *Lexikon zur Soziologie*. 3rd ed. Opladen: Westdeutscher Verlag.
Fuqua, C. 1980. "Heroism, Heracles, and the *Trachiniae*." *Traditio* 36: 1-81.
Furley, D. 1986. "Euripides on the Sanity of Herakles." In Betts, J. H., Hooker, J. T., and Green, J. R., eds. *Studies in Honour of T. B. L. Webster*. Bristol: Bristol Classical Press. 1: 102-13.

Galinsky, K. 1972. *The Herakles Theme: The Adaptations of the Hero in Literature from Homer to the Twentieth Century*. Oxford: Blackwell.

Gantz, T. 1993. *Early Greek Myth: A Guide to Literary and Artistic Sources*. Baltimore, MD: Johns Hopkins University Press.

Garner, R. 1988. "Death and Victory in Euripides' 'Alcestis.'" *Classical Antiquity* 7 (1): 58–71.

Garrison, E. P. 1995. *Groaning Tears: Ethical and Dramatic Aspects of Suicide in Greek Tragedy*. New York: Brill.

Gentili, B. 1977. "Eracle 'omicida giustissimo.' Pisandro, Stesicoro e Pindaro." In Gentili, B. and Paioni, G., eds. *Il Mito greco: atti del Convegno internazionale: (Urbino, 7–12 maggio 1973)*. Roma: Edizioni dell'Ateneo & Bizzarri. 299–305.

Gigante, M. 1956. *Nomos basileus*. Vol. 1. Ricerche filologiche. Napoli: Edizioni Glaux.

Golden, M. 1998. *Sport and Society in Ancient Greece*. New York: Cambridge University Press.

Goldfarb, B. 1992. "The Conflict of Obligations in Euripides' 'Alcestis.'" *GRBS* 32 (2): 109–26.

Grethlein, J. 2012. "Homer and Heroic History." In Marincola, J., Llewellyn-Jones, L., and Maciver, C. A., eds. *Greek Notions of the Past in the Archaic and Classical Eras: History without Historians*. Edinburgh Leventis Studies 6. Edinburgh: Edinburgh University Press. 14–36.

Griffith, M. 2015a. "Satyr Play and Tragedy, Face to Face (and East to West?): The Pronomos Vase." In *Greek Satyr Play: Five Studies*. Berkeley, CA: California Classical Studies. 129–45.

Griffith, M. 2015b. "Sophocles' Satyr Plays and the Language of Romance." In *Greek Satyr Play: Five Studies*. Berkeley, CA: California Classical Studies. 109–28.

Griffith, M. 2015c. "Slaves of Dionysos: Satyrs, Audience, and the Ends of the *Oresteia*." In *Greek Satyr Play: Five Studies*. Berkeley, CA: California Classical Studies. 14–74.

Groningen, B. A. van. 1930. "Ad Aeschyli Κήρυκας." *Mnemosyne* 58 (1/2): 134.

Grote, D. 1994. "Callicles' Use of Pindar's Νόμος Βασιλεύς: *Gorgias* 484B." *The Classical Journal* 90 (1): 21–31.

Guillon, P. 1963. *Le bouclier d'Hēraclēs et l'histoire de la Grèce centrale dans la période de la première guerre sacrée*. Aix-en-Provence: Éditions Ophrys.

Gutzwiller, K. J. 1981. *Studies in the Hellenistic Epyllion*. Beiträge zur klassischen Philologie. Königstein/Ts.: Hain.

Habash, M. 2002. "Dionysos' Roles in Aristophanes' 'Frogs.'" *Mnemosyne* 55 (1): 1–17.

Hahnemann, C. 1999. "Mount Oita Revisited: Sophokles' 'Trachiniai' in Light of the Evidence of Aischylos' 'Herakleidai.'" *Zeitschrift für Papyrologie und Epigraphik* 126: 67–73.

Hainsworth, J. B. 1985. *The Iliad: A Commentary*. Edited by G. S. Kirk. Vol. 3. New York: Cambridge University Press.

Hall, E. 1998. "Ithyphallic Males Behaving Badly, or, Satyr Drama as Gendered Tragic Ending." In Wyke, M., ed. *Parchments of Gender: Deciphering the Body of Antiquity*. Oxford: Clarendon Press. 13–37.

Hall, E. 2006. "Horny Satyrs and Tragic Tetralogies." In *The Theatrical Cast of Athens: Interactions between Ancient Greek Drama and Society*. Oxford: Oxford University Press. 142–69.

Hall, E. 2009. "Deianeira Deliberates: Precipitate Decision-Making and *Trachiniae*." In Goldhill, S. and Hall, E., eds. *Sophocles and the Greek Tragic Tradition*. New York: Cambridge University Press. 69–96.

Hall, J. M. 1997. *Ethnic Identity in Greek Antiquity*. New York: Cambridge University Press.

Halleran, M. 1986. "Lichas' Lies and Sophoclean Innovation." *Greek, Roman, and Byzantine Studies* 27 (3): 239–47.

Hankey, R. 1990. "'Evil' in the *Odyssey*." In Craik, E. M., ed. *Owls to Athens: Essays on Classical Culture Presented to Sir Kenneth Dover*. Oxford: Clarendon Press. 89–95.

Hardwick, L. 2003. *Reception Studies*. Greece & Rome, New Surveys in the Classics. Oxford: Oxford University Press.

Hartigan, K. 1987. "Euripidean Madness: Herakles and Orestes." *Greece & Rome* 34 (2): 126–35.

Haubold, J. 2005. "Heracles and the Hesiodic *Catalogue of Women*." In Hunter, R., ed. *The Hesiodic Catalogue of Women: Constructions and Reconstructions*. Cambridge: Cambridge University Press. 85–98.

Hawhee, D. 2002. "Agonism and Arete." *Philosophy & Rhetoric* 35 (3): 185–207.

Heerink, M. 2012. "Apollonius and Callimachus on Heracles and Theiodamas: A Metapoetical Interpretation." *Quaderni urbinati di cultura classica* 101 (2): 43–56.

Heerink, M. 2015. *Echoing Hylas: A Study in Hellenistic and Roman Metapoetics*. Madison, WI: University of Wisconsin Press.

Heiden, B. A. 1989. *Tragic Rhetoric: An Interpretation of Sophocles'* Trachiniae. New York: P. Lang.

Henderson, J. 1991. *The Maculate Muse*. 2nd ed. New York: Oxford University Press.

Herman, G. 2006. *Morality and Behaviour in Democratic Athens: A Social History*. New York: Cambridge University Press.

Hernandez, M. P. N. 1993. "Heracles and Pindar." *Metis* 8 (1): 75–102.

Heubeck, A., and Hoekstra, A. 1990. *A Commentary on Homer's* Odyssey. Vol. 2. Oxford: Clarendon Press.

Higgins, W. E. 1977. "A Passage to Hades: The *Frogs* of Aristophanes." *Ramus* 6: 60–81.

Hoff, R. von den. 2005. "'Achill, das Vieh'? Zur Problematisierung transgressiver Gewalt in klassischen Vasenbildern." In Fischer, G. and Moraw, S., eds. *Die andere Seite der Klassik: Gewalt im 5. und 4. Jahrhundert v. Chr.: Kulturwissenschaftliches Kolloquium Bonn, Kunst- und Ausstellungshalle der Bundesrepublik Deutschland, 11.–13. Juli 2002*. Stuttgart: Steiner. 225–46.

Holmes, B. 2008. "Euripides' Heracles in the Flesh." *Classical Antiquity* 27 (2): 231–81.

Holt, P. 1989. "The End of the *Trachiniai* and the Fate of Herakles." *The Journal of Hellenic Studies* 109: 69–80.

Holt, P. 1992. "Herakles' Apotheosis in Lost Greek Literature and Art." *L'antiquité classique* 61: 38–59.

Hooff, A. J. L. van. 1990. *From Autothanasia to Suicide: Self-Killing in Classical Antiquity*. London: Routledge.

Hooker, J. T. 1980. "The Apparition of Heracles in the *Odyssey*." *Liverpool Classical Monthly* 5: 139–46.

Hordern, J. H. 2004. *Sophron's Mimes: Text, Translation, and Commentary*. New York: Oxford University Press.

Hose, M. 1991. *Studien zum Chor bei Euripides, Teil 2*. Stuttgart: B.G. Teubner.

Hose, M. 2008. *Euripides: der Dichter der Leidenschaften*. München: Beck.

Hunt, P. 2016. "Violence Against Slaves in Classical Greece." In Riess, W. and Fagan, G. G., eds. *The Topography of Violence in the Greco-Roman World*. Ann Arbor, MI: University of Michigan Press. 136–61.

Hunter, R. L. 1983. *Eubulus: The Fragments*. New York: Cambridge University Press.

Hunter, R. L. 2014. *Hesiodic Voices: Studies in the Ancient Reception of Hesiod's Works and Days*. Cambridge: Cambridge University Press.

Huxley, G. L. 1969. *Greek Epic Poetry from Eumelos to Panyassis*. Cambridge, MA: Harvard University Press.

Irvine, J. A. D. 1997. "Keres in Stesichorus' 'Geryoneis': P. Oxy. 2617 fr. 1 (a)-(b) = SLG 21 Reconsidered." *Zeitschrift für Papyrologie und Epigraphik* 115: 37–46.

Isler, H. P. 1970. *Acheloos: eine Monographie*. Berne: Francke.

Jackson, S. 2003. "Apollonius of Rhodes: Death on Tenos." *Quaderni urbinati di cultura classica* 73 (1): 121–7.

Janko, R. 1986. "The Shield of Heracles and the Legend of Cycnus." *The Classical Quarterly* 36 (1): 38–59.

Janko, R. 1992. *The Iliad: A Commentary*. Vol. 4. Cambridge: Cambridge University Press.

Janko, R. 2000. *Philodemus: On Poems, Book 1*. New York: Oxford University Press.

Janko, R. 2013. "The Hexametric Incantations against Witchcraft in the Getty Museum: From Archetype to Exemplar." In Faraone, C. A. and Obbink, D., eds. *The Getty Hexameters: Poetry, Magic, and Mystery in Ancient Selinous*. Oxford: Oxford University Press. 31–56.

de Jáuregui, M. H. 2016. "The Meanings of Σώιζειν in *Alcestis*' Final Scene." *Trends in Classics* 8 (2): 205–25.

Jauss, H. R. 1977. "Interaktionsmuster der Identifikation mit dem Helden." In *Ästhetische Erfahrung und literarische Hermeneutik*. München: W. Fink. 212–58.

Jauss, H. R. 1982a. *Toward an Aesthetic of Reception*. Translated by Timothy Bahti. Minneapolis, MN: University of Minnesota Press.

Jauss, H. R. 1982b. "Interaction Patterns of Identification with the Hero." In *Aesthetic Experience and Literary Hermeneutics*. Translated by Michael Shaw. Minneapolis, MN: University of Minnesota Press. 152–88.

Jauss, H. R. 1989. *Question and Answer: Forms of Dialogic Understanding*. Translated by Michael Hays. Minneapolis, MN: University of Minnesota Press.

Johnson, J. 2002. "Compassion and Friendship in Euripides' *Herakles*." *Classical Bulletin* 78 (2): 115–29.

Jones, C. P. 2010. *New Heroes in Antiquity: From Achilles to Antinoos*. Vol. 18. Revealing Antiquity. Cambridge, MA: Harvard University Press.

de Jong, I. 1987. *Narrators and Focalizers: The Presentation of the Story in the* Iliad. Amsterdam: B.R. Grüner Pub. Co.

de Jong, I. 2014. *Narratology and Classics: A Practical Guide*. Oxford: Oxford University Press.

Jourdain-Annequin, C. 1992. *Héraclès-Melqart à Amrith: Recherches Iconographiques: Contribution à l'étude d'un Syncrétisme*. Paris: Libr. orientaliste P. Geuthner.

Jourdain-Annequin, C., and Bonnet, C., eds. 1996. *Héraclès, les femmes et le féminin: IIe rencontre héracléenne: actes du Colloque de Grenoble, Université des sciences sociales (Grenoble II), 22-23 octobre 1992*. Bruxelles: Institut historique belge de Rome.

Kajava, M. 1997. "Heracles Saving the Shipwrecked." *Arctos* 31: 55–86.

Kamerbeek, J. C. 1966. "Unity and Meaning of Euripides' 'Heracles.'" *Mnemosyne* 19 (1): 1–16.

Karanika, A. 2011. "The End of the Nekyia: Odysseus, Heracles, and the Gorgon in the Underworld." *Arethusa* 44 (1): 1–27.

Kelly, A. 2010. "Hypertexting with Homer: Tlepolemus and Sarpedon on Heracles (*Il.* 5.628–698)." *Trends in Classics* 2 (2): 259–76.

Kelly, A. 2015. "Stesichorus' Homer." In Finglass, P. and Kelly, A., eds. *Stesichorus in Context*. Cambridge: Cambridge University Press. 21–44.

King, K. C. 1991. *Achilles: Paradigms of the War Hero from Homer to the Middle Ages*. Berkeley, CA: University of California Press.

Kingsley, S. 2018. "Justifying Violence in Herodotus' *Histories* 3.38: *Nomos*, King of All, and Pindaric Poetics." In Bowie, E., ed. *Herodotus: Narrator, Scientist, Historian*. Trends in Classics. Berlin: De Gruyter. 37–58.

Kirk, G. S. 1974. *The Nature of Greek Myths*. Harmondsworth, UK: Penguin.

Kirk, G. S. 1977. "Methodological Reflexions on the Myths of Heracles." In Gentili, B. and Paioni, G., eds. *Il Mito greco: atti del Convegno internazionale (Urbino, 7–12 maggio 1973)*. Roma: Edizioni dell'Ateneo & Bizzarri. 285–97.

Kirk, G. S. 1990. *Iliad: A Commentary (Books 5–8)*. Vol. 2. New York: Cambridge University Press.

Kirkpatrick, J., and Dunn, F. 2002. "Heracles, Cercopes, and Paracomedy." *Transactions of the American Philological Association* 132 (1/2): 29–61.

Kirkwood, G. M. 1994. *A Study of Sophoclean Drama with a New Preface and Enlarged Bibliographical Note*. Ithaca, NY: Cornell University Press.

Klees, H. 1998. *Sklavenleben im klassischen Griechenland*. Stuttgart: F. Steiner.

Knox, B. 1999. "Always to Be Best: The Competitive Spirit in Ancient Greek Culture" presented at the Professor John C. Rouman Classical Lecture Series, October 13, University of New Hampshire, Durham.

Kock, T. 1880. *Comicorum atticorum fragmenta*. 3 vols. Leipzig: B.G. Teubner.

Koenen, L., and Merkelbach, R. 1976. "Apollodoros (Περὶ θεῶν), Epicharm und die Meropis." In Hanson, A. E., ed. *Collectanea Papyrologica: Texts Publ. in Honor of H. C. Youtie*. Papyrologische Texte und Abhandlungen Bd. 19. Bonn: Habelt. 3–26.

Köhnken, A. 1965. *Apollonios Rhodios und Theokrit; die Hylas- und die Amykosgeschichten beider Dichter und die Frage der Priorität*. Hypomnemata; Untersuchungen zur Antike und zu ihrem Nachleben, Heft 12. Göttingen: Vandenhoeck & Ruprecht.

Köhnken, A, 1983. "Mythical Chronology and Thematic Coherence in Pindar's Third Olympian Ode." *Harvard Studies in Classical Philology* 87: 49–63.

Koning, H. H. 2010. *Hesiod, the Other Poet: Ancient Reception of a Cultural Icon*. Leiden: Brill.

Konstan, D. 1997. *Friendship in the Classical World*. New York: Cambridge University Press.

Kratzer, E. 2010. "The Double Herakles: Studies on the Death and Deification of the Hero in Fifth-Century Drama." Dissertation, Los Angeles: University of California.

Kratzer, E. 2015. "Mortality Is Hard to Wrestle With: Cosmology and Combat Sports in the *Alcestis*." Edited by Thomas Scanlon. *Classics@* 13. https://chs.harvard.edu/CHS/article/display/6053.

Kraus, C. S. 1991. "'Logos Men Est' Arxaios': Stories and Story-Telling in Sophocles' *Trachiniae*." *Transactions of the American Philological Association* 121: 75–98.

Krumeich, R., Pechstein, N., and Seidensticker, B., eds. 1999. *Das griechische Satyrspiel*. Texte zur Forschung Bd. 72. Darmstadt: Wissenschaftliche Buchgesellschaft.

Kuntz, M. 1993. "The Prodikean 'Choice of Herakles': A Reshaping of Myth." *The Classical Journal* 89 (2): 163–81.

Kurke, L. 1991. *The Traffic in Praise: Pindar and the Poetics of Social Economy*. Ithaca, NY: Cornell University Press.

Kyle, D. G. 2014. *Sport and Spectacle in the Ancient World*. Chichester: John Wiley & Sons.

Kyriakou, P. 2002. "The Violence of Nomos in Pindar fr. 169a." *Materiali e discussioni per l'analisi dei testi classici* (48): 195–206.

Kyriakou, P. 2006. *A Commentary on Euripides' Iphigenia in Tauris*. New York: De Gruyter.

Lada-Richards, I. 1998. "'Foul Monster or Good Saviour?' Reflections on Ritual Monsters." In Atherton, C., ed. *Monsters and Monstrosity in Greek and Roman Culture*. Nottingham Classical Literature Studies v. 6. Bari: Levante. 41–82.

Lada-Richards, I. 1999. *Initiating Dionysus: Ritual and Theatre in Aristophanes' Frogs*. Oxford: Clarendon Press.

Lämmle, R. 2013. *Poetik des Satyrspiels*. Heidelberg: Universitätsverlag Winter.
Lang, M. L. 1983. "Reverberation and Mythology in the *Iliad*." In Rubino, C. A. and Shelmerdine, C. W., eds. *Approaches to Homer*. Austin, TX: University of Texas Press. 140–64.
Lapalus, É. 1934. "Le Dionysos et l'Héraclès des *Grenouilles*." *Revue des études grecques* 47: 1–20.
Laurens, A.-F. 1990. "IX.J. Herakles and Hebe." In *LIMC*. V.1: 160–5.
Lawrence, S. E. 1978. "The Dramatic Epistemology of Sophocles' 'Trachiniae.'" *Phoenix* 32 (4): 288–304.
Lazzeri, M. 1995. "Osservazioni su alcuni frammenti della *Gerioneide* di Stesicoro." *Bollettino dei classici* ser. 3, fasc. 16: 83–102.
Lazzeri, M. 2008. *Studi sulla* Gerioneide *di Stesicoro*. Napoli: Arte Tipografica.
Lefèvre, E. 2001. *Die Unfähigkeit, sich zu erkennen: Sophokles' Tragödien*. Leiden: Brill.
Lerza, P. 1978. "Su un frammento della *Gerioneide* di Stesicoro." *Atene e Roma* 23: 83–7.
Lesky, A. 1925. *Alkestis, der Mythus und das Drama*. Wien: Hölder-Pichler-Tempsky.
Lexicon Iconographicum Mythologiae Classicae (LIMC). 1981–2009. 8 vols. Zurich, Munich, Dusseldorf: Artemis and Winkler Verlag.
Liapis, V. 2006. "Intertextuality as Irony: Heracles in Epic and in Sophocles." *Greece & Rome* 53 (1): 48–59.
Liddell, H. G., Scott, R., and Jones, H. S. (*LSJ*). 1996. *A Greek-English Lexicon*. Oxford: Oxford University Press.
Lissarrague, F. 1995. "Héraclès et les satyres." In *Modi e funzioni del racconto mitico nella ceramica greca, italiota ed etrusca dal VI al IV secolo a.C.* Salerno: Centro Studi Salernitani. 171–201.
Lloyd-Jones, H. 1971. *The Justice of Zeus*. Berkeley, CA: University of California Press.
Lloyd-Jones, H. 1972. "Pindar Fr. 169." *Harvard Studies in Classical Philology* 76: 45–56.
Lloyd-Jones, H. 1990a. "The Meropis (SH 903 A)." In *Greek Epic, Lyric, and Tragedy: The Academic Papers of Sir Hugh Lloyd-Jones*. Oxford: Clarendon Press. 21–9.
Lloyd-Jones, H. 1990b. "Heracles at Eleusis." In *Greek Epic, Lyric, and Tragedy: The Academic Papers of Sir Hugh Lloyd-Jones*. Oxford: Clarendon Press. 167–87.
Lloyd-Jones, H. 1993. *The Oresteia*. Berkeley, CA: University of California Press.
Lobel, E. 1961. "2450. Pindar, Uncertain Category (? Διθύραμβοι)." *The Oxyrhynchus Papyri* 26: 141–54.
Lobel, E. 1967. "2617. Stesichorus, Γηρυονηΐς?, And Other Pieces?" *The Oxyrhynchus Papyri* 32: 1–29.
Loraux, N. 1987. *Tragic Ways of Killing a Woman*. Translated by A. Forster. Cambridge, MA: Harvard University Press.
Loraux, N. 1990. "Herakles: The Super-Male and the Feminine." In Halperin, D. M., Winkler, J. J., and Zeitlin, F. I., eds. *Before Sexuality: The Construction of Erotic Experience in the Ancient Greek World*. Princeton, NJ: Princeton University Press. 21–52.
Lord, A. B. 1965. *The Singer of Tales*. New York: Atheneum.

Luce, S. B. 1930. "Studies of the Exploits of Herakles on Vases. II. The Theft of the Delphic Tripod." *American Journal of Archaeology* 34 (3): 313–33.

Lunt, D. 2009. "The Heroic Athlete in Ancient Greece." *Journal of Sport History* 36 (3): 375–92.

MacDowell, D. M. 1972. "The *Frogs*' Chorus." *The Classical Review* 22 (1): 3–5.

MacKinnon, J. K. 1971. "Heracles' Intention in His Second Request of Hyllus: *Trach.* 1216–51." *The Classical Quarterly* 21 (1): 33–41.

Maehler, H., and Snell, B., eds. 1989. *Pindari carmina cum fragmentis*. Bibliotheca scriptorum Graecorum et Romanorum Teubneriana. Leipzig: Teubner.

Maingon, A. D. 1980. "Epic Convention in Stesichorus' 'Geryoneis: SLG' S15." *Phoenix* 34 (2): 99–107.

Maitland, J. 2007. "Ion of Chios, Sophocles, and Myth." In Jennings, V. and Katsaros, A. eds. *The World of Ion of Chios*. Leiden: Brill. 266–81.

Mann, R. 1994. "Pindar's Homer and Pindar's Myths." *GRBS* 35: 313–37.

March, J. R. 1987. "Deianeira and Herakles." In *The Creative Poet: Studies on the Treatment of Myths in Greek Poetry*. BICS Supplement. London: Institute of Classical Studies. 49–77.

Martindale, C. 1993. *Redeeming the Text: Latin Poetry and the Hermeneutics of Reception*. Roman Literature and Its Contexts. Cambridge: Cambridge University Press.

Mastronarde, D. J. 1968. "Theocritus' Idyll 13: Love and the Hero." *Transactions of the American Philological Association* 99: 273–90.

Matthews, G., and Goodman, S., eds. 2013. *Violence and the Limits of Representation*. Basingstoke, UK: Palgrave Macmillan.

McDonald, M. 1990. "Iphigenia's 'Philia': Motivation in Euripides 'Iphigenia at Aulis.'" *Quaderni urbinati di cultura classica* 34 (1): 69–84.

Meineck, P. 2012. "Combat Trauma and the Tragic Stage: 'Restoration' by Cultural Catharsis." *Intertexts* 16 (1): 7–24.

Meineck, P., and Konstan, D., eds. 2014. *Combat Trauma and the Ancient Greeks*. New York: Palgrave Macmillan.

Mette, H. J. 1983. "Perithoos-Theseus-Herakles bei Euripides." *Zeitschrift für Papyrologie und Epigraphik* 50: 13–19.

Michelini, A. N. 1987. *Euripides and the Tragic Tradition*. Madison, WI: University of Wisconsin Press.

Mikalson, J. D. 1986. "Zeus the Father and Heracles the Son in Tragedy." *Transactions of the American Philological Association* 116: 89–98.

Montiglio, S. 2000. *Silence in the Land of Logos*. Princeton, NJ: Princeton University Press.

Montiglio, S. 2011. *From Villain to Hero: Odysseus in Ancient Thought*. Ann Arbor, MI: University of Michigan Press.

Moorton, R. F. 1989. "Rites of Passage in Aristophanes' 'Frogs.'" *The Classical Journal* 84 (4): 308–24.

Morrison, J. V. 1997. "Kerostasia, The Dictates of Fate, and the Will of Zeus in the *Iliad*." *Arethusa* 30 (2): 276–96.

Most, G. 2003. "Epinician Envies." In Konstan, D. and Rutter, N. K., eds. *Envy, Spite and Jealousy: The Rivalrous Emotions in Ancient Greece*. Edinburgh: Edinburgh University Press. 123–42.

Mueller, M. 2016. "The Disease of Mortality in Hesiod's *Theogony*: Prometheus, Herakles, and the Invention of *Kleos*." *Ramus* 45 (1): 1–17.

Murray, G. 1946. "Heracles, 'The Best of Men.'" In *Greek Studies*. Oxford: Clarendon Press. 106–26.

Muth, S. 2008. *Gewalt im Bild: das Phänomen der medialen Gewalt im Athen des 6. und 5. Jahrhunderts v. Chr*. Berlin: Walter de Gruyter.

Nagy, G. 1999. *The Best of the Achaeans: Concepts of the Hero in Archaic Greek Poetry*. Baltimore, MD: Johns Hopkins University Press.

Nesselrath, H.-G. 1990. *Die attische mittlere Komödie: ihre Stellung in der antiken Literaturkritik*. New York: Walter de Gruyter.

Nestle, W. 1936. "Die Horen des Prodikos." *Hermes* 71 (2): 151–70.

Nightingale, A. W. 1995. *Genres in Dialogue: Plato and the Construct of Philosophy*. New York: Cambridge University Press.

Nilsson, M. P. 1932. *The Mycenaean Origin of Greek Mythology*. Vol. 8. Sather Classical Lectures. Berkeley, CA: University of California Press.

Nilsson, M. P. 1941. *Geschichte der griechischen Religion*. München: Beck.

Noys, B. 2013. "The Violence of Representation and the Representation of Violence." In Matthews, G. and Goodman, S., eds. *Violence and the Limits of Representation*. Basingstoke, UK: Palgrave Macmillan. 12–27.

Ogden, D., ed. forthcoming. *The Oxford Handbook to Heracles*. Oxford: Oxford University Press.

Olson, S. D., ed. 2007. *Broken Laughter: Select Fragments of Greek Comedy*. Oxford: Oxford University Press.

Omitowoju, R. 2002. *Rape and the Politics of Consent in Classical Athens*. New York: Cambridge University Press.

Ormand, K. 1999. *Exchange and the Maiden: Marriage in Sophoclean Tragedy*. Austin, TX: University of Texas Press.

Ormand, K. 2014. *The Hesiodic* Catalogue of Women *and Archaic Greece*. New York: Cambridge University Press.

Ostwald, M. 1965. "Pindar, *Nomos*, and Heracles: (Pindar, Frg. 169 [Snell2]+POxy. No. 2450, Frg. I): Dedicated to Harry Caplan." *Harvard Studies in Classical Philology* 69: 109–38.

O'Sullivan, P., and Collard, C. 2013. *Euripides'* Cyclops *and Major Fragments of Greek Satyric Drama*. Oxford: Aris & Phillips.

Padilla, M. 1992. "The Heraclean Dionysus: Theatrical and Social Renewal in Aristophanes' *Frogs*." *Arethusa* 25: 359–84.

Padilla, M. 1998. *The Myths of Herakles in Ancient Greece: Survey and Profile*. Lanham, MD: University Press of America.

Padilla, M. 2000. "Gifts of Humiliation: Charis and Tragic Experience in *Alcestis*." *American Journal of Philology* 121 (2): 179–211.

Page, D. 1973. "Stesichorus: The Geryoneïs." *The Journal of Hellenic Studies* 93: 138–54.

Panofsky, E. 1930. *Hercules am Scheidewege und andere antike Bildstoffe in der neueren Kunst*. Berlin: B. G. Teubner.

Papadopoulou, T. 2005. *Heracles and Euripidean Tragedy*. New York: Cambridge University Press.

Parke, H. W., and Boardman, J. 1957. "The Struggle for the Tripod and the First Sacred War." *The Journal of Hellenic Studies* 77: 276–82.

Parker, L. P. E. 2007. *Euripides Alcestis*. New York: Oxford University Press.

Parry, H. 1965. "The Second Stasimon of Euripides' *Heracles* (637–700)." *American Journal of Philology* 86 (4): 363–74.

Pavese, C. 1968. "The New Heracles Poem of Pindar." *Harvard Studies in Classical Philology* 72: 47–88.

Pavese, C. 1993. "On Pindar, Fr. 169." *Harvard Studies in Classical Philology* 95: 143–57.

Payne, M. 2006. "On Being Vatic: Pindar, Pragmatism, and Historicism." *American Journal of Philology* 127 (2): 159–84.

Philips, F. C. 1978. "Heracles." *The Classical World* 71 (7): 431–40.

Pike, D. L. 1984. "Pindar's Treatment of the Heracles Myths." *Acta Classica* 27: 15–22.

Pinker, S. 2011. *The Better Angels of Our Nature: Why Violence Has Declined*. New York: Viking.

Platter, C. 1994. "Heracles, Deianeira, and Nessus: Reverse Chronology and Human Knowledge in Bacchylides 16." *The American Journal of Philology* 115 (3): 337–49.

Platter, C. 2007. *Aristophanes and the Carnival of Genres*. Baltimore, MD: Johns Hopkins University Press.

Podlecki, A. J. 2005. "Aiskhylos Satyrikos." In Harrison, G. W. M. and Ambrose, Z. P., eds. *Satyr Drama: Tragedy at Play*. Swansea: Classical Press of Wales. 1–19.

Poliakoff, M. B. 1987. *Combat Sports in the Ancient World: Competition, Violence, and Culture*. New Haven, CT: Yale University Press.

Pozzi, D. 1999. "Hyllus' Coming of Age in Sophocles' *Trachiniae*." In Padilla, M., ed. *Rites of Passage in Ancient Greece: Literature, Religion, Society*. Bucknell Review. Lewisburg, PA: Bucknell University Press. 43, no. 1: 29–41.

Pralon, D. 1996. "Héraclès-Iole." In Jourdain-Annequin, C. and Bonnet, C., eds. *Héraclès, les femmes et le féminin: IIe rencontre héracléenne: actes du Colloque de Grenoble, Université des sciences sociales (Grenoble II), 22–23 octobre 1992*. Études de philologie, d'archéologie et d'histoire anciennes. Bruxelles-Rome: Institut historique belge de Rome. 31: 51–76.

Rabel, R. J. 1997. *Plot and Point of View in the* Iliad. Ann Arbor, MI: University of Michigan Press.

Race, W. H. 1989. "Elements of Style in Pindaric Break-Offs." *The American Journal of Philology* 110 (2): 189–209.

Rankine, P. 2011. "Odysseus as Slave: The Ritual of Domination and Social Death in Homeric Society." In Alston, R., Hall, E., and Proffitt, L., eds. *Reading Ancient Slavery*. London: Bristol Classical Press. 34–50.

Rawlings, L., and Bowden, H., eds. 2005. *Herakles and Hercules: Exploring a Graeco-Roman Divinity*. Swansea: The Classical Press of Wales.

Recke, M. 2002. *Gewalt und Leid: Das Bild des Krieges bei den Athenern im 6. und 5. Jh. v. Chr*. Istanbul: Ege Yayınları.

Riess, W. 2012. *Performing Interpersonal Violence: Court, Curse, and Comedy*. Berlin: De Gruyter.

Riess, W., and Fagan, G. G., eds. 2016. *The Topography of Violence in the Greco-Roman World*. Ann Arbor, MI: University of Michigan Press.

Robbins, E. 1982. "Heracles, the Hyperboreans, and the Hind: Pindar, 'OL.' 3." *Phoenix* 36 (4): 295.

Roberts, D. H. 1988. "Sophoclean Endings: Another Story." *Arethusa* 21 (2): 177–96.

Robertson, M. 1969. "*Geryoneis*: Stesichorus and the Vase-Painters." *The Classical Quarterly* 19 (2): 207–21.

Robertson, N. 1980. "Heracles' 'Catabasis.'" *Hermes* 108 (3): 274–300.

de Romilly, J. 1980. "Le refus du suicide dans l'*Héraclès* d'Euripide." *Archaiognosia* 1: 1–10.

de Romilly, J. 2000. *La Grèce antique contre la violence*. Paris: Editions de Fallois.

Rosen, R. M. 1995. "Plato Comicus and the Evolution of Greek Comedy." In Dobrov, G. W., ed. *Beyond Aristophanes: Transition and Diversity in Greek Comedy*. Atlanta, GA: Scholars Press. 119–37.

Rozokoki, A. 2008. "Stesichorus, *Geryoneis* S 11 SLG: The Dilemma of Geryon." *Wiener Studien* 121: 67–9.

Ruijgh, C. J. 1995. "D'Homère aux origines proto-mycéniennes de la tradition épique. Analyse dialectologique du lange homérique, avec un excursus sur la création de l'alphabet grec." In Crielaard, J. P., ed. *Homeric Questions: Essays in Philology, Ancient History, and Archaeology, Including the Papers of a Conference Organized by the Netherlands Institute at Athens (15 May 1993)*. Amsterdam: J.C. Gieben. 1–96.

Ruijgh, C. J. 2011. "Mycenaean and Homeric Language." In Duhoux, Y. and Davies, A. M., eds., *A Companion to Linear B: Mycenaean Greek Texts and Their World*. Louvain-la-Neuve: Peeters. 2: 253–98.

Russo, C. F. 1965. *Hesiodi Scutum*. 2nd ed. Florence: Nuova Italia.

Rusten, J. S., and Henderson, J., eds. 2011. *The Birth of Comedy: Texts, Documents, and Art from Athenian Comic Competitions, 486–280*. Baltimore, MD: Johns Hopkins University Press.

Rutherford, I. 2001. *Pindar's Paeans: A Reading of the Fragments with a Survey of the Genre*. New York: Oxford University Press.

Schechter, H. 2005. *Savage Pastimes: A Cultural History of Violent Entertainment.* 1st ed. New York: St. Martin's Press.

Schein, S. 1984. *The Mortal Hero: An Introduction to Homer's Iliad.* Berkeley, CA: University of California Press.

Schein, S. 1988. "ΦΙΛΙΑ in Euripides' *Alcestis*." *Metis* 3 (1): 179–206.

Schein, S. 1990. "Philia in Euripides' *Medea*." In Griffith, M. and Mastronarde, D., eds. *Cabinet of the Muses: Essays on Classical and Comparative Literature in Honor of Thomas G. Rosenmeyer.* Atlanta, GA: Scholars Press. 57–73.

Schweitzer, B. 1922. *Herakles, Aufsätze zur griechischen Religions- und Sagengeschichte.* Tübingen: Mohr.

Schwinge, E.-R. 1962. *Die Stellung der Trachinierinnen im Werk des Sophokles.* Göttingen: Vandenhoeck & Ruprecht.

Scodel, R. 1979. "Ἀδμήτου Λόγος and the *Alcestis*." *Harvard Studies in Classical Philology* 83: 51–62.

Scully, S. F. 1973. "Φιλία and Χάρις in Euripidean Tragedy." Dissertation, Toronto: University of Toronto.

Seaford, R. 1988. *Euripides: Cyclops.* New York: Oxford University Press.

Segal, C. 1961. "The Character and Cults of Dionysus and the Unity of the *Frogs*." *Harvard Studies in Classical Philology* 65: 207–42.

Segal, C. 1977. "Sophocles' *Trachiniae*: Myth, Poetry, and Heroic Values." *Yale Classical Studies* 25: 99–158.

Segal, C. 1981. *Tragedy and Civilization: An Interpretation of Sophocles.* Cambridge, MA: Harvard University Press.

Segal, C. 1994. "Bride or Concubine? Iole and Heracles' Motives in the *Trachiniae*." *Illinois Classical Studies* 19: 59–64.

Segal, C. 1995. *Sophocles' Tragic World: Divinity, Nature, Society.* Cambridge, MA: Harvard University Press.

Segal, C. 2000. "The Oracles of Sophocles' 'Trachiniae': Convergence or Confusion?" *Harvard Studies in Classical Philology* 100: 151–71.

Seidensticker, B., and Vöhler, M. 2006. *Gewalt und Ästhetik zur Gewalt und ihrer Darstellung in der griechischen Klassik.* Berlin: De Gruyter.

Shapiro, H. A. 1983. "'Hêrôs Theos': The Death and Apotheosis of Herakles." *The Classical World* 77 (1): 7–18.

Shapiro, H. A. 1984a. "Herakles, Kyknos, and Delphi." In Brijder, H. A. G. ed. *Ancient Greek and Related Pottery: Proceedings of the International Vase Symposium in Amsterdam 12–15 April, 1984.* Allard Pierson Series. Amsterdam: Allard Pierson Museum. 271–4.

Shapiro, H. A. 1984b. "Herakles and Kyknos." *American Journal of Archaeology* 88 (4): 523–29.

Shaw, C. 2014. *Satyric Play: The Evolution of Greek Comedy and Satyr Drama.* Oxford: Oxford University Press.

Shay, J. 1994. *Achilles in Vietnam: Combat Trauma and the Undoing of Character.* New York: Maxwell Macmillan.

Shay, J. 2002. *Odysseus in America: Combat Trauma and the Trials of Homecoming*. New York: Scribner.

Sheppard, J. T. 1916. "The Formal Beauty of the *Hercules Furens*." *The Classical Quarterly* 10 (2): 72–9.

Silk, M. S. 1985. "Heracles and Greek Tragedy." *Greece & Rome* 32 (1): 1–22.

Sjoqvist, E. 1962. "Herakles in Sicily." *Opusculana Romana* 4: 117–23.

Sommerstein, A. H., ed. 1989. *Aeschylus' Eumenides*. New York: Cambridge University Press.

Sommerstein, A. H. 1996. *Aristophanes: Frogs*. Warminster: Aris & Phillips.

Sourvinou-Inwood, C. 1988. "Myth as History: The Previous Owners of the Delphic Oracle." In Bremmer, J., ed. *Interpretations of Greek Mythology*. London: Routledge. 215–41.

Stafford, E. 2005. "Héraklès: encore et toujours le problème du heros-theos." *Kernos* 18: 391–406.

Stafford, E. 2012. *Herakles*. New York: Routledge.

Stamatopoulou, Z. 2017. "Wounding the Gods: The Mortal Theomachos in the *Iliad* and the Hesiodic *Aspis*." *Mnemosyne* 70 (6): 920–38.

Stanford, W. 1947. *The Odyssey*. London: Macmillan.

Stanford, W. 1954. *The Ulysses Theme: A Study in the Adaptability of a Traditional Hero*. Oxford: Blackwell.

Stanford, W. 1963. *Sophocles: Ajax*. London: Macmillan.

Steiner, D. 2010. "The Immeasures of Praise: The Epinician Celebration of Agamemnon's Return." *Hermes* 138 (1): 22–37.

Stevens, L. C. 1958. "Rabelais and Aristophanes." *Studies in Philology* 55 (1): 24–30.

Stinton, T. C. W. 1990. "The Scope and Limits of Allusion in Greek Tragedy." In *Collected Papers on Greek Tragedy*. New York: Clarendon Press. 454–92.

Storey, I. C. 2005. "But Comedy Has Satyrs Too." In Harrison, G. W. M., ed. *Satyr Drama: Tragedy at Play*. Swansea: Classical Press of Wales. 201–18.

Sutton, D. F. 1980. *The Greek Satyr Play*. Meisenheim am Glan: Hain.

Swift, L. 2010. *The Hidden Chorus: Echoes of Genre in Tragic Lyric*. New York: Oxford University Press.

Swift, L. 2011. "Epinician and Tragic Worlds: The Case of Sophocles' *Trachiniae*." In Athanassaki, L. and Bowie, E., eds. *Archaic and Classical Choral Song*. Berlin: De Gruyter. 391–414.

Swift, L. 2012. "Paeanic and Epinican Healing in Euripides' *Alcestis*." In Rosenbloom, D. and Davidson, J., eds. *Greek Drama IV: Texts, Contexts, Performance*. Oxford: Aris & Phillips. 149–68.

Taplin, O. 1993. *Comic Angels : And Other Approaches to Greek Drama through Vase-Paintings*. New York: Oxford University Press.

Temmerman, K. De, and Emde Boas, E. van, eds. 2018. *Characterization in Ancient Greek Literature*. Mnemosyne. Supplements 411. Leiden: Brill.

Thompson, S. 1955. *Motif-Index of Folk-Literature*. Rev. and enl. ed. Copenhagen: Rosenkilde and Bagger.

Torrance, I. 2017. "Heracles and Hercules: Ancient Models for PTSD in Euripides and Seneca." *Maia* 69: 231–46.

Trundle, M. 2020. "Violence, Law and Community in Classical Athens." In Fagan, G. G., Fibiger, L., Hudson, M., and Trundle, M., eds. *The Cambridge World History of Violence*. Cambridge: Cambridge University Press. 1: 533–49.

Tsitsibakou-Vasalos, E. 1990. "Stesichorus' *Geryoneis*, SLG 15 I–II." *Hellenika* 41: 7–31.

Tsitsibakou-Vasalos, E. 1991. "Stesichorus, Geryoneis S. 11.5–26: The Dilemma of Geryon." *Hellenika* 42: 245–56.

Tzanetou, A. 2012. *City of Suppliants: Tragedy and the Athenian Empire*. Austin, TX: University of Texas Press.

Uhlenbrock, J., and Galinsky, K. 1986. *Herakles: Passage of the Hero through 1000 Years of Classical Art*. New Rochelle, NY: A.D. Caratzas.

Uhlig, A. forthcoming. "Satyrs in Drag: Transvestism in Ion's *Omphale* and Elsewhere." In Antonopoulos, A., Christopoulos, M., and Harrison, G., eds. *Brill's Companion to Satyr Drama*. Leiden: Brill.

Untersteiner, M. 1954. *The Sophists*. Translated by Kathleen Freeman. Oxford: Blackwell.

Verbanck-Piérard, A. 1989. "Le double culte d'Héraklès: légende ou réalité?" In Laurens, A.-F., ed. *Entre hommes et dieux: le convive, le héros, le prophète*. Paris: Les Belles Lettres. 43–65.

Verrall, A. W. 1905. *Essays on Four Plays of Euripides: Andromache, Helen, Heracles, Orestes*. Cambridge: Cambridge University Press.

Versnel, H. S. 2011. *Coping With the Gods*. Leiden: Brill.

Walcot, P. 1979. "Cattle Raiding, Heroic Tradition, and Ritual: The Greek Evidence." *History of Religions* 18 (4): 326–51.

Wees, H. van. 1992. *Status Warriors: War, Violence, and Society in Homer and History*. Amsterdam: J.C. Gieben.

Wees, H. van 2008. "Violence." *The Journal of Hellenic Studies* 128: 172–5.

Weil, S. 2003. *Simone Weil's The Iliad, or, The Poem of Force: A Critical Edition*. Edited by James P. Holoka. Translated by James P. Holoka. New York: P. Lang.

Weiler, I. 1974. *Der Agon im Mythos: zur Einstellung der Griechen zum Wettkampf*. Darmstadt: Wissenschaftliche Buchgesellschaft.

Weiss, N. 2019. "Generic Hybridity in Greek Tragedy." In Foster, M., Kurke, L., and Weiss, N., eds. *The Genres of Archaic and Classical Greek Poetry: Theories and Models*. Leiden: Brill. 167–90.

Wender, D. 1974. "The Will of the Beast: Sexual Imagery in the *Trachiniae*." *Ramus* 3 (1): 1–17.

West, M. L. 1966. *Theogony*. Oxford: Clarendon.

West, M. L. 2003. *Greek Epic Fragments from the Seventh to the Fifth Centuries BC*. Loeb Classical Library. Cambridge, MA: Harvard University Press.

West, M. L. 2014. *The Making of the* Odyssey. Oxford: Oxford University Press.

Whitman, C. H. 1951. *Sophocles: A Study of Heroic Humanism*. Cambridge, MA: Harvard University Press.

Wilamowitz-Moellendorff, U. von. 1895. *Euripides: Herakles*. 2nd ed. Berlin: Weidmannsche Buchhandlung.

Wildberg, C. 2002. *Hyperesie und Epiphanie: ein Versuch über die Bedeutung der Götter in den Dramen des Euripides*. Zetemata. München: Beck.

Willcock, M. M. 1964. "Mythological Paradeigma in the *Iliad*." *The Classical Quarterly* 14 (2): 141–54.

Wills, G. 1969. "Why Are the Frogs in the *Frogs*?" *Hermes* 97 (3): 306–17.

Winnington-Ingram, R. P. 1980. *Sophocles: An Interpretation*. New York: Cambridge University Press.

Wohl, V. 1998. *Intimate Commerce: Exchange, Gender, and Subjectivity in Greek Tragedy*. Austin, TX: University of Texas Press.

Wolfsdorf, D. 2008. "Hesiod, Prodicus, and the Socratics on Work and Pleasure." In *Oxford Studies in Ancient Philosophy*. Oxford: Oxford University Press. 35: 1–18.

Woodford, S. 1966. "Exemplum Virtutis: A Study of Heracles in Athens in the Second Half of the Fifth Century B.C." Dissertation, New York: Columbia University.

Woodford, S. 1971. "Cults of Herakles in Attica." In Mitten, D. G., Pedley, J. G., and Scott, J. A., eds. *Studies Presented to George M.A. Hanfmann*. Mainz: Verlag P. von Zabern. 211–25.

Xydopoulos, I. K., Vlassopoulos, K., and Tounta, E., eds. 2017. *Violence and Community: Law, Space and Identity in the Ancient Eastern Mediterranean World*. New York: Routledge.

Yasumura, N. 2011. *Challenges to the Power of Zeus in Early Greek Poetry*. London: Bristol Classical Press.

Yoshitake, S. 1994. "Disgrace, Grief and Other Ills: Herakles' Rejection of Suicide." *The Journal of Hellenic Studies* 114: 135–53.

Zardini, F. 2009. *The Myth of Herakles and Kyknos: A Study in Greek Vase-Painting and Literature*. Verona: Fiorini.

Zeitlin, F. 1990. "Playing the Other: Theater, Theatricality, and the Feminine in Greek Drama." In Winkler, J. and Zeitlin, F., eds. *Nothing to Do with Dionysos? Athenian Drama in Its Social Context*. Princeton, NJ: Princeton University Press. 63–96.

Žižek, S. 2008. *Violence: Six Sideways Reflections*. New York: Picador.

Index

Achelous 79–83, 88–89, 91, 104
Achilles 10, 19, 25, 41–42, 58, 78, 85, 178
Achilles in Vietnam (Shay) 3
Admetus 147–55
Aeacus (doorkeeper) 165–70
Aegisthus 41, 89
Aegle (Hesperid) 12
Aeschylus 32, 54–55, 89, 137, 170
Agamemnon 8, 25, 39, 41
Agamemnon (Aeschylus) 89
agathos 67, 76, 119
agōn 79, 127, 156
aisimon (fate) 36
Ajax 8, 200n.38, 202n.62
Alcestis (Euripides) 13, 17, 108, 131, 133, 146–56, 171, 210–11n.54
alexikakos (averter of evils) 1, 134
Amphiaraus 9
Amphitryon
  as father of Heracles 22, 24, 28–29, 52
  and Heracles 114, 119–20, 123–25, 157–58
  Heracles' toiling and Labors 109
  lamenting state of personal friends 110
  skepticism of 115
  preventing slandering of Heracles 111
Aphrodite 28, 80, 83
Apollo
  and Alcestis 153
  and death of his son Asclepius 147
  and the Delphic tripod 23, 30–34
  and Euripides' *Orestes* 103
  and Heracles 147
  killing of the Python 32–33
  Laomedon's refusal to pay 37–38
  oracle of 35
Apollonius of Rhodes 179–80
apotheosis 10–11, 23, 15, 20, 30, 42–6, 54, 61, 67–8, 76, 102–5, 114, 130, 156, 158

Apples of the Hesperides 12, 54, 98, 112, 130
Aquila Theatre company 3
Areithous ('Maceman') 64
Arendt, Hannah 4, 15, 50, 122
Ares 15, 23, 29–30, 34–36, 36, 55
Aretē 113–14, 121, 173, 175–76, 179, 214n.7
Argolid 11, 52
Argonautica (Apollonius) 12, 179–80
Argos 25, 27, 126
Ariadne 136
aristeia (Diomedes) 28
Aristides, Aelius 72
Aristophanes
  centrifugal style of comedy of 170–71
  and destabilizing of Heracles 176
  and Dionysus 164–65
  and *Frogs* 145, 157–58
  and generic manifestations of Heracles 179
  and Heracles of epic, tragedy and comedy 13, 17, 131
  and literary carnivalization 133
  and the stereotypical comic Heracles 212n.80
  and theatrical illusion 169
  and *Wasps* 142
Aristophanes and the Carnival of Genres (Platter) 133, 158
Arrowsmith, W. 108
Artemis 69, 112, 175
Asclepius 147–48
Atalanta 81
Atē 25
Athena
  and fight of Heracles and Cycnus 35–36
  and Hera 26, 121
  Heracles as champion 23
  and the Lernaean Hydra 22, 52
  and Poseidon 61–62, 194n.45

relationship with Heracles 11, 15, 25, 45–46
and Zeus 61
Athenaeus 135, 142
Athens
    and Attic religious rituals 158
    and comedy 132, 140–42
    popularity of apotheosis motif in 42–43
    and violence 6
Atlas 112
Atreus 89
Attic black-figure vases 11
Attic dramatic festivals 132
Attic forensic oratory 5
Attic religious rituals 158
Attic vase painting 6

Bacchylides 157
Bakhtin, M. M. 131–33, 135, 146, 158, 171, 178, 208n.3
Bär, S. 24
Barlow, S. A. 126
Barrett, W. S. 58, 60, 194n.39
Beaulieu, M. 54
Bellerophon 52
Benjamin, Walter 5, 15, 47, 76, 78, 122, 132, 171
Better Angels of Our Nature, The (Pinker) 2
bia 3, 55, 147, 149
biē 19–20, 42
Birds (Aristophanes) 142, 161
Boardman, J. 11, 31
Bond, G. W. 114
Boreads 180
Bowie, A. M. 160
Brize, Philip 64–65
buffoon, Heracles as 1, 6, 7, 12, 13, 17, 18, 47, 132, 134, 136, 139, 141, 146, 147, 149–53, 159, 167, 168, 170, 171, 175–6, 178
Burnett, A. P. 122
Busiris 12, 134–35
Busiris (Epicharmus) 134–35, 151
Busiris (Euripides) 138

Callicles 72, 75
Callirhoe (Geryon's mother) 51–52, 58–59
Campbell, D. A. 163
Cape Cenaeum 93–94, 96, 101

Cape Taenarum 138
Carey, Chris 115
Casolari, F. 134
carnivalesque, the 132, 134–6, 146–7, 152–3, 156, 169, 171, 175, 178
Cassandra 89
Catalogue of Women 11
Cattle of Geryon
    eliminating the monstrous 50–56, 192n.11
    and Hesiod 50–54
    introduction 49–50
    and Pindar 68, 70–72, 74, 76
    stolen by Heracles 58–59, 61–62, 130, 193n.32, 194n.40
    treatment by Stesichorus 56–67
Centauromachy 160
Centaurs 95, 100, 111–12, 120–21, 134, 136, 160
Cerberus
    and capture from Hades 16, 26, 45, 109, 114, 126, 130, 137–38, 165, 171
    and fifty headed version 50
    and Heracles 167–68
    and Orthus, the brother of 54
    task to lead to Mycenae 129
    victim of a marauder 166
Cerberus (Stesichorus) 157
Cercopes (Eubulus) 144
Ceryneian Hind 178
Ceto 50
Chalk, H. H. O. 108
Charon 163, 168
Cheiron 94, 200n.41
Chimaera 52
'Choice of Heracles' (Prodicus) 144, 173
Chorus 94, 104, 111–16, 120–21, 123, 126, 148–50
Chrysaor 51–52, 59
City Dionysia 136
Clay, Jenny Strauss 21, 50, 52, 56, 192n.5
Clytemnestra 89, 95
Colchis 179–80
comedy
    and *Alcestis* (Euripides) 146–56
    and Epicharmus 134–36, 208n.12
    Frogs (Aristophanes) 156–59
    Heracles remembered 165–71, 213n.113

Heracles in retirement 159–62, 212nn.80, 85
  introduction 131–33
  the mock Heracles 162–65
  Old and Middle 141–46
  renewing violence through laughter 133–34, 208n.5,6
  satyr play 136–41, 208–9n.14
competition 2, 16–17, 30, 32, 68, 77–93, 98–101
cottabus (drinking game) 142
Creophylus of Samos 20, 39
Cretan Bull 117
Critias 166
Critique of Violence (Benjamin) 5
Cronus 29
Crotty, Kevin 74–75
cult 8–9, 11, 31, 46, 108, 119, 129–30, 132, 134, 149, 158, 159
Cyclops 8, 147
Cyclops (Euripides) 136, 139
Cycnus 33–36, 56, 112
Cycnus (Stesichorus) 56
Cypris 152

daimon (destiny) 150
Davies, M. 56, 60
Death 147–49, 153–56, 171
Deianeira
  end of Heracles' life 177
  in exile in Trachis 77
  and Heracles 79–93, 95–101, 104–5
  and Iole 16
  jealousy of 39
  and Sophocles' *Trachiniae* 104–5, 198nn.6, 12, 20–1, 27, 199–200nn.35–6, 42, 201n.45
Deimos 36
Deipnosophistae 133
Delphi 30–34, 56
Detienne, M. 71
Dikē 93
Diodorus Siculus 146, 160, 211n.70, 212nn.84, 89, 213n.113
Diomedes (in *Iliad*) 28, 63–64
Diomedes (Thracian king) 73–75, 112, 118, 150, 156, 163
Dione 28–30, 40–41
Dionysus 136, 141, 156–71, 212n.88

Dobrov, Gregory 157, 166
Doerries, Bryan 3
dromoi 112
drunkenness 134, 153, 159
dyskleia 127

Easterling, P. E. 78
Echidna 50
eidōlon 44
Eleusis 158, 160
Empusa 164–65
enkrateia (self-control) 174
Ephialtes 29
Epi Tainario (Sophocles) 157
'Epic vs Novel' (Bakhtin) 133
Epicharmus 133–36, 138, 151
epinician
  genre of 1, 13, 16, 46, 78, 80, 82, 105, 108–9, 111, 115–22, 129, 133, 143, 155, 175–9
  Heracles 131, 147, 156
  odes 16, 178
  victor 5, 7, 13, 18, 47, 107, 147–50, 154, 156
  violence 129–30
Erginus of Orchomenos 137
Erinys 93
Eros 77, 87, 89–90
Erymanthian Boar 117, 160
Erytheia 49, 51, 53–55, 58, 76
Euboea 94, 115
Eubulus 144
Eudaimonia 173, 175–76, 179
eukleia 127
Eumenides (Aeschylus) 32
Euripides
  and Aeschylus 170
  and *Alcestis* 13, 17, 131, 146–57, 171
  composition of song for Alcibiades 203n.8
  and *Cyclops* 136
  and *Heracles* 16, 107–30, 160–61, 178
  Heracles the bull 180
  and *Iphigenia among the Taurians* 32
  and *Syleus* 141
  and the *Trachiniae* 103
Eurydice 149, 157
Eurystheus
  final Labor of Heracles 109, 115

and Heracles 121
Heracles' delusional pursuit of 117
Heracles and Hades 25–26
Heracles stronger than 81
Heracles subordinated to 45, 90, 174
killing of 116
and the Labor of the Hind 69
palace of 119
Heracles to Erytheia 49
Eurystheus (Euripides) 138, 157
Eurytion (herdsman) 21, 49, 51, 58–59
Eurytus, king of Oechalia 30, 39–40, 86, 88
Evenus river 82
exakontizō (stabbing) 123

Farmer, Matthew 157
Finglass, P. 56, 60, 63, 195n.52
First Sacred War 31
Foley, H. P. 116
Fontenrose, J. 8
Fowler, D. 66
Franzen, C. 58
Frog-Swans 163
Frogs (Aristophanes)
    characters discussing tragedy in 211n.74
    and the comic Heracles 133
    destabilizing of Heracles 176
    and Heracles of epic, tragedy and comedy 7, 13
    Heracles' many roles 170–72
    Heracles' signal act for 160
    and hybrid Frog-Swans 163
    multiplicity of Heracleses in 131
    and Plathane the innkeeper 145–46
    polyphony of genres in 156–59

Gaia 32
Galinsky, Karl 14
Garden of the Hesperides 112
Garner, R. 154
Gentili, B. 74
Geryon 16, 21, 49–76, 112, 120, 166, 193n.33, 194nn.43, 49
Geryoneis (Stesichorus) 16, 49, 56–67, 76, 166, 177, 192–93nn.18, 24
Giants 29, 44, 68, 97, 111, 126
Gigantomachy 29
Girdle of Hippolyta 112, 136

Glaucon 60
Glaucus 180
gluttony 134, 135, 144, 146, 161, 171
golden cup of the Sun 58, 193n.25
Golden Fleece 179
Goldfarb, B. 147
Gorgias (Plato) 72
Gorgythion 66
Grethlein, J. 24
Griffith, M. 136, 139, 141

Habash, M. 163, 169
Hades
    cattle of 49
    and Cerberus 109, 138
    Dione and Heracles' attacks on 15
    and Dionysus 164
    and Heracles 28–30, 102, 110, 154, 158, 167
    Heracles return from 26, 45, 54, 124, 157–8
    and Persephone 170
    and a race of four legs 114
Hadesfahrt 157
Hahnemann, C. 102
Hall, Edith 140
Hebe 10–11, 42–44, 114, 130
Hector 25–26, 58, 62
Hecuba 58–59, 193nn.28, 30–1
Helen 56, 139
Hera
    and Athena 26, 121, 206n.57
    continuous plotting of 22–23
    divine enmity of 19
    and Hebe 10–11
    Heracles' assaults on 15, 28–29
    Heracles the enemy 23, 42–43, 46, 52, 122, 125–27, 130, 207n.74
    and Heracles' greatest defeat 119
    and Hypnos 27
    Labors of Heracles 81
    and Lyssa and Iris 116
    madness of Heracles 17, 178
    snakes of 138
    and Zeus 53
Heraclea (Panyassis) 20, 157, 160
Heraclea (Pisander) 20, 160
Heracleidae 103
Heracles at the House of Pholus 136

Heracles (Euripides)
    and the apples of the Hesperides 12
    and the Centauromachy 160
    epinician persona of 13, 143
    greatest triumph/most horrific act 16
    Heracles the bull 180
    introduction 107–9, 203n.2
    kallinikos victor 150
    and Lycus 195n.54
    Lycus and the Hydra 163
    madness of Heracles 168
    and role of the victor 178
    violence against enemies 109–16, 204nn.14, 16, 23, 205nn.35–36
    violence against friends 116–22
    violence against himself 123–29
"Heracles' Katabasis or Cerberus" (Pindar) 157
Heracles and Euripidean Tragedy (Papadopoulou) 14
Heracles' Quest for the Belt 136
Heraclidae (Aeschylus) 54
Heracliscus (Sophocles) 144
Herakles Inside and Outside the Church (Stafford) 14
Herakles (Stafford) 14
Herakles Theme, The (Galinsky) 14
'Hercules Project' (Stafford) 14
Hermes 29, 45
Hermione 103
hero-god 11, 43, 68
Herodotus 75
Hesiod 15–16, 19–20, 23, 54–55, 60, 67, 74–76, 111
Hesione 37
Hesperides 12
hiketēs 119
Himerans 58
Hind of Artemis 68–69
Hippodamia 81
Hippomenes 81
Holt, P. 102
Homer 3, 15, 20, 56, 64, 195n.54
Homeric Hymn to Apollo 32
Hound of Hades 166
hybris 42
Hydra *see* Lernaean Hydra
Hylas 179–80
Hyllus 93–101, 103–5, 201n.54, 202n.68

Hyperboreans 68–69
Hypnos 26–27

Iliad (Homer)
    attacks on the gods 19
    death of Gorgythion 66
    death of Heracles 41–46
    denigration of archery 63
    and Diomedes 64
    excessive punishment of Hector's corpse 178
    and Heracles' apotheosis 11
    Heracles between the Gods in 24–28
    Heracles the *theomachos* 28–30, 30–36, 184n.34, 185nn.40–44
    Heracles as a warrior 20, 174–75
    introduction 3
    Nestor and Peleus 78
    Nestor's tale 54
    prominent roles of Heracles in 23–24
    the sacker of cities 37–41
    Sarpedon's speech to Glaucon 60
instrumental violence 4, 15–18, 20, 23, 47, 49–50, 75, 107, 119, 122–4, 175, 177–81
Iolaus 52–53
Iole 16, 77, 82, 84, 86–92, 95, 98, 102–4, 177, 202n.62
Ion of Chios 140, 146
Iphigenia 89
Iphigenia among the Taurians (Euripides) 32
Iphitus 30, 40–41, 46, 82, 86–87, 94, 101, 126, 140, 169
Iris 62, 116–17, 119
Ithaca 40
Itymoneus 54

Janko, Richard 56
Jason and the Argonauts 179–80

Kakia (vice) 18, 173, 175–76, 179
kakos moros 45
kallinikos 16–17, 108–14, 116–17, 122–25, 128–30, 143, 150
katabasis 156–57, 160–61, 164, 168
Kelly, A. 38
Kerykes (Aeschylus) 137
kētos 37

Kirk, G. S. 14, 64
kleos 22, 42, 45, 85
Kuntz, Mary 174, 214n.3
Kurke, Leslie 109

Labor of the Cattle of Geryon 16, 49–76
Labor of the Mares of Diomedes 73–4, 112, 150
Labor of the Stymphalian Birds 120–1
Labor of the Apples of the Hesperides 54
Lada-Richards, I. 56, 160
Lang, Mabel 26
Laomedon 37–39
laudandus 71
lekythos 120
Leon (Aeschylus) 137
Lernaean Hydra
    and Athena 22
    and the Chorus 112
    death of 54
    and Geryon 58
    and Hera 52–53
    and Heracles 163
    a marsh snake 110
    prehistoric origin of myths 6
    venom of 64–65, 77, 94, 196n.61
Lichas 85–90, 92, 94, 199n.25
Linus 78, 144–6, 161, 174
Linus (Alexis) 144–6, 161
Lissarrague, F. 136
Lloyd-Jones, H. 32, 72
Loraux, N. 125, 140
Lucian 169
Lycurgus 64
Lycus, king 109–12, 114–17, 119, 123–24, 204n.15
Lydia 87, 144
Lyssa 116–17, 119, 168, 180, 206n.45

MacDowell, D. M. 163
Maingon, A. D. 66
Maitland, J. 140
manifestation, violence as a 2, 5, 16–18, 20, 29, 47, 78, 105–6, 122–3, 134, 171, 175, 177, 180–1
Mares of Diomedes 73–4, 112, 150, 163
Martindale, Charles 9
material bodily lower stratum 132, 134, 144, 146–7, 152, 156, 167, 175, 178

means-ends calculus for violence 4–5, 17, 78, 105, 119, 122, 166, 171, 177, 180
Medea 92
Medea (Euripides) 92, 200n.39
Medusa 52
Megaclides 63
Megara 101, 110–11, 113, 115, 118, 120–21, 127, 204n.19
Meineck, Peter 3
Melanippus 9–10
Meleager 78
Memorabilia (Xenophon) 173
Menoetes 49, 59
Middle Comedy 132, 134
Minyans of Orchomenos 109, 175
Modern Hercules, The (Stafford) 14
Moirai, the 147, 149
monster-slayer, Heracles as a 7, 12, 15–16, 19–23, 49–56, 67, 75–6, 82, 111, 117, 160, 163–5, 171, 177–8
Montiglio, Silvia 71
Moorton, R. F. 163, 165–66
Mount Oeta 10, 101, 103
Mulius 54
Muth, Susanne 6, 65, 196n.59
Mycenae 112, 116–17, 119, 121, 129
Myrtilus 81, 198n.11
Mysia 179
myth, general dynamism of 6–10

Nagy, G. 42
Nemean Lion 6, 21, 52–54, 58, 110, 112
Neoptolemus 103
neotas 114
Nessus (centaur) 16, 77, 82–85, 88, 93–94, 100, 104, 177
Nestor 54, 64, 78
Niobe 122
nomos 50, 72, 74–75, 197n.86
nostos 109

Oceanus 53–55, 58
Odysseus 10, 40, 44
Odysseus in America (Shay) 3
Odysseus Theme, The (Stanford) 14
Odyssey (Homer)
    council of the gods in 62
    and Heracles' apotheosis 11

Heracles kills a guest-friend 20
    introduction 3
    Laertes and Eurycleia 92
    and the sack of Oechalia 23, 37
Oechalia 23, 39–41, 85–88, 95, 104–5, 180
Oedipus 8, 102
Oeneus 79, 88
Oenomaus 81
oikos 16, 81–85, 88, 92, 95, 98, 100, 105, 110, 113, 165, 179
Old Comedy 134, 141–6
Olympic Games 8, 68–69, 119
Olympus
    apotheosis in 44–6
    and Dionysus 159
    and Geryon 61
    and Heracles 26, 28, 33, 61, 102, 104, 130
    introduction 1, 10–12
    and Semele 157
Omphale (Ion of Chios) 140–41
Omphale, queen of Lydia 30, 40, 86–87, 90, 140, 169–70
On Violence (Arendt) 4, 50
Onomacritus 44
oral poets 6
Orchomenos 109, 137
Orestes (Euripides) 103
Orpheus 148–49, 154, 157
Orphic music and writings 149
Orthrus *see* Orthus (dog)
Orthus (dog) 21, 49, 51, 54, 58–59, 64
Ostwald, M. 72–73
Other, the 58
Otus 29
Oxford Handbook to Heracles 14
Oxyrhynchus 133

Pagasae 30
Page, Denys 58, 60, 66
paian 148
Palinode (Stesichorus) 56
Panyassis of Halicarnassis 20, 157, 160
parerga 128, 137, 207n.77
Paris 37, 63–64, 173
parodos 148
Parry, H. 115
Patroclus 42

Peirithous 157
Peirithous (Euripides or Critias) 166
Peisistratus 11
Peleus 78
Pelops 81
Penelope 40
Performing Interpersonal Violence (Riess) 3
peripeteia 115
Persephone 154, 157, 165–67
Perseus 10, 52
Pheres 150
philia
    as applied to rescuing Theseus 114
    conflicting with *xenia* 147, 152
    and a disruption of 96
    of Euripides' *Heracles* 175
    expression of traditional 111
    Heracles' extends beyond human race 111
    importance of the communal 122
    a mechanism for *kallinikos* revival 123, 125, 128–29
    obvious violations of 116
    relationship with the Thebans 109
    and reversal for Heracles 119, 121
    ties of to defend close relatives 113
    and violence 180
Philo 139
Philoctetes 103
Philoctetes (Sophocles) 103
philoi 17, 112–15, 122–23, 129, 154, 156, 178, 180
philos 17, 108–9, 111–17, 121–24, 127, 130, 178
Phobos 36
Phoebus 32–33, 148
Phoenix 103, 202n.70
Pholus (centaur) 136
Phorcys 50
Phrynichus 147
Pindar
    composing a dithyramb 157
    epinician odes of 13, 46, 130, 178
    first *Nemean* ode of 144
    and Geryon's death 16
    and the myth of Geryon 50
    and the Olympic Games 108, 119
    and third *Olympian* ode 68–9, 71, 177

treatment of Heracles 11, 43, 68–76, 115, 175, 195n.88
undermining instrumental violence 177
Pinker, Steven 2
Pisander of Rhodes 20, 160
Plathane (maid) 167–68
Plato 72, 75
Plato Comicus 142–43
Platter, Charles 133, 158
ponoi 112
Poseidon 37, 61–62
post-traumatic stress disorder (PTSD) 3
Problems of Dostoevsky's Poetics (Bakhtin) 133
Prodicus 17–18, 144, 173–76, 179, 214n.8
Prometheus 22
Pronomos Vase 136
Pseudo-Apollodorus 30, 33, 49, 135, 136, 146, 160, 189n.52, 190n.65, 193n.32, 211n.70, 212nn.84, 89
Pythia 32–33

Rabelais and his World (Bakhtin) 135
Rabelaisian folk culture 132
Race, W. H. 71
Rankine, Patrice 81
Riess, Werner,
introduction 3, 15–16
semantic grammar of violence 19, 183n.2, 184n.16
Robertson, Martin 64
Rosen, R. M. 143
Rusten, J. S. 145

Sack of Oechalia (Creophylus) 20
Sarpedon 37–39, 42, 60
satyrs 140–41, 146
Seaford, R. 136
Segal, C. 36, 160
Semele 157
sex 80–83, 132, 134, 136, 139, 140–44, 141, 153, 170
Shay, Jonathan 3
Shield of Heracles (Hesiod) 15, 23, 34–36, 56
Silenus 136
Siphnian Treasury, Delphi 31
skene 163
Socrates 173, 176, 214n.2

Sophocles 13, 16, 77–105, 110, 137–38, 144, 157, 161, 177, 202n.64, 67
Sositheos 141
Stables of Augeas 117–18, 139, 190n.63
Stafford, Emma 11, 14
Stesichorus 16, 49, 56–67, 62–67, 70, 73–76, 157, 166, 177
Stymphalian birds 120–21
Suda 20
Sutton, D. F. 136, 138, 141
Swift, L. 78, 108–9, 111, 117, 121, 148, 154
Syleus 134, 138–39, 141
Syleus (Euripides) 138, 141

Temple of Zeus, Olympia 117–18, 121, 206n.49
Teucer 66
Theater of War Productions 3
Thebes 9, 11, 96, 101, 109–10, 113, 116, 120, 126, 137, 144
Themis 32–33
Theocritus 179–80
Theogony (Hesiod),
Heracles as a monster-slayer 111, 177–78
introduction 7, 11, 16
and seizure of Cattle of Geryon 49–50
violence as a civilizing force 19–23, 183n.11
theomachos 19–20, 23, 28–30, 37, 71, 177
theoxenia 134
Theseus 10, 17, 108, 114, 124, 127–30, 157, 207n.67
Thessaly 112
Tiryns 49, 54, 94, 96, 101
Tlepolemus 37–39
Topography of Violence in the Greco-Roman World, The (Riess/Fagan) 3
Trachiniae (Sophocles)
conclusion 104–5
and death of Heracles 177
death of a victor 93–104, 200n.38, 201n.57, 203n.74
Heracles and Achelous 79–82
Heracles and Nessus 82–85
Heracles' own household violence in 149
heroic competition in 155
introduction 13, 16, 77–79

Iole and Deianeira 88–93
and Ion of Chios 140
sack of Oechalia 85–88, 180
self-aggrandizing Heracles of 113
Trachis 77, 82, 93, 95–96, 102–3
Trojan War 9, 25, 46
Troy
destruction of 39
the gods' investment in conflict at 23
heroes of the Trojan War 25
sacking of 8, 24, 37, 41
Tydeus 9–10
Tzetzes, John 138–39

Uhlig, A. 140
Underworld, the
capture of Cerberus 45, 130
and Dionysus 162–63, 169
Dionysus and Xanthias 170
and Erytheia's location 53
and Euripides 156
and *Eurystheus* 157
and Heracles 46, 133, 154, 157–58, 161
and Odysseus 43–44
and Persephone 166–67
releasing of Eurydice 149
and Theseus 114, 124–25

victor, role of 16, 49, 67, 78, 81–3, 89–104, 117, 157, 160, 164, 166, 171–2, 177–8
victory
anxiety about 18, 78–9, 178
athletic 8, 13, 46, 68–71, 76, 115, 142
on battlefield 7, 10, 35
in comic plots 17, 131–6, 141–6, 175
in competition 33
over death 54, 153–4
and glorious victor (*kallinikos*) 16–17, 107–30, 143, 150, 165
as justification for violence 54, 177
prizes of 35, 39, 51, 54, 77, 87, 155
symbol of 6, 13, 76, 78
Violence and Community (Xydopoulos/ Vlassopoulos/Tounta) 3
Violenze Antiche (Foraboschi) 3
Virgil 157

Wasps (Aristophanes) 142
Wedding of Hebe (Epicharmus) 135–36
Weil, Simone 23–24
Wilamowitz-Moellendorff, U. von 108, 203n.3, 205n.25
Wills, G. 163
Winnington-Ingram, R. P. 39

Xanthias 156–59, 161, 165–67, 169–70
xenia 40–41, 118–19, 135, 147, 152
Xenodoce 139
xenoi 108
Xenophon 17, 173, 176

Yoshitake, S. 128

Zeus
abandonment of Heracles 124
and Amphitryon's remonstrations with 114–15
and Asclepius raising the dead 148
and Athena 11, 61
the champion and protégé of 19, 46
controlling his son's fate 86–87
and Deianeira 100
and Dionysus 159
disapproves of attack 'by stealth' 94
and Eurystheus 69
father of Heracles 1, 9, 13, 23–26, 35, 42, 45, 52–53, 75–76
and Gaia's defiance 32–33
and Geryon 71, 75
and Hera 53
and the Hyperboreans 175
inscrutable will of 103–4
introduction of Heracles 43
killing of Asclepius 147
a more ordered universe under 49–50
and the Olympic Games 68
and power of Eros 90
promoting the rule of 21–22
sacrifices to on Mount Cenaeum 96
service of his agenda 7
and the *Theogony* 20–21
and two sons fighting 30, 34
Zeus Abused (Plato Comicus) 142
Zeus Soter 110–11

www.ingramcontent.com/pod-product-compliance
Lightning Source LLC
Chambersburg PA
CBHW072141290426
44111CB00012B/1941